BROKEN *and* SHARED

BROKEN *and* SHARED

FOOD, DIGNITY, AND THE POOR ON LOS ANGELES' SKID ROW

Jeff Dietrich

MARYMOUNT
INSTITUTE PRESS

TSEHAI
Publishers & Distributors

Broken and Shared: Food, Dignity, and the Poor on Los Angeles' Skid Row
Copyright © 2011 by Robert Jefferson "Jeff" Dietrich, 1946—. All rights reserved.

Marymount Institute Press books may be purchased for educational, business, or sales promotional use. For more information, please contact our special sales department.

Marymount Institute Press,
a Tsehai Publishers Imprint, Loyola Marymount University,
One LMU Drive, Suite 3012, Los Angeles, CA 90045

www.tsehaipublishers.com/mip
mip@tsehaipublishers.com

ISBN: 978-0-9839616-2-8

First Edition: November 2011

Publisher: Elias Wondimu
Editor: Theresia de Vroom
Director of Marketing and Assistant Editor: Ellen Hoffs
Typesetting and Layout Design: Tessa Smith (www.tessasmithdesign.com)
Cover Design: Kerri Blackstone (www.kerriblackstone.com)

Library of Congress Catalog Card Number
A Catalog record for this book is available from the Library of Congress.

British Library Cataloguing in Publication Data
A Catalogue record for this book is available from the British Library.

10 9 8 7 6 5 4 3 2 1

Printed in the United States of America on acid-free, recycled paper.

*This book is dedicated to my wife Catherine Morris,
who has made my life possible.*

It is also dedicated to my mothers:

*Marguertie Vandeleur Brooks Dietrich,
the gracious, southern, lady who talked to me in the womb
and thus gave me the mother tongue*

and

*Dorothy Day,
Founder of the Catholic Worker,
mentor and "barren woman," who is mother of us all.*

CONTENTS

LIST OF ILLUSTRATIONS

FOREWORD

By Martin Sheen

In December 1959 I had been a struggling young actor in New York City for nearly a year when I lost my "day job" as a stock-boy at the American Express Company. Then suddenly I was hired as a general understudy and stagehand at off-Broadway's renowned Living Theatre by its founders, husband and wife team Julian Beck and Judith Malina. While they could only offer me a pittance of $5.00 per week, they tried to compensate by directing me downtown to Christie Street, where a friend of theirs ran a "soup kitchen" serving free hot meals every evening to anyone in need, with no questions asked, and happily I became a regular "guest." The place was the Catholic Worker, and their friend, of course, was Dorothy Day. This began my life-long involvement with and deep affection for the Catholic Worker Movement, including the Los Angeles Catholic Worker (LACW) where I came to know and revere Jeff Dietrich.

For forty years Jeff and his wife Catherine Morris have formed the core leadership of the LACW located in the heart of Los Angeles' Skid Row, where 3,000 street people are fed and clothed weekly. The small compound at the corner of 6th Street & Gladys, affectionately referred to by the street folk as "The Hippie Kitchen," includes a free dental clinic and a small medical center.

The Catholic Worker Movement was founded by Dorothy Day and Peter Maurin in 1934 with the hope of reawakening the gospel message of active peacemaking and social justice within the Catholic Church, and it has had a profound effect.

Nourished through prayer and reflection, individual worker communities are generally formed by idealist young pacifists who live together in voluntary poverty to serve the poor, performing the corporal works of mercy, and offering hospitality. Of equal importance, they address the root causes of poverty and injustice by speaking truth to power through nonviolent forms of action against every form of violence and injustice that crushes the poor, devalues life, and destroys the environment. Of course, such a mandate can and often does lead to unpleasant confrontations with

Jeff Dietrich

4. Jeff Dietrich (right) with Dom Helder Camara and Martin Sheen at a press conference for the National Catholic Worker gathering at the Nevada Nuclear Test Site to celebrate Dorothy Day's 90th birthday, November, 1987. Photo by James Ryman

both church and state authorities with harsh consequences, including serious jail time. Worker communities, however, generally accept the notion that if their work is not costly, they are "left to question its value," and the LACW is no exception.

As one of its original members, Jeff has fully lived every aspect of the worker's mission, including spending long periods in jail. He has kept a personal diary nearly all his life, where he faithfully records his experiences and reflections, many of which appeared over the years in the *Catholic Agitator*, the LACW's bimonthly publication that Jeff has edited since its inception in 1972.

Now the Marymount Institute Press has chosen for this volume the very best of these reflections, which were originally recorded almost as they were happening and not subject to distant memory. As such they offer not only an accurate history of the LACW, but also a history of the Skid Row community and of the politics and culture that evolved over the last four decades in "Third World America".

Perhaps chief among these reflections and essays are Jeff's prison letters, a harsh and necessary reminder of the personal cost of peace making and social justice activism, which may give pause to future generations as Jeff's level of commitment goes far beyond 'civil disobedience' and reaches 'criminal' behavior. Yet the entire work is no less inspiring and deeply compelling. From his early days resisting the draft and protesting the war in Vietnam, through his personal, spiritual evolution and commitment to "comfort the afflicted and afflict the comfortable," he writes with self-deprecating humor and extraordinary insight, exposing his faults, confronting his fears, and confirming his faith.

"I believe the gospels are the best story we have," Jeff writes in his introduction: "They are the singular counter-narrative to our consumerist, war-mongering, media saturated, technologized, dehumanized, death-oriented culture."

Even for the most conservative among us there is little doubt that we are all responsible for each other, and the world is exactly the way it is because consciously or unconsciously we have made it so. But as things decline more and more rapidly with the world's economy in shambles, very few are aware of just how devastating the residual effects are on the poor who are ground down and served up daily to the gods of our idolatry: perpetual war, corporate greed, and personal indifference.

Clearly the need to bring compassion, peace making, and social justice into the fray has never been greater, but when faced with such a reality, who can be blamed for turning away in despair or self-preservation? And yet the open invitation from the gospel still reaches our hearts after 2,000 years and we are left to wonder: "Whatever you do to the least of mine you have done so to me."

Simply stated, this is the story of Jeff Dietrich's lifelong effort to unite the will of the spirit with the work of the flesh. But by his own admission he "doesn't seem to have accomplished much." On the contrary, things have only gotten worse since he joined the LACW forty years ago. Nonetheless he still shouts to us from the deep end with enviable joy: "Come on in, the water is fine."

PREFACE

WHERE THE SPIRIT DARES
BY DANIEL BERRIGAN, SJ

When I set to work on this preface, two moods quickly surfaced. The first was sober indeed, a debt of friendship. I had sentenced myself to uncounted hours facing down the carnivorous eye and this in the hottest summer this side of inferno. Nonetheless, I went to work. Doggedly.

But not for long, that half aggrieved distemper. It fled the page. It simply could not thrive in face of the sounds, sights, pots and pans banging away, choices maladroit and heroic, moods, friendships, glimpses of heaven touching earth, stark days, tears giving way to laughter, the near giving up, dogged starting over. I pondered Jeff's text; these things held me enchanted, page after page, hours on end. I was at the mercy of a magister of recall, a verbal magician, who is also, gift beyond price, a friend.

Jeff's history dwells on the first forty years of a community known as the Los Angeles Catholic Worker. Jeff has been there, together with other near indomitables. He has done that, yearly, daily, and hourly since.

Imagine a somewhat prosaic event. Time passes and events are colored by the glow of myth: that first meal forty years ago, cooked, and served. And presto—gone in an hour! A first overnight guest, long gone...the first Eucharist. The flavor is vivid, the faces and words, the hope against hope.

From the start, Christ is native to the scene, the first among equals, the prime hungry and homeless, the *Christ of the Bread Lines*, the line, that in forty years never once has diminished, the hellish law of increase perpetually verified as ego, avarice, weapons, and wars like pinpoint bombings, falling "like lightning" upon the innocent and the expendable.

One thing is constant and life-giving in Jeff's text. For forty years, he and Catherine and their friends have kept seeking the nascent vision, poking away, uncovering the rich loam of Dorothy Day's letters and diaries. So armed and disarmed, time and again, their community brings to bear the holiness and wisdom of Dorothy Day. For forty years, her star is ascendant above the roof of the Los Angeles Catholic Worker.

THE CHRIST OF THE BREAD LINES 1950

3. *The Christ of the Bread Lines* by Fritz Eichenberg, 1950, woodcut

Again and again, her wisdom rings true: "Stand with those at the bottom of the monstrous pyramid;" "Make of every generation a first generation, first in fervor and innocence and intent;" "When all else fails, pray. When prayer fails, pray more;" "Don't make money from money," an entire eschatology expressed as an aphorism, "Human misery is not the will of God. There's ample creation to heal, clothe, educate everyone born. But there's not ample creation for every one, and for war."

For such wisdom and gratitude, a muted alleluia.

AUTHOR'S ACKNOWLEDGEMENTS

I would like to thank Dan and Chris Delany, mentors and founders of the Los Angeles Catholic Worker; Martha Lewis, my co-editor, moral compass and first reader always; Mike Wisniewski, my co-editor and right-hand guy, who always makes me look better than I actually am.

Many thanks to Martin Sheen, for decades of financial and moral support; to Daniel Berrigan, SJ; Philip Berrigan and Liz McAlister; John Dear, SJ; Kathy Kelly; Stephen Kelly, SJ; Ladon Sheats; and Fr. Louis Vitale, OFM, for their prophetic spirit, friendship, and faithfulness.

To Ched Myers, who opened the womb of the Word to me; and Susan Pollack, my first co-editor, friend and supporter.

With gratitude to my entire LA Catholic Worker Community: Catherine Bax; Clare Bellefeuille-Rice; Lisa Bilek and Dick Hannigan; Ann Boden; Patty Carmody; Rebecca Casas; Faustino Cruz, Tina Delany and Paul McCudden and family; Toni Flynn, who gave me the idea for this book; David Gardner; Rev. Elizabeth Griswold; Paul Gross and Lisa Redman; the late Dr. Pat Heffron, my personal gynecologist; Grace Hill-Speed; Kent Hoffman; Larry Holben; Sandi and Pat Huckaby; Margaret Johnson; Theo Kayser; Arnal Kennedy, poet, story teller and dishwasher extraordinaire; Jesse Lewis; David Lumian; Meredith Males; Allison McGillivray; Nancy Minte; Kurt Morrow and Sybilla Bryson; Ann Mulder; Donald Nollar; David Omondi; John Owen, "Hippy Kitchen" waterman forever; Jonathan Parfrey; Rio Parfrey; Joyce and Jim Parkhurst; Kieran Prather; Cath Robson; Alecia Stuchlik; Joan and Tony Trafecanty; Sheena Tseko; Ann Turner; Ross Weaver; Tim Wertzberger; and Sam Yergler.

Much gratitude to ALL volunteers at the LACW soup kitchen over the decades, without whom we could not exist.

Thanks to the artists Christa Occhiogrosso and Gary Palmatier. Thanks also to Kevin Cody, for arranging our printing and years of friendship and support; to Greg McDonald for printing the *Agitator* for free for many years; and Don Milici, for years of great photos, friendship and support.

With gratitude to all the members of our "Sister Houses": Julia Occhiogrosso and Gary Cavalier, Katie Kelso, and John Yevtich; Mary Beth Appel and Johanna Berrigan; Kate Chatfield and Peter Stiehler; Alice Lindsmeier

Jeff Dietrich

and Eric DeBode; Helen and Curt Grove; Tensie Hernandez, Dennis Apel, and Jorge Manly; Leia and Dwight Smith; Manuel Hernandez; Kim Williams and Steve Baggarly; Eduard Loring and Murphy Davis, and Nelia and Calvin Kimbrough; Liza and Bryan Apper; Larry Purcell, "El Jeffe del Norte," Steve and Ann Bremser; Paul Engler, and Sam Pullen.

Many thanks to other long-time Catholic Workers: Frank Cordaro, resister, archetypal Catholic Worker, priest, confessor, and spiritual advisor; Shelley and Jim Douglass; Willa Bickham and Brendan Walsh; Kassie Temple, my favorite critic; and Joanne Kennedy.

With thanks to Alice Callaghan, co-conspirator and bulldog for the underdog; Janice Jensen and Jason de Groot, who taught me that it was cool to be an outlaw, artist and intellectual; and my lawyers Carol Sobel and Bob Myers. To Wes Howard-Brook, theologian and friend. Thanks to the members of the Los Angeles Community Action Network (LACAN): Becky Dennison, General Dogan, and Pete White, dedicated advocates for the people on the street; Dan Jiru and all the "Hunger Walkers" from St. Paul High School.

Thanks, also, to Fr. Greg Boyle, SJ, my pastor and first volunteer at the LACW soup kitchen; Fr. Chris Ponnet; Zen Master Robert Aitken, who encouraged this book; Dr. Rich Meehan, long-time LACW dentist, friend, and supporter; and Ted Von der Ahe, long-time friend, volunteer, and supporter.

Much thanks to my father Cliff, and siblings, Joe, Brooks, Susan, Nancy, Anne, and my uncle Bobby, priest forever.

To Theresia de Vroom and Elias Wondimu, my editor and publisher. You have invested more time, money, and love into this project than any single author could possibly desire or deserve. I thought I was just getting a book published, but what I received from you was my own self-revelation as a writer and a whole person. For this gift, my deepest and heartfelt gratitude.

Jeff Dietrich

xxii

ACKNOWLEDGEMENTS

The production of this book has been a true labor of love as well as an undertaking of mammoth proportions, larger than any our fledgling press has embarked upon. This book represents more than forty years of writing and thinking, naturally its creation and presentation posed many complex challenges.

The Press and author would like to acknowledge and thank John Connolly, Professor Emeritus of Theology at Loyola Marymount University (LMU), who first brought the manuscript to the attention of the Press and who compiled and edited the early drafts. Without John and Kristen Heyer, Associate Professor of Theology, University of Santa Clara, this book would probably not have been published by the Marymount Institute Press.

We thank Provincial Superior, Sister Mary Genino RSHM, and the Western American Province of the Religious of the Sacred Heart of Mary for their generosity in support of this publication.

This book brings together an eclectic array of artists. We thank the visual artists whose work illustrates the book, the late Fritz Eichenberg, along with Christa Occhiogrosso, Gary Palmatier, and Michael Stansell. We thank the five photographers who gave their time to the project with generosity and enthusiasm: Brian Braff, Bernadette Ortiz, Robert Radin, Deirdre Walpole, and Mike Wisniewski.

We thank Wole Soyinka, Nobel Laureate and President's Marymount Institute Professor in Residence, for giving us permission to use his poem about a last super.

For reasons that can only be described as bordering on the magical, the production of this book inspired a large team of people to work together, many who are not Catholic and had no prior working relationship with the author or knowledge of his work. We thank the three anonymous outside readers of the book. We thank those who proof-read the manuscript and offered editorial advice: Chake Koujoumjian, Associate Dean for Graduate Studies at LMU, Stephen Shepherd, Professor of English at LMU and Michael Madrikian, Marymount Institute Student Editorial Intern. Jane Crawford, Professor of Classics at the University of Virginia, spent the daylight hours of her six-day Oxford "vacation" editing the manuscript. Ellen Hoffs, Assistant Editor and Director of Marketing for the Marymount Institute Press not only pulled an "all-nighter" so we could add two crucial sections to the ending the day before the book went to press, but she also read the manuscript more than seems humanly possible. Reading a 450+ page manuscript even just once is a great deal of work—reading it more than twice either deserves a medal or a stint in a convalescent home—maybe both.

Our Typesetting and Layout Designer Tessa Smith, worked on the manuscript 24/7 for more than six months with enthusiasm and the greatest patience. Our Graphic Designer, Image Editor, and Graduate Assistant Kerri Blackstone made the book live. It is due to the diligence, expertise, determination, and genius of these two women that this book is a thing of clarity and beauty. Meantime, our graduate intern, Darcey Whitmore, may have invented a new field of forensic science called "bibliographic detection."

Several Marymount Institute student interns were involved in the research and manuscript preparation of the book. We thank: Semhar Dory, James Duffy, Stephanie Felix, Mahelet Gebeyhu, Jennifer Hamlin, Michael Madrikian, Sean McEvoy, Jeff McMahon, Briana De Marco, Caleb Nyberg, Misha Scott, Rebecca Siess, Paulina Slagter, and Chris Wonder.

We would like to thank Santa Clara University student Brittany Adams and the following LMU students who assisted in transcribing and editing the articles from the *Catholic Agitator*: Irma Lizardi, Mercedes Jefferis, Clayton Chmiel, and most especially, Melanie Nguyen.

Theresia de Vroom's personal administrative assistant, Ivie Arasomwan, scanned hundreds of images for the book and managed the final edits. Equally important, she kept the ship from capsizing, the coffee flowing, the phones answered, and the meals coming. Rev. James Fredericks, Professor of Theology, Advisory Board Member, and Chaplain to the Marymount Institute spent countless hours talking to the Press's editors about Dorothy Day and the Catholic Worker Movement. Jeffrey Siker, Chair and Professor of Theology, provided invaluable advice on how to 'out-Herod Herod.' Thanks to Peter B. Hirtle, Selector for US, Canadian, General European, and Bibliographic History Senior Policy Advisor and Fellow, Society of American Archivists, Cornell University Library, who gave us invaluable advice on copyright and permissions.

At Loyola Marymount University, CAO Joseph Hellige provided substantial support for the student involvement in the Press. His budget team, particularly Maria Cano and Kimberly Petok, made the finances for the book viable. Pamela Burrill, Business Manager for the Division of Student Affairs, gave us hours of sound financial advice.

We thank the Advisory Board of the Marymount Institute for their guidance: Barbara Busse, Dean of the College of Communications and Fine Arts; Phil Dorin, Professor of Computer Science; Rev. James Fredericks, Professor of Theology; Sr. Mary Genino, RSHM and Superior General of the Western Province, *ex officio*; Mary Ellen Gozdecki, Consultant for RSHM Educational Ministries, *ex officio*; Kathleen Harris, Director, National & International Scholarship Office; Beth Henley, President's University Professor of Theatre Arts; Ellen Hoffs, Director of Marketing and Assistant Editor for the Marymount Institute Press; Michael Horan, Professor of Theology; Wenshu Lee, Professor of Communication Studies; Linda McMurdock, Dean of Students; Stephen Shepherd, Professor of English.

The Senior Administration at Loyola Marymount University has encouraged and supported the endeavors of the Institute and the Press, making our work possible on a daily basis. We particularly wish to thank David W. Burcham, President of Loyola Marymount University, and Dr. Lane Bove, Senior Vice President for Student Affairs and Chair of the Marymount Institute Advisory Board.

Jeff Dietrich   Theresia de Vroom   Elias Wondimu

INTRODUCTION

If this is going to be a Christian nation that doesn't help the poor, either we have to pretend that Jesus was just as selfish as we are, or we've got to acknowledge that he commanded us to love the poor and serve the needy without condition and then admit that we just don't want to do it.

—Stephen Colbert, *The Colbert Report*, December 16, 2010

In the book of Genesis, God gives mankind life and sustenance in a paradisal garden. In no time, however, Adam and Eve discover the difference between good and evil and as a result they are cast out of their primal and idyllic home forever. And so they would walk naked, homeless, and ashamed into a world where they would not only come to endure extraordinary suffering, but also retribution and incomprehensible isolation.

Skid Row in Los Angeles, California is anything but an Edenic garden. There are no fruit trees or flowering plants, no gentle animals or undulating rivers—just concrete, fences, police patrols, and fundamentalist missions. The economic and governmental forces that make Skid Row a reality reinforce a narrow and modern-day distinction between good and evil, the result of which is the complete dehumanization and abandonment of men and women who have one thing in common: they are poor.

At the intersection of 6th Street and Gladys Avenue sits the Hospitality Kitchen. Outside its walls, the immediate and "real world" of Los Angeles' Skid Row is barren, violent, bleak, soul-devouring, and dangerous; inside the compound it is a *hortus conclusis*, an ideal memorialized by painters, poets, and theologians of the Middle Ages and the Renaissance—the enclosed garden—the new Eden, the space that renews and regenerates—the space that re-dignifies its visitors by recognizing them as beings made in the image and likeness of God.

Three times each week for the last forty years, Jeff Dietrich and his wife, Catherine Morris, have brought homeless guests into their garden and into their house of hospitality. It is a place where their guests, like those of any other gracious hosts, are given food, drink, and respect, a place where they can listen to music, talk, get basic medical attention, and most importantly, reclaim their dignity. It is a place where they can re-enter the Garden, and for a few hours, recover their inheritance as children of God.

A great deal has been written about the Catholic Worker Movement by its founders, its observers, and its historians. The Catholic Worker Movement indeed provides the foundational ideology and the locus of Jeff Dietrich's activism; it is where his life, his writing, and his thinking have their roots and find their home—it is what this book is all about.

As a result of living with and among the poor, through his work with the Catholic Worker Movement, Jeff Dietrich's perspective is prejudiced on their behalf. His viewpoint helps him see the fallacies and absolute detriment in what most of us, and even the poor themselves, believe to be in their best interest. He argues that systems, usually conceived as positive in the service of justice and progress, are, in reality, disadvantageous to poor and marginalized people. Further, that these very systems, ranging from the justice systems to various welfare/rehabilitation systems, to ideologies of technology and progress, are designed not only to subdue and pacify the underclass but also to keep them in their place. Thus and in sum total, they exist for the benefit of the elite and to the disadvantage of the poor.

At the same time the reader considers Jeff Dietrich the activist, we should also like the reader to imagine Jeff Dietrich, the writer. We hope thereby to situate him in a broader context as his work has a great deal in common with that of writers, thinkers, and artists over time, who at the core of their being understood the profound significance of need; the tragedy that is poverty; the blinding unjustness of privilege and wealth; the value of the gift and the providential nature of generosity; the renewing watershed of the natural world; the need for personal, intellectual, and artistic solidarity with the poor; and finally, that food is sacramental and redemptive.

Therefore, Jeff Dietrich's work stands with contemporary social and cultural critics as various as Noam Chomsky, Andrew O'Hagan, Lewis Hyde, Christopher Lasch, and Michael Pollan. His work understands that the only way out of apocalyptic tragedy is to recognize as Shakespeare's King Lear finally does, that we have "taken too little care of this," that the most common and pervasive injustice on which civilization itself is founded is the quotidian and systematic neglect, degradation, and abuse of the poor. He also understands, as Lear finally does, that redemption lies in giving up everything for nothing. Jeff Dietrich's work knows what the fourteenth-century poem *Piers Plowman* knew, which is that only in the most vivid dreams of poverty can we see God. He knows what poets like Robert

Frost, William Wordsworth, and W.B. Yeats did, that in the experience of the common man, the language of poetry is born. Like Jonathan Swift or Wole Soyinka, he understands that satire and wit are among the most effective tools of resistance to corruption and the abuse of power. He knows along with Claude Lévi-Strauss, Sir James Frazer, Aesop, and Sigmund Freud, that in the smallest details of a story, the truth of humanity lies buried. Jeff Dietrich knows what Charles Dickens imagined, that "great expectations" are really the sum of small and providential acts of kindness through which orphans, convicts, and strangers become family. And finally, in his writing about the problem of feeding the hungry on a daily basis he realizes what M. F. K. Fisher told us many years ago, that knowing *How to Cook a Wolf* can come in handy.

Jeff Dietrich, like Jacob in the Bible story and by his own admission, was "raised in a tent of women." As a result, his writing is naturally, organically, and strikingly feminist. It is born out of the work of Dorothy Day and Peter Maurin, founders of the Catholic Worker Movement, but it is also rooted in the presence of many women in his formative life and in his long collaboration with his wife, Catherine; together they are the driving force, the heart and soul of the Los Angeles Catholic Worker. Perhaps some of the most important and moving pieces in this book are the radical feminist interpretations of the Gospel story on subjects as various as the pregnancies of Mary and Elizabeth, the "great faith" of the Canaanite woman, and a reading of the Gospel of Luke as "a gospel of women."

This book is both encyclopedic and eclectic in nature. Like the Bible itself in which it is steeped, this book has many parts, and many kinds of writing—short vignettes, portraits of individuals, short essays, longer essays, letters, and appeals. The reader may choose to take it up start to finish, or read it like many people read the Bible, dipping in and out.

The essays in this book were published over a forty-year period. They were researched and written largely when the long day's work, expected of all Catholic Workers, was done, late at night or in the early hours of the morning, week after week, year after year. The writing is studied, complex, powerful, honest, sophisticated, fair, sometimes angry, sometimes tender, always humble, sometimes proud. The writing is deceptively straightforward and, unlike the ubiquitous bulk of journalistic and academic writing available today on shelves and computers screens, it is writing which is careful with the truth; and it is writing that can afford to wear its learning lightly.

If Jeff Dietrich's gift were that of a painter, he would have a great deal in common with Vincent van Gogh, who, like Dietrich, was largely self-

Jeff Dietrich

taught; who lived his entire adult life in poverty; who painted against all odds; who wrote voraciously, and read the parables of Jesus every day; who believed in the "university of the poor," and whose two greatest paintings were not of sunflowers or stars at night, but of the poor eating potatoes, at the start of his non-existent "career" as an artist, and of the *The Good Samaritan* in the last year of his life. Vincent van Gogh was largely unknown in his lifetime. We hope that with the publication of this book, Jeff Dietrich will no longer share this distinction with him.

The cover illustration of this book is Carravagio's painting, *The Supper at Emmaus*, 1601. It is a painting that dramatizes the moment of recognition or re-cognition, the moment of re-knowing and knowing again. In the painting, two poor men recognize Christ at the moment he breaks bread with them. All the while, the innkeeper never takes his eyes off his guest. In the painting the shadow behind Christ is clearly that of the innkeeper. Jeff Dietrich is the innkeeper. On a day-to-day basis it is he, along with his community, who maintains a place where the poor can be fed, clothed, comforted, and recognized. This book, if nothing else, is an account of what the innkeeper sees.

Theresia de Vroom

Professor of English
Editor of the Marymout Institute Press
Director of the Marymount Institute for Faith, Culture and the Arts
Loyola Marymount University

Forever Young:
Forty years as a Catholic Worker

Catholic Agitator, April, 2010, pp. 1, 2, and 8[*]

May you grow up to be righteous
May you grow up to be true
May you always know the truth
And see the lights surrounding you
May you always be courageous
Stand upright and be strong
May you stay forever young

—Bob Dylan

Like many of my generation of Vietnam War resisters, I was a fugitive from the law on September 15, 1970, when I exited the plane at Kennedy International Airport. I was a young long-haired hippie draft resister, who thought that you could not trust anyone over thirty. I had recently refused induction into the military, left the country, hitchhiked through Europe and Africa, and six months later when I came back to the States, I fully expected to be arrested. Somehow, miraculously, I slipped through customs without notice. I had $3.00 in my pocket when I stepped to the curb at Kennedy International and stuck my thumb out with more bravado than I actually felt, seeking a ride back to my home, 3,000 miles away in Los Angeles. I had the same $3.00 in my pocket two days later outside of St. Louis, when a psychedelic VW bus picked me up. "We're going to a peacemakers' confer-

---

*   Portions of this essay appeared in the *Catholic Agitator*, marking the fortieth anniversary of the founding of the LACW community.

1

ence," they said and took me to what sounded like a dubious gathering in the woods not far from the city.

It could easily have been a rainbow hippie gathering or a flower child love-in, but instead it turned out to be something far more substantial and profoundly life changing. Ironically, the Peacemakers were old people—I thought they were ancient, but they probably were only in their late forties at the time. Founded in the midst of World War II by three Union Theological graduates, who went to jail rather than fight, the Peacemakers were a self-described "anarcho-pacifist" organization, whose members had continued their lifelong resistance to war and injustice by demonstrating, marching, sitting-in, and refusing to pay taxes. They had participated in the southern Freedom Rides, committed civil disobedience against every Cold War weapon system introduced by the US. Beaten, jailed, and reviled, still they persisted in their stubborn resistance.

Such heroism by "old people" was edifying for the newly minted radical I fancied myself to be. But even more revelatory for me was my encounter at the conference with some young people from the Catholic Worker. Though I had been raised a Catholic, gone to regular Sunday mass, and attended Catholic schools most of my life, no mention of Dorothy Day and the soup kitchen subversives of her radical Catholic Worker Movement had penetrated the sanitized suburbs of my youth. The young folks from the Milwaukee Catholic Worker ran a soup kitchen and hospitality house, and they had recently come from the court room drama of the Milwaukee 14, where their founder, Michael Cullen, and thirteen others had been sentenced to lengthy prison terms for the crime of burning draft files to protest the Vietnam War. As I listened to their story, a light suddenly went on in my head. This is what Jesus would be doing if he were around today, I thought. He would be feeding the hungry, clothing the naked, and *burning draft files*!

It was what the Buddhists call Samadhi—a flashing moment of realization, I understood that all of those gospel stories I was vaguely familiar with were not just spiritual allegories; that the life of Jesus was not just some sacramental metaphor; that the Sermon on the Mount was not just a quaint collection of spiritual poetry; that Christianity was not just a set of dogmas and prohibitions; that we were not supposed to worship Jesus—we were supposed to practice Jesus. We were supposed to be feeding the hungry, clothing the naked, and burning draft files. It was the most radical thing I could imagine, and it was being done by Catholics, a group that had been thoroughly purged as irrelevant from my recently formed radical soul.

I still had the same $3.00 I started with when I arrived back in LA ten days later. In a kind of epic journey of self-discovery, strangers had taken care of me, fed me, housed me, transported me across the country, and I had been gifted with an insight that very shortly led me to the front door of the newly founded Los Angeles Catholic Worker where I was, only thirty minutes after my arrival, made editor of the community's not-yet published newspaper, the *Catholic Agitator*. Each day we fed the poor of Skid Row, greeted county jail releases with coffee and donuts, and regularly protested the Vietnam War.

On Sundays, we gathered around the dining room table, with friends and supporters, with bread and wine, to read the gospel stories and celebrate a simple liturgy. In the context of our daily life of community, service, and resistance to war, the stories and liturgy came alive to me in a way they never had in the high church environment of silken vestments, linen altar cloths, and smoky incense. I prayed that I would be able to stay at least a year at the Catholic Worker before the FBI arrested me for draft refusal, because I knew that when I was brought before a judge, I wanted to be able to say with conviction, "I am not a coward. I do not refuse to serve, I simply refuse to serve the way you want me to serve. Like Jesus, I choose to serve life and not death. I am ready to go to jail." Ironically, I had found a home in the Church that I had so thoroughly rejected as irrelevant. I had caught a glimpse of the original founding spirit. I had found a place to ground my radical sensibilities—a radical foundation that stretched back 2,000 years to Jesus, and even further to Moses and the prophets.

Beautiful Losers

To be a Catholic Worker does not mean that we believe we can transform the poor or the domination system itself but rather that we believe we can transform ourselves. The most important thing for us is to live our lives as if the gospels were true, calling us back to a more sustainable vision of community, simplicity, and resource.

We try to live our lives by the story of Jesus, but that story is not a success story; it is, rather, a failure story. Jesus was betrayed by his best friend, denied by his lead disciple, deserted by his followers, and ridiculed by his once-adoring crowds. He died a painful and humiliating death on a cross. And his resurrection was not a triumph but rather an affirmation of his "failure project"—that radically inclusive program in which the "successful affluent" would redistribute their resources in community with the "unsuccessful poor" such that "all ate and were satisfied" (Matthew 14:20).

Our vision is shared with other "Beautiful Losers"— Jesus, Gandhi, St. Francis of Assisi, Monsignor Romero, Martin Luther King, and Dorothy Day, who lived, and in many cases died, for what in reality is impractical, unquantifiable, unachievable, but nonetheless essential to our humanity. In the end, our vision concerns the one who loses in a way that is eloquent and beautiful because it has a consistent integrity with the sublime vision of scripture. It is called *grace*.

While we have success stories, we do not feature them because to feature our few success stories would only serve to mask the extent to which our capitalist-consumerist economy makes it impossible for the majority of poor to even exist at all, must less to succeed.

Most poverty organizations begin their appeal letters with obligatory success stories and positive achievement statistics. But we refuse to pander to our supporters in a manner that might let them assume that the experience of poverty is the result of individual poor people who have failed, rather than the failure of, in fact, an entire system.

Our one-world, global-excess economy is designed to suck the maximum wealth possible from poor and working people, to say nothing of middle class people, and deposit it in the bank accounts of the wealthiest 1 percent of the world's population. We do not live in a democracy, a nation of and for the people. We live in a meritocracy, a nation of and for the successful. And we have a cultural script in our heads that says that "this is the land of opportunity," where everyone can make it if they just try—the land where immigrants succeed, where the poor can pull themselves up by their bootstraps. This common script is reinforced by the evening news, the morning paper, talk radio, the internet, and the election of the first African American president only reinforces that script.

But the truth is that President Obama and the homeless young woman who graduated from Harvard, and the black rapper from Watts who won a Grammy, and the pituitarily endowed basketball player from Harlem who led his NBA team to a championship are not the norm—they are the calculated exceptions. And their success only serves to underscore the abject failure of the vast majority of poor people, who are characterized as too lazy, addicted, or self-indulgent to succeed.

Blaming The Victim

There is a tendency, particularly among Fox News "journalists" and their followers, and truthfully among the public at large, to blame the poor for their own situation—*their sloth, their addictions, their anti-social values—*

4

and for their complicity in what has been termed by sociologists in the employ of conservative think tanks as a "culture of poverty." It is such a pervasive message because it is a comforting one that abrogates our collective responsibility for the plight of the homeless and the poor. And while drug and alcohol addiction are endemic among the homeless poor, there are just as many alcohol and drug addicts among the population at large, the difference being that they are housed and thus invisible, and in many cases their drugs come with a prescription that legalizes their situation.

Increasingly, the commendable "tough love" language of Alcoholics Anonymous has become the linguistic camouflage of police state repression that redirects much needed social service dollars to jails and prisons rather than to housing and social services. In fact, building supportive housing units for the homeless is a far more effective use of public dollars than incarcerating the homeless.

Jesus Christ started his ministry by curing the afflicted and exorcising their demons on an individual basis. But gradually he began to notice that their problems were not mere individual problems; they had a root cause. And so, not unlike Dr. Martin Luther King, who intended to take his local campaign, healing the wounds of racism and exorcising the demons of Jim Crow to Washington to demand jobs and economic justice, Jesus took his own local ministry of healing and exorcism to Jerusalem—upsetting the tables of the money changers and confronting the civil and religious authorities so that poor people could be healed, replenished, and restored. The fact that Martin Luther King and Jesus Christ came to the same end does not mitigate the veracity of their intentions.

It now has been forty years since I first encountered the Catholic Worker, and I still feed the hungry, clothe the naked, and shelter the homeless. Although I have never burned draft files, I have poured blood and oil on the steps of the Federal Building, downtown Los Angeles to protest the Persian Gulf War; cut the fence around the Nevada Nuclear Test Site to protest nuclear weapons; occupied the bell tower of the cathedral and appropriated the Cardinal's bulldozer to protest the Church's extravagant building project; blockaded the bathroom of City Hall to get porta-potties for those who sleep on the streets; and placed my body under the giant tires of a dump truck to protest the city's theft of property from the homeless. In all, I have been arrested over forty times for various civil disobedience actions.

Some years ago, as part of a court-ordered sentencing report, a federal probation officer wrote of me: "Mr. Dietrich is a sixty-year-old man who

5. Jeff Dietrich, Marina del Rey, California, 2011. Photo by Bernadette Ortiz

works in a Skid Row soup kitchen. He is given $15 a week and has no bank account or assets and is thus incapable of paying a fine. Over the years, he has been arrested scores of times and seems to be undeterred by incarceration. It is my opinion that further incarceration of Mr. Dietrich would serve no purpose, and would, in fact, be a waste of the government's resources."

Next year I turn sixty-five, and in preparation for my "retirement years," the Social Security Administration dutifully sent me a statement of my earnings. In 1970, the year that I came to the Catholic Worker, I earned $2,553.82; in 1971, I earned $0; in 1972, I earned $0; in 1973, I earned $0; and so on right down to 2009, when I also earned $0. For my entire life I have earned a big fat zero.

Some might ask, what's the point? You have created nothing, you have earned nothing, you have not ameliorated injustice. There are more hungry

6. Jeff Dietrich on vacation in Laguna Beach, California, 1979. Photo by Ardon Alger

people on the streets of Skid Row than ever and there is another war going on that is more intractable than the one in Vietnam. What do you have to show for your forty years of toil? It is one thing for an idealistic youth to devote a few years after college to community service. That is commendable and even helpful when applying for graduate school. But beyond that, it is something of a waste of time, talent, resources and an expensive education. After all of the protesting, after all the years of work for social change, after all the decades of unremunerated service, what did you accomplish? By any reasonable standard, you are a failure.

Though I am older now, I still operate out of the youthful assumptions that originally attracted me to the Catholic Worker, that basic sense of simplicity and immediacy of the gospel put into practice, that call us to give up everything and become a disciple of Jesus and serve those in need, confront war and injustice, be a human being, and do this outside the context of an institutional apparatus, whether that be State or Church or foundation or nonprofit corporation. To meet human needs in a human way—this is what appealed to the youthful pilgrim in me. Moreover, while I have not seemed to have accomplished anything permanent, the Catholic Worker was not founded with an eye towards permanence. It simply is a living witness to the gospel ethic of humans responding humanly to one another. In a culture obsessed with the beauty and glamour of youth, Dorothy Day understood that it was the idealism and courage of youth that attracted young people to the challenging life of the Catholic Worker. She understood that the gospels in practice, enfleshed in the world, were perennially a project of youthful fervor—they were, in the words of poet and songwriter Bob Dylan, "forever young;" forever appealing to those who were willing to give up everything, to risk their lives and their futures on the possibility that feeding the hungry, sheltering the homeless, and burning draft files was the most compelling, efficacious, and audacious thing that one could do. Such people were usually uninvested in careers or jobs or professional advancement, the substantive elements of the culture, and thus by definition, "young."

I believe the gospels are the best story we have. They are the singular counter-narrative to our consumerist, war-mongering, media-saturated, technologized, dehumanized, death-oriented culture. The story of the gospels—the triumph of goodness and mercy over the powers of death and domination—cannot be proven; and we cannot accept the story on faith alone; but we love the story so much that we want it to be true. To will the story into existence by our own living testimony to its veracity, thus giving witness to our deepest hopes for humanity—that is what attracted me as a young person to the Catholic Worker, and that is what attracts young people still to this day.

It is simply a love of the story and the existential recognition that the "making of the story real" is the best and perhaps only hope of humanity. What we do here at the Catholic Worker is so small and insignificant, this practice of the insubstantial, this act of living poverty, this hope against hope. But it is absolutely essential to the salvation of the world that we give witness to an alternative reality—that we say with our whole lives and our whole beings that there is another way to live, a more human and compassionate and meaningful way to live. I hope that I have lived my life conformed to this gospel ethic, shaped by this movement that continues to call young people to respond to a suffering world, to comfort the afflicted and afflict the comfortable.

But the truth is that while young people are attracted to the Catholic Worker, very few young people actually stay at the Catholic Worker long enough to become "old people." Along with a handful of others, I am a rare exception.

If I believed in luck, I would count myself a fortunate man indeed; but I do not believe in luck, therefore, I count myself exceedingly blessed. But even though I feel blessed, I do not consider myself particularly saintly or wise or spiritually evolved, in fact, quite the opposite. I do believe I am probably a more compassionate, sensitive, and courageous person than I would have been had I not spent my entire life at the Catholic Worker. And, though I am an "old person" now, I still aspire with fervor to the gospel project of being "forever young."

Jeff Dietrich
Los Angeles
September 2011

PART ONE

FAITH AS STORY AND COMMUNITY

All we have are these stories and each other.

Daniel Berrigan, SJ

INTRODUCTION

The entire Christian faith can be reduced to its essentials: stories and community. Faith is nothing more than the Gospel stories and the people who have gathered around the stories, compelled by a desire to make them real, to be affirmed and challenged by them, to conform their own lives to that narrative. It may seem stark and apocalyptic-like that at the end of the world, stories and friends are all that we have.

Storytelling is the essential human activity. It is the story we tell ourselves that gets us out of bed each morning, gets us through the day, forms us as a person. Faith is nothing more than the stories in which we believe, the stories that shape our lives, the stories that give us meaning. I don't believe in faith with a "capital F." Real faith has little to do with creeds or dogmas or doctrine or even church attendance. Real faith is about which story we tell ourselves, to which story do we give testimony with each action of our waking day. In which story do we put our faith?

We all know, because we heard it in church or learned it in Sunday school, or maybe we even saw the movie the "Greatest Story Ever Told." It is a story about how God sent his son to die for us, and how we can be Wall Street bankers, build nuclear bombs, pledge allegiance to the flag, and kill people in foreign lands as long as we accept Jesus as our personal Savior.

But the Gospels are not the greatest story ever told: the Gospels are the greatest alternative story ever told. When we encounter the Gospels as a great alternative story, rather than the greatest story, our faith becomes more than an emotional affirmation of Jesus or an obedient assent to dogma. It becomes, rather, a passionate desire to make the story real. When we start to put ourselves in the role of disciples who have been called to live the story as personal adventure, abandoning the safe harbor of fishing boats (Mark 1:16) and the security of tax collecting booths, the two car garage, the townhouse, the professional career, when we begin to understand that this is a living story whose conflicts with authorities, encounters with suffering, and trials of precarity are not mere dead history, but remain imminent and compelling unto this moment, then we live as people of faith.

Like the disciples, we walk "on the road" with Jesus. To give up everything and follow him is not sacrifice, but adventure. We begin with the same naïve enthusiasm as the disciples, equally unaware that the demons of the dominant story still move within us. We have left behind comfort, security, and privilege, but we still yearn for public acclaim, adulation, and perhaps even the modest fame of being a published author. Like the disciples, we want to "sit one at your right and the other at your left" (Mark 10:37). However, the male disciples abandon Jesus at the threat of the cross. It is the women disciples who remain to follow the lifeless body to the grave, becoming the first witnesses to the Resurrection and the first evangelizers of the Gospel.

While the triumphal Resurrection may be the centerpiece of the "Greatest Story," it is the brutal cross of Roman repression that forms the centerpiece of the great alternative story. And according to this story, it is only by hanging out at the cross, only by hanging out with the lepers and losers, rebels and reprobates, the hungry and the homeless, the desperate and the dispossessed, only by acknowledging the power of death at the center of the dominant story and acting like the courageous women disciples, committed to compassion and social transgression, that we get a fleeting glimpse of the Resurrection.

And every morning when we get up, we have to ask ourselves, for which story are we willing to risk everything: our comfort, our security, even our very lives, because the story we tell each other is both our faith and our salvation, since "All we have are these stories."

8. *The Last Supper* by Fritz Eichenberg, woodcut. Reproduced in the *Catholic Agitator*, 1975

Letters from County Jail*

Catholic Agitator, December, 1979, pp. 2 and 3

Catholic Agitator, November, 1980, pp. 4 and 5

Thursday, November 1, 1979

Dear Catherine,

Whenever I go out of my cell, I realize that there is a major portion of the population that I would find very difficult to deal with. I get a little frightened. I wish I would finally get into my permanent situation so I can find out if I can handle it. I am doing a lot of praying. I never felt more totally in the hands of God. I miss you so much.

Friday, November 2

This evening I washed the smell of fear from my T-shirt even as I tried to wash it from my own body. Furtively and quickly, I washed, not out of modesty, but out of fear that someone would observe my small, spare frame. I feel like a tiny rabbit among so many hungry hounds; the clanging of metal upon metal, my heart jumping each time; the cold cement against my feet; the piercing draft working its way through thin blankets; the swaggering braggadocio of the inmates; life is indeed cold and hard and brutal. At this basic level, any act of kindness is a gift of gold.

Today while I was working (I am a "runner" or errand boy for Deputy Jones), Jones gave me a cup of coffee. I was profoundly grateful not just for the coffee, but for the recognition of our shared humanity. So I waited until no one else was around and shared with him my apprehensions. "Oh, you'll be OK in Tank D. Don't worry. If you were a young kid or if you were black, you might have some problems, but you'll be OK."

---

*   The following are excerpts from Jeff Dietrich's letters to his wife and the community while he is serving a six month sentence in the Orange County Jail for blocking the doors of the Military Electronics Expo '79 held in Anaheim, California.

Jeff Dietrich

My apprehensions stem from the sudden realization that I am very obviously the smallest and weakest guy in a tank with forty others.

Very little in my past experience has prepared me to deal with the raw, brutal, macho lifestyle of the jail house. "If they talk shit, just talk shit right back to them!" Can you imagine talking shit to guys with twenty-inch biceps? That's how I measure the relative security of my environment—by the average size of the biceps and forearms.

So far the weight of the sentence has not borne down upon me. I've been too busy being scared about each new change, and whether or not I would survive. I continue to survive one day, one hour, one minute at a time. I pray unceasingly; I pray continuously. Not for world peace or social justice. I pray for survival. I pray for mercy. I pray for courage and strength, a touch of kindness, an inkling of compassion. My life has never been so completely out of my control. I am closer to the poor and powerless than I have ever been. It is not a position I relish.

Saturday, November 3

"Do you have a degree or something?" asked Tim. "I mean you don't seem to fit in here. You look smarter than everyone else." Found out! Well, I try. God knows I try but I can't get the swagger down. The shoulders are too narrow, arms too small, no tattoos. A Chinese dragon, anyone? Or a swastika, or perhaps the Virgin or a skull?

I can't talk in low conspiratorial whispers, unintelligible grunts between clenched teeth, lips not moving so the guard won't notice. "Watcha say, Simon? What's happening, hombre?" I am doing it all wrong. I smile when I hand out bedrolls: "Welcome to the County's free hotel." "How about a little chef salad?" I say when I help hand out food to those in isolation cells.

If we ever have illusions that love and nonviolence will carry the day, then all we need to do is go to jail to have those illusions shattered. The world is based on power, coercion, force. It is hard to see this on the outside, because we think that men's lives are directed by reason. But here most pretensions of civilization are stripped away and the fist and the club rule. I do not believe we can change it. The human heart is corrupt and deceitful. Only by God's grace will the world be transformed.

For years I have prayed for humility, a virtue which does not come easily to me. But this process of stripping away leaves me with nothing. The years of study, work, travel, aesthetic sensibility, organizational skills, leadership abilities, openness, enthusiasm, count for nothing here. I can't even perform a simple task like serving food the right way or making my bed properly, or keep from losing my towel.

I think of you constantly, Catherine. I know that my life is full of grace. Otherwise, I would never have found you. I would have moved through life without purpose or direction like so much flotsam and jetsom.

Monday, November 5

Last night the big guys invited me to do some weight lifting with them! Can you believe it? Well, it's not exactly the way it sounds. The weight they were lifting was me! They lay under the bed at one end while I sat on the top. They "pumped" the bed. Great fun, huh? Oh well. I might not be a peer, but it's nice to be accepted on some level.

I feel a lot more at ease now that I have a job and a routine. So far it is a whole lot better than I thought it would be. Sometimes I even forget that I am in jail, and then I look up and see the bars and it seems so strange, startling, like being in a cage in the zoo.

I read the editorial in the *Times* today. I was excited and encouraged. However, I honestly feel that the Judge Fitzgerald understands the situation better than the *Times*. The *Times* says that we are nice, responsible protestors and not a threat to society.

But as Christians, activists, and agitators, we wish that we were a threat to society—against war and injustice and intolerance. Judge Fitzgerald has, in a sense, paid us the great compliment of taking us more seriously that we take ourselves.

Tuesday, November 6

My new-found confidence was short-lived. Last night "Mumbles," the guy in the bunk across from me, told me some horror stories. Fights, suicides, gang bangs in the showers. No wonder I can't get any Vaseline for my chapped lips. It confirmed my initial impressions that violence is seething just under the surface. His advice, "Don't protest in here. Just do your own time." Frankly, I hope the occasion never arrives in which I might feel impelled to protest. What a coward I am at heart!

I got sent to the County Health Department today for a chest x-ray. Talk about feeling like a criminal. First, the handcuffs, then the leg irons. Then along with two armed guards, we ambled into the health clinic, while everyone inside and in the parking lot averted their eyes.

More letters from people who think that I am strong and dedicated. If they only knew how scared I am. People really want to believe that it's possible to be brave, noble, pure. I *hope* that it is.

Wednesday, November 7

Funny that before now writing had always been a chore to be avoided. But now there is nothing that gives me more pleasure. When there is nothing else to do and no one with whom to share your thoughts and reflections, there isn't much choice. Also, the enforced discipline of the situation, which is virtually monastic, almost requires that one become more focused and introspective.

Each event that happens becomes more significant, bathed as it is in the light of reflection and introspection. The other day some fellow inmate was riding down the escalator singing "Day by Day" as it echoed and reverberated off the walls of the stairwell; even though he couldn't sing it all, it seemed a profound, almost holy experience.

Part of my job is serving lunch and dinner to the "In-cells," those in protective custody; sex offenders, gays and snitches; the rejects of the rejected. We also serve soup and two slices of bread to the guys in the "hole." Today there were seven of them. I thought I would at least try to smile and be cheerful while I served this meager fare, as I am the only human contact they have. But the door doesn't open. A small rectangular window below waist level is pulled down and the bread and soup are set there. A single hand reaches out and the food is gone. No hello, no thank you, no contact, no human warmth, no communion. Surely man does not live by bread alone. Never have I been moved so passionately by the sight of a single hand. All I could do was silently pray, and the words "Give us this day our daily bread and forgive us our trespasses as we forgive others" took on a new significance. I had finally reached, within the secret recesses and labyrinths of this jail, the silent center and perfect still point of human suffering. Behind those thick steel doors, entombed in concrete, curled in a tight fetal position on a cold metal bed lies the suffering body of Christ.

Where, in God's name, is His compassionate and faith-filled Church? Where are the priests to minister to His wounded Body? Who will bring the sacraments to the wretched and rejected? Who will roll back the stone and enter the tomb? Who will bring the Good News of the Resurrection and Christ's eternal Love to rekindle lost faith, lost hope?

Do not the cries of the suffering and rejected ones pierce the very concrete and steel? Have you ears that do not hear, eyes that do not see?

(Mark 8:18) Is your heart turned to stone? Do you stand before us as the judges do: cynical, haughty, powerful, and deem us unworthy, unfit to be a part of His Church? Woe to you who minister only to the rich and are unmindful of the poor, the sick, the prisoner.

Today is a milestone. It's been two weeks since I came in here. Two weeks and my survival skills certainly seem to have improved, perhaps a little too much. Yesterday after visiting hours, they herded all of us, about forty, into that small cell, as usual, before having us ride single file back up the escalator. Standing at the door of the cell was John, a guy I knew from the first tank that I was in. My first reaction was to go up and say hello, but on second thought, I crouched down in the far corner.

John is the suspect in the sensational Orange County rapist case which has received extensive coverage in the Orange County papers. His picture was on the front page of the *Register*. After extensive talks with him, I am convinced he is innocent.

However, rape is not an acceptable crime in jailhouse society and I did not think it would do me any good to be associated with him. John went out at the head of the line, I went out last. I heard later that he was "jumped" while on the escalators and punched a couple of times.

I am not sure of the ethics of such situations, but I am certain that my behavior doesn't qualify me for any hero buttons!

Friday, November 9

As the "Reluctant Resistor"* it has taken many years to get myself in real "trouble" because, even though I know intellectually that it is the right thing, in my chicken heart of hearts I did not want to go to jail. I suppose, if there had been anyone around here even remotely like Berrigan or James Douglass, I would have been in this situation long ago. This may come as a shock to some people but I've never felt like a leader. I am really much better at being a follower. I have persistence, diligence, dedication, commitment. I don't feel comfortable being an initiator.

A factor that I keep coming back to is Judge Fitzgerald. I don't feel any anger towards him at all. At least not any more anger or frustration than I would feel at anyone else in our society. We are so isolated from the suffering and misery of the poor and war-torn. We are so caught up in the material distractions and pleasures of our culture that the prospect of nuclear devastation and its attendant horrors is a completely abstract concept.

---

* Also the title of Jeff Dietrich's first book, a collection of letters from jail written to his wife and community.

Anyway, there seems to be some dynamic at play here that transcends the legal process and causes me to react in a way that I might not otherwise behave. Perhaps it's just a personality conflict. Perhaps it's more than that.

Last year, Judge Fitzgerald's skepticism and his mocking manner which sought to identify us as neurotics with a martyr complex, made me all the more determined to come back the next year. Now this year the same attitude combined with his efforts to punish us until we promise not to come back next year are making me feel like I want to do it again even though I had previously decided that I wouldn't do it in 1980.

We don't know what the dynamics are in this whole thing, but I do know that, up to now, I've been taking tiny baby steps, testing my balance, testing the evenness of the ground, each small step only a slight calculated risk. Until now. Now it's suddenly a giant step that I really wasn't counting on. The ground is unfamiliar and my balance unsure. I don't feel the least bit in control of this game.

I keep asking God to protect me. I try to say "not my will but your will be done, O Lord." But then I keep thinking, what if I don't like what the Lord's will has in store for me? What if it's too hard? What if I can't handle it? I try to have faith and believe that the Lord did not bring me to this place only to abandon me in my hour of greatest need. The temptation is great, but I cannot believe that my life on this planet is a cosmic joke, which is what it would be if it were to end in nuclear holocaust.

Sunday, November 11

Yesterday three or four of the guards were asking me if it was worth it to be in jail for so long. I really couldn't think of an adequate answer. How could I talk about something as ephemeral as God acting in our lives or intervening in history? At such times these sentiments ring too loudly of foolishness and absurdity. These men want to hear about results: mass demonstrations, political candidates, election returns, not the "foolishness of God that is wiser than the wisdom of men." How do I speak of the necessity of making personal sacrifice? Change does not come from the barrel of a gun or the decrees of the legislature. It comes out of the suffering and sacrifice. And so it goes…the ancient ritual is played over and over again. Birth, death, resurrection. The light shown in the darkness and the darkness overcame it not. Only the sacrifice of the innocent victim will suffice. In some small measure I am now participating in that ancient drama. I am being punished, but I committed no crime. In fact, I have done a service to mankind. I am a prisoner but I have no guilt.

It is a game that is both exciting and frightening. It is the ultimate game, because, at its more intense levels, it doesn't allow for any "time-outs." It's not often that people in our culture have the opportunity to immerse themselves totally in an experience, to become one with that experience. In fact, our way of life is designed specifically to prevent us from having anything close to an authentic experience.

We are so afraid that we might experience suffering, misery, poverty, death that we have built buffers against these things that keep us from experiencing joy, happiness, satisfaction, transcendence, and life. Ultimately, we keep a lot of psychiatrists employed.

Monday, November 12

Mass is supposed to be said tonight but nobody I've talked to has heard about it. Maybe it's like the movies that we're supposed to see on Fridays, but never do. I really would like to receive communion.

What a great gift the Eucharist is. There is something there which speaks so simply and clearly to my life. Sometimes I think I am saved by poetry. Without an understanding of poetry, how can we grasp the spirit of Christ's message? Christ speaks to us through myth, metaphor, symbol, the language of poetry.

The Eucharist is such an excellent, perhaps even perfect, metaphor. It appeals to me intellectually, emotionally, physically, spiritually. A simple meal of bread and wine. It could have been bread and water, but that is prison fare, a subsistence meal. Bread and wine, that is a celebration! Bread for the body, wine for the spirit. Body and blood.

Tuesday, November 13

One of the guys who works in the kitchen is really incensed at my position as a protester of military weapons. He is always on the verge of physically accosting me. "What are you, some kind of Communist?" "No, I am a pacifist and a Christian," I said. "Christian! If you are a Christian, what are you doing in jail? Oh, I know. You are a protester and society is against protesters, right?" "No, I am in jail, because I broke the law. I tried to block the entrance to a Military Arms Convention." "What the hell do you think we're gonna do without arms? How are we gonna defend ourselves? If it weren't for arms, you'd be speaking Communist by now and working in some shoe factory!" "Well," I said, "I feel if we don't do something about it we will undoubtedly destroy the entire planet." "If that's the way it has to be, that's the way it has to be. If I can't have it, they can't have it."

That's it in a nutshell. We are totally possessed by fear and greed; our path is firmly fixed. I don't want to sound too pessimistic, but I believe that this man expresses the dominant opinion in the United States. Against such heartless sentiments, how do we prevail?

Wednesday, November 14

Dear Catherine and Community,

Today while I was serving lunch in the hole one of the inmates called out to the deputy that he was about to have a seizure. The deputy, much to my surprise, called on the phone for a nurse. It took almost a half hour for the nurse to come. Good thing it wasn't an emergency. The deputy and I waited in silence, usually I kind of banter or make light conversation, but not in the hole.

There were a lot of grilled cheese sandwiches on the food cart and I wanted to eat some of them. Somehow it seemed sacrilegious to eat in this place. Furthermore, the slight odor of vomit and the fetid atmosphere of human suffering take the appetite away. It was not a good place to eat but it was a good place to pray. So I walked up and down the cold, sterile corridors and prayed and felt very strongly the presence of the Lord.

The hole is located on the fourth floor mezzanine, between the third and fourth floors. If you turn right, you enter the hole. If you turn left, you enter the Chapel! The Chapel, like everything else here, is sterile and lifeless. I couldn't help but reflect upon this irony: that the house of God is located so near to the house of punishment. I can say without a doubt that the Lord is present ever so much more strongly in the latter than in the former. One is the true Church of the Catacomb; the other is just simply buried.

Tomorrow is Thursday! A great joy. I will see Catherine.

Ernie (he's the barber) says I do my time easy. We'll see in a couple of months if I do easy time. But it is kind of interesting that for almost ten years I have been striving and struggling to do the work of the Lord and now I do the most important work I have ever done, simply by doing nothing. So, in that sense, it certainly is easy time.

I need to be more trusting, however. I continue to ask the Lord to protect me. You know—don't let me get beat up or stabbed or raped. Probably that's very juvenile and indicates a low level of spiritual development. Probably on an existential level it is more acceptable to pray for courage and fortitude. For the virtues that are already within all of us. Because while the Lord may see fit to subject us to any number of trials, He will give us the grace to prevail. I hope I have that kind of faith anyway.

Recently my concern has been not so much that something would happen to me but that I would witness something happening to someone else and be too frightened to respond. As I prayed the other night, it occurred to me that I would have to respond with the same moral outrage to the violation of personhood in here as I would on the outside. Whether the violation is committed by an individual or a government, it is the same. I know that that seems elementary, but it occurred to me with such clarity that I felt as if I had more strength to do the actual deed no matter what the consequences, and it gave me a sense of peace.

Thursday, November 15

This is our third week in jail and I feel good. Truly a gift from God! I feel that if I come out of this whole thing in one piece—I still don't have absolute faith— nothing will be able to stop me. I will have experienced about the worst they have to offer, which so far isn't so bad. I keep thinking of the children of Israel whom King Nebuchadnezzar threw into the burning furnace. It was seven times hotter than the hottest furnace. And those children, God's children, who had refused to bow down to the golden idol were simply standing unharmed in the middle of the furnace. I think it's possible to not just survive, but even to grow and flourish. A perfect revenge upon the system. This, however, is a provisional evaluation. I'll be able to give you a more definite answer when I get out of here.

I had a good surprise today. Because our cell was late in getting up to the roof (that's where we get outside), I was back from work in time to go. As you can imagine, no one else was doing any running except for me. Long distance running is not one of the popular sports around here. There I was running around the roof like some fool. After I didn't stop for thirty or forty minutes, people began to give me funny looks. But it was good to run, to take my shirt off and feel the cool evening breeze on my body. It was sensuous to breathe hard and feel my heart pounding and sweat stinging my eyes. After a while I stopped just to look at the trees below, the blue sky and the bright reds of the dying day.

Honestly, it is not possible to appreciate life until we no longer have it. We cannot have life until we give up our life. I think so much about my life: the gift of community, my relationship with Catherine, meaningful work, the *Agitator*. Never have things seemed so important to me. When we are living from day to day we take things for granted. Our bodies, our senses, the natural beauty of the world, love, warmth, community. Now these are seen as from a tomb and they seem so special, precious. I see, as if I had new eyes. I cannot take this life for granted. Perhaps this is the meaning of resurrection: that when we are deprived of life we come to appreciate it with a renewed understanding, as one who comes back from the grave.

Tuesday, November 20

I pray at times when the void seems to open up before me and suddenly I am totally alone with my fears. I pray when I serve chow in the hole. I pray when I am locked in small cages for hours with a group of other men. I pray when I march in single file through the chow line and I can sense the undertone of violence and terror and desperation crackling through the air like static electricity. I pray when I ride down the escalators and walk through the mausoleum halls alone and the cold cement and steel begins to wrap itself around my heart. I pray when the guards put their hands upon my body so that I feel like an animal or a piece of dirty laundry. Only prayer can make sense out of this experience, only prayer can transform this experience.

Wednesday, November 21

When I went to work this morning I noticed that Sam wasn't among those who went down the escalator with us. "Hey, where's Sam?" "They called him out at 6:00 a.m. this morning. Took him to the pen today." I was disappointed. I had hoped to say goodbye to Sam. Sam wasn't exactly a great pal of mine, but he tolerated and accepted me, and I appreciated that as much as anything else that's happened to me recently.

Sam was a big, heavy-set Mexican *vato* about thirty-five years old, with enormous tattoos all over his body. He was in bunk #1 and he was sort of tacitly in charge by force of his superior personality, you might say. The first night I was in the module, I was taking a furtive shower after the lights went out hoping that no one else would want to use the shower while I was in there. The curtain was suddenly pulled back in such a ferocious manner that I almost jumped out of my white, white skin. Sam's abundant Pancho Villa-style mustache appeared to curl in disgust at the sight of my naked white body. I had visions of the classic Humphrey Bogart bandito encounter in *Treasure of the Sierra Madre.* "What's in the bags, American?" Sam was so disgusted that he didn't even come in. I got out as quickly as I could.

I saw Sam several times in the course of my work each day. He would come into my store room for extra blankets and towels. He would speak very jovially to my partner, Chips, but completely ignore my existence. After a suitable length of time, however, Sam finally deigned to take enough notice of me to make me the butt of jokes and witticisms. "Looks like this newspaper was messed up by a demonstrator or something." The relationship was ultimately never what you would call warm, but it was tolerant, for which I was grateful, because it made me feel somewhat "at home," as if I might be able to make it here after all.

Just two days before they came and got Sam, I was taking my evening shower when he stepped in to use the shower next to me. I felt a little stupid because I was standing under the nozzle washing my undershirt and socks and that just didn't seem very cool. But Sam got in, took off his shorts and started to wash them, so I felt much cooler, like I was into the scene. I said hello to him. He said hello to me. Then there was just silence and running water. After a long while I finally got up my nerve and asked, "How long you in for, Sam?" "I'll probably be out of here by Wednesday. They're taking me to the pen." "How come?" "For a burglary. And the shit of it is I don't even remember doin' it." "What do you mean?" "Oh I ain't saying' I haven't done anything, cuz I done a lot of stuff, but I always remember what I done." "So if you don't remember this one, you probably didn't do it right?" "Right! But I got so many priors that I couldn't afford to fight it. And they had a witness who swears that she saw me there. It's not like I never done anything. I just don't remember doin' this one. So anyway I pleaded guilty and took the three years cause if I fought it and lost, the judge would'a given me nine years." "You been to the joint before?" I asked. "O yeah, three times before. It ain't so bad." "You married?" "No." "Well, maybe that's a good thing," I said, feeling stupid for having said it, but not able to think of an appropriate response. I stood drying off trying not to look directly at Sam's hairy body, or the tattoo of a woman on his backside or his uncircumcised genitals. Awkward silence again prevailed as I tried desperately to think of some encouraging sentiment to exit by. Something sympathetic and yet still tough. "I'll pray for you, Sam," I said as I stepped out of the shower. That wasn't exactly what I had in mind. It just kind of came out while I wasn't thinking. It was the kind of thing that you would say at a funeral. It always sounds so false, hollow, inappropriate. Sam just kind of smiled like it was funny and wouldn't be much help where he was going, but it somehow was important to him anyway.

I've been praying for Sam ever since. Maybe I'll be praying for Sam for the rest of my life.

* * *

As the lights go out at night I am not so much lonely as just alone. I have never had quite this sense of self before, a feeling of compression, distillation, essence.

The boys have taken to gathering in the bathroom after lights out for exercise and bullshit. The addition of a couple of new faces has made it a little more raucous and exceedingly more macho.

Thursday, November 22, Thanksgiving Day

Another milestone. Four weeks are past. By the way, four weeks don't equal a month here. Four weeks are twenty-eight days. It'll be three more days before I am here a month. But many of the guys already consider me "short." That does not refer to physical stature. It indicates that you only have a short time left to go on your sentence.

I was thinking about the unique sense of self that emerges out of a situation like this when one is cut off from family, friends, and other support systems. I remember that I have actually had one other similar experience like this that also effected a major change in my life's direction.

After I refused induction into the armed services in 1970, I felt very much cut off from the mainstream of life in my own country. That act was the culmination for me of several years of anger, frustration, and alienation. Not knowing what else to do and feeling certain of eventual incarceration, I decided to pursue a long-time dream of traveling in Europe. The act of refusing induction was frightening, but not so frightening as the prospect of traveling alone in a foreign country. But I intentionally chose to travel alone as a conscious test of my abilities to sustain myself.

Until that time (I was twenty-four), I felt that I was extremely dependent, particularly in an emotional sense, upon family and friends. This, then, was an effort to break those ties and see where it would lead me. Parenthetically, it was also a dropping out experience, as it was very popular at that time to become a hippie and take to the highways. In many ways, I date the beginning of my life, perhaps it's not too dramatic to say "rebirth," from the time I refused to enter the military and decided to make this trip abroad.

I felt as though I was laying myself open to whatever happened. Breaking out of my safe, sheltered environment, breaking ties with family, friends, the past. It was a trust in some as yet undefined spirit. It was a letting go. Until that time I was afraid of everything that was unfamiliar, unknown, strange. Now I would pit myself against the unknown. In retrospect, it was something of a pilgrimage, or more accurately the beginning of a pilgrimage upon which I still journey. In the beginning, it was a pilgrimage into the unknown, requiring all of the feeble faith that I could muster, faith that the unknown would not denounce me. Faith that strangers would be kind; faith that it was safe to sleep by the roadside, in city parks and wheat fields; faith in my ability to survive; faith in the goodness and charity of others.

Before I left for Europe, I stopped with a friend in Boston. It was there in a bookstore that the most important event of the trip occurred. I learned how to pray again. This is kind of embarrassing to admit, but I owe my conversion (for that's what I think happened) to an at the time popular, though now long forgotten, book on the drug culture. I would like to be able say that it was Thomas Merton or Dorothy Day or St. John of the Cross who brought me back to Christ, but I can't. The name of the book was *Beyond the Drug Experience* by Robert S. de Ropp. Which was pretty much where I was at the time. So it appealed to me when it talked about mantras and meditation. One of the mantras it mentioned was the Jesus Prayer, which I chose for myself, possibly because of a latent feeling for Christianity, but more probably because I like J.D. Salinger's book *Franny and Zooey*. The book talked about repeating the mantra over and over until it became as natural and unconscious as breathing and every breath was a praising of God. Well, I've never really developed to that level of spirituality. But I immediately grasped the practicality of this style of praying. If one were constantly occupying one's mind with prayer, it would be easier to combat self-perpetuating anxieties and fears, particularly those associated with being alone. It also stops the mental tape recordings of scenarios from the past and stupid, repetitious jingles from TV commercials. All of this was in addition to what I still regarded as the somewhat dubious spiritual value. So I began to pray constantly. It was an act of the Holy Spirit.

By the time I got to Europe (it took almost two weeks because I went by way of boat from Iceland), I was so lonely that I was almost in physical pain. It took about a month before I got used to it. Though it was an extremely difficult time for me, it was also very good in some of the same ways that it is good to be in jail. It was a time alone, a time of reflection and prayer and for many of the same reasons. I kept a journal then as I do now.

There was a kind of compression and distillation of inner strength, a focusing, a depth of understanding and perception to the point that when I returned home some of my friends simply did not understand me. I was almost a different person, stronger, more direct, more perceptive and articulate, because I spoke from a place within myself. I think these moments of enlightenment come only very rarely and the insights can be very easily dissipated. I was fortunate in finding an environment that nurtured these insights.

Friday, November 23

Yesterday, we had a big Thanksgiving dinner. It was good, too much sage in the dressing and too much ginger in the pumpkin pie, but otherwise everything tasted fine and there was a lot of it. We were even given extra time to eat it, and if you liked to smoke there was a big cigar waiting for you as you left the chow hall.

But it was a very sad experience. I wasn't depressed or anything. It was just such a poignant reminder that a celebration is more than just material abundance. Celebration comes from the hearts of the celebrants. It is more than sharing food and drink. It is sharing each other. When there is no community, there is no celebration. To break a dry crust of bread with loved ones is a greater celebration than sharing a banquet with those whose hearts are closed.

This does not mean that community cannot happen among strangers, merely that an atmosphere of oppression and alienation does not readily lend itself to effective community. It was a hollow holiday.

Saturday, November 24

Last year at about this time, Kent, Marty, Jon, and I were sitting in a holding tank at county court. Kent had just shared a passage from the Acts of the Apostles. The Apostles had been beaten and jailed for repeatedly preaching the Gospel. When they were thrown in jail this time the doors were opened by an angel so that they could return to their preaching. It was at that time that I decided to come back to the Convention Center the next year. Actually I was kind of disappointed in myself for not going back immediately upon release. But Kent pointed out that it was the last day of the convention and it was almost over. So I allowed him to ease my conscience with the prospect of returning the next year. So here I am and what I want to know is when does the part happen where the angels come and release us?

I really am not certain that this is the most important thing that I can do with my time or if it is going to make any difference in terms of the arms race. Perhaps I could be more effective "on the streets" organizing for next year, speaking, educating, planning, researching, etc. On the face of it, it certainly would be a better use of my time to be at the kitchen caring for the hungry and homeless and helping to take the load off of other community members. I guess the efficacy of an act like this must in great measure be taken on faith, because we may never know the results of the act or its effect on human lives and actions. We do not know if people will ever be moved

9. Jeff Dietrich at the Federal Building, downtown Los Angeles protesting US intervention in Central America, 1985. Photo by James Ryman

by the sight of the Spirit working in our lives. Or if the apparent course of history will be even slightly modified. It is purely a matter of faith.

But there is one sense of the effectiveness of our actions that has been verified by personal experience. On the outside, no matter what I was

31

doing, community organizing, serving the poor, demonstrating for peace and justice, it was not enough. There was always a subtle feeling of guilt because I was participating even in a marginal way in a culture of warfare and death. While I have not by any means transcended guilt, I have never been more at peace with myself. To be in jail because of one's commitment to peace, this is the closest I have come so far to a lack of complicity in the crimes of our culture.

The Lepers on Crocker Street

Catholic Agitator, February, 1990, pp. 1 and 2

It looks like a war zone, with sleeping bags and bed rolls strewn in disarray, and supine bodies asleep where they have fallen dead to the world. The acrid smoke of campfires stings the eyes and the gutter-fat odors of garbage and human offal assault the nostrils like the Nazi *blitzkrieg.*

Even though the sun has been up in the rest of the city for at least two hours, here on Crocker Street the two-story, gray concrete wall of the Pacific American Fish Company turns its unblinking stare upon the cocaine and crack addicts of this seamy Skid Row drug encampment, blocking the warmth of the sun and shuttering this cement canyon into a permanent twilight zone.

There is a bizarre, foreign-looking quality to these 200 or so feet of concrete sidewalk crammed to overflowing with filthy humanity, like a cattle car rushing to the slaughter house. Surely, these must be the streets of some Third World Calcutta, where people endure a vermin-like existence with oriental stoicism, living in public places, a full half-world away from the broad avenues and boulevards of American enterprise and opportunity.

It is easy to rekindle the feelings of revulsion and righteousness of the nineteenth-century British imperialist encountering for the first time the filthy opium dens and squalid humanity clinging precariously to the fringes of the Empire.

Not unlike these British officers, who did their best to maintain a façade of civilization in wilderness outposts, the officers of the LAPD are deploying a holding pattern, rather than push for victory in their battle against drugs and deviance. Thus, there are regularly scheduled harassment and arrest actions in which a score or so of the inhabitants might be forced to kneel with hands behind their heads while officers swagger about, making a show of force and civilization complete with, knocking over camp fires and

Jeff Dietrich

throwing possessions into the street, searching suspects, and occasionally making an arrest or two. But, for the most part, there is an unstated recognition that this is a battle of appearances only, a waving of the flag of law and order in the badlands of chaos and degeneracy. On most days, you can drive by anytime of the day or night and see the unmistakable glow of "crack pipes," the frenzied exchange of cash, and a score of spent butane lighters which give silent but eloquent testimony to the persistence of deviance.

Like the Good Humor* man driving into Dante's *Inferno*, the old Catholic Worker Chevy van rolls into these badlands a couple of mornings a week to serve coffee and fresh-baked raisin bread to the early risers. Of the various nomadic activities that we are experimenting with while our new soup kitchen is being built, this is the most challenging and the least favorite. The people are aggressive and rude and we have to keep our "street smarts" on constant alert, like the half-cocked hammer of an imaginary pistol, ready to pack it up at the first sign of the trouble that can flash through this crowd like a Fourth of July brush fire. Last week, when a drug deal went sour, knives and screw drivers and lead pipes wrapped in electrical tape appeared quick as secret hand-shakes at a Shriners' convention. It was over in a flash. They had the little culprit up-ended and screaming like a spider monkey in heat, shaking him until the requisite amount of cash was gleaned from the inner sanctum of his pockets. Here on Crocker Street, we feel as though we have stepped into a morass of problems of such depth and gravity that they make our meager gifts of bread and coffee seem about as helpful and effective as a popsicle in hell.

The ancient Hebrew name for hell is Gehenna. It meant, literally, garbage dump. In the daytime it was just a heap of decaying, odiferous matter rotting in the sunlight at the outskirts of town. No civilized person ever went there during the day except to quickly dump his refuse and perhaps pause to urinate. In the dark of night, however, it was a different matter. It became the grocery store and gathering place of the most disgusting and degenerate low-life of Hebrew culture: the lepers, who were literally the outcasts of this community.

Of course, the ancient Hebrew people were not nearly so advanced in their understanding of the human condition as contemporary folk and thus did not realize that leprosy is a physical disease. Rather, they believed that it was a condition precipitated by the sinfulness of the individual. Thus, in Hebrew culture, the victim of the physical disease of leprosy—which in ancient times could be a symptomatic condition as benign as adolescent

---

* A popular brand of American ice cream that was sold from trucks driving through neighborhoods.

34

skin eruptions—was heartlessly ejected to the margins of the community for his "sinfulness."

Today, we are under the impression that such superstitious behavior would never be tolerated in our more progressive society. But the city of Los Angeles is extremely adept at administering just this type of garbage dump therapy to the homeless addicts of Skid Row. The city of Los Angeles has an extremely effective drug therapy program. Amazingly enough, it is staffed by unlicensed "drug counselors" on loan from the Street Maintenance Department. They are supervised by two senior drug and substance abuse counselors from the Los Angeles Police Department, who offer free group therapy at the Los Angeles County Jail. Their therapeutic equipment consists of two five-ton yellow dump trucks, a T-228 caterpillar skip loader, a pick-up truck, and a squad car. Together they operate as a kind of rapid deployment task force. Twice a week, they rush about in military-type caravan from one Skid Row encampment to the other, cleaning up the city's drug problem with the speed and efficiency of Patton's tank corps rushing to the Rhine.

If this seems like a ludicrous and inappropriate way of dealing with the serious drug problem in our city, you are correct. You are equally correct in assuming that there are more serious responses taking place. But you are wrong if you think that their level of success, compassion, or humanity is a great deal higher than the garbage dump approach.

Both the liberal social service programs and the Christian fundamentalist missions that earn their keep—some rather nicely, by the way—by salvaging the shipwrecked lives caught on the shoals of Skid Row share the same Calvinist theology that undergirds our larger social system and places the burden of economic and spiritual sinfulness directly upon the shoulders of the individual. Repent and be saved, repent and be employed—it is the same message. As long as we can convince ourselves that the situation is the result of the individual person's sinfulness, or pride, or laziness, then the larger community is comfortably absolved of any responsibility for the miserable condition.

We at the Catholic Worker believe that the drug addicts of Crocker Street are in the same situation as the lepers of first-century Palestine. They have been cast out of the community for a sin that they did not commit.

The poor are the ones most affected by the rapid changes in technology, culture, and the economy. It is among the poor that we are able to observe the seamy underside of our most precious cultural idols: technological and economic progress. The glowing effusiveness of futurologists like Alvin

Toffler and John Naisbitt, who liken our future of constant technological change and economic growth to a series of waves, and our critical survival skills as the ability to surf that so-called wave of the future, are as naïve as the nineteenth-century scientist and industrialist whose own utopian projections were devoid of the disastrous environmental consequences that we suffer today.

It is on places like Crocker Street that the wave has already crashed, leaving the poor bereft not only of jobs but of dignity, self-worth, family, community and a sense of purpose. Of course the poor take drugs. Their situation is hopeless. Drugs are not the problem. They are merely the symptom of a despair and lifelessness at the center of our culture. We are deluding ourselves if we think that it is possible to teach the poor how to surf when they have never learned to swim.

Over the last two and a half decades, under the pressure of revolutionary changes in the fields of transportation, communication, and information processing, we have rapidly shifted from a national economy to a world economy. In this situation, the "surfers," who engage in what Harvard economist Robert Reich calls "symbolic-analytic work"—lawyers, bankers, executives, consultants, scientists, writers, editors, etc.—have increased their share of GNP to 40 percent, while representing only 20 percent of the job force. On the other hand the "swimmers", who engaged in "routine production work" have had their share of the GNP reduced from 30 percent to only 20 percent. These manufacturing type jobs once represented a full 50 percent of the American work force. Today, they represent only 25 percent ("Why the Rich are Getting Richer and the Poor are Getting Poorer," *UTNE Reader* p. 42).

The people on Crocker Street know intuitively that this "wave of the future" will not reverse itself. It will only gather momentum and the "surfers" will ride faster and faster while the "swimmers" will surely drown in the sea of despair and drugs. They also realize that neither the liberal social worker nor the conservative fundamentalist preacher, nor for that matter a Democratic presidential candidate, will offer them the true salvation that Jesus Christ demanded for the lepers of this time; that is, full participation in the economic, social, and spiritual life of the community.

The true faith of our nation lies not in the worship of Jesus Christ, the God of life, but rather in the worship of the gods of power: technological progress and unrestrained economic growth, which progressively relegates to the dung heap the large masses of simple folk who will never be ordained into the higher level of abstract symbolic function demanded of its arcane priesthood. As Hazel Motes, the demented preacher in Flannery O'Connor's novel, *Wise Blood*, said, "Nobody with a good car needs to be justified" (quoted in *Collected Works*, p. 64). Our faith in power is justified by its manifest effectiveness. Our faith in Christ is justified only by the simple spirit of life that flows through us, and life is never effective.

Thus, in good conscience, we can offer the "lepers" of Crocker Street neither the "cheap grace" of mission salvation nor the tawdry hope of phony job training programs. While we know that what we do have to offer is manifestly meager, it comes without restrictions. We do not demand repentance or job readiness or clean streets. Along with the meager gifts of bread and coffee, we offer a few brief moments of an authentic human contact that neither judges nor condemns, but recognizes the improbable connectedness of our common human brokenness.

Sundance and All the Indian Raiders

Catholic Agitator, August, 1976, p. 5

"The raiders, they're there, they're up in the hills above Los Angeles! We've got submachine guns and M-16s. We're gonna ride down tonight and we're gonna take over. But don't you guys worry; you'll be protected because you help the poor and the Indians."

Like some drunken prophet, Sundance would shake his fist at the empty sky and relate his apocalyptic vision of Indian revolutionaries riding out of the hills to mete out justice for the poor and oppressed and condemnation to the rich and powerful. Often he would relate his images with such power and conviction that I never quite knew where drunken fantasy left off and reality began.

Of course, reality was and is that Sundance, like so many of the Indians, particularly on Skid Row, is a victim of the disease of alcoholism. During the commemoration of the massacre at Wounded Knee a few years ago, Sundance was always on the verge of leaving Los Angeles to join his besieged Indian brothers and sisters.* But there was always an excuse: "The Chippewa and Sioux must get together first." "We have to organize blankets and supplies before we can leave." "The FBI is following us," and on and on until, of course, the expedition never materialized. It was just another drunken fantasy.

Of all the people that we encounter on Skid Row the Indians are the most destroyed, the most exposed, the most naked. They do not fit into the white man's culture and their own civilization has been completely destroyed. It would have been better if the people had died with their

---

* Commemorating the 1890 massacre of at least 150 men, women, and children of the Lakota Sioux Tribe on the Pine Ridge Indian Reservation in South Dakota. The ceremony has grown increasingly larger every year. Riders subject themselves to the cold weather as well as the lack of food and water as they retrace the path that their family members took to Wounded Knee. They carry with them a white flag to symbolize their hope for world peace.

culture. It would have been kinder; it would have been more humane than this slow death by alcoholism and brutality. What is a man who has no place in the world, who has no history because it has been destroyed or negated, who has no God because it was "pagan," who has no dignity because it was taken, who finds no meaning in life because it is one's culture that shapes life and gives a sense of place and permanence in infinite time and space? Our place in the world, our perception of time and space is determined by our culture. It is as if we had put on a special coat that protects us from a vast and sometimes hostile universe. Lacking this special coat, the Indian is naked and defenseless.

It is not without a grave sense of guilt that I ladle out a bowl of beans to Johnny Blackgoat, whose patrimony was the big horn sheep and the great mountain elk, whose home is now covered with cement and strangled by high tension lines and barbed wire. We have squandered Johnny's patrimony and his homeland. We have paid him off with a bunch of glass beads and a whole lot of cheap wine with which to kill himself. Surely the heavenly hosts cry out for justice.

Justice is the crux of Robert Sundance's struggle. Sundance has been arrested over 175 times for being drunk in public. In his court case Sundance has championed the cause of all of the poor in Los Angeles who are arrested for what has been legally defined as the disease of alcoholism. Over 75,000 drunk in public arrests are made in LA each year, 30,000 in the Skid Row area. Often these men are arrested, jailed and released without ever seeing a judge or magistrate. When they do come before a judge, only the most foolhardy or courageous will plead innocent. A plea of innocent means a thirty-day wait in county jail before trial, while a guilty plea means a "kickout" in a few days. If Sundance and his lawyers from the Center of Law in the Public Interest are successful, the alcoholic will be taken out of the criminal justice system and placed in the Public Health system where he belongs.

The so called "Sundance Decision" (1978) was a victory for Skid Row homeless by decriminalizing public drunkenness; it required police to take public inebriates to treatment centers rather than jail.

Sundance is sober now. He doesn't talk too much about the raiders; mostly he talks about his trial. How long will he remain sober? My guess would be as long as he can work for Justice.

No Resurrection Without the Poor

Catholic Agitator, May, 1998, pp. 4 and 6

Mean Ed is a crack addict, a drug dealer, and a passionate despiser of all white people—and since Catholic Workers are the only white people that he comes in contact with, we bear the brunt of his ferociousness. I have been spat upon, punched, threatened with a knife, a pair of scissors, a length of lead pipe, a bicycle chain, and a particularly lethal No. 2 pencil. When he comes to our soup kitchen, he deliberately starts fights, cuts the line, and slanders white and black people alike. Though he helps himself to the resources of our facility, he consistently maligns us and rebuffs all overtures of friendliness. So we were not exactly saddened when the police recently busted Mean Ed for drug dealing. "The poor you will always have with you," and they are often a pain in the neck.

It is easy to understand why current public policy dictates that the poor be eliminated from our streets and parks and public gathering places. It is easy to understand why the police aggressively collect shopping carts, destroy street encampments, and arrest panhandlers. The poor are a pain in the neck.

By the same token, it is easy to understand, but more difficult to accept, that our Church has removed the poor in the process of building its new Cathedral. When Jesus said, "the poor you will always have with you," he was speaking not to municipalities or state-run institutions; he was speaking to the Church.

As the cost of the new Cathedral soars from a promised cap of $45 million to a new high of $163 million, the fund raising process begins to resemble that of the Music Center and the Disney Concert Hall, with the donor list reading like an ad for "Lifestyles of the Rich and Famous." Every millionaire from Rupert Murdoch to Roy Disney to Betsy Bloomingdale is standing in line to fork over the big bucks. The poor you will always have with you, but not when it comes to building cathedrals.

The poor are a pain in the neck, but without the poor there is no cross, there is no Resurrection, no Easter, no Christianity. Without the poor we separate Christ from his Church. In order to raise $163 million, one must eliminate the negative and accentuate the positive. One must sell the Resurrection at the cost of the cross. The rich and powerful have always been in the market for such cheap grace. The rich do not need the cross; they can buy salvation.

Though it often seems bewildering to me that Cardinal Mahony and the Catholic Worker claim allegiance to the same Church, it is nevertheless true. And in that Church we both have separate job descriptions. The Cardinal is a good and faithful man and a powerful leader; he is doing the job that cardinals do, and he is doing it well. He is enhancing the power of the Church by building a grand cathedral that will be the rival of any downtown skyscraper. He is establishing himself and his Church as a prominent political and social force. He is cementing his relationship with the rich and powerful.

Our job as Catholic Workers is somewhat less glamorous but no less important: it is to be obedient to our consciences and faithful to scripture, and to humbly but boldly remind the Church that the kind of fund raising necessitated by grand projects like this has a tendency to uncritically affirm the rich and powerful while selling out Jesus by denying the vocation of the cross and forgetting that the poor will always be with you.

While we continue to have much discrete and clandestine support, we remain the solitary public Catholic voice in opposition to this project. While we realize we are on tenuous ground in our protest, it remains a fascination to me that everyone who criticizes us, from the Cardinal himself to the ordinary lay person, quotes scripture in support of the Cathedral rather than Church history, tradition, and doctrine, to unambiguously support church construction.

The scriptural passage most often quoted is the Anointing of Jesus. From the perspective of the Cathedral supporters, the Cardinal is the woman who anoints Jesus, the Cathedral is the expensive oil, and of course the Cathedral detractors (namely the Catholic Workers) are the disgruntled disciples tisk-tisking at this gracious gesture. There is no question that this would seem to be the literal meaning of the text. But like so much fundamentalist proof, the reading is out of context, superficial, simplistic and uncritical of the status quo. It defies the imagination to think that the Jesus who fed the hungry, rebuked the religious establishment, and never went to Church except to disrupt the liturgical peace of the pious would actually approve of a $163 million Cathedral!

To properly understand the anointing of Jesus we must recognize that there are two sets of disciples in the Gospels. There are the well known male disciples, but in addition to the males, there is also a set of lesser known "women disciples."

In the Gospel story, the male disciples, from a literary perspective, seem to be almost comic foils. Jesus preaches nonviolence, and the disciples want to call down heavenly fire on the villages who rejected them. Jesus tells them to "feed the hungry," and they want to send off the hungry multitudes in the wilderness to "buy food." Jesus says, "Let the children come to me" (Matthew. 19:14), and the disciples are the ones blocking the way. Jesus says that in the kingdom the one who would be first must be last and we must be the servant of all, and the disciples want to: "sit one at your right and the other at your left" (Mark 10:37) when you come into your kingdom. Jesus says, "It will be hard for one who is rich to enter the kingdom of heaven. It is easier for a camel to pass through the eye of a needle," and the disciples say, "Who then can be saved?" (Matthew 19:23-25).

The basic message of Jesus is to care for the poor, confront the powerful, and forget the self. The male disciples seem to miss the point at every juncture, while the female disciples appear to embody every aspect of the message.

The bleeding woman breaks all social conventions to reach out and touch Jesus. It is her faith and courage that "heal her." The Syro-Phoenician woman boldly argues with Jesus and gains the healing of her daughter and the expansion of Jesus' ministry to the Gentiles. And it is the "scandalous" woman that anoints Jesus who thus proclaims and affirms the vocation of the cross.

The anointing of Jesus is much more than a mere sumptuous gesture of love and respect. As Jesus points out, "She has anticipated anointing my body for burial" (Mark 14:8). While the male disciples have been instructed on three separate occasions that the "Son of Man will be handed over to be crucified" (Matthew 26:2), they consistently reject the entire concept. On the other hand, this scandalous woman knew intuitively that the entire confrontative life of Jesus would lead logically to the cross.

The story of the anointing of Jesus reminds me of the young African Americans who sat-in at the lunch counters of Nashville, Tennessee, confronting the forces of southern segregation in the 1950s. David Halberstam quotes protester Diane Nash of Chicago, who said "how terrified she was before the first sit-in. She had sat in her dorm the night before, thinking of how formidable the forces aligned against them in Nashville were: the rich store-owners in the business community, the all-powerful white politicians, the white police and the white judges who served them. 'We are just children,' she had thought. 'How naïve and foolish of us to take on so powerful an apparatus.'" ("We Were Led by the Children," *Parade*).

These young people knew that in confronting these forces of concentrated wealth and power of the Southern oligarchy, they risked death. Such confrontations never cause one to be anointed with precious oil, but rather less sumptuous substances: catsup, lighted cigarette butts, boiling coffee.

Jesus was anointed with blood, spit, and derision. But just as the sacrifice of the African American youths in the South brought about a profound moral renewal and a healing of the social body of America, so too has the sacrifice of Jesus inspired for two millennia the better angels of our nature.

The central point of the story is that the anointing of Jesus is a confirmation of the vocation of the cross by a courageous and prophetic woman disciple. The passage begins with a description of the plot by the priests and scribes to kill Jesus, and ends with Judas rushing out to betray him to those very same people.

The powerful women disciples follow Jesus to the cross and beyond the cross to the empty tomb. The women disciples are courageous, compassionate, and faithful, but the male disciples are fearful, hard-hearted, and disillusioned. They deny, desert, and sell Jesus out to the rich and powerful for money. We have often heard that the Gospels display a "preferential option for the poor," but the Gospels display a preferential option for women as well. It is not that women are inherently better than men, it is simply that historically and socially men are formed by the cultural paradigm of power and domination, while women are formed by the paradigm of service and self sacrifice.

Thus, the women disciples are intuitively more open to the message, while the men, despite the constant teachings of Jesus, are more obtuse and closed-minded because their cultural formation causes them to form delusions about the authentic nature of Jesus' ministry and makes the cross look like Jesus' failure rather than his glory. In much the same manner, the male disciples of the Church continue to sell out Jesus to the rich and powerful, forgetting that "the poor you will always have with you" (Matthew 26:11).

Despite our collective disdain for Mean Ed, Joyce, a new member of our community, would often visit him at the end of the day with a clandestine gift of pie or cake. And he would occasionally snarl something at her that approximated a sign of gratitude. When Ed was taken off to jail she went to visit him. Fully expecting to be rebuffed for her efforts, she was

10. Catherine Morris praying, *Catholic Agitator*, 1984. Photo by Ardon Alger

shocked when he appeared delighted and grateful for her presence. He was charming, talkative, friendly. He asked her to come to his court appearance where she found out, much to our amazement, that he had actually been framed by the police and was innocent of all but a minor charge. Like the women in the Gospel, Joyce followed Mean Ed to the cross of county jail, and much to her surprise she found the resurrected "Human One" awaiting her there.

At Easter time we love the comforting platitudes of the empty cross, the promise of "cheap grace" and painless resurrection. But the reality is the tortured body of the victim. The centrality of the cross means that God became human and allowed himself to become a victim, thus elevating the status of all victims and calling into question the status of all elites and the wealth and power upon which their status is based.

The resurrection means risking death and derision and following Christ to the cross and beyond the cross to the grave. It means that the God who hung on the cross will be with us when we stand with the victims. It means that love is stronger than death. It means that God is on our side and that "we shall overcome" when we insist, like the young African Americans in Nashville, that "the poor will always be with us" (Matthew 26:11), despite the fact that they are often a pain in the neck.

Wrestling and Reconciling

Catholic Agitator, June, 1999, pp. 1 and 7

My brother Joe committed suicide in 1972. It was at least his third or fourth attempt, but this time he was successful. He ran across the Hollywood Freeway and got hit by a semi-truck loaded with cement crypts from Joplin, Missouri. On prior occasions, he had put his wrist into an electric band saw, stuck his head into an oven, and in a particularly spectacular occurrence, while serving time in a minimum security jail, he climbed atop an outdoor gas tank and, spraying gas in a large circle about the tank, lit a great conflagration around himself.

In our modern world we have psychiatrists who can diagnose these unsettling events. My brother was a schizophrenic, which could perhaps be traced to a chemical imbalance in his neurological system. But the guilt that I have carried with me for my brother's death is not easily abrogated by a facile medical diagnosis. I know that it is not my fault, but I also realize that in some essential way I am to blame. Families are weird.

It is this very weirdness of families, according to scripture, that is the root cause of violence and death in the world. Intrafamilial jealousy, strife, competition, and enmity leading ultimately to fratricide and war are at the very heart of the scriptural stories, especially in the book of Genesis.

Perhaps the reason that so many Christians find the book of Genesis bizarre and intimidating is because it hits too closely to home, subverting pietistic notions of Christian family values. Rather, it assumes the dysfunctional nature of even the best and most faithful family ever to exist—the patriarchal lineage of Abraham, the primal founder of our Judeo-Christian tradition.

So ambiguous and conflicted are these figures, one wonders why they are present in sacred scripture at all. Abraham abandoned his wife Sarah to Pharaoh's harem; Sarah was vindictive and unjust to her maid Hagar;

Rebekah plotted against her husband; Rachel lied and stole from her father; and Jacob lied, cheated, and deceived his father, his uncle and his brother. These stories shake our faith. Indeed, it requires almost an act of faith to believe that there is in fact a moral center to the entire narrative.

But that is because all of us were raised not on authentic Biblical stories, but on the mythological stories that distill both ancient myth and the Bible itself to make a moral point and create heroic figures for children. But the Bible is not myth or moral law, and even less is it a children's story. It is adult literature on a scale that would make even Jackie Collins blush. It is family saga that puts *Dallas* to shame. It is sexual indiscretion straight out of *Melrose Place*.

Yes, these stories have a moral center, but like any good writer, the authors of Genesis have refused to bash their readers over the head with it. Rather, in the same way that Jacob struggled with the angel at Jabbok, we are required to struggle with the narrative, until it has wounded us.

Popular culture would have us believe that family is the source of love, affection, and nurturing goodness. But from a Biblical perspective, family is rather the "genesis" of violence, and death born of sibling rivalry and fraternal strife. After the Fall, death came into the world in the form of fratricide. Cain was jealous of Abel and his anger caused him to murder his brother. "Am I my brother's keeper?" (Genesis 4:9) Cain asked. Obviously not.

But the story of Jacob offers hope for change, rebirth, reconciliation for nations and families alike. Jacob is perhaps the most ambiguous character in all scripture. He is the "smooth one," shrewd and deceptive. He deceives his father, he cheats his brother twice, but for some reason God desires him over his brother Esau.

While Jacob is the "smooth one," Esau is the "hairy one," he is an outdoorsman familiar with weapons and hunting; while Jacob stays close to the tent and is loved by his mother, Esau roams the wilderness and is loved by his father. Esau is the tough guy, while Jacob is the "mama's" boy. Esau is physically strong, Jacob is intellectually astute. Esau is like Arnold Schwarzenegger, a brutish man of few words who uses violence to achieve his goals, while Jacob is like Cary Grant, a charming, witty, intelligent thief who uses brains rather than brute force to achieve his goals.

Even as twins in Rebekah's womb, the jostling and competition between Jacob and Esau begins as they actually wrestle before their birth. Jacob is the second born, but in spite of this God has promised that he, and not Esau the eldest, would receive the legacy of Abraham and Isaac. Nevertheless, Jacob, wanting to be in control, takes matters into his own hands, and thus sets in motion the cycle of sibling violence that dates back to Cain and Abel.

With his mother as his advisor, Jacob embarks upon a deceitful plot that will secure his ascendancy. His mother has overheard her husband, the aging and blind Isaac, requesting his favorite son Esau to kill and prepare a wild game stew "that I may eat of it and then give you my blessing" (Genesis 27:25). Rebekah now urges her favorite son Jacob to disguise himself as Esau and substitute a delicious lamb stew that she has prepared, thus deceptively securing this formal blessing and the inheritance that comes with it. But in doing so, he has also incurred the enmity of his brother Esau and now must flee for his life to the home of his uncle Laban in Haran.

It is in exile in Haran that Jacob meets his match. His uncle Laban is even more deceitful and larcenous than Jacob. Laban tricks him into marrying Leah, instead of her beautiful sister Rachel, for whom he has labored seven years. Now he must labor seven more years to have Rachel, the wife of his choice. Though Laban continues to trick him out of his wages, God protects Jacob and he is able to escape his bondage to Laban with the blessings of prosperity and progeny. He then decides to go back to "the land of his Father" so that he might be reconciled with the brother that he has so painfully wronged.

The climax of the cycle, and perhaps even to the book of Genesis itself, comes when Jacob spends a fearful night alone beside the river Jabbok, awaiting the dawn and possible death at the hands of his angry brother, who has sworn to kill him. In this atmosphere of anxiety, tension, and darkness, Jacob is confronted by an other-worldly creature with whom he enters into an all-night wrestling match.

It is impossible to plumb the depths of this scene, so bizarre and evocative is it. But clearly it is emblematic of who Jacob is, who God is, and what it means to be a faithful people of God. It turns out that the creature is of divine origin and, after an all-night struggle, is unable to defeat Jacob fairly. But towards dawn, the creature cripples him with a foul blow to the hip, and thereupon renames him. "You shall no longer be spoken of as Jacob but as Israel," he said, "because you have contended with divine and human beings and have prevailed" (Genesis 32:29). Jacob has been "reborn" as Israel. This wrestling on the Jabbok throughout the night has been the birth pangs of a new man, who is the very personification of the Hebrew people.

Jacob's experience of wrestling with and being wounded by the Angel is symbolic of wrestling with and being wounded in exile by his deceptive uncle Laban. Further, his experience parallels and foreshadows the experience of the Hebrew people wounded in their struggle for liberation with the Egyptian Pharaoh.

The experience of woundedness in exile and bondage is paradigmatic for the Hebrew people. Just as it is the experience of woundedness that precipitates and gives birth to reconciliation for Jacob/Israel, so too for the Hebrew people the tender memory of oppression and woundedness in slavery must always give birth to compassion for the poor and reconciliation with enemies.

Jacob is the prime example of what Henri Nouwen calls the "Wounded Healer." "Compassion," writes Nouwen, "is the possibility of man to forgive his brother, because forgiveness is only real for him who has discovered the weakness of his friends and the sins of his enemy in his own heart and is willing to call every human being his brother" (*The Wounded Healer*, p. 41).

Authentic reconciliation and healing can thus occur only through the painful recognition of our own woundedness. Richard Rohr, the noted spiritual director of the Center for Action and Contemplation, once said at a Los Angeles Catholic Worker Retreat, that as one becomes healthier and more integrated, one becomes less efficient and effective. In this story, after his encounter with the angel, Jacob is now more completely integrated and thus less effective.

Jacob has been wounded now, and rather than go ahead of his brother as he has struggled to do since sharing the same womb, he now must walk behind with the "frail children and the sucklings" while his brother goes on ahead. "Let my lord then, go ahead of me, while I proceed more slowly at the pace of the livestock before me and at the pace of my children" (Genesis 33:14). Jacob the striver, Jacob the supplanter, the one who desires to put himself forward must now walk more slowly because he is wounded, and his woundedness is his salvation.

When Jacob finally meets with his brother he says, "Meeting you is like seeing the face of God." Indeed, at the Jabbok, Jacob has seen the face of God and lived. And now, the text implies that reconciliation between brothers is like meeting the face of God. For the moment, the cycle of violence that began with Jacob's jealousy of his brother and his subsequent deception of his father has ended in an experience of unexpected grace. Also miraculously terminated for the moment is the cycle of fratricidal jealousy and strife that has advanced steadily through the book of Genesis since Cain and Abel.

In an interview with Bill Moyers, Bishop Tutu of South Africa spoke of his own painful encounter with the unbearable suffering of his people as it

11. Jeff Dietrich and Michael, a Catholic Worker guest, on the street in front of the Hospitality House Kitchen, 1975. Mural by Gary Palmatier

was illuminated by the Truth and Reconciliation Commission. It revealed the unspeakable torture of genitals, mouth, anus, and feet, as well as the programmatic use of violence and terror to control black populations. He spoke of weeping as he listened day after day to stories of unbelievable pain and suffering.

He went on to say that a recent South African poll has indicated that the majority of white South Africans, those who never suffered under apartheid, believed that reconciliation is not possible. On the other hand, the vast majority of black people, whose suffering was unbearable, believed that reconciliation *is* possible. "Only those who have been wounded have the capacity to forgive," said Bishop Tutu.

While reconciliation between Jacob and Esau is an intra-family affair between brothers, it is important to remember that on a more macro-cosmic level, according to scripture, Esau was the founder of the Edomites, or Arab tribes, while Jacob was the patriarchal founder of the Hebrew people. The scriptures call for reconciliation between Arabs and Jews who are from the beginning brothers. Thus does the story give us hope that Palestinians and Israelis might be reconciled as well.

My brother Joe was smarter, stronger, and better looking than his older brother, but he did not know it because he was second born and thus in his mind would forever be second best. He could not live up to the example of the first born, who in his mind was smarter, faster, bigger, and better loved by his mother. His anger, frustration, and violence turned inward and he took his own life. As I mature, I look to the story of Jacob for a rejection of the arrogance and pretension of first born sons, and, wounded myself in the struggle for liberation and integrity, I look forward to reconciliation and forgiveness even beyond the grave.

Yes, I am my brother's keeper.

Power of Suicide at the Heart of the World

Catholic Agitator, July, 1990, pp. 1 and 2

His breathing came in labored, spasmodic gasps. First the chest would heave a great sigh, then the head would snap back upon the pillow with such force that the jaws popped open automatically, sucking air like a greedy baby. Then came the gurgling sounds. Each hungry breath pushed his face deeper into conformity with the clear plastic oxygen mask that gave him the only sustenance he cared about now.

Any fool could see that Isaiah was dying. But when confronted, the doctors insisted that he was doing fine, and why didn't we all go home and get some sleep. Lots of people had pulled through this. And besides, having eight visitors was against hospital regulations. Their bland professional palliatives stood in marked contrast to our grieving countenances. Isaiah died four hours later.

It is almost impossible for health care professionals to accept the reality of death. In fact, for all the professionals who keep our country running smoothly, the denial of death is essential. As Walter Brueggemann writes, "The royal consciousness leads people to numbness, especially to numbness about death. It is the task of prophetic ministry and imagination to bring people to engage their experiences of suffering to death" (*The Prophetic Imagination*, p. 41).

As Catholic Workers we find ourselves engaged with suffering, despair, and death on a daily basis. We believe that this is the authentic reality of the culture. But the message of the culture consistently confirms in powerful ways the very opposite. Until we can understand with some clarity that the "truth of the culture" is grounded in the worship of false gods, we are condemned to a schizophrenic existence.

The theology of Jacques Ellul offers us the prophetic clarity of naming with exquisite perfection the idolatries of contemporary culture. As the theologian William Stringfellow said, "For Ellul...the affirmation of death as ultimate reality and—hence—the ground for immediate moral decision...[he recognizes] an idolatry of death in which all men [and women] and all societies are caught up" ("Introduction," *The Presence of the Kingdom*, p. 4).

Ellul believes that the contemporary manifestation of this idolatry of death lies in our worship of the "sacred ensemble of techniques," as he calls technology. "From the moment that technics [techniques], the State, or production, are facts, we must worship them....This is the very heart of modern religion" (*The Presence of the Kingdom*, p. 37).

Simply put, technique is the systematic reduction of all human thought, action, and organization to the logic and efficiency of the machine (See *Catholic Agitator*, June 1990).

This situation is monstrous because it amounts to the virtual enslavement of humanity to the *principalities and powers*—the spiritual force of evil in the world. If we are not "awake and aware," we will enthusiastically cooperate with this demonic power. "If we let ourselves drift along the stream of history, without knowing it, we will have chosen the power of suicide, which is at the heart of the world. But we cannot have many illusions" (Ellul, *The Presence of the Kingdom*, p. 30-31).

To the extent that our actions are founded upon the mythology of the contemporary reality rather than the Word of God, we reinforce this demonic direction. The mythologies of progress, revolution, and youth are the foundation of all our cultural ideologies. All of the motivating forces of the culture, from advertising copy to political propaganda to the idealization of humanitarian impulses in medicine, education and public service are founded upon these false mythologies.

We cannot fight the world of power and technique (technology) with more and greater power and technique. Our situation is not unlike the Allied forces of World War II fighting the demonic forces of Nazism with the same tactics of Hitler: mass bombings, propaganda, and terrorism of civilian populations. They won the physical war, but the demonic spirituality of Hitlerism triumphed in the bombings of Hiroshima and Nagasaki and the subsequent willingness of US foreign policy to transform the entire globe into a nuclear concentration camp.

God does not work through "technical means." Most contemporary Christians, especially Catholics, harbor an unconscious Chardinian theology. Teilhard de Chardin was the Jesuit paleontologist who believed that technology was an extension of natural biological evolution, and that as it developed and became more sophisticated, so too would human consciousness. This process would eventually lead to the encirclement of the entire globe by the *noosphere*,* a cloud of higher consciousness culminating in the second coming of Christ.

But this view of culture and technology is, if not blasphemous, antispiritual. Any overview of the Hebrew-Christian scripture would clarify that, except in rare cases, God only works through human beings. The Holy Spirit does not work through the electoral process, through war, revolution, scientific progress or the space program. Neither does the Holy Spirit work through mass movements, political reform or institutions. The Holy Spirit only works through people.

We cannot use the means of the world to bring in God's Kingdom of peace and justice. We cannot bring in peace and justice, writes Ellul, we can only be peace and justice. The Christian must be "the leaven in the loaf," "the light in the darkness," "the sheep among wolves." In other words, if we want the Kingdom of God to be a reality, then we must use the means of the Kingdom to achieve that end. If we seek first God's Kingdom and righteousness, then all the other things, like peace, justice, sisterhood and brotherhood will be added unto us.

Ellul's theological perspective radically liberates us from having to respond to the false challenge of either violent revolution or liberal reform with which the world is constantly seducing us. Now we don't have to kill all of the capitalists, nor do we have to go to graduate school to get an MSW, nor do we have to become a non-profit corporation and raise millions of dollars or make millions of converts. In short, we don't have to be effective!

We have been liberated to be the means of God, a channel for the Holy Spirit to act in the world. But this does not mean that we can just *be*, it means that we must be engaged with the suffering reality of the world, the sinfulness of the world, the injustice of the world. We must be present in the places of darkness, manifesting the Kingdom, opening a channel for the Holy Spirit to come into the world.

This is the essence of the tension that Ellul writes about. As Christian realists, we must be engaged with a sinful world, but aware that it is not possible for us to do anything about it. Our situation is not unlike the women who stayed with Jesus at the foot of the cross. Their love was stronger than their illusions, unlike the male disciples who had expected to become regional administrators in the new "Jesus corporation," the women had more authentic orientation, and thus remained faithful to the end.

---

*   A term that refers to Chardin's notion of higher consciousness.

Jeff Dietrich

12. Poster by Gary Palmatier, 1975

We live in a crucified world. We cannot make it uncrucified any more than the women could rescue Jesus from his cross. But, like the women, we will not abandon that suffering reality. The response of the women was to mourn and to grieve, to enter into the darkness of suffering.

We picked up Isaiah's body at the coroner's office and brought him to our house. We sat with him throughout the night, watching and praying. In

54

the morning we put him in the old blue van and drove him over to Dolores Mission for the funeral. Finally, we buried him in a plot at the back corner of Sacred Heart Cemetery. We grieved the injustice that only in death could this homeless man finally have a home. We grieved the dying of a culture that numbs itself to the pain of the poor, and blinds itself to the reality of death.

Brueggemann writes that "Anguish is the door to historical existence... only those who embrace the reality of death will receive new life" (*The Prophetic Imagination*, pp. 56-57). We believe that the denial of death and the subsequent narcissism that causes our insatiable consumption of products and experiences defines the essence of contemporary culture. As Christopher Lasch writes,

> There is a growing despair of changing society, even of understanding it....Industrial civilization gives rise to a "philosophy of futility," a pervasive fatigue, a "disappointment with achievements" that finds an outlet in changing the "more superficial things" It addresses itself to the spiritual desolation of modern life and proposes consumption as a cure.

The Culture of Narcissism, p. 73

But we refuse to take the cure. Trivial entertainments, superficial relationships and compulsive shopping are not the cure; they merely address the symptoms of our schizophrenic condition. We seek unitive wholeness and with Brueggemann we recognize "that all the satiation was a quick eating of self to death" (*The Prophetic Imagination*, p. 47). We refuse to be numb and narcotized—the prophetic call is to be aware and awake. We will not worship at the altar of the false god of technique. We will not accept the bland palliatives of the technocratic priesthood. When we encounter suffering, we will mourn. We will respond with compassionate engagement. Wholeness comes when we refuse any longer to deny death. Wholeness comes when we respond to the Word of God which calls us out of the bondage of death and oppression to life and liberation. In the words of Deuteronomy "I have set before you life, death, the blessing and the curse. Choose life, then, so that you and your descendants may live" (Deuteronomy 30:15-16).

The Devil's Pact*

Catholic Agitator, August, 2001, p. 1

June 26, 2001, Kern County Jail

Dear Community,

Nino doesn't sleep very well. He lives in the bunk below me, and he tosses and turns all night. When he finally does sleep it is fitful, with his massive hands and feet sprawled over the edge of the bunk. It is as though he is fighting a war in his sleep, and indeed, that is exactly what is happening. For seven years Nino fought in the Iran/Iraq war. He showed me the angry gash of shrapnel wounds still sprinkled with a purple dust of metal filings, and the perfect round bullet wounds like vaccination scars on his chest and abdomen. He demonstrated the maneuver of simultaneously pulling down a gas mask and jabbing his thigh with a hypodermic of antitoxin as the chemicals explode in mid-air. The ground is so polluted in those areas that the rain itself continues to be red and poisonous a decade after the war's end. After a thirteen-month stay in the hospital, he was discharged with a lifetime prescription of psychotropic drugs. "I am not same man I used to be," he says in his broken English. "When I was young, I was fanatic. Many people in Iran are fanatic. Now I think is better to talk than to fight."

Not surprisingly, Nino and Jesus are of a single mind on this issue. They both understand that the difference between fanatical faith and authentic faith is the willingness to use force rather than gentle persuasion. That is why Jesus rejected the violent kingdoms of the world offered to him by Satan in the wilderness. He refused to further his messianic project by the use of violence, and for almost two centuries, his first followers practiced love and cheek-turning rather than crusades and inquisitions. Not until the time of Constantine did the Church finally succumb to the temp-

---

* These letters were written to the Los Angeles Catholic Worker Community while Jeff Dietrich was in the Kern County Jail awaiting sentencing for trespassing onto Vandenberg Air Force Base on May 20, 2001 to protest George W. Bush's National Missile Defense Program.

tation and make "a pact with the Devil." As James Carroll writes, "When the power of the empire became joined to the ideology of the Church, the empire was immediately recast and reenergized, and the Church became an entity so different from what had preceded it as to be almost unrecognizable" (*Constantine's Sword*, p. 171).

Central to this perverse transformation was the image of the cross, which under Constantine became both the static instrument of Christian self-affirmation and the idolatrous symbol of deadly state power that murdered all who would not accept its salvific efficacy.

Beginning with the Council of Nicaea (325), the Constantinian Church de-historicized and de-politicized the scriptural basis of Christianity by reducing Jesus' teachings to Hellenistic/philosophical categories of personal and ontological salvation. Constantine's need to ground his universal empire in a universal spirituality was the driving force behind the formation of a standardized, universal Christian theology and the development of an absolute Church authority to enforce it.

After Constantine, Carroll writes, "The metaphors that early Christians used to describe their experience of and faith in Jesus of Nazareth were reinvented in the categories of Hellenistic metaphysics....Neoplatonism posited a dualism that would become Christianized as between grace and sin" (*Constantine's Sword*, p. 578). Thus, salvation came to mean the healing of an ontological rift between God and man, body and soul in the ethereal realm of eternity, rather than the fulfillment of God's promise to Abraham in the here and now of human history.

St. Paul's brilliant theology of sacrificial atonement transformed Christ's defeat on the cross into victory, his death into life-giving martyrdom, and empowered first-century Christians to bravely endure crucifixion. But it de-historicized the cross, and set it within the context of a triumphal Church and a newly benevolent empire, which recast Rome as a benign policeman and the cross as a symbol of automatic salvific power rather than empowerment for martyrdom. This abstract, idealized cross became a symbol of a victorious Church and the sacred foundation of a divinely mandated state, emblematic of veneration rather than the dynamic of discipleship, emphasizing idolatry rather than self-sacrifice.

"The transformation of the cross was complete," writes Carroll, "not a sign of real suffering any longer, nor even, with Paul, of spiritualized victory, but a sign of power in the world" (*Constantine's Sword*, p. 571). This Constantinian cross is the direct antecedent to the American Evangelical theology which claims that Christ *had* to die, that he was not a *victim* of the

Roman death penalty, but rather a victim of Divine wrath. Christ had to die to heal the ontological rift between an angry God and a sinful humanity, thus saving all sinners and opening the gates of heaven. While this theology may justify sinners who are saved by its passive cross, it also justifies Constantine and Hitler and George W. Bush. And it further justifies just wars and unjust wars, crusades and inquisitions, death camps and death penalties. It justifies and sanctifies the making of victims by the divinely sanctioned state. It falls here to the temptation of Satan. It is a pact with the Devil. And so I join my friend Nino, who in his battle-scarred wisdom says, "I think is better to talk than to fight." It is also better to be in jail with the victims of state-sanctioned violence, than out of jail with the victimizers.

PART TWO

FOOD AND SALVATION

Journey

I never feel I have arrived, though I come
To journey's end. I took the road
That loses crest to questions, yet bears me
Down the other homeward earth. I know
My flesh is nibbled clean, lost
To fretful fish among the rusted hulls—
I passed them on my way
And so with bread and wine
I lack the sharing with defeat and dearth
I passed them on my way.
I never feel I have arrived
Though love and welcome snare me home
Usurpers hand my cup at every
Feast a last supper.

Wole Soyinka

I am the bread of life,
whoever comes to me will never hunger.

John 6:35

Exorcising Jesus

Catholic Agitator, June, 2008, pp. 1 and 6

It is dogma of the highest order that Jesus was like us in all respects except sin, but a closer look at the Gospel of Matthew might call that dogma into question. In the story of the Canaanite woman (15:22-28) Jesus appears to be possessed by the very demons that he has so adroitly exorcized thus far in his public life.

The story of the Canaanite woman is pivotal in what commentators call the "third narrative block" in Matthew's Gospel, which stretches from 13:58 and the rejection at Nazareth and ends at 17:27 with a "fishy" story about paying taxes. In between are found two wilderness feedings, one to the Hebrews and one to the Gentiles, two "theophanies" (walking on water and the Transfiguration), two mass curings, two conflicts with the religious authorities, two exorcisms, and two prophecies of the cross.

It would be difficult to overestimate the centrality of this Canaanite woman, this solitary female figure of "great faith" set as she is in the midst of a multitude of men who are portrayed either as faithless (the disciples) or blind (the religious authorities) or murderous (Herod).

The story of the Canaanite woman is intimately connected with the themes of food and faith which dominate this entire narrative block. The visit to Nazareth introduces the theme of "no faith," while the beheading of John the Baptist at Herod's dinner party introduces the theme of food, albeit in a decidedly negative manner.

Perhaps it is because I have spent almost my entire adult life in a soup kitchen that I want to argue that the driving force of the section is food. In Roman occupied Palestine in the first century AD, the ruling elite controlled 50 to 67 percent of the wealth. Food and survival was the primary issue for peasants and the "unclean" and expendable classes, who constituted almost 90 percent of the population, but received only 2 percent of the wealth.

Jeff Dietrich

According to William Herzog:

> Their goal [the aristocracy] remained the plunder of their peasant population, leaving the peasants only the minimum required for survival. These farmers were forced to send their children into the streets as itinerant day laborers who might work during harvest or planting season, but had to beg the rest of the year. Many expendables became criminals or joined bands of social bandits, which insured their survival until they were hunted down and killed.

Parables as Subversive Speech, p. 65

The Canaanite woman was no doubt a member of just this segment of the population that formed the lynch-pin of Matthew's story, where the issues of faith and food converge in a conflict between the economics of empire and the economics of the Kingdom.

The beheading of John announces the escalation of political repression and the imminent threat of reprisals against Jesus and his movement. Everything revolves around food and Herod's murderous dinner party sets the tone. It personifies and satirizes the economics of empire that produce hunger, starvation and death, and must be seen in contrast to the Kingdom economics of satisfaction and abundant life, as enacted by Jesus in the two wilderness feedings. The wilderness feedings are meant to evoke the radical anti-empire origins of the Hebrew people in the Exodus story, with their experience of manna and the alternative economic practice of Sabbath sharing.

Jesus' invocation of the radical liberation memory of the Hebrew people precipitates a response from the religious authorities in charge of pacifying the population with platitudes of orthodoxy and dogma. But Jesus completely rejects commonly accepted orthodoxy, which, as always, props up a corrupt status quo and supports the power elite. Jesus is not a priest or scribe or seminary-educated theologian, and thus completely rejects that element of religion that wants to separate the righteous from the sinners. In fact, Jesus rejects religion altogether in favor of the wild, free, anti-empire God, who speaks not from churches, but from mountaintops—whose Word comes not to priests in satin robes, but to prophets in tattered camel hides.

The purity codes of conservative piety support the status quo of empire by separating out and consigning to death the unclean and expendable, thus allowing the surplus wealth extraction of empire to function smoothly. So the Pharisees and Scribes from Jerusalem are not really concerned by the fact that there are multitudes of starving, desperate people in the land; they are concerned with religious propriety. "Why," they ask Jesus, "do your disciples...not wash their hands when they eat?" (Matthew 15:2).

Jesus calls them hypocrites and blind guides and commits complete civil disobedience by nullifying all of their codes and laws, calling them mere human precepts. He declares all foods "clean." It is not what goes into the mouth that makes him unclean but what comes out of the mouth from the heart that makes a man unclean. For from the heart come evil intentions: adultery, fornication, theft, perjury, slander. These are the things that make a man unclean. But to eat with unwashed hands does not make a man unclean (Matthew 15:17-20).

It is all about food and food distribution and eating. It is all about survival. The Empire wants to extract the maximum wealth possible, and the religious elite have a theology that, rather conveniently, supports that project. Later Jesus warns the disciples to beware of the yeast of the Pharisees, another food image, by which he means the teachings of religion that support the deadly project of empire.

The story of the Canaanite woman appears on the very heels of Jesus' most liberating statement in the entire Gospel. She comes, pleading for the life of her daughter, who is demon-possessed.

But Jesus is in a crabby mood. In fact, he is so crabby that he is downright rude to this woman and rejects her plea in a most uncompassionate manner. "I was sent only to the lost sheep of the house of Israel....It is not right to take the food of the children and throw it to the dogs" (Matthew 15:24, 26). He is insulting her; he has as much as called her a bitch. She is a Gentile, a Canaanite, a "dog"— she is unclean, impure, unworthy. Ironically, Jesus, the most radical guy in all of Hebrew history, has just nullified the purity codes that separate the worthy from the unworthy. He has recognized that such segregation codes are deadly and have nothing to do with the heavenly Father. And yet, here he shows himself to be filled with the same demons of nationalism and patriarchy that he had just criticized in the religious authorities. But the woman is desperate and will not be silent. She keeps calling out in the most annoying manner, sounding, in the Greek translation, like a crow.

While we cannot know for certain the exact nature of her daughter's demonic possession, I want to suggest that given the context of the story, with its elements of food and food prohibitions, and the scarcity techniques of empire and the separation techniques of religious collaborators, that it must certainly have had something to do with a lack of food.

The Canaanite woman was probably a widow, without family or resources, with no male figure—no husband or father or brother, to speak for her. In this overwhelmingly patriarchal culture it is unprecedented for a woman to speak directly to a man; she could have been stoned.

Her response to Jesus' insult is extraordinary and her quick retort worthy of the finest debater: "Please, Lord, for even the dogs eat the scraps that fall from the table of their masters" (Matthew 15:27). Jesus is stopped in his tracks, knocked over, so to speak. In a single instant she has exorcised from Jesus the demons of nationalism, religious righteousness, segregation, and patriarchy. Just as Jesus restored the Gerasene demoniac to his right mind, she has restored Jesus to his right mind. And Jesus replies, "Woman, great is your faith! Let it be done for you as you wish. Let your wish be granted" (Matthew 15:28). And from that moment, her daughter was well again.

She has exorcized Jesus and transformed the entire Kingdom Project. If it had not been for the Canaanite woman, there would have been no second wilderness feeding to the Gentiles. Because of her, the liberating message of the Kingdom would include not just the lost sheep of the house of Israel, but all of the lost sheep, all of the expendable victims of empire who have no food, all of the victims of empire whose children are consigned to starvation. Henceforth, there would be no more unclean people, no expendables, no dogs, no excuse for treating anyone as less than human.

The legacy of the Canaanite woman continues to this day. Her faith, which is to say her courage, was born of desperation, poverty, and love of her child, and is lifted up by Jesus. It is all about food and faith. The Liberation Project of Jesus, now extended to the Gentiles, has frightened the authorities. And they will respond as empire always responds to those who terrorize them.

Twice in this section, (Matthew 16:21 and Matthew 20:18), Jesus says he must go to Jerusalem where the authorities are going to crucify him. But Peter says, "God forbid, Lord! No such thing shall ever happen to you" (Matthew 16:22) to which Jesus responds, "Get behind me, Satan!...You are thinking not as God does, but as human beings do" (Matthew 16:23).

The Canaanite woman has shown great faith, which means that she has a fearlessness born of desperation. But the disciples are fearful and have little faith. They are still caught up in the snares of empire: they want power and privilege, status and security. But the perks of empire are always purchased at the cost of the victims of surplus wealth extraction. And nationalistic religion always supports the victimizing project of empire.

14. Jeff Dietrich working in the soup kitchen, 1975. Photo by Hank Lebo

The Canaanite woman has reminded Jesus that the lost sheep of the house of Israel are not the only victims of empire. Amazingly, it is not until this woman has cast out Jesus' demons of nationalism and religious prejudice that he is able to totally identify with all the victims of empire and thus articulate the fullness of the Kingdom Project in his prophecy of the cross. This is confirmed in the ultimate Biblical theophany on the mountaintop with those two anti-empire wild men, Moses and Elijah, and God herself, who says, "This is my beloved son. Listen to him" (Mark 9:7). And, oh yeah, the Resurrection. It's all about food and faith, and as Dom Helder Camara said, "When I give food to the poor, they call me a saint. When I ask why the poor have no food, they call me a Communist" (*Essential Writings*, p. 11).

Food comes first. When we start to redistribute food as if every human being had a God given right to it, nationalistic religion will vilify us and the forces of empire will fall upon us with the weight of the cross. But God herself has confirmed the insight of the Canaanite woman, that there are no dogs and there are no expendables—no unclean—only human beings who have a God-given right to food and to a dignified life.

And the promise of the Resurrection is that you just can't kill the spirit of liberation. Like Moses and Elijah and Jesus and Francis and Gandhi and Dorothy and Archbishop Romero, who said, "I will rise in the Spirit of the people" (Sobrino, *Archbishop Romero*, p. 43), it cannot be stopped by the forces of empire or ecclesial propriety, it just goes on and on.

Can't Get No Satisfaction:
The Political Economy of Empire and the Beheading of John the Baptist

Catholic Agitator, June, 2007, pp. 1, 2 and 6

Shortly after Jean Bertrand Aristide was elected president of Haiti, he addressed the United Nations, articulating the Ten Commandments of Democracy. "The tenth commandment of democracy," he said," is everyone around the same table." Most of us realize that Jesus also invited everyone to the same table, but very few First World people realize that Jesus had pretty much the same understanding of table fellowship as Jean Bertrand Aristide. For Jesus, as well as Aristide, the table is emblematic, not only of food sharing, but of social and political participation as well.

In Chapter 14 of Matthew, we find these relationships masterfully juxtaposed in two powerful food stories: The Feeding of the Five Thousand (Matthew 14:13-21) and the Beheading of John the Baptist (Matthew 14:1-12). One represents the empire's "anti-food story" of decadence and death, while the other is Jesus' "pro-food story" of abundance and life. The "anti-food" story recounts the beheading of John the Baptist, in which the young girl, Salome, upon receiving positive acclaim for her alluring dance, requests, at her mother's behest, the head of John the Baptist on a platter. The story is meant to be a satirical parody of power relations at the center of empire, where important political decisions are made in a drunken stupor—where vengeance, lust, and face-saving are the primary motivations for decision making. Herod is the son of "Herod the Great," but for purposes of the Gospel, pretty much all Herods are the same. They are the stand-in for empire, the puppet kings of Rome, and the most reviled figures in all of Israel. Like his father before him, who built the Temple in Jerusalem, Herod the tetrarch had a great fondness for large building projects that enhanced his reputation while depleting the national resources and impoverishing the people with double and triple taxation. He is feared and despised, with a reputation for brutality as well as cunning. He is the one whom Jesus called "that fox" (Luke 13:32).

This is not the typical dinner party arranged by, say, Martha Stewart, where the centerpiece of a sumptuous table setting might be dominated by roast suckling pig or a whole fresh Atlantic salmon. To bring a human head to the dinner table, rather, conjures images from a horror film. It is quite the opposite of food. And it is meant to disgust and revolt us. Like having your dinner served in a slaughterhouse, it takes your appetite away. Matthew wants us to recognize that the political economy of empire is the source of blood and murder and does not satisfy authentic human hunger. It is meant to evoke images of a degenerate Roman orgy. It also presents Herod as a leader without integrity, tricked by a mere child into making a self-destructive political decision, executing John the Baptist.

Only the elite have been invited to this table of decadent drunken revelry, but it is at this table that life and death decisions are made. While we know this is a parody of the dissolute life of the degenerate Herodian monarchy, it remains a profound reflection on the powerful, who even today, behind the veneer of bourgeois Christian morality, meet at tables in back rooms and exclusive restaurants to make life and death decisions over "power lunches" and expense account dinners—where lobbyists and developers and military contractors provide lap dancers and prostitutes for politicians and bureaucrats, and decisions are made that consign the poor, the immigrant, and the homeless to death, along with those who speak on their behalf: the prophets, John the Baptist, Jesus, Gandhi, and Martin Luther King.

When Jesus heard of John's death "he withdrew in a boat to a desolate place by himself" (Matthew 14:13). Like any reasonable person, Jesus has fled to avoid, at least for the time being, the fate of John. But the crowds find him in this desolate wilderness. Matthew has deliberately juxtaposed these two similar but opposite food readings, the beheading of John the Baptist and the feeding of the 5,000. One takes place at the very center of the power structure, while the other takes place at the very margins of power, in the wilderness. Unlike Herod's party, this is not an exclusive gathering—all are invited.

It has often been noted by commentators and sermon-givers that a huge portion of the Gospels revolve around stories of eating and the table. The typical church sermon is fond of noting these narratives as examples of Jesus sitting down to eat with both the rich and the poor, as if Jesus blesses the status quo of unjust wealth distribution. Nothing could be further from the truth. Whenever Jesus went to the home of rich Pharisees and Scribes, he went as a prophet and a critic, insulting his host and everyone at the table, calling them hypocrites, thieves, and prophet-murderers—a truthful, though non-convivial, dining experience. On the other hand, when he reclined at the table with his disciples, he was often in the presence of the socially marginated. In fact, one of the charges against him was that he dined with prostitutes, tax collectors, and drug addicts.

Contrary to the rigid economic and class structures of the time, Jesus practiced what theologian John Dominic Crossan has called, "open Commensality." "Commensality," writes Crossan, "means the rules of tabling and eating as miniature models for the rules of association and socialization" (*Jesus: A Revolutionary Biography*, p. 68). In first-century Mediterranean cultures, "commensality" was strictly relegated to members of one's own social class and hierarchy. Lest we should start to believe too strongly in our own egalitarian values, Crossan is quick to remind us that the social strictures of eating and "commensality" continue unabated into our own century. In the face of our human perverse tendency to organize ourselves into social and class hierarchies, Crossan writes that Jesus practices an "'open commensality,' an eating together without using the table as a miniature map of society's vertical discriminations and lateral separations" (*Jesus: A Revolutionary Biography*, p. 69).

The "Feedings in the Wilderness"are the primary example of Jesus' socially radical practice of "open commensality," in which Matthew juxtaposes this extraordinary number of mostly poor people with Herod's tiny gathering of wealthy elites. The feedings are meant to recall the Manna story in Exodus, in which the Hebrew people are rescued by God from the persecutions of empire, fleeing from the slavery of Egypt into the freedom of wilderness, where they are saved from pursuing Egyptian soldiers and fed on manna.

While pious commentators focus on the "miracle of Manna," the important element of the story is the "lesson of Manna," which goes to the heart of the economics of distribution. "He who gathered a large amount did not have too much," says the author of Exodus, "and he who had gathered a small amount did not have too little. They so gathered that everyone had enough to eat. Let no one keep any of it over until tomorrow morning" (Exodus 16:16-19). This passage articulates the economic practice of sharing and non-hoarding, and it is the heart of what is called "Sabbath economics," encoded in the law of Leviticus (Leviticus 25). It is the very opposite of the economics of empire, in which the wealthy and powerful steal and murder and hoard such that starvation, sickness, and death are the norm for the poor of the world.

When Jesus disembarked from the boat, Matthew says, "his heart was moved with pity," which is a link to Matthew 9:36, recalling the description of the crowds as "sheep without a shepherd." With the citation of this passage, Matthew is evoking the prophet's scathing critique of the leaders of Israel: "Woe to the shepherds of Israel who have been pasturing themselves!" says Ezekiel. "Should not shepherds, rather, pasture sheep? You have fed off their milk, worn their wool, and slaughtered the fatlings, but the sheep you have not pastured. You lorded it over them harshly" (Ezekiel 34:2-4). The leaders of Israel have fattened themselves on the flock while disregarding their responsibility to care for the people. But Jesus responds in compassion as an authentic shepherd should—by feeding the sheep.

Typically, the marketplace economics of empire based on greed, war, and competition do not reward the "Good Shepherd" economic practice of compassion and inclusivity. Rather, the economics of empire, like Herod's birthday party, always produce death. Herod's primary job is to act as tax collector; he sends tax money back to Rome, and on top of that he collects an extra tax for himself, leaving the "Lost Sheep of Israel" impoverished and depleted.

In our own day, according to historian Chalmers Johnson, the economics of empire have depleted the national treasury with a military budget of almost one trillion dollars! Johnson writes:

> Imperialism and militarism have thus begun to imperil both the financial and social well-being of our republic....I believe there is only one solution to the crisis we face. The American people must make the decision to dismantle both the empire...and the huge (still growing) military establishment that undergirds it.

"Ending the Empire," *TomDispatch.com*

In contrast to the economics of empire, Jesus calls us to practice the Sabbath economics of the Exodus wilderness tradition, in which resources are distributed to all so that 'everyone had enough and all were satisfied' (Matthew 15:37).

The key elements of the wilderness feeding story are compassion, distribution, satisfaction, and inclusion. Jesus acts with compassion, blesses the bread, breaks it, and distributes it to his disciples, who pass it along to the people and all ate and were satisfied. The basic idea in this wilderness story, as well as the Manna story, is that all creation is a gift, and if we give thanks and pass the gift on rather than hoarding it, then there will be enough and all will be satisfied.

In contrast, the political economy of empire does not produce satisfaction. In fact, it reminds us of the classic rock and roll hit by the Rolling Stones, *Can't Get No Satisfaction,* which is a scathing critique of our modern consumerist culture based on the artificial stimulation of desire through the manipulation of mass media images. By definition, the market economy of empire is a substitution for authentic satisfaction, addressing only the false needs that it creates for the superfluous products it produces, while leaving the vast majority of the world's population in starvation and destitution, bereft of authentic satisfaction.

Satisfaction will only come when we practice the radical inclusiveness envisioned by the prophet Isaiah: "You who have no money, Come, receive grain and eat; Come, without paying and without cost, drink wine and milk! Why spend your money for that which is not bread; Your wages for what fails to satisfy" (Isaiah 55:1-2).

Though many commentators would consign Isaiah's vision to the realm of the spiritual, something that happens to us in heaven when we die, he was in fact calling the Hebrew people to a renewal of the radical Sinai covenant, which demanded an earthly economy of satisfaction for all. And that will happen when we begin to heed the words of Jean Aristide and Jesus in the wilderness and "invite all around the same table."

Bread for Ducks but No Bread for the Poor

Catholic Agitator, April, 1973, p. 3

Our finances are fast approaching the desperate stage. Our bank account is down to $6.00. We are $400 in debt and there are at least $300 in outstanding bills with more expected in the very near future. Also, our food bills keep rising astronomically. We are now serving 300 to 500 men a day. This amounts to over 3,000 meals a week. To make matters even worse, the general economic state of the nation has forced us to spend much more money on inflated food prices.

One example of the exorbitant food prices is onions. Since our food budget doesn't allow for too much meat, we must use something to liven up the otherwise bland food. In the past this has always been onions. But in one week the price of onions has soared from $3.00 to $12.00 for a fifty pound sack. Now it is questionable whether we can even afford to buy this most basic of ingredients. Indeed, we already have had to cease putting them into our tossed green salad.

Even more basic than onions is our bread situation. The large bakery that was supplying us with free day-old bread has recently halted this humanitarian activity in favor of the more lucrative procedure of selling it to the county for duck feed. This seems to us an injudicious choice of priorities when there is bread for ducks, but no bread for the poor! Being unable to find a regular source of cheap or free bread, we have been forced to spend much needed funds in buying crackers, which are not nearly as satisfying as bread.

The President tells us that the economy is improving while the unemployment rate in Watts is still 27 percent. Economists argue about guns or butter and we cannot afford bread or onions. I can give my opinion of the economy in one word: *quack!*

If your economic situation is any better than ours, please help. Please share so that the work may continue, because the work is good and you are part of it. Without you it would not have started and it would not be possible to carry on.

Strike

We have always known that our work was good and that it was unusual. But until we took to the streets with our blood bank strike, we were not aware just how unique we really are.

No other place on Skid Row serves as many men as we do. Most missions have a meal ticket system which limits the times per week a man may eat. And, of course, all missions require the men to sit through a sermon, which is often degrading and always loud. The sermon usually consists of a condemnation of those who are drunk. This is not the kind of Christianity we subscribe to. We do not believe that Christ came to find fault with those who are jobless and those who are drunk.

Since the beginning of the strike we have been the subject of a number of sermons in at least one Skid Row mission. One of the preachers publicly denounced us because we do not preach the Gospel. "But I guess we can forgive them," he said, "because they are Catholics."

Please do not think that, simply because we are Catholics, we are unconcerned with the spiritual. Since the beginning of the strike we have on occasion invited a priest to say Mass for ourselves and the strikers. It must be the first time in many years that the Eucharist has been present on Skid Row. That first Mass said on the opening day of the strike was an incredibly moving experience. We gathered around the cutting table on which we prepare all of the food. To me the Mass has never seemed more appropriate, surrounded as we were by pots, pans, and food, and men from the streets who would soon be walking the picket line with us.

The Mass that day was symbolic of a new relationship that has come about between ourselves and the men as a direct result of the strike. It is no longer a question of one party always being the giver and the other always being the taker. Because of the nature of the strike a mutual relationship has developed. The men cannot strike without us and we cannot do anything without them. We must work together.

The California Transfusion Service, the blood bank we are picketing, is located on the north side of Fifth Street in a store front in between the Hotel Lorraine and the Pioneer Café, which has recently been turned into a Chinese restaurant. By 7:00 a.m. the sun has already risen, but our hands and feet are still numb with the cold. We have been walking our small circle

15. Skid Row residents picket a blood bank on 5th Street during the Blood Strike, 1973. Photo by Annie Leibovitz, Credit: © Annie Leibovitz/Contact Press Images courtesy of the Artist

in front of the blood bank for an hour. We rose at 4:45 a.m. to prepare breakfast for the six or seven strikers who will brave the early morning chill to walk with us on the line.

By 5:45 a.m. we have begun the eight block walk from our kitchen to the blood bank, armed with picket signs. The street lamps are still shining and you can see your breath in the early morning darkness. We walk past the Panama Hotel, on up past the Singapore Bar and Tillie's Kitchen. Men are huddled together in front of liquor stores and bars trying to keep warm while waiting for that first beer or half pint of wine at 6:00 a.m. The temporary employment offices, sometimes called slave marts, are packed with men hoping for any kind of work. If the scene looks familiar, as if from a dream or movie, perhaps it is because you've seen it in half a dozen recent Hollywood productions. The film companies often use this area for their location shots. It is so quaint, filled with old buildings and forgotten men, whose suffering is much easier to relate to through the medium of stereotypical Hollywood films.

After having worked on Skid Row for three years, I had thought that my own stereotypes were a thing of the past, but working so closely with some of the men has shattered certain illusions.

One of these illusions was that Skid Row is filled with despair and nothing could be done with such hopeless men. While we have by no means transformed Skid Row or changed the multitudes of men who live there, the energy of our presence has generated a spark of hope in the hearts of many and some few have responded with a sense of dedication and tenacity that has gratified us beyond belief.

The Indians still gather in the alcove of the Hotel Lorraine to drink wine and sing chants from half-forgotten rituals. And Pollack still spends the day bumming nickels and dimes, loping to the liquor store to buy half pints, and keeping a sharp eye peeled for the paddy wagon while he and Oscar and "the boys" drink and talk and laugh. But Mike Stone, and Luis, and Jerry, and Leroy, and Charles, and Victor walk round and round in that damn circle in front of the blood bank lifting our hearts and stirring the ashes of hopelessness up and down the street.

Please Save Our Soup Kitchen

Catholic Agitator, December, 1987, p. 1

The good news is that we can save our earthquake damaged building. The bad news is that it will cost at least $100,000. The city of Los Angeles has ordered us to submit plans for, and begin work on, rehabilitating our soup kitchen in a timely manner or we must proceed with demolition.

We are people of faith. We live by faith but we are intimidated by the prospect of having to raise such an enormous sum of money. Here at the Catholic Worker the money comes in and the money goes out to the poor. We take no salary, we live with the poor, we eat what comes into the kitchen, we have no medical insurance or life insurance. Rather, we believe that we are called to live on faith. For us this means that if we are faithful to the Lord, if we serve His people, if we feed the hungry, shelter the homeless, and comfort the afflicted, then everything else will be provided for. We do not need to worry.

We are trying to keep our part of this faith commitment. Each day we take the tables and chairs out of our kitchen and set them up in our back parking lot and with the soup line set against the brick-tumbled north wall of our building, we begin to serve 500, 1,000, 1,500 hungry men and women.

There are flowers on the table and a smile for everyone and lots of funny comments about picnicking and dining cafe style. There is a sincere air of gratitude, even celebration, because we did not let them down. Despite the earthquake damage, we continued to serve. We have kept faith that God will keep faith with us. But our faith is not as strong as it should be, and we worry because it is so much that we are asking for.

Ten years ago, when we were similarly worried about raising the initial sum to buy our building, we had a providential visit from Mother Teresa of Calcutta. While standing on the street by our building in front of the huge mural of the crucified Christ, we told her of our concerns, "Do not worry," she said. "You are doing something beautiful for God. He will take care of you."

16. Catherine Morris and Jeff Dietrich with Mother Teresa in front of the Catholic Worker Soup Kitchen, 1977. Mural by Gary Palmatier. Photo by Yoya Bertun

Jeff Dietrich

"This is what you must do. You must write down what you need on a piece of paper. Then you must take this note and tie it to a statue of Saint Joseph, for he is your patron saint."

I must say I was skeptical, but I nevertheless complied. Within two weeks the entire sum of $55,000 had been procured just in response to a simple letter to our tiny mailing list!

So now that we need to raise twice as much money as before, it seemed appropriate to take Mother Teresa's advice again. I wrote down what we needed on a piece of paper, took it over to St. Joseph's Church, and tied it to the tall white statue of our patron saint in front of the rectory. But I was caught right in the middle of this act of primitive spirituality by a couple of passing shoppers who stared at me as if I were demented.

Afterwards, as I walked into the church to pray, I realized that the reason that I was so embarrassed was that I had been caught in the act of doing what the poor do every day. The poor light candles, petition the saints, and tie notes to statues because they realize in their desperation that they have no one else to turn to but God. We are called to that simple, humble, faith that complete dependency on God alone. With that kind of faith, we will not worry; for God, working through you, our generous supporters, will provide what we need, what the poor need. Thank you in advance for your generosity, for your faithfulness. May the peace of Christ be with you through this Christmas season.

Yours in faith,
Jeff Dietrich
For the Los Angeles Catholic Worker Community

Demonic Transubstantiation

Catholic Agitator, June, 1996, pp. 1 and 2

"Hey, don't give me nonna that hard crust stuff, man. I ain't no Frenchy." For the majority of folks who eat at our soup kitchen, bread is not hard and crusty, it does not have poppy seeds or sesame seeds, it is not black or brown, it does not have the flavor of rye or yeast. In fact, it has no flavor or character, or mass or density, or substance at all. It is soft and white and bland and as flavorless as a cotton ball. It is bread in name only, made by machines for a people who have lost all memory of bread.

This is not a judgment on the people who eat at the Catholic Worker soup kitchen, it is just a minor example of the subtle but pervasive manner in which technology "transubstantiates" life into a mere simulation of itself, erasing all memories of what has gone before.

In recent months we have read articles about artists and monastics, Catholic Workers and peace activists, embracing the Internet. It is not the technology itself that concerns us so much as the fact that these particular people who are apparently embracing this new technology with such enthusiasm should, by virtue of their "alternative" vocations, be more skeptical than they apparently are.

They should not so glibly repeat the hype and promise of technical progress. They should know that everything that is being said today about the positive benefits of the Internet was first said about the automobile and then about radio and television. "It will bring us closer together, give us more and better leisure time, improve our intellect, save lives, promote community, give us more freedom, greater autonomy, and personal power." How many times do we have to hear that same sales pitch before we realize that we are being sold a bill of goods? Soon they will forget the taste and substance of face-to-face community. Soon the only real community will be the net, just as the only real bread is Wonder Bread.

Jeff Dietrich

Those who criticize new technology are often characterized as naïve or romantic. But in truth, it is the ones who uncritically embrace new technical innovations that are being naïve and idealistic. They put their hope in the power of technology to solve the very problems that it has caused in the first place: alienation, pollution, unemployment, and an epidemic of cancer-related diseases. Technique is monistic. That is, it is all one piece. All techniques are inseparably united and cannot be detached from the others. Nor can the technical phenomenon be broken down in such a way as to retain the good and reject the bad. Every technical advance is matched by a negative reverse side. Jacques Ellul writes:

> History shows that every technical application from its beginnings presents certain unforeseeable secondary effects which are much more disastrous than the lack of the technique would have been.

The Technological Society, p. 105

Though we cannot know all of the unforeseeable consequences of the information superhighway, we can certainly recognize the secondary effects of our current highway system: air pollution; traffic fatalities that every five years exceed the number of Americans killed in World War II; war, intrigue, and death to secure oil in the Middle East; endless suburban sprawl, and more acres of asphalt than farm land. Here in Los Angeles anyone without an automobile is *de facto* a second-class citizen without access to the better paying jobs and decent housing that have migrated down the freeways to the suburbs. The same will also be true of everyone who finds himself stuck on the on-ramp of the information superhighway. It's a dead-end street for the poor.

The late Christopher Lasch points out that the "new mericratic elites" are already cruising down the information superhighway, losing all sense of connectedness with community, place, and the common good. "Their loyalties...are international rather than regional, national, or local. They have more in common with their counterparts in Brussels or Hong Kong than with the masses of Americans not yet plugged into the network of global communications" (*The Revolt of the Elites and the Betrayal of Democracy,* p. 35).

Our blindness to the disastrous "secondary effects" of technology is a result of our theological attachment to the technical phenomenon. We tend to think of technology as a neutral instrument. But in fact, it is the physical embodiment of our cultural values of rationality and efficiency, and our collective desire to overcome the forces of nature: toil, suffering, and death.

As such, it is a response to the "Fall." It is a manifestation of our attempt to attain salvation without repentance or discomfort.

Thus, we must recognize that our struggle is not against technology in itself, but rather against the "spirituality of technology," against technology as a *principality and power*. Ellul writes that technology, or "technique" as he calls it, is the "sacred organizing principle of our culture," somewhat like the force that Christianity exerted on the culture of Medieval Europe.

In the past, technological growth was restrained by the culture. All traditional cultures are essentially religious and conservative, skeptical of anything new and innovative and focused primarily upon preserving the patterns and practices of the past. As a consequence, technology developed at a very slow pace and never disrupted cultural structures up until the Industrial Revolution.

It is axiomatic that human institutions develop at a far slower pace than technical innovations. Just ask any businessman and he will tell you that in our world today, change is the only constant. The survivors are the ones who have positioned themselves to ride the cresting wave of the future. On the other hand, the vast majority of the world's population will drown because they need the buoyancy provided by stable institutions.

It is often assumed that the prosperous working class of the industrial nations was created by the progressive development of technology. But the truth is that this prosperity was created not by machines but by the struggle and sacrifice of dedicated workers and the advent of the labor union. But the institution of the labor union took over a hundred years to evolve, while the positive benefits that they created have been destroyed in less than a generation by the onslaught of new information technologies. The constant cycle of technological change is disastrous for the poor. Long before any human institution can evolve to address this current technology there will be a new destabilizing technical development.

Ellul is not a very satisfying writer because he refuses to give us any solution to the problems of a "technological society." He simply reminds us that as Christians we are called to be "in the world but not of it." Ellul is painfully aware that we cannot simply reject technology and that it is impossible to give a pure witness to the simple non-technical life. But we can refuse to sing the songs of technology, we can refuse to repeat the mythology of technical progress, we can refuse to put our hope in the god of technology. And when we use technology, we can use it "confessionally," acknowledging our complicity in the degradation of the planet and the oppression of the poor.

Jeff Dietrich

Though I am a big fan of *Star Trek* and *The X-Files*, I do believe that Carl Jung is correct when he says that the current interest in space travel and flying saucers is a projection of desperate people seeking salvation, no longer in God or repentance, but in a fantasy of space-traveling extra terrestrials. Correspondingly, Wendell Berry maintains that, or

> we cannot look for happiness to any technological paradise or to any New Earth of outer space, but only to the world as it is, and as we have made it. The only life we may hope to live is here....We can only wait here, where we are, in the world, obedient to its processes, patient in its taking away, faithful to its returns....And all that we deserve, of earthly paradise will come to us.
>
> *A Continuous Harmony,* p. 151

Our salvation lies in eating the true bread of life, not bread baked by machines and filled with chemicals—the bread of remembering, not the bread of forgetfulness.

Planting the Seeds

Catholic Agitator, August, 1992, p. 1

Clarence Jordan, the rural theologian, founder of Koinonia Farm, and graduate of Union Theology Seminary, often said that he did not believe that Jesus was a carpenter. He believed that Jesus was a farmer. I only wish that I could imitate the low Southern intonations of Clarence's voice for you as he drawled out the word "farmer" into a seven-syllable noun that conjured up images of poor, rural sharecroppers trying to scratch out a meager living from the dusty, red Georgia clay.

I sometimes feel as though we too are farmers here at the Catholic Worker, attempting to scatter the seed of God's word and work in a sometimes rocky, arid soil, hoping against hope for the "Abundant Harvest" that Jesus promised in the fourth chapter of Mark's Gospel.

I treasure a note from a personal hero of mine, the poet/farmer Wendell Berry, in which he compares his own work of "healing the wounds of the land" to our work of "healing the wounds of the inner city." Both, he said, require the steadfast faithfulness of personal commitment and personal presence.

It is just this vision of healing and faithfulness, commitment and presence that we attempt to share with the ten interns who come to live with us for two months each summer.

Over the last seven years, the summer program has become one of our major projects. At first, it seemed like a simple thing to do: just invite a few folks for the summer, let them look around, live with the community, share in the work and, presto, at the end of two months they will understand the whole thing.

Well, that turned out to be pretty naïve. While it is essential to offer a living model of Christian community and an example of contemporary prophetic witness, that is really not enough.

85

People need to be told what it is they are seeing, so in the last few years, we have developed a three-part program: we tell people who we are (Catholic Worker history and philosophy), we tell them what we think the world is like (Western history and sociology), and finally, we tell them what we think God is about (theology and scripture study). Gradually, our summer program is beginning to look a bit like a college seminar course. But, unlike college, it is a living experience of theology in Christian community and can at times be a bit intimidating for novices, who initially assume that we must be either Mother Teresa clones or unemployable clowns.

We are, in fact, merely human beings, no better and no worse, with both blessings and brokenness. In community, when we live so closely together, we cannot pretend to be saints, or gurus, or experts, and that can be disappointing for people who sometimes expect us to be all three rolled into one. Sometimes the summer interns are like Jesus' neighbors and relatives in Nazareth. Their skepticism makes it impossible for the community to perform any miracles. But that is a phase, and it usually passes. In the end, we are usually accepted as simple farmers trying to spread the seed of God's word and are graciously forgiven for the pretentious human fertilizer that sometimes gets scattered along with the seed.

It is always our hope, each year, that we will reap an abundant harvest of full-time community members who will stay and work with us throughout the coming year. So, of course, it is disappointing after all of that work of plowing and planting, pulling up rocks and watering, that we have no interns who plan to stay with us.

But, much as we would prefer it otherwise, our job is merely to plant the seed; it is not for us to determine when or where, or even if, the harvest will occur: "Our work is to sow. Another generation will be reaping the harvest" (Day, *Selected Writings*, p. 92).

Creative Cooking

Catholic Agitator, May, 1981, p. 4

Every Tuesday is "hospital food day" at the Catholic Worker kitchen. Though we are always in need of volunteers at the Kitchen, we are usually a little embarrassed when eager neophytes show up ready to help chop fresh carrots, celery, and potatoes for our enormous soup cauldrons and we announce that, "Today we need your assistance in the preparation of hospital food!"

The new volunteer looks hesitantly at the red or brown liquid mass slowly seeping out of the bag into the concrete floor, feels the unfamiliar heft of the twelve inch french knife in her hand and probably gives more than a fleeting thought as to why she decided to come in the first place, making a mental note not to accept any more invitations for Sister Janet's social justice field trips.

These mental reveries are rudely disturbed as a Catholic Worker, knife in hand, rips into the plastic bag with a gusto born of experience and spews liquid of unknown quality into the aluminum catch pan. The new volunteer whispers a silent gasp, as if her own body had been stabbed. A hand reaches into the bag pulling out several defrosting meat loaves, dripping with tomato sauce, and distributes them around the chopping table with the alacrity of a fish monger parceling out the day's catch.

Inspired by the casual attitude of the other choppers, the new volunteer overcomes her initial timidity and begins to dissect the meat loaf, still wondering, however, why the appellation "hospital food"?

"Hospital food" is at the very heart of what Hospitality Kitchen is all about. Though it conjures images of cadavers and formaldehyde, it is actually a major source of healthful and nutritious food. At first glance it may be lacking aesthetics, but that is in fact part of the primary challenge of hospital food. As Christians, we are called to look beyond outward appearances to

Jeff Dietrich

discern the inner reality. So too with hospital food. In scripture, the rejected stone is the one that finally forms the corner stone of the new structure.

In our society, whatever is rejected is immediately categorized as garbage. To some, hospital food may look like garbage merely because it has been rejected, but to those trained in perceiving the inner reality, hospital food already looks like what it will become, a banquet for the rejects.

For the last six years, Sister Samuel at St. Francis Hospital has been saving left-over and discarded food that passes through their kitchen. Let me hasten to add that this is food that has never been served to patients; in fact, it has never left the kitchen. Because the daily patient load of the hospital fluctuates, the cooks can't be certain how much food should be prepared, so to be sure they have enough they deliberately over-cook. Until Sister Samuel's happy advent, this food was slated for the large green dumpsters at the back of the hospital.

Some years ago, when she was planning to retire, Sister Samuel hit upon this project as a kind of second career. She had always been disturbed at this enormous waste of food and with the heightened awareness of the problem of world hunger, she resolved to do something about it. We were a bit dubious when she first contacted us, but we were desperate. At that point in our history, even a sack of potatoes was a luxury. We were ready to try anything. Ultimately, hospital food has proven to be the best thing that has ever happened to the Hospitality Kitchen, but it was hardly love at first sight. Like every good relationship, it took some "working out." After all, how could one develop an immediate affection for 2,000 pounds of frozen left-overs? It was all packaged neatly in a hundred cardboard boxes, lined with sheets of plastic—but what do you do with a hundred frozen blocks that weigh twenty pounds each? We had no adequate freezer or refrigerator space, so we had to use it all immediately—we learned very quickly that you cannot just drop twenty-pound blocks of frozen food into boiling water. It turns out like Baked Alaska; the outside burns, but the inside is still frozen solid.

Though the first meal we served was a disaster, we remained undaunted. This was the perfect challenge for our Catholic Worker creativity; not unlike the old Russian folk tale about the man who made soup from stones, we were determined to make soup out of glacial left-overs. Our dilemma was finally resolved by the "water cure." We would fill up our triple sink with hot water and after the frozen chunks had defrosted for awhile, we would chop through them with our large french knives, reducing the entire mass to a fine slush with a consistency similar to snow-cones.

Once the food had been reduced to its cookable state, we then had to face the problem of aesthetics. At this point you are probably thinking that I have made the same error as Charlie Tuna who confused aesthetics, that is good taste, for tasting good.* Actually, hospital food is quite tasty, though unattractive in its natural state. The challenge is to make it look like something other than a prop from a 1950s horror movie.

A few basic guidelines were quickly developed; cardinal among them was "no beets!" While beets may be nutritious and purportedly tasty, a mere handful of them can transform fifteen gallons of stew into a purple nightmare. The same rule, for obvious reasons, also applies to pea soup. By now, it must be apparent that correct color combinations are the key to cooking hospital food. Red, brown, and cream are the primary colors. The pot of red food generally looks something like spaghetti or baked beans, while the brown one tends to have the appearance of beef stew or noodles Romanoff. We try to make the cream-colored pot into chicken à la king, but sometimes it just turns out looking like oatmeal with chicken lumps floating in it.

Whether or not we achieve our aesthetic objectives seems to be of little concern to our clientele. They always think that the meal tastes great simply because it had about 200 pounds of meat in it. We also think hospital food is great, even though it can be challenging and even dangerous at times, when one of those plastic bags breaks and you find your entire body covered in a clammy mucus of half-frozen cream of mushroom soup.

Yet, with all of its problems, whether aesthetic or logistic, hospital food is still the best thing that ever happened to us. And thanks to Sister Samuel, hundreds of hungry people are eating nutritious food that once was considered fit only for dumpsters.

---

* The 1960s cartoon fish and mascot for *StarKist Tuna*, who thought he had good taste and therefore qualified as the perfect specimen for a can of *StarKist*. But in the TV ads Charlie was always rejected. A note attached to a fish hook was lowered at the end of each commercial that said, "Sorry, Charlie," making it clear that *StarKist* was not looking for tuna with good taste, but tuna that tasted good.

Eating the Forbidden Fruit:
The Problem of Industrial Agriculture

Catholic Agitator, October, 2009, pp. 1, 2, and 6

Modern industrial agriculture is unsustainable. "It has been pushed to the limit..." writes Dale Allen Pfeiffer. "Our farm crops have been genetically reduced to weak, high yield hybrids that are susceptible to any number of pests, and that offer minimum nourishment" (*Eating Fossil Fuels,* p. 39).

Our farmlands have been concentrated into an agribusiness dedicated to maximizing short-term profit, while incidentally undermining our ability to support ourselves with local agriculture. And industrial-style farming has wreaked havoc on the environment and on our health.

According to Michael Pollan, 22 percent to 33 percent of climate change gasses can be traced to the food system, and all of those diseases that we so take for granted as what will kill us—heart disease, cancer, diabetes—were virtually unknown 150 years ago, before agriculture was "modernized" (*In Defense of Food,* p. 10).

Our unhealthy diet, based on corn sweeteners and cheap grain-fed beef, has led to an obesity epidemic, especially among the poor, who are heavy consumers of cheap, fast, and processed foods.

Our agricultural system threatens the health of our planet as well, precipitating the destruction of the Amazon rain forest and the creation of an oceanic dead zone the size of the state of New Jersey, where the Mississippi River, filled with pesticides, oozes into the Gulf of Mexico. Industrial agriculture, focused on the genetically modified seeds of the four primary grains (corn, wheat, rice, oats) of our contemporary monoculture (the agricultural practice of producing or growing one single crop over a wide area), demands ever greater quantities of fossil fuel, both for fertilizer as well as pesticides, in order to operate at a time when sky-rocketing oil prices and global warming threaten everything.

Modern industrial agriculture grew out of the "Green Revolution" in the 1960s and the work of geneticist Norman Borlaug, popularly credited with providing heretofore unimaginable quantities of food and saving millions from starvation. However, this high-yield agriculture, dependent upon expensive, genetically modified seeds, costly farm equipment, oil-based fertilizers and pesticides, forced American small-scale farming into debt and out of business.

Vast surpluses of grain were exported to poor nations, and farmers there, unable to compete with cheap American grain, also were destroyed. In the end, hunger was not eliminated through this "scientifically sound" response to a human problem.

We forget, of course, that agriculture is a relatively recent invention. As Richard Manning writes:

> For most of our human history, we lived by gathering or killing a broad variety of nature's offerings. Farming did not improve most lives. Agriculture was not so much about food as it was the accumulation of wealth. It benefited some people and those people have been in charge ever since.

"The Oil We Eat," *Harpers Magazine*, p. 38

In the Bible, agriculture first appears as a consequence of the Fall: "By the sweat of your face shall you get bread to eat, until you return to the ground from which you were taken; for you are dirt, and to dirt you shall return" (Genesis 3:19). Adam and Eve, once sustained by the herbs and fruits of paradise, were expelled from the garden and turned to farming grain.

What was the "forbidden fruit of the Fall," the "fruit of the knowledge of good and evil?" According to Evan Eisenberg, Rabbi Meir of the second century AD, gives a remarkable answer: "It was wheat, for when a man lacks knowledge people say, 'That creature has never eaten bread of wheat'" (*Ecology of Eden*, p. 95). Rabbi Meir's notion sounds less odd in Hebrew than it does in English, for the word translated 'fruit' can mean any kind of produce. And if the forbidden fruit is indeed wheat, the role of the snake becomes clear: in ancient times snakes were used to protect granaries from rodents.

The cultivation of wheat for bread and beer-making did in fact first appear in the Near East some 10,000 years ago. Eve, blamed for taking the first bite of the forbidden fruit, dimly recalls that surely women, who were the "gatherers" and not the "hunters," first dabbled in the domestication of plants.

Agriculture became, over time, the foundation for cities, with their armies, their bureaucrats, their great ancient canals, their store houses, their weary peasants and slaves, their famines and plagues.

The Fall into agriculture has continued. What do we do about this disastrous system?

One could say that the entire scriptural opus is a critique of that system. Starting with the recognition in Genesis that the Fall was a fall into agriculture, the authors of scripture realized that we cannot go back to the garden. They understood that agriculture is a poor substitute for the garden and that, if left to its own rapacious devices, it would, as it did in Egypt and Babylon, destroy the environment, enslave the populace, and accrue great wealth to the few while starving the many.

Much of the wisdom of Jewish law is derived from keen observation of the surrounding nations and the painful experiences of their own captivity in both Babylon and Egypt. Both nations were economic powerhouses with highly intensive plantation-style agriculture, not unlike our industrial farms today. The Jews watched as this highly intensive monoculture ultimately depleted the soil, and irrigation systems led to salinization of once fertile land.

In contrast to empire, the alternative Hebrew system created a set of regulations that required the land be given a rest every seven years, and that every fifty years the land be redistributed. This kept the soil healthy and undermined the development of large plantations. Therefore, during this time Israel was composed of a multitude of small farmers with a personal interest in caring for their land.

Unlike the great empires of Egypt and Babylon, with their verdant valleys watered by great rivers and extensive canal systems, Israel's rocky hillsides and mountainous soil was dependent upon rainfall and the loving attendance of a multitude of small farmers who practiced a style of human-scale peasant farming that persisted throughout the ages until the beginnings of the twentieth century. Our scriptures are about nothing if not about food. That's why Jesus refused to turn stones into bread in the Second Temptation in the Wilderness, creating life out of non-life. We are so impressed with our own technological "miracles" that we actually think that we are God and that we are creating something out of nothing. But, as environmentalist Richard Manning writes, "there is only so much energy. You can change it from motion to heat, from heat to light, but there will never be more of it and there will never be less of it. The conservation of energy is not an opinion; it is a fact. This is the first law of thermodynamics" ("The Oil We Eat," *Harpers Magazine,* p. 37). We have only the earth, sun, and photosynthesis. We are human beings. The word humus means soil. There is only the energy of the sun preserved in seeds, grain, rice, corn, and plants in subterranean deposits of decomposed dinosaurs and long dead prehistoric forests.

Special as we humans are, we get no exemptions from the rules. All animals eat plants, or eat animals that eat plants; this is the food chain, and pulling it is the unique ability of plants to turn sunlight into stored energy in the form of carbohydrates. This is the basic fuel of all animal life. There is no alternative energy.

Our current industrial agriculture has created the miracle of the green revolution with heavy infusions of plant energy stored in fossil fuel. This is a transfer of energy, *not* a miracle of turning dead stones into food. But it is an uneconomic energy transfer that uses ten calories of energy to create one calorie of food; and it turns out that we have been eating our most valuable asset: oil.

Jesus refused to participate in the domination system's technological sham because he knew the problem with hunger was not one of production, but rather of distribution.

The "Feedings in the Wilderness"offer a model of how the distribution problem can be solved, as each person unwraps his small portion and begins to share with his neighbor. "They all ate and were satisfied" (Matthew 15:37).

The story of the "Abundant Harvest" (Mark 4:8) must be understood as a model of Kingdom economics that operate when small farmers are able to make their living without the oppressive fees and taxes exacted by empire. According to theologian Ched Myers:

> The parable...represents a dramatic shattering of the vassal relationship between vassal and landlord. With such a surplus, the farmer could not only eat and pay his rent, tithes and debts, but indeed even purchase the land and thus end his servitude forever. "The kingdom is like *this*," says Jesus: it envisions the abolition of the oppressive relationships of production that determined the horizons of the Palestinian farmers' social world. Such images strongly suggest that Mark is articulating an ideology of the land, and revolutionary hopes of those who work it.

Binding the Strong Man, p. 177

In our contemporary era, the forces of agribusiness and industrial farming are parallel to the first-century Palestinian landlords who evoked the condemnation of the great prophet: "Woe to you who join house to house, who connect field with field" (Isaiah 5:8).

In the wake of the contemporary critique of industrial farming, it is more than appropriate for this publication to recall the peasant farmer and Catholic Worker co-founder, Peter Maurin.

Though often dismissed by urban Catholic Workers, his vision of what he called a "Green Revolution" was quite the opposite of the fossil-fuel infused "Green Revolution" of our industrial farming system. Born as a peasant farmer in southern France, Peter valued the tradition of small-scale peasant farming that now is extolled as exemplary by many critics of our failing agricultural system today. The Jewish Festival of Succoth begins soon, a time when Jews celebrate their deliverance from slavery by recalling that their ancestors lived in tents for forty years in the wilderness. We too might reflect during this season on the lessons from the wilderness—the call to share bread with our neighbors, to give rest to weary farm laborers, and to the land as well—and strive to be a different kind of free people.

Exorcising the Demonic Food
of Warmaking*

Catholic Agitator, May, 2003, pp. 4 and 5

Tuesday, April 1, 2003, Metropolitan Detention Center

Dear Community,

As I sit in this jail, my two principal activities, aside from praying and fasting, are watching the TV news coverage of the war and reading the Bible. What strikes me most powerfully as I watch TV is the strident moral certainty of President Bush and Defense Secretary Rumsfeld as well as the generals running this atrocious war. Not only do they feel that God is on their side, but that moral virtue itself is in their favor. In these dark times, the sometimes puzzling phrase of the theologian William Stringfellow— the "Moral Reality of Death"—suddenly makes more sense than ever.

Certainly Stringfellow's insight that these leaders have grounded their moral principles not on the God of life, but on the demonic works of death is confirmed by the Gospel of Luke.

In Luke 11:11-12:3, Jesus speaks directly to our current situation, exposing the cycle of violence and uncovering the religious hypocrisy that gives a false moral foundation to the demonic activities of war and death. I call the passage "The Demonic Food of Our Fathers."

The keys to understanding the passage are the "Jesus and Beelzebub" verses (11:14-23), in which Jesus is accused of "casting out Satan by the power of Satan," and the "Dinner with the Pharisees" (11:37-53), in which Jesus reveals the religious leaders as murderers. In the center of the passage are the mysterious "Light of the Body" verses (11:11-12) and the "Leaven of the Pharisees" (12:1-3).

---

* At the beginning of the Iraq war, Jeff Dietrich was jailed for praying the rosary on the steps of the Federal Building, downtown Los Angeles.

When we go to Church on Sunday and hear the "Snakes and Scorpions" verses: "What father among you would hand his son a snake when he asks for a fish? Or hand him a scorpion when he asks for an egg?" (Luke 11:11-12), it is always the occasion for an innocuous sermon on the importance of being a good father and providing for the needs of our children.

But it is essential to note that the passage is not addressed to fathers and children, but to fathers and sons. And further, that it is specifically addressed to the disciples and not to fathers in general, because fathers in general do indeed feed snakes and scorpions to their sons.

Unlike mothers, who nurture their children on "the milk of human kindness," it is traditionally fathers who nurture their sons on the bile of violence, teaching them to grow up and be men. It is fathers who train their sons in the violence of contact sports, the arts of war, and survival in a harsh dog-eat-dog world.

While we cannot specifically identify what snakes and scorpions symbolize, it is clear that they are associated with the demonic, because Jesus had already told his disciples, "I have observed Satan falling like lightning from the sky. I have given you power 'to tread upon' serpents and scorpions and nothing will harm you" (Luke 10:18-19).

Overcoming the power of Satan is the theme of the next passage (11:14-23), in which Jesus is accused of using the power of Beelzebub, the chief of demons, to cast out demons. But Jesus quickly turns the tables on his opponents by denying the charge and raising what is actually the deeper and more profound issue: unifying the house divided. "Every kingdom divided against itself will be laid waste," says Jesus, "and no town or house divided against itself will stand" (Matthew 12:25). Thus Satan's kingdom would fall if Jesus were exorcising by the power of Satan. But for Jesus, the real question is: "How do your own people exorcise demons?"

To illustrate how his opponents use the power of Satan to drive out demons and unify the "household," Jesus tells the story of the stronger man attacking the *strong man*: "When a strong man fully armed guards his palace, his possessions are safe. But when a stronger than he attacks and overcomes him, he takes away the armor on which he relied and distributes the spoils" (Luke 11:21-22).

It is almost as if Jesus has taken his words from the daily headlines or the nightly CNN newscast. The *strong man* could be Saddam Hussein, guarding his house with "weapons of mass destruction," and the stronger man could be George Bush, attacking, disarming, and dividing what he has stolen along with Exxon, Unocal, Halliburton. In the process, George Bush has unified his own household around patriotic solidarity and cast out the demons of political dissent by silencing Congress and marginalizing the peace movement.

No, Jesus is not watching the nightly news. He is simply identifying the archetypal pathology of the worldly kingdoms that constantly employ the tools of Satan: war, violence, coercion, and death, to cast out demons and unify the household. The particular players may change, but whether it is Hitler, Caesar, or George Bush, the demonic pathology remains the same.

Oddly enough, however, Jesus does not spend much energy critiquing the *strong man*. He reserves his entire critical effort for the religious leaders, the Scribes and the Pharisees. Perhaps he knows, as George Bush and every *strong man* knows, that war and violence need divine sanction to achieve validity. Without it, strong men are just brutes who murder and plunder.

Moral justification is always provided by the religious leaders. And it is just this religion of moral hypocrisy that Jesus condemns during his dinner with the Pharisees when he says, "Woe to you! You build the memorials of the prophets whom your ancestors killed....This generation might be charged with the blood of all prophets shed since the foundation of the world, from the blood of Abel to the blood of Zachariah who died between the altar and the temple building" (Luke 11:47-51).

Imagine going to a dinner party only to accuse your host of being party to murder! But Jesus is no respecter of polite social conventions. Rather, he is a champion of truth, who rips away not only social conventions but all hypocrisies to unveil the lie at the foundations of human culture, and most specifically at the foundation of religion itself.

According to René Girard, what Jesus has unveiled is the ritual murder of human sacrifice that lies at the foundation of human culture and is inscribed in every religion. Girard writes:

> Not to recognize the founding character of murder...is to perpetuate the foundation....People do not wish to know that the whole of human culture is based on this mythic process of conjuring away man's violence by endlessly projecting it upon new victims. All cultures and all religions are built on this foundation, which they then conceal, just as the tomb is built around the dead body that it conceals.

Things Hidden Since the Foundation of the World, pp. 163-164

Of course, the Scribes and the Pharisees did not practice human sacrifice, nor for that matter does any contemporary religion engage in such repugnant practices. But all religion continues to maintain an unconscious connection to its roots in "sacred violence" through the perpetuation of a "sacrificial consciousness," which projects human violence onto the false image of an angry, violent, vengeful god who demands sacrifice. This sacrificial mentality is seen most clearly in the Christian theology of "Blood Redemption," which asserts that "Jesus had to die for our sins" in order to appease a petulant God still angry at the sin of Adam.

This sacrificial mentality, shared by all religious leaders, not just the Scribes and Pharisees, provides the basis for the theological justification of the *strong man's* murder and plunder or George Bush's liberation of Iraqi oil.

It is just this blindness that Jesus addresses in the mysterious "Light of the Body" passage (Luke 11:33-36). This passage is usually the occasion for reflection on some mystical inner light, but in truth there is nothing mystical about it at all. It is really about our ability to see what is actually in front of us. The real issue is not light, but eyes. Jesus says, "The lamp of the body is your eye. When your eye is sound, then your whole body is filled with light, but when it is bad, then your body is in darkness" (Luke 11:34).

According to Jesus, the religious leaders are in darkness and thus blind, because there is something that they do not see. What they do not see is brought to light with startling clarity in Luke's Good Samaritan passage (10:29-37), in which a Levite and a priest, both religious leaders, *looked* but did not *see* the man "stripped, robbed, beaten, and left for dead by the side of the road." Only the Good Samaritan responded in compassion. "Although you [the Lord] have hidden these things from the wise and learned" religious leaders (10:21) they have been revealed to the childlike Samaritan.

What the Samaritan sees that the religious leaders are blind to is the victim by the side of the road in need of compassion. Of course, the ultimate victim in this story who is stripped, robbed, beaten, and left for dead by the side of the road, is Jesus himself. Seeing the victim is the key to knowledge (10:32). The religious leaders, the wise and the learned, have knowledge of the Law and the prophets, but they are impaired by their blindness to the victim at the heart of their sacrificial theology.

Again, it is a question of eyes. If we do not read scripture, history, and the world in front of us with the eyes of the victim, then our " whole bodies will be full of darkness," (Matthew 6:23) and we will continue to give divine sanction to war, violence, and the continuous cycle of producing more and more victims.

This moral blindness to the victim is the food of the religious leaders; it is the "beware of the leaven of the Pharisees" (12:1) that Jesus warns us

17. Jeff Dietrich leads "Mourn on the 4th of July," 2008 peace parade on the Santa Monica Pier. Pictured: Fr. Chris Ponnet, Theresa Yugar. Photo by Mike Wisniewski

against. This tiny yeast of blindness to the victim spreads through the entire loaf, creating the food of death.

Though Jesus attends no less than three dinner parties with the religious leaders in the Gospel of Luke, these are not occasions for noting, as so many commentators have, Jesus' receptivity to all people, including the rich and powerful religious leaders. These are, rather, occasions for noting that Jesus constantly rebukes the blindness of these leaders, and most importantly, he never eats with them. He has refused the demonic food that fathers feed to their sons, the cycle of violence and war covered over by the deadly yeast of the Pharisees.

It is the same food that is fed to us each night on CBS and CNN as we watch, transfixed by the slaughter of the victims. As disciples of Jesus, we must follow the example of our leader and steadfastly reject this demonic food, though we know full well that refusal to eat may cause us to share in the fate of the crucified one.

So I continue to sit here in my jail cell, fasting and praying, rejecting the food of our national violence, seeking instead my sustenance in the Holy Word of scripture. I am grateful for this opportunity to give humble witness to the Gospel of non-violence and the God of Life. I am deeply grateful for your prayers and support and most especially for your continued commitment to our presence among the victims of our own city.

In Sure and Certain Hope of the Resurrection,
Jeff

Recovering Radical Memory*

Catholic Agitator, May, 2002, p. 1

For us at the LACW, Passover has come to mean that we bring our memories to the table and celebrate the radical roots of our heritage. Each of the foods on our table represents a symbolic memory of our heritage of liberation, so you might be wondering why I have brought this large Mexican cactus to the table. A Mexican cactus doesn't have anything to do with the Jewish Passover. But in truth, it represents the very core of Passover celebration.

In bible study last week, we reflected on the story of the chosen people eating manna in the wilderness, and we speculated that manna might actually be a hardy variety of edible plant that grew abundantly in the Sinai Desert, not unlike the wild dandelion and mustard greens consumed by the poor African Americans of the American South.

Suspecting that such wild food might also be consumed by poor people in Mexico, we asked Manuel, who grew up in Mexico, for input. Indeed, he said that all poor Mexicans eat *nopales*, a nutritious cactus that grows abundantly in the deserts of Mexico. We further inquired whether there might be some derogatory term attached to people who eat such food. "Yes," he replied. "We say *El Nopal en la frente*, which means '*nopales* on the forehead.'"

When the poor country folks come into the city, they want to quickly conform to the demands of urban sophistication and wipe those *nopales* off their foreheads. They want to be part of the urban power scene and quickly forget where they came from.

But I thought that is exactly what Passover is. Passover means putting *nopales* back on our foreheads and remembering that our radical heritage is not the heritage of urban sophistication and power. It is not the heritage of Pharaoh and royalty. No! Tonight we remember that we all come from

---

*   Jeff's welcome statement at the 28th Annual Los Angeles Catholic Worker Passover Seder.

18. Protest of the Persian Gulf victory parade on Sunset Boulevard, as it passes in front of Blessed Sacrament Church. Pictured: Jeff Dietrich, Betsy Perluss, Tensie Hernandez, Mary Blanche, Sandi Huckaby, 1991. Photo by Mike Wisniewski

poverty. Tonight we remember that all of our ancestors, whether they are Italian, Irish, Polish, or African American, had *nopales* on their foreheads; we remember that our biological ancestors came from poverty and oppression; we remember that our spiritual ancestors came from poverty, oppression, and slavery in Egypt.

I think "*nopales* on the forehead" are like phylacteries, the tiny wooden boxes containing scriptural quotations that orthodox Jews wear tied to the top of their foreheads—worn to remind them of who they are and where they come from, so that they will never be absorbed into an alien culture.

Tonight we are called to remember who we are and where we come from. Tonight we remember that our ancestors were slaves who came from poverty and oppression. And when we recover our radical memories, our hearts are broken open in compassion for the poor, the oppressed, the slave, the homeless, the victim.

This Passover, our hearts are heavy indeed. We mourn the Passover deaths of Israeli terrorist victims, even as we mourn the deaths of American terrorist victims.

But we believe that the memory of these victims is not served by the making of more victims. The worldwide War on Terror, wherever it takes place, is a world-wide war on the poor. It is Pharaoh's solution to the terrorist problem. It will not make the world safe—it will only breed more terror.

The Passover story urges us to recover our story, our memory as refugees and slaves and open our hearts in compassion to the poor and powerless, even as we reject the power solutions of Pharaoh.

We reject Pharaoh's chariots and horses. We reject his armies and tanks, his rockets and bombs, his B-52s and F-16s. And we put *nopales* on our foreheads and stand in solidarity with the poor and the powerless and trust the Living God, who topples the mighty, liberates the slave, and avenges the victims with a mighty hand. And I might add here that there are a lot of Pharaohs in our own Catholic Church who could benefit from putting *nopales* on their foreheads and remembering that their founder was poor and powerless and stood in solidarity with the victims of political as well as sexual tyranny. Shalom! "Next year in Jerusalem! Next year, may all be free!"

Christmas Appeal:
The Poor Are Still with Us

Catholic Agitator, August, 2008, pp. 1 and 2

Christmas, 2008

Dear Friends,

We have no money. Our bank account is depleted by rising food costs and longer lines.

We need your help. But we know that you, too, are at the end of your economic rope because our nation's collective wealth has been squandered on financial bailouts and foreign wars. Like you, we pray that sanity might soon prevail.

In the meantime, the poor are still with us. Today I watched as a man in our dining garden carefully spooned his meal of chili beans and green salad onto tortillas, making six burritos. "Oh, they're not for me," he said, "they're for homeless friends."

This Christmas, even as you experience tough times, we urge you to remember the poor who pack burritos into knapsacks to take to their friends, knowing that whatever small gift you can donate to us is spread throughout the homeless community in a kind of heavenly leaven that cannot be devoured by Wall Street titans or the dogs of war. It is a gift that will last for eternity and possibly redeem us all.

Thank you. Many blessings.
Jeff Dietrich

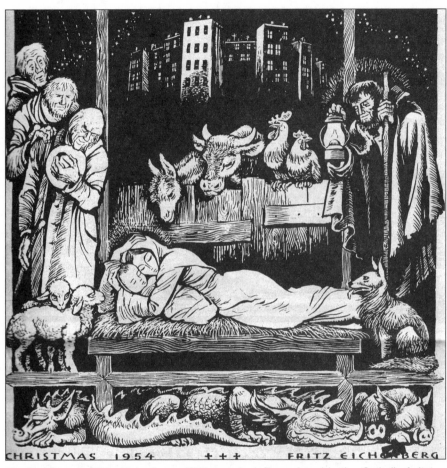

19. *Christmas* by Fritz Eichenberg, 1954, woodcut. Reproduced in the *Catholic Agitator*, 1996

PART THREE

THE CHURCH

And God, who is able to prevail, wrestled with him,
as the Angel did with Jacob, and marked him;
marked him as for his own.

Izaak Walton,
The Life of John Donne (1640)

Introduction

As one who has spent his entire adult life in reaction to the orthodox Church of his mid-century childhood, it is ironic that I am one of the few members of the Los Angeles Catholic Worker who still attends regular Sunday Mass at a Catholic Church. Until recently, I must admit to only sporadic church attendance, preferring to let my wife carry the banner of Catholic Worker fidelity while I took the opportunity for a much needed Sunday sleep-in. But when even my fiercely loyal wife jumped the ecclesiastical ship, I felt duty bound to renew my regular Sunday presence.

Though the stilted, impersonal Church of my childhood, with its Latin Masses, formal liturgies, and clerical culture has been, thankfully, ameliorated by the reforms of Vatican II, the machinations of the recent Church sex scandals reveal a depth of institutional duplicity and betrayal of victims, and of the Gospel itself, that cry out for profound change.

If it were not for Dorothy Day and the Catholic Worker Movement, I probably would not be in the Church at all...but because of her, I have found a home where I least expected, in the Catholic Church. And, through a life lived in community, with the daily practice of the works of mercy and a profound reconnection with the eucharistic tradition as metaphor and motivator for a life of service, I have come to appreciate the Catholic tradition in a way I never would have thought possible. Though I find myself in constant conflict with the Church, I am inspired by Dorothy, who understood that the only way to reform the Church was for us to live our lives as if we were the Church we desired the Church to be.

Many years ago, in the midst of an intractable community conflict, we engaged the services of a Harvard-trained community conflict negotiator. She turned out, much to our surprise, not to be a slick professional, but a very unpretentious Sister of St. Joseph of Orange. Nevertheless, Sr. Kathleen Schinhofen gave us profound advice. "Human beings," she said, "do not call communities together. It is the Holy Spirit who calls communities together, and the Holy Spirit has endowed your community with unique gifts that you are required to discern and share with the Church and the world."

We came to realize that our gift to the Church was to try, as Dorothy Day did, to live this new vision of church; not a Church without scandal, not a Church of perfection, not a Church of saints, but a Church of human beings with all their flaws and brokenness, who had caught hold of the original fervor and fire of the discipleship project, the original Kingdom of God movement: a Church that cares for the impoverished and confronts the causes of their impoverishment. Unfortunately, such a volatile gift is not always well received by those who are in charge, and this is a reflection of the eternal conflict between the institutional Church and the prophetic Church. This is, in fact, the very dynamic of scripture itself, the conflict between the institutional priesthood and their critics, the uncredentialed prophets from the non-institutionalized margins.

Nonetheless, over the years it gradually dawned on me that the very reason that we could give these under-appreciated gifts to the Church at all was because we had already received gifts from the Church herself. It is the Church from whom we first learn the Gospels. It is the Church who gives us the Communion of Saints, the Eucharist, liturgical sensibility, a tradition of prayer, and through the monastic movement, a history of community.

My favorite Christian theologians tend to be Protestant because they are steeped in the scripture. But my favorite Christian practitioners tend to be Catholics: Dorothy Day, Mother Teresa, the Berrigans, St. Francis of Assisi—I suspect that this is because, while Protestants have scripture, Catholics have a tradition that encompasses liturgy, community, prayer, and practice.

Out of the partial and imperfect knowledge that we received from the Church, our community was able to fashion a rudimentary recapitulation of what it might have meant to live as disciples in the Early Church. Many of our new, young community members are not, in fact, Catholics but Protestants, who have come to us out of what has been called the "emerging church movement," inspired by a reconnection with the radical

21. Dorothy Day outside St. Joseph Church, just released after two weeks in the
Fresno County Jail for protesting with the United Farm Workers, still under a
court order to remain in California, *Catholic Agitator*, 1973

Gospel and a desire to live in a community committed to service. When these seekers want to find out how to put this vision into action, they find minimal resources within their own tradition, and inevitably many of them find their way to the doorsteps of various Catholic Worker communities, ours included.

So, I get up every Sunday morning and I go to mass, not because of the great sermon (because it usually isn't), not because of the great music (because it rarely is), not because of the liturgy (often lackluster). I don't go to Mass to be edified or illuminated or even challenged by the Gospels, because that almost never happens. I do not go even for a spiritual experience. I go so that I might be faithful to the imperfect but essential gifts that I have been given. I go because of the Communion of Saints, the cloud of witnesses. I go, because despite its imperfections and scandals and its suburban-comfort homilies, there is really no other ecclesial entity I have found that is better. I go because in the Catholic tradition even rich, comfortable Catholics know intuitively and sacramentally in a way that other religious expressions do not, that feeding the hungry, clothing the naked, and sheltering the homeless, is the core of the Christian project.

I go to church because Dorothy Day went to church. I go to church because Mother Teresa went to church. I go to church, because Dan Berrigan, at eighty-nine, still goes to church. I go to church because most of the 8,000 people on our tiny mailing list are exclusively Catholic. And for the last forty years, I have had the privilege of living a life of scandalous simplicity, community, service, and resistance, and I have been supported financially and spiritually by those Catholics who think that what I am doing, what the Catholic Worker is doing, is what Jesus would be doing if he were around today, and what the Church should be doing until "He returns in His glory." And I am thus compelled by my gratitude to be in "holy communion" with those Catholics who go to Mass every Sunday.

A Vision of the Church as Mother of the Poor

Catholic Agitator, January, 1979, pp. 1 and 2

"Something really strange happened last night," Dan Brown told us on Saturday morning when we walked into the kitchen. "Come outside and look." We walked over to the Regal Hotel next door. There was an outline of a human form drawn in chalk half on the sidewalk and half on the street. A vivid red trail ended at the exact spot. In the street, thin lines of burnt-out ashes marked the spot where a dozen flares had burned in a semi-circle around the chalk-marked area. "There were police all over the place last night," Dan said. It didn't take much intelligence to figure out that there had been another murder on Skid Row.

It was Raul Martinez—eighteen years old, just up from Mexico to find a job. He died in an attempt to save a friend from a knife attack. Raul was stabbed five times. Then the assailant finished the job by properly carving his initials on the face of the still warm body. Raul's ever present smile and easy charm had made him a favorite of many here at the Kitchen. His death was hard to accept.

Our joys so quickly turn to despair when confronted with the violent reality of poverty. Not only is Raul dead, but the maniacal Skid Row stabber has claimed his twelfth victim in a month, forcing the men from the streets at night—the only home they have. I can hardly face the line of 500 hungry men and women. Joy turns to despair, despair to anger. I feel abandoned. Why are we, with a few exceptions, the only Catholic organization on Skid Row?

Where are those who are ordained to serve? Where are those who are vowed to poverty? Where are the vast resources of the Church? Why is it that Catholic Charities, with their enormous resources, send us people to care for? Why is it that parish priests call us in the middle of the night for housing referrals? Are their rectories over-crowded with the poor? I think not. Where are the Church's priorities? Whom does she serve?

The Church serves the rich. Her priority is maintaining the status quo and her resources are simply committed to suburban parishes. Millions of dollars are invested in land, mostly in suburban Los Angeles.

I can't say that I have ever been real positive about the Church. When the anger wells up in me and I feel like an abandoned child, the words of the prophet Amos come to my mind: "I hate, I spurn your feasts, I take no pleasure in your solemnities" (Amos 5:21).

Over the years, there have been countless nuns and priests who have stood before me and said, "You know, you guys are the real Christians. You are the ones who are really doing the work of Christ." Well, if they really believe what they are saying, why do they go back to their comfortable and affluent rectories and convents?

The poor are not served by waving styrofoam wafers at suburban parishioners. We wonder if it is possible for the clergy to challenge affluent Americans to change their lifestyles while living in the same middle-class manner as their congregation. Will the gospel of peace ever be preached strongly enough to cause parishioners to give up jobs in war-related industries? Will the gospel of justice ever be preached as stridently as the "gospel of anti-abortion?" It's not that abortion isn't important, because it is. It is crucial to the gospel message of respect for life, but it has become the myopic concern of middle-class Catholics to the exclusion of all other Church teachings regarding social justice, simplicity, peace and the arms race. It is easy to elicit concern for murder of the unborn, but difficult indeed to raise consciousness about the institutionalized violence and injustice of the American system.

Certainly the proper forum for these concerns is the pulpit. However, it is unlikely that from the pulpits of Los Angeles "justice [will] surge like water, and goodness like an unfailing stream" (Amos 5:24). Especially when one considers that the major decisions of the Los Angeles Archdiocese are all made by the Chancellor, Monsignor Hawkes,* a highly successful businessman who gave it all up to serve the Lord. Apparently, the good Monsignor feels it is his major calling to keep the servants of the Lord in the black. If the Los Angeles Archdiocese had a Dow Jones industrial rating, it would be one of the blue chips. I have never met Msgr. Hawkes, but I feel that I know him well, as he has been vividly described to me on numerous

---

* Monsignor Hawkes was the chief administrative officer and treasurer of the Archdiocese of Los Angeles, under Cardinals McIntyre and Manning.

22. Guest at the Hospitality House Kitchen, 2011. Photo by Robert
Radin

occasions. The dream of many a priest or nun, who thought that he or she
could serve the poor through the Church, has been shattered in his office.

St. Vincent Center's medical clinic on Skid Row has been waiting for
his go-ahead for ten years. A request for one of the scores of abandoned
convents to provide a women's shelter in Los Angeles is met with equal
dispatch. Fear of legal suits, the need for insurance, and security are the
basis for decision-making, not the needs of the poor. "Hear this, you who
trample upon the needy and destroy the poor of the land! The Lord has
sworn....Never will I forget a thing they have done!" (Amos 8:4,7).

"Bless me, Father, for I have sinned. It has been two weeks since my last confession. I masturbated five times, I touched a girl twice and missed Mass once."

"Where?" "At St. Mary's, Father."

"Oh, on her breasts."

"O my God, I am heartily sorry for having offended Thee."

Ten Our Fathers and ten Hail Marys later I am again united with Christ and the Blessed Virgin.

I was twenty years old before it occurred to me that morality might involve more than the sex organs. After a lifetime of religious education, that, in itself, should stand as an indictment of the Church. The great moral crisis of my life was the war in Vietnam. In deciding not to go to war and embrace the Gospel of peace, the Church was a deficit. I was refused conscientious objector status by the local draft board specifically because I was Catholic.

I had left the Church some years previous because I was struck by the manifest distinction between the teachings of Christ and the life of the Church on the parish level.

It all seemed so silly. All of the smoke and incense and men in satin and lace skirts waving around wafers as if they were some kind of magicians. Certainly not my image of Christ.

Father O'Hearn, our parish priest, bought a new Buick every year. One could hardly imagine him, with his well-tailored suits and Gucci loafers, wandering from village to village preaching the good news to the poor or suffering the little ones to come unto him. In fact, we used to live in fear of his periodic tours of the religion classes at St. Mary's. He once reduced the entire 8th grade to tears because none of them could make the sign of the cross to his satisfaction. This was the man held up as an example of Christ in our lives. God help you if you ever had to serve Mass for him. He was merciless and exacting. But Father O'Hearn was a good businessman. His sermons concentrated on the need for more money and the Sunday collection increased. The debt was paid and the parish plant refurbished. The good father was eventually promoted to a more affluent parish, much to the relief of the entire grammar school and all of the altar boys.

By the time I found my way to the Catholic Worker, I had progressed beyond mere disdain for the Church to a highly sophisticated level of indifference.

But while awaiting the fall of the corrupt ruling class, which for me also included the Church, this Catholic Worker stuff seemed OK. Everything they did appealed to my young radical heart, feeding poor people, visiting the jail, resisting the war. But why all of the Catholic stuff? Why the Mass? Why the prayers? Why call it the Catholic Worker? Why not the radical archo-syndicalist Worker? What the hell does Catholic have to do with revolution?

With each passing day it became clearer why Dorothy Day had forsaken her Marxist friends and converted to Catholicism. It's not that she was no longer radical; she simply found deeper roots for her radicalism and a home for her spiritual longings.

Within the context of the Worker much of the absurdity of Catholicism began to make sense. We spent our days as we still do, preparing and serving a meal to hundreds of men and women on Skid Row. Exhausted, we would gather at the end of the week to celebrate an informal Eucharist. It was all so clear and simple; Christ meant the Eucharist to be a symbol of our lives. Just as Christ sacrificed His life for us and feeds us with His body, so we also sacrifice ourselves and feed the poor. This is what we celebrate, that through our sacrifices the broken body of humanity can become one in Christ.

The great sin of Catholicism is to confuse substance and form. The sacraments of the Church are such beautiful symbols in and of themselves that the substance, which is our daily lives of service, is lost, and we slip into idolatry.

At last I was home. There was no longer any distinction between our daily lives of service to the poor and our communion with Christ in the Eucharist. My radicalism truly had roots. Now it could take hold and flourish. While other young radicals fell by the wayside as their notions of the Woodstock nation faded, I had the strength to struggle for a greater kingdom. Certainly I have derived great comfort and strength from my reunion with the Church.

Dorothy Day often said that "Though she is a harlot at times, she is our Mother" (*Selected Writings*, p. 339).

She comforts us, she nurtures us, but she also abandons us to face the death of Raul Martinez alone, the insanity of the Skid Row stabber, the violence and injustice of poverty.

The Church Sex Scandal: Three-quarters of a Billion Dollar Settlement

Catholic Agitator, August, 2007, p. 2

The clergy sex scandal. I do not want to write about it—it is not one of our issues. But on the occasion of the historic sex abuse settlement of the Los Angeles Archdiocese, I feel that we must say something so that our readers might not conclude that we are unthinking supporters of the institutional Church. We are not. But, of course, we are so predisposed to criticizing the Church that we hesitate to enter the field where so many critics have obviously tread before us.

As readers of this paper, you must know that I periodically find myself in jail for various protest actions. In jail I hesitate to disclose that I am Catholic for fear of being misidentified as a pedophile priest. This scandal has definitely affected our humble ministry for peace, to say nothing about the larger ministry of the Church itself, to speak out for the poor and the immigrant and for peace and justice.

I keep hoping that it is possible that I do not know all of the facts, and that Church leadership may have information that I do not possess. But even if that is the case, even if, in the best case scenario, the bishops and prelates are trying to act in the highest interests of the victims of clergy sex abuse and the larger Church, their actions scream otherwise.

Like our foundress Dorothy Day, we both love the Church and hate the Church for the scandal that she is.

I hope that my frequent criticisms reveal that love. I am part of this scandalous Church. I am part of the Catholic Worker, and I am outspoken and critical in the improbable hope that this scandalous Church might come closer to the vision Jesus had in mind for it.

Nevertheless, in my thinking about the Church regarding this scandal, I do not impose such high standards. I think rather of George Tenet, former director of the CIA, who in his resignation speech took full responsibility for the "deficient intelligence" that led us into the war in Iraq. I do not believe for one second that George Tenet or the CIA delivered faulty information to George Bush or to Dick Cheney.

But I do believe that he was embroiled in the midst of a scandal created by others and inflamed by an antagonistic press, just as our Church is. I believe that George Tenet was a company man and a stand-up guy, and like a good soldier, he fell on his sword for the greater good, as he saw it, of the CIA and the nation. I am still waiting, and I believe that the American Church is still waiting, for an American prelate that will stand up and take responsibility for this scandal—a scandal they may not have personally caused but that happened on their watch—and have at least as much integrity as the director of the CIA, one of the most reviled entities in the world.

The Great Cathedral Caper

Catholic Agitator, August, 1996, pp. 1 and 2

When the police finally came, they yelled up to us, "Be sensible. Come down from there and talk to us." We all laughed. If we were sensible, we never would have scaled the walls of the old abandoned Cathedral and climbed into an open window and scrambled up the rickety stairs of the dilapidated bell tower in the first place. If we were sensible, we wouldn't be sitting 200 feet above the ground on top of an earthquake damaged structure, hanging onto an enormous banner that reads, "We reclaim the Church for the poor." Only devious criminals or obstreperous school boys do such things. Sensible people obey the law and mind their own business.

That is why throughout the Gospel Jesus refers to himself not as a sensible person but as a criminal who binds the *strong man* or a thief in the night who strikes at the most unexpected hour. Jesus knew that to get the religious authorities to pay attention to the good news he had to be subversive.

Indeed, subversion seemed the only way to get the Church to pay attention to our own concerns. As the Cardinal moved relentlessly forward with his plans to tear down the old Cathedral and build a new $50 million one in the midst of the largest concentration of homeless people in the United States, without the slightest recognition of that problem, and as Church officials repeatedly referred to the poor and homeless of that area in terms of "blight" and "eyesore," it seemed important to break into the conversation with another perspective. And I have to admit that it was pretty exhilarating to be sitting atop the Cardinal's bell tower being filmed by every media helicopter in the city and proclaiming that not all Catholics wanted a new Cathedral.

After our arrest at the Cathedral, the Cardinal let it be known that he was willing to speak to us. Since we had already had an amicable but unproductive meeting with him, I had misgivings about this second encounter. It seemed more like a trip to the principal's office than a dialogue session.

Following a brief reiteration of our respective positions, the Cardinal, smiling all the while like a Republican presidential candidate on the campaign trail, launched into a tirade that left us wishing he had merely turned us over to the Grand Inquisitor's torture rack rather than verbally lacerating us into the equivalent of psychic hamburger.

"I've always had problems with the Catholic Worker," he said. "You need the poor." By which he meant that we were somehow codependent with the pathologies of the poor and that we needed them for our own diminished sense of self-esteem. He went on to remind us that he worked with the largest population of the poor in the city—poor families—while we worked with the smallest. But we tried to point out that it was just exactly this smaller population of 5,000 homeless poor who, like Lazarus, were virtually living on his very doorstep.

But to argue theology with a cardinal in his own office is like fighting Mohammed Ali with both your hands tied; you're just bound to lose because he has all the right moves, and pretty quickly he hit us with his best shot. "I don't even think that you are Catholic," he said, "Neither with a big 'C' nor a small 'c'." *Boom!* He knocked us clean out of the ring, down the aisle, and pretty much out the door of the church itself.

It went down hill from there as we lobbed Biblical quotations back and forth at each other. We tossed off one from the book of Kings in which God tells King David that he doesn't need a temple. And the Cardinal hurled back at us God's specific blueprint for the Temple from the book of Ezekiel. Then he went on to say that we were negative, confrontational, and uncooperative. And we suggested that he give a further reading to the prophets and the confrontations of Jesus with the authorities.

While our dialogue actually seemed more like a monologue, I think it does offer some profound insights. Foremost among these is the recognition that other than the Church, there are few organizations that would allow a rag-tag bunch of protesters like ourselves in the front door, much less into their executive offices.

The second is that it seems like we are dealing with two pretty conflicting visions of what constitutes church. On the one side there is the Cardinal's sophisticated, technocratic approach to power politics and social change; on the other side is our own personalist, direct-action (dare we say it?) Gospel-based orientation.

Jeff Dietrich

23. Cover collage by Jeff Dietrich. *Catholic Agitator*, 1996

Our technocratic cardinal offers a perfect paradigm for the postmodern twenty-first-century Church. He is an autocrat who runs his church like an efficient CEO, with all of his parishes tied into a tight computer network, and were it not for a formal protest by the Catholic Worker and others, he would have his own helicopter as well. He is feared and courted by politicians of both left and right. He knows how to manage public relations to his advantage and articulates the social agenda of the Church in a forthright manner. And while he takes laudable public stands on the death penalty, social welfare cutbacks, immigration, and raising the minimum wage, as well as the more expected anti-abortion position, it is often done in a self-serving and image-conscious manner. But he is, unfortunately, about the best that we can expect to get in the Church as it is presently constituted.

In the end, though, he presents an image of Church leader as shrewd, calculating, and affectless—a kind of modern-day Richelieu. He is disliked by many of his priests, who seek a more pastoral, collegial approach to management. And while he is indeed concerned about the poor, it is always at the structural level and never at the personal level.

But as appalling as it is for me to say this, we *need* Cardinal Mahony and his cold, heartless, technocratic church; and though I don't think it would ever occur to him, he needs us as well.

These two conflicting visions of Church have been warring with each other ever since Peter and Paul went at it over the issue of circumcision. The Cardinal needs people who are brash, foolhardy, and fearless enough to climb up ladders and hang out of bell towers, and break into buildings like a thief in the night in an effort to sneak the Word of God back into his Church and thumb their noses at his authority like obstreperous school boys. On the other hand, we must never forget that this cold, heartless, technocratic Church in all of her corruption and defilement is the repository of faith, the distributor of sacraments, and the primordial proclaimer of the Gospels, without whom we would never have heard the Word of God in the first place. My sense is that the Holy Spirit wants both of these visions to continue in perpetual, loving, faithful, and symbiotic conflict with each other unto the end of time and the coming of the Celestial Temple—"made not by the hands of man" (Hunter, *Ripple**)—out of which will flow the onrushing waters of healing and mercy and justice. Amen.

---

*   Lyrics by Robert Hunter, to a song composed by Jerry Garcia, the Grateful Dead, 1970.

The Silence of the Patriarchs from A to Z

Catholic Agitator, November, 2004, p. 1

Tall, thin, and gaunt, Cheryl is an inveterate crack user. She is also pregnant. Even among hard-core street addicts, Cheryl is regarded as bad news. She can cause a fight at the slightest hint of an insult—"I don't take shit from nobody," is her battle cry.

When she shows up at our soup kitchen, we go on high alert to quickly intervene before she causes a major riot. Like a lot of women on the street, she trades sex for drugs, so this isn't her first pregnancy. Even the guys on the street think that she is something of a loose woman and refuse to have anything to do with her. Things haven't changed much—pregnant, unwed mothers, whether in twenty-first century Skid Row or first century Palestine, are still objects of scorn, derision, and violence.

We all know the story of how Mary got pregnant through the power of the Holy Spirit and became the Mother of God, but our understanding of that Annunciation story is so sanitized and anemic that it rarely occurs to us that Mary was herself an unwed mother. A loose woman.

For centuries now, the patriarchal Church has used the cult of Mary to reinforce the quiet obedience, even the servility of women; but a closer reading of the Gospel of Luke, Chapter 1, the Annunciation and Visitation passages, assures us that such a reading represents quite the opposite intent of the Gospel of Luke.

Luke begins his story with two parallel birth announcements—one to Zechariah (Luke 1:5-26), a man in the "priestly division of Abijah," a traditional and holy line of male priests—and the other to Mary (1:26-38), a lowly, unknown teenage girl. These are two completely contrasting individuals: an older man who can trace his lineage back to Moses and a mere girl of absolutely no social status whatsoever. Both are chosen to play an essential part in salvation history, but one, the girl, is destined for the more prominent role.

Both Mary and Zechariah express disbelief at these two seemingly impossible birth scenarios, with Zechariah saying, "How shall I know this? For I am an old man and my wife is advanced in years," and Mary saying, "How can this be, since I have no relations with a man?" But despite the similarity in their disbelief, it is Zechariah and not Mary who is struck "speechless and unable to talk" (1:20).

It seems a bit unfair, almost a kind of divine prejudice against Zechariah, that he would be the only one to be struck dumb. Thus, the story starts off with an implied question, which is: why is Zechariah struck dumb and not Mary? The story requires an examination of not only the similarities, but also the differences between the two accounts.

Personally, I've never been a big fan of the "Virgin Birth" story. It seems to reinforce the Church's negative view of sexuality, a patriarchal preference for virginity, a predominate emphasis on the miraculous "divine nature" of Jesus to the detriment of his earthly mission to "liberate the poor" and establish the "kingdom" of justice. On the other hand, I found the story of Zechariah and Elizabeth more in keeping with the entire corpus of Judeo-Christian scripture. The Zechariah and Elizabeth story is the recapitulation of the Abraham and Sarah story—the original "impossible birth" scenario—and essentially the beginning of salvation history. Why not keep with the same story? Why do we have to go with this miraculous Virgin Birth stuff?

Well, the obvious difference between the two passages is the glaring absence of a father figure in the Virgin story, the elemental importance of which has been consistently overlooked by the predominately patriarchal commentators throughout history. The entire Gospel of Luke, indeed the entire life and mission of Jesus himself, pivots around the question of ambiguous paternity. Who is the true father? This question cannot be answered until we contemplate the "silence of Zechariah."

In Luke Chapter 11, Jesus charges the "scholars of the law" with the "blood of all of the prophets shed from Abel to Zechariah"—in other words, all of the blood shed from the first murder in the Hebrew scripture to the last murder in the Hebrew scripture. Which is to say, he accuses the scribes of the murder of every prophet from beginning to end, from A to Z.

I want to suggest that in this story, the birth narrative of Luke, Zechariah, the father of John the Baptist (not to be confused with Zechariah the Prophet), is for Luke, both symbolically and literally, the absolute last patriarch, while Abraham, whose story this resembles, is the first. And further, that the silence of Zechariah is emblematic of the silence of all the patriarchs from A to Z. At this moment all the "earthly fathers" are silenced. It is an historically unprecedented and quite literally pregnant pause. *His-Story* stops.

Though human culture has been around for close to a million years, civilization, patriarchal culture, and history itself have only existed since the rise of the Fertile Crescent city-states 5,000 years ago. And since that time, history has been predominantly the history of warfare and violence, written and perpetrated by men. Now in the beginning of the Gospel of Luke, the patriarchal perpetrators of history are silenced. And in that silence where men don't talk, we can finally hear an alternative voice, as prophetic women find their voice when priests, patriarchs, warriors and presidents are finally gagged.

The obvious and authentic purpose of the parallel birth announce-ments is nothing less than a repudiation of the patriarchal project alto-gether. It is not that Abraham and Zechariah are bad guys. Nothing could be further from the truth—they are an essential part of salvation history. But they are nonetheless guys, and predisposed to the historical flaws of guys: war, violence, and football. God doesn't hate guys—God just thinks that the previous few thousand years of testosterone-dominated patriarchal history haven't gone so well, and he wants to displace them a bit. So God chooses to bypass fathers and forego the use of their sperm all together.

Thus, Mary is directly impregnated by the Heavenly Father and not by an "earthly father," setting off the controversy of dubious paternity. Who is the true father of Jesus, the murderous earthly fathers (11:50-51) or the Merciful Heavenly Father (6:36)? I propose that the Gospel of Luke is, from the very beginning, not only a gospel of women, but it is indeed first and foremost a repudiation of patriarchal domination.

The silence of the patriarchs from A to Z clears the stage of history and for the first time in scripture allows pregnant, prophetic women and unborn children to speak: John leaps in his mother's womb, thus prompting Eliza-beth to announce the coming of the "Blessed One," while she utters her archetypal rejection of the reign of patriarchal lineage and says, "No! He will not be named Zechariah after his father! His name is to be John!" Then Mary proclaims the most significant liberation discourse in all of scripture, the *Magnificat*.

Feminist theologian Elizabeth Johnson has observed that,

> Known as the Magnificat from its opening word in Latin translation, this canticle can barely contain her joy over the liberation coming to

fruition in herself and the world through the creative power of the Spirit. As noted earlier classical Mariology has rarely dealt with this prayer. Its radical depiction of Mary's "no" to oppression completes her earlier "yes" to solidarity with the project of the reign of God. By sealing this page of scripture, such theology managed to suppress the portrait of Mary as a prophet and to forestall the upheaval that would ensue from oppressed peoples, including women, taking a similar stance.

Truly Our Sister, p. 258

Indeed, Mary's canticle is the essential declaration of liberation, and thus, the prophetic pronouncement of the unraveling of all patriarchal regimes. The prophetic handmaiden of the Lord proclaims:

He has shown might with his arm, dispersed the arrogant of mind and heart. He has thrown down the rules rom their thrones, but lifted up the lowly. The hungry he has filled with good things; the rich he has sent away empty.

Luke 1:51-53

Johnson cites the essayist and poet, Kathleen Norris, who "treasures Mary as an original Biblical interpreter, linking her people's hope to a new historical event" (*Truly Our Sister*, p. 273).

Even as Zechariah is silenced and thus rebuked, Mary the lowly servant girl has the insight to accept this burden, this cross. She is the quintessential unwed mother, the whore, the prostitute, the stand-in for all women raped by Roman legions, and all of the legions and armies of the world that have come before and after.

In this very first passage she has taken up the cross and taken on all the burden of those who have been called slut or whore. The new history starts with the outrageous utterance of a brave girl/woman hero who said: 'Yes. Yes I will take on this cross of male dominance and sexual violence. I will risk the possibility of stoning, of village gossip, of repudiation and rejection, of poverty, of walking around with my tumescent belly protruding before me publicly proclaiming that I am a sinner. I will stand in solidarity with all of the despised welfare mothers, with all of the raped unwed women on street corners and in times of war, with all women despised and shunned and yes, even murdered by the patriarchal establishment.'

Though we are conditioned by 5,000 years of patriarchal domination to conceive of Mary in the traditional categories of Virgin and

Jeff Dietrich

24. Untitled woodcut by Fritz Eichenberg. Reproduced in the *Catholic Agitator*, 1991

Mother, this is in fact the opposite intention of the story. Rather, this story is the announcement of God's new project, the new song, the new creation. And while it may begin in the temple with a member of the male priesthood, these traditional patriarchal categories are immediately repudiated and subverted by God's decision to abandon propriety and patriarchy with the choice of Mary, the pubescent servant girl, the Galilean rebel, the unwed teenage mother. It is as if God were saying, "Come on. Get a clue!" Nothing could be more radical. Or as Johnson writes: "This poor unconventional peasant woman's free and autonomous answer opens a new chapter in the history of God with the world" (*Truly Our Sister*, 257).

Theologian Brigitte Kahl has pointed out that pregnancy is the primary motif of Luke, Chapter 1. Not only are both Elizabeth and Mary pregnant, but the "silence of Zechariah" lasts the entire nine months of his wife's pregnancy, terminating only when he confirms his wife Elizabeth's prophetic rejection of patriarchal lineage by writing: "He is to be called John" (1:60). And immediately Zechariah is able to speak a prophetic canticle, the Benedictus (1:67-79), comparable to Mary's song of liberation. "Learning to believe," writes Kahl, "is a nine-month-long process of development on the part of one who embodies the order of the fathers" ("Reading Luke Against Luke", p. 81).

Luke's Chapter 1 thus introduces a bizarre theme in the Gospel, what I call "the pregnancy of the patriarchs," which continues throughout the next 24 chapters. In the Gospel, Luke depicts women through images of yeast and seed and fertile soil, in a vivid reflection of Mary herself, as individuals immediately receptive to the Spirit who produce abundant fruit "out of the store of goodness in [their] heart[s]" (6:45). However, the male disciples, like Zechariah, are unable to hear Jesus' radical, anti-patriarchal message of compassion, service, and forgiveness. Because they are biologically predisposed to the message of patriarchal power, they are inherently unreceptive to the Spirit. Interestingly, the Gospel of Luke begins and ends in the patriarchal space of the Temple of Jerusalem. Even though the male disciples have listened to and observed Jesus for 24 chapters and watched as the patriarchal proprietors of the Temple murdered him, they still return to the wrong place.

Like Zechariah, the male disciples require a lengthy gestation period before they can be filled, or dare I say impregnated, with the Holy Spirit of the Creator God. Even at the end of the Gospel, the male disciples still don't get it. It is not until after Pentecost that the Holy Spirit is finally able to fill Peter and Stephen with powerful, anti-patriarchal songs of liberation (Acts 3:12-26; Acts 7:1-60), comparable to the one sung by the unwed teenage mother in the very first chapter of Luke. The guys finally get it—but it takes a while before they can bear fruit.

In the meantime, Cheryl and her unborn child still bear the cross of male dominance and sexual violence along the mean streets of Skid Row. And while she asserts, "I don't take shit from nobody," she remains an object of judgment, a focus of shame, a potential victim of male violence. But as she walks along those streets of Skid Row, she is accompanied by the one who first shouldered the cross so that the Son of God might enter this world, bringing salvation through compassion and the silencing of the patriarchs.

The Power of the Cross:
The Glory of the Mountain Top[*]

Catholic Agitator, September, 1997, pp. 1 and 6

"I have been looking for you," came the friendly but ominous voice. I had been hoping all weekend that this moment would never come, that we could slip in and out of this massive conference without his ever seeing us. But now here I was staring at his shiny black shoes, my eyes making the seemingly endless journey up the black-clad body, past the silver belt buckle, past the gold pectoral cross, past the white Roman collar, and finally wondering, as I looked onto his intense dark eyes, if bishops, like basketball players and princes, are chosen for their height.

Cardinal Mahony, looking down from his lofty, regal height upon my vertically-challenged body, explained that the new Cathedral project to which the Catholic Worker has expressed considerable public opposition, was a "done deal, so couldn't we get together and talk about what the Church could do for your organization?" "We're doing fine," I said, "But maybe the Church could do something for the homeless poor." "Excellent," he said, "I'll be waiting for your phone call!"

The general sentiment around the Catholic Worker house was cynical at best. "He is a jerk." "He is just trying to buy us off. But we can't just refuse to talk with him, it will make us look bad." So we wrote him a letter that said in essence, "OK, we'll meet with you, but we'll never change our minds about the Cathedral project. We think that it is an injudicious use of funds, an insult to the poor, and we have no intention of ever being dissuaded." We figured that would discourage him.

But it didn't. Almost immediately a letter came back from the Chancery Office. "I would like to come to your soup kitchen to celebrate Mass for you on August 6th, the Feast of the Transfiguration." Now the cynicism turned

---

[*]   A version of this piece appeared in the *Los Angeles Times*, September 19, 1997.

to panic and paranoia. "He can't do that to us. We're onto him. He is trying to trick us into being Christian. He is trying to trick us into sitting down together and breaking bread. Well, he won't get away with it."

On the night before the Cardinal's visit my dreams reflected the anxiety that we all felt. I dreamed that I was in a vast stadium with thousands of people looking on; I was awaiting the Cardinal. He entered the arena, and a hush fell over the crowd when the Cardinal threw himself to the ground and began walking on his knees towards me like some peasant woman at the shrine of Guadalupe. I was pissed. I knew that he was trying to out-humble me—the humble Catholic Worker, the servant of the poor—and he was winning. Even if I throw myself to the ground, I'm still the loser because I can't possibly humble myself more than a Prince of the Church on his knees before a lowly Catholic Worker. "I hate this guy," I am thinking, even as I throw myself to the ground and he embraces me to the roaring of the crowd. "I hate this guy, and I'm a loser."

The actual visit wasn't nearly so dramatic, but in some ways it was just as edifying. The Prince of the Church arrived alone and unattended. We gave him a tour of our soup kitchen and dining garden. He vested by the kitchen sink and seated himself on a simple wooden stool at our chopping table, which Catherine had prepared with flowers from the garden, candles, a Guatemalan cloth, and symbols of our prophetic concerns about homelessness, nuclear weapons, and the death penalty.

The Mass itself was pretty innocuous, and the homily was neither insulting to our intelligence nor abusive of our opposition. But one could not help but sense that the Cardinal's understanding of the Transfiguration story focused entirely upon "the Glory of God." And that the contemporary equivalent of that experience would be embodied in the structure of a new Cathedral for the city of Los Angeles.

Afterwards, as we shared bagels and cream cheese, the Cardinal finally got around to the purpose of his visit: "I know that you are opposed to the building of a new Cathedral," he said, "and you know that I am equally committed to the project. My concern is that this issue not prevent us from working together on issues that affect the poor."

Though we had never worked together on anything before, I was encouraged by his statement and responded by re-articulating our position. "You are our pastor and it is not an easy thing for us to put ourselves in opposition to you and this project. We do not do it for malicious or self-serving reasons. We do it out of our concern for those whom we serve. Today you spoke of God's glory, but our experience is not so much one of

God's glory, but of God's suffering in the person of the poor and the homeless. And it is from that daily experience of the Cross that we speak."

Much to my surprise the Cardinal replied, "That is an important message for the Church to hear and you must not stop speaking it."

As he departed, shaking hands with everyone in the community, the Cardinal inquired about our serving schedule and said that he would return. Somehow I suspect that he will not. We are not naïve; we realize that the Cardinal is a shrewd and politically savvy player, and that there is no doubt that his visit to our soup kitchen was motivated by a desire to mitigate even our minimal opposition to a project upon which he has staked his reputation and his place in history. And as an anonymous, but highly placed source recently told us, "You are the only fly in his ointment."

But even if he is doing it out of the basest motivations, even if he is a cynical, Machiavellian politician, even if he is manipulative and unfair, he is still doing the right thing. He has acknowledged the humanity of his opponents and the truth of their position, and for that I have to give him credit, though it is the last thing in the world that I would desire to do. I would prefer to just generally dislike him because he represents a vision of church that I find repugnant. I don't want to sit down and break bread with him. I don't want to heal our wounds. I don't want to close the breach. I don't want to acknowledge that we are part of the same family.

But the Cardinal's visit forces me to consider the humanity of my opponent. Just as he has done us the courtesy of acknowledging our humanity, I have to recognize that there is a part of me that desires to oppose him simply because he is an authority figure and I have unresolved issues about authority. Much as I might like, I cannot simply demonize or dismiss him as a heartless functionary of a hierarchical Church. Much as I might find it distasteful and uncomfortable, the Cardinal has personalized our struggle.

But our differences are nonetheless real, and in large measure they are reflected in our conflicting interpretations of the Transfiguration story. The Cardinal believes that the Transfiguration is a simple miracle story about God's glory. But the point of the story is not the *glory* of God, but the *voice* of God, which says, "This is my beloved son. Listen to him" (Mark 9:7). The disciples are simply not listening to Jesus. He has just told them about his imminent Crucifixion and they have said in effect, "No way, man."

They are not focused on the cross. Instead they are focused on glory. "Grant that in your glory," said James and John, "we may sit one at your right and the other at your left" (Mark 10:37). When they see Moses and Elijah on the mountain of Transfiguration, their response is, "Rabbi, it is good that we are here! Let us make three tents" (Mark 9:5). Like the disciples, the historic tendency of the Church has always been to build a structure around the glory of God. But when we institutionalize God's glory rather than embracing the power of God's suffering on the cross, we are not listening to Jesus.

The temptation has always been to remain upon the mountain top because the "mountain top experience" gives off a reflected glory and thus power to its acolytes. But Jesus was looking for disciples who would walk the way of the cross, not acolytes who would fan the fading flames of glory.

We know that in opposing this cathedral project, we fly in the face of 1,500 years of Church tradition embodied in its cathedrals and churches as well as its liturgies and laws. But throughout that history there has always been a tiny minority of prophetic people who held to the notion that the church Jesus Christ had in mind could not be built with bricks and mortar and steel and stained glass. But rather, it is built out of works of mercy and compassion and justice. Thus, we take our stand with Francis of Assisi who answered God's call to "rebuild the Church" with a life of poverty and service. And with the martyred Monsignor Romero who said, "The temple shall remain unfinished until all are housed in dignity."

We will continue to reject the Cardinal's cathedral until this worthy goal is achieved. But this struggle with the Church is no mere political battle. It is more akin to a family fight around the dinner table. Passions are high, tensions are personal, unresolved inner demons are ubiquitous. But still there is this sense of an unbreakable bond between ourselves and the Cardinal, renewed in the sharing of food and the acknowledgement of mutual humanity. This historic tension between the glory of God on the mountain top and the suffering of God in the person of the poor on the streets may never be resolved, but on the other hand, may it never be abandoned.

Their Story Seemed like Nonsense: Women in the Gospel of Luke

Catholic Agitator, February, 2005, pp. 1, 2, and 6

The Gospel of Luke is something like the Catholic Worker—the guys sit around talking about theology while the women do all of the work. No, that's not quite true—at the LACW the guys do a lot of work, too. All of us clean toilets, make beds, sweep the floors, take care of the guests, and make food. We make *a lot* of food. But basically the work of the Catholic Worker is "women's work;" it is just such work that forms the very heart of the Gospel of Luke. Luke calls it *diakonon* or *service*; everyone else just calls it women's work or domestic servitude. But for Luke, this attitude of humble service is the source of transformative grace in the world. It is the foundation of discipleship—the "mustard seed of the kingdom."

Though we have been conditioned by patriarchal theologians for 2,000 years to think that the focus of the Gospels is the twelve male disciples, the truth is that Luke's Gospel, from beginning to end, is a gospel of women. It is the women disciples who hear and respond immediately to Jesus' message, while the male disciples consistently miss the point, almost to the level of absurdity. Not only is Luke's Gospel pro-woman, but it is at the same time anti-patriarchal. That does not mean that the Gospel is anti-male; rather, it is oppositional to the political, economic, and religious power structures of the world that are founded and administered, Condoleezza Rice notwithstanding, almost exclusively by men.

Chapter 1: The Unwed Mother

Mary, the unwed teenage girl who becomes impregnated by the heavenly Father and not by any earthly father, states the theme of the Gospel in the very opening passages. The Gospels have become so domesticated that theological interpreters have for centuries missed the obvious intent of this scandalous passage, covering it over with sappy images of the Virgin Mother and the Holy Family. From its very inception, or should I say "conception," Christianity has been at odds with the patriarchal, male power establishment that ran not only the Jewish and Roman world of Jesus' time, but continues to run the world today.

Patriarchal theologians have always portrayed Mary's *Yes* to her pregnancy as an act of obsequious obedience to authority, endemic to all women. But in truth, her *Yes* to the heavenly Father is a repudiation of all earthly fathers and an affirmation of the Liberation Project of the heavenly Father, who has chosen to bypass earthly fathers all together.

Mary articulates the ultimate demise of the patriarchal project in the greatest liberation song of all time, the *Magnificat*

> The Mighty One has done great things for me,
>
>> and holy is His name.
>
> His mercy is from age to age
>
>> to those who fear him.
>
> He has shown might with His arm,
>
>> dispersed the arrogant of mind and heart.
>
> He has thrown down the rulers from their thrones,
>
>> but lifted up the lowly.
>
> The hungry He has filled with good things;
>
>> the rich he has sent away empty.
>
> Luke 1:49-53

Mary has prophesied the end of all patriarchal power and the beginning of a new era of liberation for the poor, the sick, and the outcast.

The Mother-In-Law

The healing of Peter's mother-in-law, found in Chapter 4:38-39, is such a brief passage that it seems hardly worth noting. But it may in fact be one of the most important sections of the Gospel, because it introduces the single most important element of discipleship: *diakonon*. At face value, it appears to be a typical patriarchal parable: Jesus cures a sick woman, she gets well, and she returns to the kitchen to prepare dinner for the men-folk. End of story.

But there's more to it. The curing of Peter's mother-in-law is paired with the exorcism in the synagogue that immediately precedes it (4:31-37), and the two are linked by the word "rebuke." Jesus "rebukes" the demon in the synagogue just as he "rebukes" the fever in Peter's mother-in-law, an odd response to a fever by the way. Suggesting that the woman's sickness is connected with the "unclean spirit" in the synagogue.

So, what's the big deal? What is not so obvious initially is that Peter's mother-in-law is a widow. She is living in her son-in-law's house without an income of her own. She is an impoverished dependent. Her status as an impoverished widow is the source of her fever, and its locus is the demon-possessed synagogue that Jesus has just exorcised. Impoverished widows are the paradigmatic focus of Jesus' ministry: the Widow of Zarephath, the Widow of Naaman, and the Persistent Widow seeking justice are all elemental figures in the Gospel narrative. But it is not until Chapter 20 that we find out that it is the Scribes, associated with the patriarchal temple establishment, who "devoured the houses of widows," leaving them impoverished, who are the problem. Thus, the sickness and poverty of widows is directly caused by the greed of the patriarchal temple establishment.

Commentators have long noted the odd placement of this story in the Gospel of Luke—Jesus meets Peter's mother-in-law even before he meets Peter, but no explanation is offered. However, from an anti-patriarchal perspective it is quite obvious what is going on. The story is set at the beginning of the initial call to discipleship narrative. Even before Jesus calls the first male disciples, Peter, James, John, Levi, and the others, he has already "called" his first female disciple—Peter's mother-in-law, the impoverished widow, "got up immediately and served." *Diakonon,* the Greek word for *service,* is the source of our word for *deacon*—it is the primary virtue of discipleship.

This is the first supper in the Gospel of Luke, and the theme of *diakonon* continues throughout until the Last Supper, wherein Jesus instructs his male disciples:

> Let the greatest among you be as the youngest and the leader as the servant. For who is greater: the one seated at table or the one who serves? I am among you as the one who serves.

> Luke 22:26-27

The first female disciple at the First Supper is already practicing discipleship, while the male disciples, even at the Last Supper, are still arguing about "which of them should be regarded as the greatest" (22:24).

Women Hear and Obey

I call Chapters 7 and 8 "the Women's Chapters," because there are twelve women listed in this section, all of whom exemplify discipleship, the virtues of fearless courage and faith, while all of the men, with a few notable exceptions, express doubt and fear.

Two chapters long, this section is bracketed on both sides by twin healing doublets that are actually raisings from the dead. At the far end is the exorcism of the Gerasene demoniac (8:26-29), coupled with the healing of the bleeding woman and the healing of Jairus' daughter (8:40-56).

The section is framed by the healing of the Centurion's slave (7:1-10) and the raising of the widow's son at Nain. But it is the healing of the Centurion's slave that seems to set off the action of the entire section, for immediately after this controversial favor for an enemy, John the Baptist sends his disciples to inquire of Jesus: "Are you the one who is to come, or should we look for another?" (7:19).

The driving energy of this section is the "sinful woman" who rudely breaks into the all-male dinner banquet to wash Jesus' feet. Many feminist commentators have objected to the passage because Luke has transformed the woman from Mark's Gospel, who anoints Jesus for crucifixion, into a "sinful woman," who washes his feet because of her loving repentance.

But I want to suggest that this woman is the key to the entire Gospel. Even as John the Baptist, the one who originally anointed Jesus for his mission, expressed doubts about Jesus, she has broken into an all-male enclave, violating every social taboo of the time, to anoint Jesus and confirm him in his way.

She has come at the very moment that Jesus has begun his journey to Jerusalem, and ultimately to the cross, and has anointed his feet with expensive perfume and with her tears. Her tears are a deep expression of her understanding of the mission of Jesus. The scene is reminiscent of the anointing of King Jehu in the Old Testament (2 Kings 9:6-7); but rather than anointing his head, this woman anoints his feet for discipleship. She knows intuitively that his journey will lead to his death. Tick, tock....In this Gospel, the women already know "what time it is."

Immediately following the anointing passage we find that, along with the twelve, some women accompany him: "Mary Magdalene from whom seven demons had gone out, Joanna, the wife of Herod's steward Chuza, Susanna, and many others who provided for them out of their resources" (Luke 8:2-3). Not only do the women follow, but they are the financial foundation of the new discipleship community. And they are there from the very beginning of the trip to Jerusalem, on to the cross and beyond to the grave.

The Guys Don't Get It

If Chapters 7 and 8 can be titled "Women Who Hear and Obey," Chapter 9 must surely be titled "Men Who Can't Hear and Haven't Got a Clue." The men are the complete antithesis of the women in Chapters 7 and 8. If the women are examples of selfless service, the men are exemplars of self-serving power: they tell Jesus to "dismiss" the 5,000 hungry people without feeding them; they want to call down fire upon the Samaritan village; they want to prevent an exorcist from casting out demons in Jesus' name, even though they are unable to cast out demons themselves.

The core of the chapter revolves around the identity of Jesus—"Who do you say I am?" When Peter seemingly gets the right answer, "You are the Messiah of God," Jesus rebukes him, just as he rebuked the demons.

Jesus rejects the title of Messiah and chooses to call himself "the Son of Man." Twice in this chapter Jesus tells the disciples that the "Son of Man must suffer greatly and be rejected by the elders and the chief-priests and the scribes and be killed" (9:22). But the male disciples can't hear what he is saying "because its meaning was hidden from them," and argue instead about "which of them was the greatest" (9:44-46).

Unlike the women disciples in the story, who are exemplars of compassion and service, the men are oriented toward power and privilege; they want a Messiah of God who will establish a kingdom and give them prestigious jobs in his new administration.

The center of the chapter is the Transfiguration—Jesus appears on the mountain top with Elijah and Moses while the voice of God from heaven proclaims: "This is my Son....Listen to him." The guys are not listening, while the women "hear and obey."

God is convinced that the world cannot be saved through the patriarchal power system and the bias towards women in the Gospel of Luke reflects that. The patriarchal system can only produce greater and increasingly oppressive domination. Salvation can only come when we begin to serve each other, rather than dominate the other.

The male disciples, like all males, are socialized for power and domination. They want to sit, one at the right and one at the left, when Jesus comes into his kingdom. But the women disciples are socialized for service. Women give birth, care for the young, prepare food, and serve at table. They care for the aged, tend the sick, minister to the dying, and wash the bodies of the dead. From incarnation and birth to Crucifixion and Resurrection, the women disciples already knew what the kingdom was about because they were already doing it.

Resurrection

When the male disciples flee in fear and despair at the point of Jesus' arrest, the women disciples' inherent commitment to service compels them to continue following Jesus to the cross and then on to the tomb. It is in this final act of *diakonon*, tending to the dead body of Jesus, that the women in Luke become the first evangelists of the Resurrection. But the response of the male disciples is that "their story seemed like nonsense" (24:11).

That is the typical patriarchal response to anyone attempting to live the resurrected life: "I am planning to join the Catholic Worker." "That's nonsense! You're wasting your college degree." "I am planning to get arrested at the School of the Americas.* That's nonsense. You won't make any difference anyway."

From beginning to end, the Gospel of Luke is about service: "Serve God, not Mammon;" "Serve God, not Caesar;" "Serve the little ones, not ourselves;" "I am among you as one who serves."

But the patriarchal "servants of Israel," the leaders of the nation, serve themselves first. And it is thus even to this day. Have you ever known a politician to leave public office poorer than he entered? But Jesus said: "among you it shall not be so" (22:26).

I am well aware that over the centuries, patriarchal theologians have misused this theme of humble service to keep women in their place, in kitchens and washrooms and bedrooms. Perhaps it is because I belong to a movement founded by a woman that concerns itself with women's work that I believe the intent of the Gospel is to liberate all of us, both men and women, from the grandiose and deadly patriarchal project of world domination, and to focus us instead on the unpretentious, life-giving instruments of God's own *diakonon* project for the salvation of the world. But of course *that* seems like nonsense!

---

* Located in Fort Benning, Georgia, the SOA trains 700-2,000 soldiers a year from Third World Countries, teaching them how to stamp out freedom and terrorize their people.

Not by Bread Alone nor by Money and Ego*

Catholic Agitator, November, 1998, pp. 5 and 6

As we shimmied along the overpass high above the 101 Freeway and climbed the barbed wire fence surrounding the Cathedral building site, we felt stupid and afraid. Depending upon your perspective, we were either unruly party crashers at the Cardinal's ground-breaking ceremony or prophetic visionaries. Our obstreperous actions culminated in the occupation of the Cardinal's bulldozer and a symbolic victory of terminating the ground-breaking ceremony for the new Cathedral.

Cardinal Mahony has generously responded by refusing to simply boot us out of the Church. He has even praised us for our "good works." For this we are grateful. But the Cardinal has indicated that the "soup kitchen myopia" of the Catholic Workers impels us to irresponsible actions that neglect the spiritual needs of the poor in favor of the material. "Man does not live by bread alone," said the Cardinal. One must have aesthetics, architecture, and cathedrals. The Church, he says, can build cathedrals and serve the poor as well.

The Cardinal's easy synthesis of bread and cathedrals, justice and architecture finds its validation in the priestly tradition of our scriptural heritage—a tradition which creates liturgies and rituals, builds temples and shrines, and sacralizes the existing order. People need order and a sense of sacred presence in their daily lives. But the fatal flaw of this perspective lies in its often too comfortable accommodation with the powerful and its tendency to validate unjust social systems.

On the other hand, the Catholic Worker seeks its validation in the prophetic tradition of the same scriptural heritage. Its adherents are typically unruly, unordained outsiders whose main focus lies in desacralizing the existing order, which they see as unjust and occasionally even blas-

---

* A version of this piece appeared in the *Los Angeles Times*, October 26, 1988.

phemous. Its practitioners include, among others, Isaiah, Amos, Joel and Jesus, who, by the way, said of the Temple that "There will not be one stone left upon another" (Mark 13:2).

The prophetic tradition has always been myopically focused on the radical Hebrew memory of slavery and poverty in Egypt. It is a memory that forms the very core of Judeo-Christian spirituality. And the Cardinal's reference to "bread alone" takes us back to the radical memory of liberation that was intended to keep the Chosen People sensitive to their own history of poverty and suffering and thus more compassionate to the poor who lived among them.

The full quotation from Deuteronomy is: "Not by bread alone does man live, but by every word that comes forth from the mouth of the Lord" (Deuteronomy 8:3), and it recalls the experience of the Israelites being fed by God with manna in the wilderness. It does not mean, as the Cardinal has implied, a dichotomy between the material needs of bread and sustenance and the spiritual needs of cathedrals and aesthetics. It means that the Hebrew people did not live by bread alone but by God's command to share and not to store up the heavenly gift of manna, thus ensuring that "all would be satisfied" through a social practice of distributive justice.

In the building of his new Cathedral, Cardinal Mahony certainly has Church tradition on his side, but it is a tradition that must be renewed in every generation by the prophetic vision of distributive justice. It is a tradition that is often scandalously comfortable with wealth and power that began with the questionable actions of a pagan emperor Constantine, donating pagan temples and basilicas as the first Christian churches. It is a tradition that continued through the Medieval era with the building of great cathedrals that, as Clint Albertson, SJ, wrote in an *Los Angeles Times* article, were intended (along with the glory of God) "to advance the glory of kings" ("A Notre Dame for Los Angeles"). It is a tradition that precipitated the greatest unhealed wound of Christianity, the Reformation, as various popes attempted to raise funds for the construction of Saint Peter's Basilica through the selling of Papal indulgences and phony relics. It is a tradition that has produced much beauty and grandeur but must be constantly critiqued by the more radical tradition of Holy scripture.

From the Tower of Babel to the pyramids of Egypt, scripture has always been skeptical of large-scale building projects, recognizing that grand buildings and great edifices go hand in hand with great wealth and political oppression. The Temple of Solomon was built with conscripted laborers, and the tyrant Herod drained the Hebrew people dry to rebuild it.

Jeff Dietrich

25. Fr. Correio rushes to intercept Catholic Workers' efforts to disrupt the Cathedral ground breaking ceremony, 1997. Pictured left to right: Jeff Dietrich, Martha Lewis, Eric DeBode, Ann Mulder, and Rev. Alice Callaghan. Photo by Mike Wisniewski

In our own time this tradition has been carried on by the princes of industry, the Rockefellers, the Carnegies, and the Gettys, who would rather build great libraries and museums than pay a decent wage to their workers. Like the Cathedral donations of Disney, Murdoch, Betsy Bloomingdale, and others, they testify to personal generosity and ego satisfaction, but not to the justice demanded by scripture.

In the end though, it is not about worship spaces or cathedrals or aesthetics: it is about symbolism. In a church that claims sacramental sensitivity and allegiance to a God who was born in a bovine feeding trough and died the hideous death of a criminal on the cross, it is symbolically and sacramentally scandalous to memorialize his life with a grand edifice. If Betsy Bloomingdale gave the Catholic Worker a brand new Rolls Royce, we would refuse it simply because it bespeaks symbolic allegiance to sumptuous affluence and concomitant injustice.

Short of a magnitude ten earthquake, the Cardinal will no doubt build his sumptuous Cathedral. But we do not believe that the project should proceed without critical input from the prophetic tradition. Irresponsible actions—the scaling of fences and the climbing of bulldozers—are often the only means for the prophetic word of justice to garner attention and disrupt the comfortable concord of wealth and spirituality, thus tweaking the conscience of a Rolls Royce Church.

Dorothy Day and the Church

Catholic Agitator, November, 1991, pp. 1 and 7

"Less music by dead guys" is the new hip slogan of a local rock music station. Seeking to lure greater numbers of ultra cool devotees to its progressive air waves, the station plays upon our cultural obsession, particularly on the part of the young, to be freed from the shackles of a stultifying past. This rejection of the burdens and baggage of history marks western civilization as singular among all cultures. So it should come as no surprise that a mere ten years after her death the figure of Dorothy Day has become something of a burden to some contemporary members of the Catholic Worker Movement who wish to be unshackled from a past that is viewed as stultifying and oppressive.

Just as Jesus is a scandal to the Church and Francis a scandal to the Franciscans, so too has Dorothy Day become something of a scandal to members of the movement she founded along with Peter Maurin in 1933. The problem revolves around the relationship of the Catholic Worker Movement to the Catholic Church, which increasingly has come under attack, not without some considerable justification for its sexism, triumphalism, authoritarianism, materialism, and just plain unchristian attitude. Some have argued rather forcefully that Catholic Worker anarchists or Catholic Worker feminists should look elsewhere for spiritual enrichment. Some have argued that not only the Church, but scripture itself is an inadequate source of guidance.

The conflicts raised by these issues are not unusual ones for organizations that have only recently lost their charismatic founder. But they are considerably exacerbated when befalling an organization that has for the last fifty-five years described itself as unabashedly anarchist. Without structure, constitution, or rule, the Catholic Worker Movement is pretty much dependent upon the Holy Spirit and the charism of its founder for guidance and illumination, and that's about as helpful as a flashlight in a snowstorm. Therefore, I approach this situation with considerable trepidation and humility, and I ask the reader's forbearance in this effort to thread through the maze of emotion, anger, and authority.

It seems to me that Dorothy understood more clearly than most that the great sickness of the time is our collective worship of progress and the future, even as our past is stolen from us like some precious jewel. While a great majority of our contemporaries might barter away this birthright for a mere pittance, the reality is that without history and tradition we are but a horde of mindless mental patients subjected to the doctors of fad and fashion.

Even as all sense of individuality erodes before the homogenizing effects of telemarketing and consumer conformity, it is the Church that provides for us any authentic sense of identity and connectedness that remains.

I remember that shortly after joining the Catholic Worker in 1970 I was visiting with my parents, who had not at the time expressed an opinion about their naïve hippie son's current project. That was just fine, because throughout my college years there had been something of a "generation gap" between myself and my moderately conservative parents, especially with regard to racism, social justice, the Church, and the war in Vietnam. So I listened with considerable interest that evening as my mother explained to my three-year-old sister what I was doing. "Your brother," she said, "helps people, like St. Francis did. He is kind of like a priest, like your Uncle Bobby." In that moment the "generation gap" had been bridged and my mother, my sister, and I were united in a single tradition. What I had been unable to explain to my parents in years of argument was understood in a single moment by even a small child.

Seventeen years later my mother began to help out regularly in the soup kitchen, and twenty years later my sister is a full-time member of the Philadelphia Catholic Worker. Authentic change takes a long time, but without the common bonds of a shared tradition, it is rare indeed.

Often, marginalized people who are angry with the Church abandon not only the Church, but scripture itself, opting instead for cultural relativism rather than gospel authority. As feminist theologian Rosemary Radford Ruether points out, "One cannot wield the lever of criticism without a place to stand" (*Sexism and God-Talk*, p. 18). For Dorothy, the prophetic liberating tradition of scripture was what Ruether has called the "normative principle of Biblical faith" (*Sexism and God-Talk*, p. 23) To abandon it is to abandon the Christian project to the clerics and bureaucrats. The Catholic Worker is, if nothing else, a movement that elevates and empowers the laity in an otherwise clergy-bound bureaucracy.

While Dorothy would no doubt part company with feminists around the issue of a frontal assault on Church hierarchy, obedience for her was not a matter of angelic submission. She believed that while the Church was our mother, she was also a whore. But she also understood that there were "other ways to handle a bishop." She grasped that the extraordinary freedom of the Church lay in its unwillingness to squelch prophetic lay movements and that a certain power accrued to lay people who enfleshed that tradition. Thus, Cardinal Spellman was reluctant to censure Dorothy on the grounds that "she might be a saint."

As an obedient, but angry daughter of the Church, Dorothy embraced its "magisterium" with a kind of prophetic tension that humbly acknowledged the Church's teaching authority, while boldly demanding a deeper commitment to the Gospel. This is what she called "out-orthodoxing the orthodox."

This issue of obedience to Church teaching is, of course, the toughest for contemporary Catholic Workers. So often, when we hear really orthodox people speak of the magisterium, it sounds as if the poor Holy Spirit has been locked in a tiny box in the basement of the Vatican to be consulted only by the Pope during encyclical season. It has sometimes been said that Dorothy's uncritical embrace of these teachings lay in her lack of sophisticated theological training. My own sense is that it stems rather from recognition that the Church's teaching on sexuality and life issues are in fact grounded in the scriptures, and that the prophetic task is not to ask the Church to be less conformed to scripture, but rather to be more conformed to scripture.

Thus, our prophetic criticism is that the Church, like the Pharisees and the Scribes, has conformed to God's law. But it has conformed to only a portion of the law, and its rigid conformity to a set of moral precepts has led to a hardness of heart, hierarchical power structures, self-righteousness, and a rejection of the fullness of God's law.

Jesus, like the prophets before him, proclaimed that the fullness of the law required not only obedience to the laws of ritual purity, sacrifice and personal piety, but also to the Sabbath laws of economic distribution that constrained the affluent from accumulating excessive wealth and protected the poor from oppression.

A prophetic Catholic Worker position does not ask the Church to compromise her teachings one iota, any more than Jesus asked the Pharisees to compromise their teachings. We do not want the Church to conform more deeply to the world; we want the Church to conform more deeply to

26. Dorothy Day and Jeff Dietrich at the Catholic Worker Farm in Tivoli, New York, 1974. Photo by Catherine Morris

scripture. We want the Church to preach against the sin of usury with the same forcefulness as when it preaches against premarital sex. We want the Church to condemn war and war-making as unequivocally as it condemns abortion. We want the Church to oppose nuclear weapons with the same energy with which it opposes artificial birth control. We want to see the Church devote the same amount of resources to the service of the financially poor in the ghettos as it devotes to the spiritually poor in the suburbs.

We are convinced that if the Church followed this program, in a very short time she would lose about 75 percent of her membership, 95 percent of her assets, as well as 100 percent of her credibility in the halls of political power. At that point she might look something like a community of brothers and sisters struggling to be signs of God's grace, which is, I suspect, what Jesus thought he was founding in the first place.

I realize that, although Dorothy did not articulate a systematic Biblical theology, it is nonetheless just such a perspective that continues to generate the prophetic energy driving the day to day Catholic Worker life and witness.

One then might logically ask, why bother keeping the Church at all? She is so patently broken and imperfect, with her tawdry history of currying favor among the wealthy and consecrating political power. Why not just toss her out and start all over again with "gospel purity"? The best answer might be that it's been done before, and not all that well. The Reformation has much to teach about love of scripture, but not about creating radical, prophetic churches.

Dorothy understood that our Church is like family, and as such she is both baggage and ballast to us. As much as we detest her baggage of sinfulness and abuse, she nevertheless keeps us anchored to our history, our humanness. Without her, we fall heir to the ego and delusion of fanatical reformers. We must not make the mistakes of so many adult children of dysfunctional families who simply deny their past. To be whole and human we must embrace our past, warts and all. If we are to sing a new song to the Lord, we cannot pretend to be hip, cool, and progressive, refusing to listen to music by dead guys. The new song sings of completeness that embraces the present and the future as well as the past.

PART FOUR

MAKING PEACE

When the tyrant has disposed of foreign enemies
by conquest or treaty, and there is nothing to fear from them,
then he is always stirring up some war or other,
in order that people may require a leader.

Plato, The Republic, 566e

When I speak of peace, they are ready for war.

Psalms 120:7

My Crisis with the Draft

Catholic Agitator, March, 1980, p. 4

Not often in our lives do we have the opportunity to make a decision of very much importance. Usually our options consist in deciding between a Chevy and a Ford, Corn Flakes and Rice Puffs, or Carter and Kennedy. The question of freedom of choice never arises because there is virtually no difference between the options and there are no consequences to the decision.

Occasionally, however, we have an opportunity to make a decision of real importance. For me, facing the draft was just such an opportunity. I believe that every other decision in my life has been based upon that single choice.

It was not an easy decision. It was not one that I wanted to make, but had I not made that one choice, my life would be entirely different. I would most likely be selling real estate in the San Fernando Valley and hustling "chicks" in a swinging singles bar. And furthermore, I certainly would not have been the least bit interested in Christianity.

In the United States our lives are clean and comfortable, secure and well-ordered. And that is just what I expected for my own life. But when we live this way we are completely isolated and set apart from the poor and suffering men and women who make up the bulk of the world's population. We are cut off from reality. We do not understand life. And in that pristine context, Christianity is virtually devoid of meaning.

In order to understand Christianity we must have empathy for the poor. Yet we cannot have this empathy unless we have experienced suffering. Until I had to confront the draft, my entire life plan consisted in avoiding any and all suffering.

It was my singular purpose to insure that I was able to fully participate in the affluent good life of this country and everything was going according to plan until the day I received a letter from my local selective service board. "Greetings," it said, "you are ordered to report to your induction center.

Bring a tooth brush and a change of clothes as you may not be returning home." My heart sank to my knees. This definitely was not part of my plan.

Ever since the Gulf of Tonkin Resolution, ugly visions of pajama-clad Asians, napalmed villagers, and burning children had begun to mar my dreams for a well-ordered, secure, and profitable future.

Until that time I had thought of the prospect of military service as just one more step in the normal process of growing up, maturing, and making money. It was just part of being an upstanding citizen, not all that pleasant, but it could be helpful in preparing for a lucrative career. This benign image of the military as a kind of post-graduate summer camp began to fade rather quickly. As the war in Vietnam grew more and more fierce, it occurred to me that the army was more than a physical fitness program. I didn't mind marching or calisthenics or target practice. But the real purpose of the army was to kill people and, try as I might, I could not conceive of myself as a killer. I would lie awake at night conjuring up slow-motion scenarios that made my skin crawl with dread. I saw myself breathlessly squeezing the hair-trigger of an M-16 rifle. I saw the lead slug slowly tumbling towards its intended target, piercing a painfully grimacing face, suddenly shattering fragile flesh, sending skin and skull, bone and brain, exploding into space like a giant quasar bursting forth light into the infinite cosmos.

All of my life I had watched John Wayne movies, *The Sands of Iwo Jima, Back to Bataan, They Were Expendable*. I had reveled in the wholesale slaughter of slant-eyed Asiatics. I watched gleefully as they were machine-gunned by the dozens or bayoneted individually or bombed by the multitudes. But this was not a movie, a fantasy. This was me, Jeff Dietrich, really and truly killing another human being. In the abstract I had nothing against killing, but as a personal reality it became totally repugnant, completely impossible. I simply could not do it.

The affluence and security that I had envisioned as my birthright were slowly submerged in a silent struggle within myself. Ultimately this inner turmoil brought me to a more compassionate understanding of a suffering world. Unbeknownst to me, I was being asked to choose between life and death. I was prepared to avoid that decision at all cost.

After I had a complete physical exam and was found, much to my dismay, to be perfectly healthy, my first plan was to go to Canada. I even visited Vancouver. Though beautiful, I found it to be a cold and friendless place. Quite simply, I lacked the courage to leave friends and family and go to a foreign land, never to return home again.

Perhaps the army wouldn't want me, I thought, if they knew how psychologically unbalanced I was. I went so far as to set up an appointment with a psychiatrist in New York whose specialty was certifying young men mentally unfit to serve in the Army, but I later abandoned the plan. I think I was afraid that he might find that I really was crazy.

As the struggle raged within, I thought briefly of suicide, but immediately rejected it on the same grounds as I had rejected shooting off my little toe—too painful.

In the meantime I had hired a lawyer, who, for $500, had promised to advise me of all options. We planned my forthcoming senior year to take optimum advantage of student deferments, stretching out my last year to include an extra semester by dropping several units in mid-term.

I applied to and was turned down for candidacy in every federal program that carried with it a deferment for civilian social service.

Upon graduation I waited to receive my first draft notice before applying for conscientious objector status, thereby hoping to postpone the moment of decision even longer. "The war is going to end any day now," I thought. "If I can just put them off for a little longer I will be safe." That was in 1970, and as you know, the war was only to grow worse for five more years.

When I was refused status as a conscientious objector, I continued to stall with the help of my lawyer by appealing that decision all the way up through the State Board of Appeals. But it began to appear as though the inevitable moment would soon arrive. I would have braces put on my teeth. I knew that at the age of twenty-four braces would not do much for my love life, but one had to make some sacrifices. So I made an appointment with the orthodontist. After taking X-rays and doing a preliminary examination he took me down a long hall into a small office. Upon locking the door, he told me in a furtive voice that I had a slight over-bite which under ordinary circumstances he would not treat. But if I wished to avoid the draft, then he would go ahead and put them on. "However," he said, "I have no intention of getting into trouble with the federal government, so these braces are going to be the real thing." He then outlined a therapeutic/cosmetic program that would involve braces on the upper and lower teeth and actually move my entire jaw forward one quarter inch. Furthermore, the whole process would cost $8,000, and take up to three years! A high price for procrastination, but I was desperate.

I continued with my plans up until the last possible moment. All the appeals and deferments had run out. The letter arrived. Lawyers and doctors and teachers and priests could not help me and I stood there alone with the letter in hand knowing that the time had come and I could not bring myself to procrastinate any longer. Even though I knew that I could avoid being drafted without suffering any adverse consequences simply by having those braces installed, I nevertheless could not bring myself to do it.

Ultimately, avoiding the consequences no longer mattered as much as trying to affirm what was right. After years of tribulation and turmoil, the actual decision was almost an anti-climax. But not quite.

I did experience a good deal of trepidation on that morning as a friend drove me to the induction center. I fully expected to be hauled off to jail that very day. The reality was considerably less dramatic.

I spent most of the day running around in the nude following various colored lines on the floor to prescribed destinations, where I was poked and prodded and tested and certified. "OK now, bend over and crack a smile," said the doctor with a slight chuckle. He thought he was pretty funny using this trite old euphemism for dilating the anal aperture. "Now I want you to turn your head and cough," he said, as he began checking for hernias, sticking his finger right through the prostate gland. "Yeow!" I screeched in high C as his rubber-clad finger probed deep into private territory.

Finally the process was approaching the end. I had most of my clothes on and a bundle of papers in my hand which I turned over to the appropriate sergeant. "You've passed all the tests with flying colors, buddy. Now are you going to refuse induction?" My heart started pounding. I broke into a cold sweat. How in the hell did he know what I was going to do? This wasn't a standard question. Why was he singling me out?

"Why do you want to know?"

"Because, if you are, I want you to sit over there on that bench. Now are you, or aren't you?" This seemed so ignominious, so uneventful. I had memorized a rather extensive speech about human brotherhood and the poor of the world that I had expected to recite before a roomful of fellow inductees before the FBI hauled me away.

"Yes," I whispered in a quiet voice. How unfair! How criminal! I was being robbed of my finest hour, I thought, as I sat down on the bench with six other young men. A few minutes later, a young second lieutenant took us upstairs where he read us the Oath of Obedience. Everyone refused to step across the red line painted on the floor, which would signify that you were in the army and subject to the universal military code.

After being politely interviewed by the FBI, I was told that I could go home. Though I was not arrested and hauled off to prison, I nevertheless felt like an outlaw, an outcast from the society that had spawned me. I

28. Jeff Dietrich with Pledge of Resistance, a campaign to gather signatures of those who would commit civil disobedience in the event that the US invaded Central America in front of the Federal Building, downtown Los Angeles, 1985. Photo by James Ryman

was barred from the traditional careers. I was cut off from all avenues of economic and social success.

However, I soon began to realize that all of my plans for a secure and affluent future had inhibited my ability to see the world clearly. I had never questioned the righteousness and justice of this social order. Now that I was myself barred from participating in it, I could see more clearly that the poor are exploited by the rich. Now that I faced the prospect of jail, I could see more clearly that the majority of prisoners are victims of injustice. Now that I was on the outside looking in, I began to feel the wrongness of this entire system.

Christ loved the poor, the suffering, the prisoner. Until we have personally experienced poverty, suffering and rejection, Christianity remains a lofty romantic ideal outside the boundaries of human possibility. It takes some great crisis to crash through that complacency, certitude, and security and to bring with it Christ's message of life, hope and struggle. For me, that crisis was the draft.

The Roots of Terrorism

Catholic Agitator, May, 1986, p. 5

Ron is standing next to me, an empty green wine bottle clenched in his fist like a hand grenade ready to explode into a million shards of glass shrapnel. Adrenaline surges through my body like a narcotic, reducing arms and legs to the consistency of overcooked pasta. Terror grips me as Ron's enormous 6-foot-2-inch bulk looms overhead. His neck muscles tighten like knotted steel and great gobs of saliva fly from his mouth as he hurls obscenities at me.

One of the advantages of working in a Skid Row soup kitchen is definitely *not* a sense of physical security or peaceful surroundings. Even on the calmest days, the anger, the violence, and certifiable insanity are always there, lying inert like a land mine waiting to go off. But it did occur to me recently, as Americans cancel vacations to Europe and think twice about spending any more time than necessary in airports and government buildings, that living in this sort of war zone gives one a certain edge over those who have never dealt with terrorists.

Not that Ron is really a terrorist in the political sense of the word. He belongs to no organization, espouses no cause or ideology, has received no formal training or discipline, and takes orders from no one. In fact, most of the time Ron actually functions in a fairly benign manner.

But today, for whatever reasons, whether it was too long a wait in the soup line, no luck finding a job, or just too much hot sun, he has turned to violence and I am terrified.

Since the bombing of Libya it has been fashionable to claim that terrorism is a cancer or a disease that can be removed by the military equivalent of radical surgery or chemotherapy. This is a simplistic solution that finds its domestic counterpart in the substitution of prisons and jails for a national commitment to jobs, education, and housing for all. The real cause of terrorism, both domestic and foreign, is rooted in the injustice of poverty, hunger, homelessness, and oppression.

I grew up not far from Skid Row in a placid, Orange County cul-de-sac community that was the apotheosis of the American Dream, secure against poverty and violence, perfect in its serenity. What attracted me to Skid Row is the blatant reality of suffering that shatters that placidity like a brick hurled through a window and offers a glimpse of the pain and suffering endured by most of the world. From Rio to Calcutta, from Soweto to Santo Domingo, most of the world is engaged in a violent struggle merely to survive from one day to the next, and the terrorist is simply the most active combatant in this battle. The battle for security in our homes and our property is natural, but the reality of the world is the reality of suffering; to ignore that is to live in a fantasy. How can we feel secure when children die of starvation, families are torn asunder by economic and military violence, when human lives and potential are sacrificed daily on the altar of economic necessity?

Flannery O'Connor, the literary mistress of the macabre, once wrote, "'She would of been a good woman,' The Misfit said, 'if it had been some-body there to shoot her every minute of her life'" (*The Complete Stories*, p. 133). It is at those moments of terror, as if there were a gun to my own head, that I have learned the power of prayer, quick, furtive, and repetitious: "Lord, deliver us from evil; Lord, deliver us from evil; Lord, deliver us from evil;" anesthetizing the brain, lowering the pulse rate, stiffening the rubbery limbs—prayer under fire, prayer in the trenches, practical prayer that reaches down to a place of strength that is beyond the fear. Pretend that no one can hear the pounding of your heart or smell the stink of your sweat. Get your voice under control; slowly reach out your hand. Now I hear my voice speaking calmly with all the bluff and bravado of an animal trainer, pretending a calm that I do not feel, knowing that any hint of fear on my part will surely invite disaster. "Ron, give me the bottle and I'll bring you a tray of food. Now go on outside and eat. You're too agitated to eat in here today."

"OK punk, but be quick about it," he says, handing me the bottle. I skillfully grasp the neck of the bottle so as not to inadvertently release the imaginary arming mechanism on this volatile green glass projectile and carefully drop it into the trash can, making a silent promise to be more vigilant about picking up such dangerous weapons when I see them lying carelessly about on the sidewalk.

This is not the first time that Ron has terrorized us, and once, after an epic struggle, we banned him for an entire year. I used to think that our method of dealing with terrorism—prayer and nonviolence—was hopelessly idealistic and impractical until I heard that a security guard in a similar Skid Row institution was murdered with his own gun after a struggle with an irate client. So much for the use of force. The reality is that you're pretty much on your own down here. The police simply cannot respond quickly enough to prevent violence from happening. So even on a practical level we figure we might as well stick to our principles.

After Ron finishes eating he is much calmer, almost affable, so I take the opportunity to tell him that he will be banned for a week because of the disturbance he caused in the kitchen.

"Well, fuck you, punk. I don't want your food anyway," he says, turning on his heel and walking away.

I am fully aware that it is 1986 and idealism as a basis of national policy is about as fashionable as bell bottom trousers and love beads, so I won't even suggest prayer and nonviolence as a means of combating terrorism.

I am convinced, however, that we cannot end terrorism by bombing children in Libya, or by jailing the poor in our own nation. Any effective program to end terrorism must begin with a commitment to feed the hungry, clothe the naked, and shelter the homeless.

No Blood for Oil*

Catholic Agitator, February, 1991, pp. 1 and 2

"As he drew near he saw the city and wept over it, saying, 'If this day you only knew what makes for peace!'" (Luke 19:41-42). Though the rulers and people of Jerusalem rejected and ultimately crucified him, Jesus nevertheless loved them so deeply that he was moved to tears by their failure to fulfill the promise of the chosen people.

In these first days of our newest war, so too do we weep for the unfulfilled promises of our own nation. Though all facile notions of American dreams fulfilled had long ago dashed themselves upon the wakeful realities of Skid Row soup lines and filthy encampments filled with rag-tag men numbed to their own despair, the myth is so strong that we still maintained a flickering hope.

Somewhere in the inner recess of our souls we had continued to harbor a notion, like a mother who cannot forget her lost child though many years, even decades, may have passed since the child's death. Somewhere in our deepest being we still had hope that America would fulfill its myth, that the American Dream might come true, that perhaps with the end of the Cold War, peace would finally come to our nation and all of the billions of dollars and vast human and natural resources devoted to weapons production would now be used to serve the people.

Now we realize that the evil empire of Soviet Marxism was a projection of the darkness within our own collective soul and that, far from being a threat, it was the single most important element in the creation of our own American empire and the demonic military machinery that perpetuates it. Now a mere eighteen months after the fall of the Berlin Wall, we have created a new evil empire in the Iraq of Saddam Hussein. As Martin Luther

---

*   On February 15, 1991, Jeff Dietrich and two other Catholic Workers, Curt Grove and Sandra Huckaby, poured blood and oil on the steps of the Federal Building, downtown Los Angeles in protest of the war in the Middle East.

Jeff Dietrich

King said in 1967, "The United States has never learned to listen to itself as if we are the enemy speaking" (quoted in Wink, *Unmasking the Powers*, p. 51). Rather, we create enemies outside of ourselves that effectively prevent our finding the darkness within and thus we remain, in the words of Dr. King, "the greatest purveyor of violence in the world" (*A Testament of Hope*, p. 636). Now do we weep for dreams that will never come true, for authentic hopes exposed as illusions? And in that weeping, in that mourning, we come to the deeper recognition that hope can never be fulfilled in nations and governments.

Let those who have ears hear and those who have eyes see. Now we must see clearly and hear clearly, now we must reject the illusions of America: mythic images of "pilgrim's progress" and revolutionary freedom, of a "New Jerusalem, and a "city upon a hill" giving light to all of the nations, of Yankee ingenuity and homespun wisdom, of science and technology, creating a Garden of Eden in the new world. All this must be mourned and released like the passing of a loved one.

The new world order of George W. Bush is sewn together from a hundred ratty pieces of these tattered shop-worn myths, and if we have not wept and mourned the passing of each one of them, we will find ourselves wrapped in this garment of national pride and patriotism like a madman trussed up in a straightjacket, immobilized, unable to act, tied to a history that leads only to death.

Paralyzed, we sit enthralled before our television sets, watching as the benign games of football and hockey are transformed into what they really are: rituals of empire, celebrations of power. Now we know why Lord Wellington said that the battle of Waterloo was won on the playing fields of Eton. Numbly, we watch as abstract war is fought at a distance, simulated war won at a distance. The myth of American moral power and technological efficiency is reaffirmed with each sortie flown, with each minute, loving description of hardware, ordinance, and machine. But all the while there is no body count of civilian casualties, no analysis or reflection, no critique, only reporters talking to each other, waiting obsequiously for a word from the authorities, like a dog waits for a bone. Who are these men huddled in basements giving reports of furtive peeks out of hotel windows? Surely not the heirs of Walter Cronkite and Edward R. Murrow, who reported aerial bombing and fire storms from the open streets of London.

No, this war is managed out of public relations offices by egregious press corps sycophants and cynical information officials. There will be no

29. Pouring blood and oil on the steps of the Federal Building, downtown Los Angeles. Pictured left to right: Curt Grove, Kieran Prather, George Manley-Gil, Sandy Lejune, Mary Lopez, Jeff Dietrich, 1991. Photo by Don Milici

images of bloodshed, starvation, and rubble to disturb the equanimity of the collective American conscience.

But in the final analysis, what is so disturbing is not the timidity or credulousness or superficiality of the press or even its deliberate lies, distortions, and jingoism. Rather, it is the almost unconscious celebration of the American myth of technical supremacy, moral righteousness, and spiritual superiority. This is the social topography, the foundation and starting point of all reporting. It is as if, to quote St. Paul, they see, and thus we all see, "at present we see indistinctly, as in a mirror, but then face to face" (1 Corinthians 13:12). All of our information is filtered through these mythic lenses and we perceive ourselves and our nation uncritically and unequivocally. Thus are we paralyzed by these celebrations of faithfulness, by our belief in a mythic system and a historical process whose final goal is domination, whose final destination is death. St. Paul says that we must "now put away childish things" (1 Corinthians 13:11). Now must we mourn the death of our childish beliefs, our false hopes, and our illusions.

Jeff Dietrich

We must mourn the death of our myths, we must mourn the passing of an America that will never be. Now do we declare ourselves to be enemies of the state, citizens of another nation empowered to act nonviolently in the name of that Kingdom. On Thursday, January 16, 1991, just 24 hours after the first bombing of Iraq, members of the Catholic Worker, in an act of civil disobedience poured 30 gallons of oil and two pints of human blood upon the steps of the Federal Building, downtown Los Angeles. Shouting, "No Blood for Oil!," we graphically proclaimed the truth that this present conflict is the shedding of innocent blood for world domination. Though the federal prosecutor claimed that we did $20,000 worth of damage, we were out of jail in five days. On January 31st we returned to do the same thing. Only by grieving the passing of our hopes, only by recognizing them as illusions, can we begin to seek grounding for that authentic hope. Only out of that hope in God's Kingdom are we empowered to act with truth and freedom to make a new history in the name of life rather than death.

Redeeming the Soul of America:
Voices from Exile

Catholic Agitator, April, 1991, pp. 1 and 6

"Hey Homes, you still in here?" The loud jocular voice of my fellow prisoner bounces off the steel walls of this jailhouse recreation room in reverberating echoes. "I thought they were gonna let all you protesters go home now that the war is over."

"No, man, it looks like I'm kind of a prisoner of war now."

"Well, I guess they must want your ass real bad, 'cause they're even lettin' all them Iraqis go. Well, all them that want to, anyway."

Even the guards here at the Federal Detention Center are a little surprised that I have not been released. Their concern is almost solicitous: "Mr. Dietrich," they say, "you need to be about your business. You should be getting home now."

But that is unlikely now that I have been officially indicted as a felon for our February 15th protest in which we dumped forty gallons of oil and two pints of human blood on the steps of the Federal Building in downtown Los Angeles.

"Was it worth it, Homes?" asks Mike, the cynical old jail veteran in a solicitous but sardonic tone that implies an affectionate contempt for simple-minded idealists like myself. "The war is over and you ain't accomplished a damn thing."

And again he asks, "Was it worth it?"

Who can say what convictions are worth? We are known as men and women of conviction only if we are willing to pay the price of that conviction. It is easy enough to protest a war. Far more difficult a task, though, is to place our entire existence in the path of war. The "cost of discipleship," as the theologian Dietrich Bonhoeffer said from his Nazi prison cell, must in some measure be commensurate with the price of war.

But to speak the truth while no one is listening, to continue protesting a war that is substantially over, to stay in jail when your presence is so obviously ineffective, is to appear foolish bordering upon the pathological.

Yet, it seems that our task, now that the war is over, is to remain in jail praying and fasting even as America cheers and celebrates. Our task, as people of conviction, is, in the words of the late Dr. Martin Luther King, "To save the soul of America" (*A Testament of Hope,* p. 233).

Though we are even now in the midst of the Lenten season, this archaic notion of doing penance no doubt seems offensive, even masochistic, to contemporary sensibilities.

But the original prophetic intent of repentance was always addressed to the corporate transgressions of the community: injustice, repression, the violence of war were the traditional targets of the prophet.

The authentic purpose of penance is to give substance to the otherwise ephemeral reality of evil in our midst, to take onto our own flesh the insubstantial spirit of malevolence which otherwise remains unconscious and thus deadly. Just as the assembly-line worker feels no responsibility for the sometimes dubious fruits of his labor, in the same way the B-52 pilot feels disassociated from the deadly effects of his labor.

Despite all of our moral pretense and ethical posturing, the real message of Desert Storm, heard by all the third world nations, is the Draconian edict of unrestrained power. The Vietnam era is indeed over and America is back with a vengeance, and we are no longer concerned with "winning hearts and minds." We will not hesitate to use our entire arsenal of technical omnipotence to enforce a vision of the "New World Order."

But our cheap, tawdry victory does not carry with it a corresponding moral value. Such a moral victory would, in the words of Dr. King, "Lay hands on the world order and say of war: 'This way of settling differences is not just'" (*A Testament of Hope,* p. 241). In the same speech, Dr. King went on to make the prescient and prophetic characterization that remains unfortunately true today: "the greatest purveyor of violence in the world today—[is] my own government" (*A Testament of Hope,* p. 233).

This new world order of the *Pax Americana,* based upon meeting the voracious consumer needs of a gluttonous, bulimic economy that devours world resources merely for the perverse pleasure of regurgitating them again, is pathological. It is the nature of such compulsive, deviant behavior to be in denial of itself. To challenge this state of non-recognition with the authentic consequences of such dangerous behavior patterns, to intervene

30. Catholic Workers protesting Desert Storm victory parade in Hollywood, 1991. Photo by
James Ryman

along the path of the addict's collision course with destruction, is the task
of people of conviction.

Despite the illusions that have been established of victory without sacrifice, of war without suffering, of battle without death, we know that actions
have consequences. We mourn the death of over 100,000 Iraqis. And while
our nation rejoices, we weep at the deep cost of such cheap victories.

It is this task, this penitential task of putting flesh upon the disembodied
spirits of unseen suffering that keeps us here. It is the desire to confront the
elusive reality of war with its unacceptable truth that causes us to remain in
this prison.

So we continue to fast, and each evening we gather in an obscure
corner of this jail under a garish makeshift shrine of the Sacred Heart, to
pray the rosary with a group of Latin Americans who do not even speak
English. They, too, are POW's for the most part, foot soldiers and under-
lings captured in the not-so-triumphant "War on Drugs." They do not pray
for world peace or economic justice. They pray for a lenient prosecutor,
a fair judge, a compassionate jury, a brief sentence, reunion with family
and friends. We join our prayers with theirs in the deepest hope and the
most profound conviction that such commingling of concerns may indeed
redeem the soul of America.

Getting Your Day in Court to be Among the Criminals*

Catholic Agitator, May, 1991, pp. 3 and 7

They come for you in the early morning while it is still dark. They come for you with a clanking of keys, with a bolt shot back in its lock like a pistol. They come for you like a criminal. They come for you like they came for Jesus.

"Dietrich, court line," they say. Even before consciousness breaks through the thick morning darkness, that troupe of tiny gymnasts in the circus pit of your stomach begin their program of back flips and handstands. It seems as though you had anesthetized their hyperactivity only moments before and drifted off to sleep. Now they are back with full adrenaline overdrive well before your sluggishly wakening consciousness can establish some minimal order. They remember, though you had momentarily suppressed it, that you are going to court today.

Today the judge will decide your fate, evaluate your life, determine whether you will stay in jail—five months, twelve months or even longer— or go home tomorrow. Such is the power of the judiciary, to sort through the discards and debris of the human community, examining them with the intensity and scrutiny of a rag picker going through the garbage heap, salvaging a few useful items, abandoning the rest to the fire.

It is only the few who submit their lives to such an evaluation, the prisoner of conscience, the prisoner of poverty. The rest have accepted their status without rebellion, the parameter of their prison wall never breached, never tested. For them, freedom is an empty concept. It is a few words, ancient words, scribbled hastily on parchment years ago, now safely sealed under glass to be worshipped but never practiced.

---

*   On February 15, 1991, Jeff Dietrich and two other Catholic workers were charged with felony destruction of federal property for pouring oil and blood on the steps of the Federal Building, downtown Los Angeles. Refusing bail, they remained in custody until their sentencing April 8. The following is an account by Dietrich of the court process.

You are awake now, dressing quickly so that you will have enough time to eat before the process begins. Though your appetite is suppressed in a flood of adrenaline, you must force yourself to eat a double breakfast, fortification for your fourteen-hour ordeal of cold cells, cement floors, scowling guards, and arrogant judges, fear, doubt and self-pity.

You start to wonder what the judge and prosecutor might be doing. Are they still in bed? Their stomachs are probably not churning in trepidation at the coming confrontation. Will they have breakfast, or will they sleep in and grab a quick bite on the way to court?

Down the elevator to the fourth floor. They strip you naked for the first time. They will strip you again when you come back. They peer into *all* of your orifices. You lift the soles of your feet to their scrutiny; you must lift your armpits and your genitals as well. It is a kind of ritual of indignity, a confirmation of your less-than-human status, just when you need all of the status and dignity you can muster.

The air is cold against your skin, but still you must walk naked through the metal detector before they give you the thin, blue shirt and polyester pants that you will wear to the court. This last act is too much, as if there might actually be something that you had hidden from their scrupulous eyes, as if you might have secreted some portion of your dignity into the dark cavity of your naked body where mere eyes cannot pierce.

But nothing remains undetected, nothing remains unidentified. Their eyes have seen it all and catalogued your insufficiencies in their cold, officious, bureaucratic detachment. Now you are permitted to re-cover your body, to re-cover your nakedness, but you cannot recover your integrity or your composure.

The exposure of your nakedness has sapped your strength, and the cold seeps into your muscles like a thief to steal the last measure of your resolve. Your body begins to shake, and you panic because you cannot stop it. Am I just cold, or am I afraid? Cold and fear conspire to do the work that cops and courts alone could not accomplish.

Before they take you down to the basement to be shackled, hand and foot, and chained to each other in an umbilical fraternity, you wait for an hour, maybe more, in the first of a series of holding tanks. Then when they are ready and not before, your body will be duly accounted for, a formal receipt for it will be accepted and notarized as responsibility is transferred from the Bureau of Prisons to the United States Marshalls who will transport you to the court with the same weariness and contempt they give to all criminals regardless of guilt or innocence.

By the time your body is delivered to the basement jail cell of the US Courthouse on Spring Street, it is 8:00 o'clock in the morning. Your arraignment is not until 2:00 p.m. You are worn out, but you cannot find a place to sit except on the cement floor. You think at first that you might be able to warm up the cement with your body heat, but it is no use—the coldness sucks your energy like a sponge. Nevertheless, you drift into a semi-sleep, suppressing the jailhouse clamor.

You are again wondering about the judge and the prosecutor: have they arrived yet, are they having a strong cup of coffee in a comfortable office, or are they lingering over a croissant and cappuccino before leaving for work?

Long before you can attain a level of unconsciousness even approximating the oblivion you had hoped for, the marshals come for your body again. This time they photograph it, fingerprint it and store its images on their files.

Now you cannot go back to sleep. Consciousness assaults you with its grim, tumultuous presence. The only distraction from your own inner turmoil is engagement with the suffering reality in front of you. Each time they return from the courtrooms above this jail cell, your companions bring tidings of great tribulation, of retribution untempered even by justice, of lives pressed down and squeezed until vitality is drained.

They are tough, unflinching, and stoic. You are suffocated in a wave of tenderness. You want to hold their hand, touch them, comfort them, but dare not. In this confraternity of masochism, tears and touching are not allowed. You must hang tough, screw it down, hold it together. "Ain't no big thing. I can do twenty years." "Man's gotta do what a man's gotta do." "I ain't gonna swivel for no judge. That's all they want you to do is roll over and beg like a dog."

They had already been losers, these men. Now they have lost the big gamble that they could beat the odds, that they could take a short cut, circumvent the lady luck who had dealt them such a bad hand. Wrong place, wrong neighborhood, wrong school, wrong cards; no aces, no kings, no chance of winning, just bluff and bravado.

You wonder if you will be as unflappable and firm in your ideals and convictions as these men are in their simple, naked confrontation with the power, majesty and hypocrisy of an inhuman system. Or will you roll over and beg like a dog?

After what seems like an eternity of waiting, they come for you again. They hook you up to the other prisoners for the trip upstairs. They will unhook you just before you go into the courtroom (lest any suspect that the rights of the innocent have been violated).

Upon entering the courtroom, all heads turn to stare at the line of prisoners escorted by an almost equal number of US marshals. You and your companions have come out of the oppressive depths of your jail cell tomb to enter this vast, majestic cathedral of law. Every element of it is cunningly contrived to evoke a Medieval sense of the insignificance of the individual in the sacred sanctuary of power. From the mottled marble walls to the elevated altar of the judge's diadem, from the "communion" rail separating the judicial priesthood and the unwashed laity to the priestly vestments of the judge himself, no other democratic institution has maintained such a pomposity of Papal trappings.

It works. You are intimidated. Like a peasant petitioner groveling before the royal throne, you summon as much dignity as your lowly station will allow.

Surprisingly, your voice takes on an uncommon tenor, a boldness you had not expected as you proudly plead guilty to opposing the nation's barbaric war. But in the end, the judge catches you off guard because he is neither cynical nor punitive. It is far worse, he is patronizing. He wants to let you go if only you will accept probation. When you refuse in no uncertain words, you are unprepared for his query and you bungle the answer. You had assumed that someone, especially a judge, would recognize your willingness to sacrifice and stay in jail as a sign of conviction. Rather, it was dismissed as simple-mindedness.

Later, back in your jail cell, you are approached by Lucas, the tough old jailhouse veteran. You are shocked. You had supposed that he was going to lecture you on your stupidity in not accepting the judge's offer to get out of jail. Instead, he sticks out his hand and says, "You're a stand up guy. I ain't never seen anybody talk to a judge like you did. You're a real man of conviction, and I just wanted to shake your hand. My daddy told me about men like you, but I never in my life expected to meet one except in a book."

It suddenly occurs to you as exceedingly ironic that while the criminal can recognize it, the judge is blind to the power of authentic conviction. You wonder for a moment if he might see things differently were he to spend the day as you have done, in this jailhouse tomb with these prisoners who, though they are labeled criminals, are nevertheless men.

Reflections on September 11:
We Are Still Pacifists

Catholic Agitator, September, 2002, p. 3

Although we are ridiculed and derided and marginalized, we are still pacifists. Though we abhor the violent calculated brutality of the perpetrators, mourn the death of the victims, and feel the pain of families, friends, and loved ones, we are still pacifists. Though we believe that our nation sustained a harsh and unfair blow, we are still pacifists. And even more so are we pacifists one year after that terrible day, September 11, 2001.

We are pacifists and Christians in the tradition of Jesus Christ, Dorothy Day, and St. Francis, and unlike the apparent vast majority of our fellow Americans, we have not lost our critical faculties and rational minds, or our capacity for ambiguity and paradox. We still remember the history of the last fifty years and we are still convinced that the most truculent terrorist nation in the world continues to be our own. And though we are sad at the death and destruction visited upon our nation, we refuse to allow our sadness and loss to be utilized as an excuse for America to dismantle democracy at home and run roughshod over the entire planet.

We believe that the "War on Terror" is simply another name for the war on the poor throughout the world. We believe that the "War on Terror" is the contemporary parallel to the war on Communism, only much, much better. It is a war that does not require sacrifice on the part of citizens, but rather requires diligence on the part of consumers. Since the end of the Cold War and the demise of the "world-wide communist conspiracy," our leaders have been searching for an appropriate enemy to galvanize the limp and wilted American patriotism, sustain the defense industry, and prevent our military from sliding into peacetime demise. What they have found in "terrorism" is an amorphous worldwide enemy who cannot be identified, a war that will never end, and an angry, terrified

31. Cover illustration by Gary Palmatier, pen and ink. *Catholic Agitator*, 1980

populace that will approve every conceivable activity and expense in the name of revenge and security.

It is difficult to remember that little more than a year ago President George W. Bush was among the least popular presidents in history, having obtained office on less than a majority vote, and was widely slated to be a lame-duck president. Today, however, no one thinks it odd or ironic that the same man, whom many suspect stole the election, is now leading the fight for "world-wide democracy." But in the year that we have been engaged in the "War on Terror," we have not confirmed the killing of, nor the capture of, more than one terrorist leader. Though we have invaded Afghanistan and plan to invade Iraq, we have no intention of exacting even so much as an apology from Saudi Arabia or Egypt, the actual origin of most of the September 11 terrorists.

In the name of winning the "War on Terror," President Bush has rejected the possibility of nuclear disarmament, approved first-strike use of nuclear weapons, broken the ABM treaty, funded the Star Wars National Missile Defense Program, and raised the military budget by 40 percent. All of this massive array of sophisticated technology and military apparatus is aimed at a group of people who were armed with box cutters and our own stolen air-planes. This is not a high-tech problem and our high-tech solution is both disingenuous and ineffective. But we prefer high-tech solutions because it is easier than the authentic solution, which requires social and economic transformation. It is not unlike our attempts to cure cancer with doses of radiation and chemicals, the very elements that caused cancer in the first place. But the only cure for terrorism is to eliminate American over-consumption and dependence on foreign oil and to spread the wealth. I agree with novelist Barbara Kingsolver, who besides calling for a national referendum on consumption and the redistribution of wealth, wants Americans to have an opportunity to vote on their permanent war economy. The outcome might allow the people of this country to live more simply and in peace.

Military Success Justifies War in the New American Century*

Catholic Agitator, May, 2003, pp. 1 and 6

Wednesday, April 10, 2003 Metropolitan Detention Center

Dear Community,

7:00 a.m.—Liberation day in Baghdad! All my fellow inmates are watching Fox News, which has spent the last hour waiting for the crowds to pull down the enormous statue of Saddam Hussein. It got boring just waiting and listening to the talking heads carry on about the liberation of Baghdad and similarities to the liberation of France and Germany and the fall of the Berlin Wall. So I stopped watching. I am sure I won't miss anything—once the statue finally comes down, we will no doubt see a thousand instant replays.

Baghdad is liberated, and I am still here in this jail, a prophet of doom discredited, a protester of war repudiated, an idealist who believes that the ends never justify the means.

George W. Bush and his tough, hardheaded, realists have prevailed—they have toppled a tyrant who, without doubt, has been the cause of great suffering to his people. When this war began, they couched its implementation in "Just War" theories and divine mandates. Now these theories are no longer necessary, because success is its own justification.

My fear is that, just as the fall of Hitler in World War II spurred American imperial aspirations in the last century, so too will the fall of Saddam Hussein spur American imperialism in the twenty-first century. But the Allies did not defeat Hitler, rather, the spirit of Nazism was the true victor of World War II. The only difference between the twentieth century and the twenty-first century is that the existence of the Soviet Union acted as

---

* Jeff Dietrich has been in federal prison since March 12, 2003 as a result of his participation in multiple "prayer actions" at the Federal Building, downtown Los Angeles.

a restraint on the American Empire. Now there is nothing to restrain us—not world opinion, not international law, not the United Nations. Might makes right. We are a law unto ourselves—in fact, we are the law. We have destroyed the fictions of international law, world opinion and the UN, and returned the world to the law of the jungle—the law of brute force.

No nation will ever attack or oppose us again—at least not directly. But they will secretly gloat when we are attacked by terrorists. They will applaud and rejoice at our every defeat and humiliation. And we will learn that, in this modern world of technological vulnerability, there is no protection against inflamed ideologues willing to die for their beliefs. There is no security. We cannot protect every airline's computer system, every nuclear power plant. The very air we breathe, the very water we drink, is a potential source of terror. It is a jungle out there. And it is a jungle that still has thousands of nuclear weapons floating around, far too many of which are easily available on the black market to determined individuals seeking to wound the biggest beast in the jungle.

We have liberated Baghdad, but more importantly, we have liberated Middle Eastern oil from the stranglehold of recalcitrant Arabs. Success breeds success. There is nothing to stop us now as we go on to liberate the next evil dictatorship of Iran, Syria, Saudi Arabia, Korea, China. Henceforth, the benefits of the world economy will flow unimpeded down the liberated roads of *Pax Americana*.

Success is its own validation; it requires no further certification. And those of us still in jail have been certified fools. For we seek validation, not in the success of empire, but rather do we seek our validation in the Word of God.

Scripture tells us that the world's first empire was located on the plains of Babylonia, between the Tigris and Euphrates Rivers: "Then they said, 'Come, let us build ourselves a city and a tower with its top in the sky and so make a name for ourselves'" (Genesis 11:4-8). That tower fell because it was built on a foundation of bloodshed and domination—the foundation of all successful empires.

In life, as in world affairs, success can be our own worst enemy, for it validates our least admirable traits: greed, aggression, self-aggrandizement, and moral blindness. And it tends to create disasters of its own making further down the line.

To avoid those disasters, the Gospel of Luke suggests a stronger foundation. Jesus says:

I will show you what someone is like who...listens to my words, and acts on them. That one is like a person building a house, who dug deeply and laid the foundation on rock; when the flood came, the river burst against that house but could not shake it because it had been well built. But the one who listens and does not act is like a person who built a house on the ground without a foundation. When the river burst against it, it collapsed at once and was completely destroyed.

Luke 6:47-49

8:00 a.m.—The statue of Saddam has fallen, and the newscasters are jubilant! The "New American Century" has begun with a crash.

The guys watching the TV, however, have just switched the channel to *The Dating Game*. I guess they're tired of watching history in the making. And so am I. But I remain grateful to be part of a community and a tradition that does not find its justification in success, that does not build its foundation on the structures of empire. I remain grateful to abide in jail at this historic moment, to pray for the victims, to do penance for the violence of our nation, and to give humble witness to a different Kingdom. A Kingdom that is never successful, but will nonetheless endure forever. A Kingdom whose foundation is built on the very rock rejected by the builders of empires.

In Sure and Certain
Hope of the Resurrection,
Jeff Dietrich, Prisoner for Peace

Catholic Workers are Still in Jail:
We are Still Standing with the Victims

Catholic Agitator, June, 2003, pp. 1 and 2

The war is long over, but our community members and friends remain in jail, or will soon be going to jail, for protesting our nation's shameful act of aggression in Iraq. East Coast Catholic Workers Steve Baggarly, Steve Woolford, and Bill Frankel-Streit are serving six months for pouring blood on the steps of the Pentagon last December. Catherine Morris, Martha Lewis, and Jim and Joyce Parkhurst have served county jail time for local street blockades, but must return to court in June, along with Eric DeBode, to answer federal charges for our Lenten prayer actions. Jeff Dietrich and David Gardner served two months and eight days, respectively, while community member Mike Wisniewski began a three-month sentence in late April for his protest action at the School of the Americas in Georgia, and Dennis Apel from the Guadalupe Catholic Worker will begin serving a two-month federal sentence for his blood-pouring action at Vandenberg Air Force Base.

At one point, over half of the Los Angeles Catholic Worker community was in jail at the same time, which forced us to close the kitchen on Saturdays for a while. But we are happy to report that, despite the fact that many of our folks may be returning to jail, we have nonetheless reopened the kitchen on Saturdays.

The most often-asked question in response to our various actions against the war is, "Was it worth it? Did you accomplish anything?" The answer is both yes and no. Yes, it was worth it. And no, we did not accomplish anything. We did not stop the war in Iraq. We did not stop the bombs from falling. We did not prevent the innocent from dying. In such extreme situations as America's recent build-up to war, effective political action is probably impossible. But that realization should not paralyze us or stop us from continuing to say no in the strongest possible manner. Silence is consent! And it was our intention to eliminate our consent in the most public and dramatic manner possible, even if that meant going to jail.

In some ways, going to jail is a means of removing, if only for a short while, one's participation in our nation's collective death project. It is also a means of giving significance to our words, of paying a price, of putting ourselves ever so slightly in harm's way, and thus standing in solidarity with the victims of war. It is a means of "picking up the cross" and following Christ.

We recognize our humble efforts as part of the same project undertaken by our friend and hero Kathy Kelly, director and founder of *Voices in the Wilderness*, who refused to abandon the people of Iraq, and remained in the city of Baghdad throughout the war, enduring the bombings and privations suffered by the citizens of that country. Kathy accomplished nothing; she did not stop the war, or the bombings, or the suffering of the innocent. But she gave powerful and heroic witness to the gospel command to stand in solidarity with the victims.

For it is always the victims who pay the cost of war—the victims in Iraq who died and continue to die from the privations of war, the victims in our own country who will bear the cost of this war in the form of massive cuts in funding for health care, education, and public transportation, while the wealthy benefit from massive tax cuts.

In the meantime, we continue to ask, "Where are the weapons of mass destruction? What was the danger of Iraq? Why did we have to invade?" And while we agree that Saddam Hussein was an evil dictator, we also believe that the fever pitch of war propaganda demonized him beyond recognition.

And I want to suggest the bizarre possibility that much of the credit for a relatively brief and low-casualty war may well be due to the so-called demonic Saddam Hussein himself. I realize that that must sound outrageous. But then I recall that the entire Iraq war scenario reminds me rather vividly of the 1962 Cuban Missile Crisis, in which another demonic man from the East, Nikita Khrushchev, with a snarly and swarthy "foreign" visage similar to Saddam Hussein's, faced off against another American president similar to George W. Bush. Young, clean-cut, rational, Ivy League graduate and purportedly compassionate, John F. Kennedy was, like George W. Bush, willing to sacrifice the world to complete nuclear devastation in order to preserve his political career. The swarthy, demonic Khrushchev was not. He blinked first and backed down, and thus lost his political career. But in doing so, he saved the world.

I have no idea what actually happened in Iraq. All I know is that a commonly accepted and highly potential Iraq war scenario maintained that Hussein would play the wild card. He would use biological weapons against invading forces. Or more likely, he would just simply lob a nuke into Jerusalem, thus beginning World War III or worse, Armageddon.

But, it didn't happen, and I refuse to attribute that outcome to the compassion of George W. Bush or the professionalism of the American military. I would like to attribute at least some of that outcome to the effects of prayer. And further, I would raise the possibility that, like Nikita Khrushchev, Saddam Hussein might be more human than our propaganda machine gives him credit for. But even more, I am convinced that the smooth-talking white guys with Ivy League educations, buttoned-down collars, and well-tailored suits are at least as dangerous, if not more so, than the swarthy, snarly, demonic guys from the East.

Jesus Wept

Catholic Agitator, March, 2004, pp. 1 and 2

"As he drew near, he saw the city and wept over it saying, 'If this day you only knew what makes for peace! But now it is hidden from your eyes'" (Luke 19:41-42).

The most poignant words in all of scripture may be, "Jesus wept," which are found in the Gospel of Luke, at the very moment of his triumphal entry into Jerusalem. Though often mistaken as a sentimental, emotional outpouring, they are in fact the archetypal prophetic response to the imminent destruction of Jerusalem. Jesus' tears recall the paradoxical response of all of God's prophets, who are, on the one hand, deeply outraged at the injustice and oppression caused by Jerusalem, and, on the other hand, deeply saddened at the coming destruction of the city—at the suffering and dying of the innocents, victims of their leaders, who have chosen the path of Empire and warfare, rather than faithfulness to Yahweh and obedience to his covenant of justice.

Perhaps nothing better describes our own complex emotions on this first anniversary of the Iraq war. On the one hand, we certainly feel vindicated by the almost daily revelations that the war in Iraq was predicated upon lies and falsehoods: that contrary to the statements of our nation's highest officials there were no weapons of mass destruction in Iraq, there were never any Iraqi links to al-Qaeda terrorists; and there was no imminent threat to national security from Iraq. Though there will be a year-long investigation of the CIA and the nation's intelligence community, it already seems pretty clear that intelligence information was manipulated at the highest levels to fit the aggressive agenda of administrative warmongers.

On the other hand, we feel like weeping: weeping for all the victims who have died since September 11, 2001; weeping for all the poor who are suffering from the cutbacks in health, education, and welfare services as a consequence of this war; weeping for the paranoia and loss of democratic liberties caused by this permanent war on terrorism; weeping for all of the death and destruction that will inevitably come if we continue to follow the path of warfare and empire that we have so boldly embarked upon with so little foresight.

Perhaps our current crop of American Empire boosters could learn a few lessons from historical events so powerfully documented in Errol Morris' excellent film on Vietnam-era Secretary of Defense Robert McNamara, *The Fog of War*. It offers a perfect corollary to our contemporary situation. Unlike our current warmongers, McNamara, even at age 85, is intellectually brilliant, self-reflective, and superbly analytical.

The film is subtitled *Eleven Lessons from the Life of Robert S. McNamara*. "The first and most important lesson," McNamara says, "is empathize with your enemy," something our contemporary warmongers never considered. Throughout the course of the Vietnam War, McNamara and his employers had assumed that the North Vietnamese were part of an international Communist conspiracy. It is only in recent years that McNamara came to the tardy realization that the Vietnamese perceived themselves to be in the midst of a civil war and not part of an international war and that our domino theory was invalid. Had McNamara and his bosses known this earlier, thousands of lives might have been saved.

Lesson number two is that rationality will not save us. "Three times during the Cuban Missile Crisis," McNamara says, "the most rational people in the world decided to destroy the entire planet and only dumb luck prevented them from doing so."

Above all else, McNamara is a manager; he crunches numbers, reads statistics, makes rational decisions, and brings order out of chaos. His greatest achievement was the massive reorganization of the ailing Ford Motor Company, which by the late 50s had fallen victim to nepotism, irrational management, and General Motors' advanced production techniques. As the first non-family member to become CEO of Ford, McNamara streamlined production, hired Harvard MBAs, and put Ford on top again. President Kennedy thought he could do the same for the Pentagon.

But while he was able to streamline and rationalize the Pentagon itself, which has many similarities to Ford Motor Company, he was unable to do the same for the Pentagon's actual product, which was not automobiles, but warfare. In warfare, "things get out of hand. There are so many factors involved in war that no one can keep track of them all," McNamara says. He learned what Tolstoy understood so many years before, that "war is chaos." The battlefield is run, not by logic, but by a deadly form of irrationality that even generals on the scene cannot control, much less manage in the Pentagon.

Though he is unrepentant about his wartime activities, McNamara is obviously not undisturbed. Still, at his core he is not a moralist or a theologian; he is a statistician and a rationalist, and his lifetime project is to "learn from my mistakes." If war is inevitable, and McNamara most certainly believes that it is, he wants to know how we go about the business of war with the least possible destruction and death and still achieve our goals. In other words, McNamara wants a more rational and humane form of warfare.

It was General Curtis LeMay, McNamara's boss in World War II, who best understood that war is never rational or humane. Using McNamara's statistics, he calculated that the most effective means of bombing Japan was to fly low rather than high and use incendiary bombs rather than high explosive bombs; the results were a devastating 200,000 deaths in the Tokyo raids alone, with a total of over a million deaths resulting from scores of similar fire-bombing raids on other Japanese cities. LeMay understood that "war is hell" and, if you want to win you must apply the logic of hell. McNamara quoted LeMay as saying, "If we had lost the war we would all have been tried as war criminals."

It was LeMay who, during the Cuban Missile Crisis, wanted to launch an all-out first strike against the Soviets and "get them before they got us." But as McNamara learned only recently, the Soviet missiles were actually already in Cuba at the time, armed and prepared to respond to just such a move as LeMay's. It was only dumb luck that prevented world annihilation.

The film portrays the limits of rationality—the moral struggle of a man who believes that in order to do good it is sometimes necessary to do evil. And though McNamara never repents, he does on several occasions shed a few tears.

His tears are like those shed by Jesus over Jerusalem. He has seen the destruction and bloodshed, the senseless violence and the death of the innocent, and he still has enough humanity left in him to weep. Of all the managers of war McNamara was the best and the brightest—far brighter than the current crop of warmongers—and he was still unable to manage war. They will no doubt fare much worse as our nation continues to dig itself deeper and deeper into a quagmire that increasingly resembles our Vietnam debacle.

Jesus, on the other hand, understood that it was not possible to "manage war." He recognized that the cycle of violence and retribution would always get out of hand. That is why he wept, saying:

> If this day you only knew what makes for peace—but now it is hidden from your eyes. For the days are coming upon you when your enemies will raise a palisade against you....They will smash you to the ground and your children within you, and they will not leave one stone upon another within you.
>
> Luke 19:41-44

The stones of Jerusalem tumbled, just as the stones of our own Empire will surely fall, because both are built on a foundation of violence and injustice. Though Jesus' teachings of economic sharing, compassion, forgiveness, and love of enemy articulated in the "Sermon on the Plain" (Luke 6:17-49) have never been seriously considered as viable foreign policy, they are nonetheless the "foundation of rock" and the "ways of peace" that Jesus said would be our only salvation from the floodtides of disaster.

Middle East, War, Nukes, and Apocalypse

Catholic Agitator, August 2006, pp. 1 and 5

At the height of the recent war in Lebanon, several of the folks who eat at our soup kitchen approached me with knowing looks on their faces, as if they were about to share a secret. But actually, they just wanted to comment on the current Middle East crisis, with the confidential warning that, "It looks like the End of Times are here. You can read all about it in the book of Revelation." While one might dismiss such simplistic interpretations of scripture as the babbling of uneducated street folks, overly influenced by the plethora of fundamentalist missions here on Skid Row who preach pre-millennialism, this theological garbage is now a dominant American theme.

The deadly mixture of Middle Eastern politics, lust for oil, and fantasies of Armageddon are bad enough, but when you throw nuclear weapons into the mix, it is insanity at its most incendiary level. The current manifestation of premillennialist theology, as espoused by so many Americans, had its inception after World War II with the birth of both the atom bomb and the nation-state of Israel. As scripture scholar Wes Howard-Brook explains:

> Premillennialist writing in the late 1940s and 1950s interpreted the bomb as solid evidence that the time of prophetic fulfillment was near. Premillennialists looked from this point forward upon attempts to limit weapons development as a futile effort to resist divine imperative....Premillennialists began to look more and more for the Second Coming of Jesus and the Rapture that would protect them from the "inevitable" nuclear war. The second, and even more portentous event for premillennialists, was the reestablishment of the nation of Israel for the first time in two thousand years....Premillennialists have always been supporters of Zionism because, their apocalyptic scenario depended entirely upon the existence of a restored nation of Israel.

Unveiling Empire, pp. 12-13

Many of the premillennialists understand the invasion of Iraq and the fall of Saddam Hussein as a fulfillment of the prophecy in the book of Revelation concerning the fall of Babylon and the "destruction of the Beast."

We could write all of these people off as a bunch of whackos if it were not for the fact that our current president is a firm believer in premillennialism, which is essentially an ideology of death.

These people are working hard to promote world destruction in the name of the God of Life. And whenever we use the name of God to justify killing, theft, self-defense, nuclear war, we are committing blasphemy.

When Dietrich Bonhoeffer, the great German theologian and advocate of non-violence, finally decided that it was necessary to assassinate Hitler and participated in the plot to kill him (for which he was executed in July 1944), he did not try to justify his actions with an elaborate theology. He acted confessionally—in other words, he confessed that it was a sin and a violation of the scriptures to murder anyone, even one as manifestly evil as Hitler.

As fallible human beings, we cannot presume to know the mind of God. Even when we do such apparently positive actions as feeding the hungry, clothing the naked, sheltering the homeless, we cannot presume that we are doing the will of God. We can only hope that what we are doing is in keeping with the will of God.

At a recent gathering, Fr. Dan Berrigan was asked to characterize the Bush Administration. He responded with simple eloquence in a single phrase: "They lack all modesty."

Were it not for the fact that the Bush Administration has embarked on a policy of world domination, nuclear rearmament, abandonment of the Anti-Ballistic Missile Treaty and the Nuclear Non-Proliferation Treaty, we might be able to dismiss them all as whacko. But the whackos are in charge, and they are actively working for the destruction of the planet so that they can get "raptured" and "bring" Jesus back.

This is a tough time for Christians who believe that Jesus came not to promote world destruction, but rather to promote world peace, and that our job as Christians is to work for world peace, pray for world peace, and ultimately to sacrifice ourselves in the struggle for world peace.

When we see three of the world's great religions, Judaism, Islam, and Christianity, all with nuclear arms, all fighting each other, all quoting the same scripture to justify their deadly actions, it is enough to make us abandon scripture and its murderous, judgmental God altogether, and embrace a benevolent atheism.

But we struggle, rather, to embrace the God of peace and nonviolence, the God of mercy, of whom Jesus said:

> Love your enemies and do good to them, and lend expecting nothing back, then your reward be great and you will be children of the Most High, for he himself is kind to the ungrateful and the wicked.

> Luke 6:35

Our project as Christians is to be children of the God of compassion. With the great Protestant theologian William Stringfellow, we believe that the theologians of empire, from the time of Constantine to the time of George Bush, have hijacked the Gospels and put them into the service of war and plunder and nuclear weapons. Unlike the theologians of empire, Stringfellow understood the authentic Babylonian reality:

> Babylon represents the essential version of the demonic triumph in a nation. Babylon is thus a parable for Nazi Germany. And Babylon is thus a parable for America. In *that* way, there is an inherent and idiopathic connection between the Nazi estate in the thirties and what is now happening in America.

> *An Ethic for Christians and Other Aliens,* p. 33

In the end, I assume that the whacko theologians of nuclear end times perceive me to be just as bizarre as I perceive them to be. The deeper question, however, is what kind of God it is that we believe in? Do we believe in a God who wants us to work diligently towards the incineration of the planet or do we believe in a God who wants us to beat swords into plowshares?

The Moral Captivity of Obama

Catholic Agitator, February, 2010, pp. 1, 2, and 6

"In a scene reminiscent of the 60s...." That was the classic tag line that reporters always used to belittle demonstrators like ourselves who "superciliously" continued to protest American militarism long after the war in Vietnam had ended. Well, today it's our turn. In a scene reminiscent of the 60s, a young, untried Democratic president with an aggressive social agenda inherits an Asian war that he knows is "unwinnable" but pushes ahead anyway, because unwinnable wars, despite their death toll, are always better than unwinnable elections. And if it is the 60s all over again, with a young Obama in Afghanistan standing in for a young Kennedy in Vietnam, then what better time to revisit the work of William Stringfellow, the theologian of the concept of *principalities and powers*.

It was the intractability of the Vietnam War that initiated Stringfellow's theology—the recognition that the vast majority of Americans, as well as the majority of American civil servants, from the Secretary of State to on-site military personnel, understood that the war in Vietnam could not be won. But the shameful lack of moral courage within the political system to stop the senseless slaughter clarified for Stringfellow that mere humans were not actually in charge of their own institutions, rather, they are controlled by *principalities and powers*.

As far as most rational human beings are concerned, all organizations and institutions, whether they be nations, corporations, universities, banks or libraries, are *ipso facto* the sum total of their human components and nothing more. But Stringfellow says No! "[It] is the illusion of human beings that they can make or create and, hence, control institutions and that institutions are no more than groups of human beings duly organized" (*An Ethic for Christians and Other Aliens*, p. 79).

Biblically speaking, the *principalities and powers* are in reality the actual spiritual manifestations of human institutions. St. Paul calls them the "spirits of the air" (Ephesians 2:2) because of their pervasive influence on human actions; the Old Testament calls them "idols."

Stringfellow writes, "The principalities and powers *are* legion....They include all institutions, all ideologies, all images, all movements, all causes, all corporations, all bureaucracies, all traditions, all methods and routines, all conglomerates, all races, all nations, all idols....Beyond any prospect of full enumeration. The principalities and powers are legion" (*An Ethic for Christians and Other Aliens*, p. 78).

But it is the state that is the preeminent *principality and power.* "The state," says Stringfellow, "is regarded historically,...empirically, [and] biblically as the archetypical principality, epitomizing the other *principalities and powers* and possessing or claiming a certain special status...in the seeming hierarchy of demonic powers" (*An Ethic for Christians and Other Aliens*, p. 110).

And, in the midst of the Fall, their moral purpose and vocational imperative has been turned upside down. Thus, rather than serving life, they now serve death. I remember well the enormous neon sign above a ten story evangelical church in downtown Los Angeles blaring the words: "The Wages of Sin is Death." But Stringfellow rebukes this simplistic perspective. "Human wickedness," he says, "in this sense...human pride—greed, duplicity, lust, dishonesty, malice, covetousness, depravity, and similar vices...is so peripheral in the biblical version of the Fall that in the pietistic interpretation that it represents the heart of the matter must be accounted gravely misleading" (*An Ethic for Christians and Other Aliens*, p. 76). For Stringfellow, the actual morality of the world in the Fall under, captivity of the principalities, is death.

Ironically, like President Obama, William Stringfellow graduated from Harvard Law School, and also like Obama, he chose to live in a ghetto; to serve the community of Harlem as a lawyer. It was that raw experience of Harlem that sharpened his theology. As a white, middle-class Harvard graduate, *principalities and powers* seemed benign for him; but for poor black people, they obviously were predatory. From the criminal justice system that imprisoned and brutalized without recourse, to the electric company that shut off heat in winter, to the phone company that terminated service and demanded deposits for restoration of service, it seemed clear that the *principalities and powers* were demonic and bent upon death.

Morality for Stringfellow has little to do with what we hear in church or on Oprah or Dr. Phil. Of course, there are personal moral standards, but the real saga of scripture has little to do with personal morality. Rather, for Stringfellow, it is cast in terms of an epic historical struggle of life against death in which we are called to act "humanly in the midst of the Fall" (*An Ethic for Christians and Other Aliens*, p. 63). This is a way of asking us, did we act like the human Jesus? Did we step up to the plate and confront the evil of our era? Did we act compassionately towards victims, remembering always that Jesus was the consummate and paradigmatic victim of *principalities and powers*? Or, did we simply go along with the crowd? Were we "Good Germans" or were we the "silent majority"? Were we just good functionaries of *principalities and powers* or did we risk our comfort and security to do the right thing, the human thing?

I imagine the questions a child might ask a parent about significant historical events when they come home from school: "What did you do in the war daddy?" "Well, I refused to kill and I went to jail." "What did you do about segregation?" "Well, I was a freedom rider and I went to jail." "What did you do about nuclear weapons?" "Well, I cut the fence around the nuclear test site, and I went to jail." For Stringfellow, resistance to the demonic powers is the essence of Christian morality.

It was the experience of meeting members of the Christian resistance to the Nazi regime in post WWII Europe that gave formation to much of Stringfellow's theology. It was the example of Christians acting under the most extreme circumstances that formed his particular theological outlook. For Stringfellow, the primary Christian ethic, "to live humanly in the midst of the Fall," was embodied by these Christians who practiced hospitality to Jews, held clandestine Bible study, and practiced daily resistance in tiny everyday ways as a means of maintaining their humanity in the midst of the darkness of Nazi repression. It was only in resistance to the Nazi regime's ascendant death project that one could maintain one's humanity.

Therefore, for Stringfellow, the entire purpose of the *principalities and powers* in their fallen estate is the confusion and demoralization of humanity (*An Ethic for Christians and Other Aliens*, p. 97). "In consequence," Stringfellow writes, "a Biblical person is always wary of claims...for allegiance, obedience and service under the rubric called patriotism. Such demands are often put in noble or benign or innocuous terms. But in any country the rhetoric and rituals of conformity and obedience to a regime or ruler latently concern idolatry...even though that name is not generally invoked" (*An Ethic for Christians and Other Aliens*, pp. 113-114).

While Stringfellow's theology is grounded on St. Paul's elaboration of the *principalities and powers*, it is based even more on the book of Revelation, that powerful vision of the fall of Babylon, which for its author John, a political prisoner of Rome on the island of Patmos, was a thinly veiled reference to the aforementioned Empire.

For the Evangelist John, as well as for Stringfellow, Babylon is the stand-in not only for Rome, but for all Empires: Egypt, Assyria, Babylon, Rome, Greece, Great Britain, the Nazis, and the United States of America. And thus for Stringfellow, the United States is the pre-eminent empire, "America *is* Babylon!" (*An Ethic for Christians and Other Aliens*, p. 34).

America is Babylon, and the language of Babylon, Biblically speaking, is "Babel" or confusion, "Babel means the inversion of language, verbal inflation,...coded phrases,...hyperbole,...falsehood, blasphemy...Babel *is* violence" (*An Ethic for Christians and Other Aliens*, p. 106). When we read Mr. Obama's rationale for the war and occupation of Afghanistan as a "Just War," we can hear the posturing and posing and blasphemy of one who is the blissful moral captive of the violence of Babylon.

As former *New York Times* reporter and author Chris Hedges writes:

> The president spoke in Oslo...of "just war" theory, although the wars in Iraq and Afghanistan do not meet the criteria laid down by Thomas Aquinas or traditional Catholic just-war doctrine. He spoke of battling evil, dividing human reality into binary pokes of black and white as Bush did, without examining the evil of pre-emptive war, sustained military occupation and imperialism. He compared al-Qaeda to Hitler, ignoring the difference between a protean group of terrorists and a nation-state with the capacity to overwhelm its neighbors with conventional military force. "The instruments of war do have a role to play in preserving the peace," Obama insisted in Oslo. The US, he said, has the right to "act unilaterally if necessary" and to launch wars whose purpose "extends beyond self-defense or the defense of one nation against an aggressor." Obama's policies, despite the high-blown rhetoric, are as morally bankrupt as those of his predecessor.

> "Gravel's Lament: Fighting Another Dumb War," *TruthDig.com*

Thus Obama's position represents what Stringfellow would label blasphemy. It means using God's name or moral truths to justify the Project of Empire and Death, and it is the only unforgivable sin in scripture.

Of course, human beings, and even presidents, can resist the powers; they can act humanly instead of like automatons or functionaries of their office. It is always possible for human beings to act humanly in the midst

Jeff Dietrich

32. Catholic Workers protest the awarding of the Nobel Prize for Peace to Barack Obama at the Federal Building, downtown Los Angeles. Pictured left to right: John Yevtich, David Omondi, Jeff Dietrich, Catherine Morris, Mike Wisniewski, 2010. Photo by Sam Yergler

of the Fall, but it is rare and improbable for presidents and heads of state to sacrifice their very political survival to do the right thing. We might have hoped that Obama would be better than Bush or Kennedy or Johnson and put an end to the senseless slaughter of unwinnable Asian and Middle East wars, but Stringfellow reminds us that, "the survival of the principalities is the secret purpose of war....Their [America's leaders] servility...depletes them as human beings. They become captivated, dominated, possessed by the demonic" (*An Ethic for Christians and Other Aliens*, p. 93). For Stringfellow, and for the entire opus of scripture, we must look not to our political leaders for salvation—rather we ourselves must resist the powers and "act humanly in the midst of the Fall" (*An Ethic for Christians and Other Aliens*, p. 63).

Osama bin Laden:
The Wicked Witch is Dead

Catholic Agitator, June, 2011, p. 3

Ding-dong, witch is dead. Ding-dong, the wicked witch is dead. That is all I could think of as the pictures of the revelers in Washington and New York came on to the screen. Bin Laden was dead, *ding-dong, the wicked witch was dead,* evil itself had been destroyed, and virtuous America is finally victorious!

However, at what cost have we achieved this victory? It has taken 10 years, two failed wars, the entire apparatus of the CIA, the NSA, and every other intelligence agency in the US and Europe, to say nothing of our so-called ally Pakistan, and a trillion plus dollars to find and eliminate Osama bin Laden. In the meantime, the US treasury has been depleted, 6,037 US military personnel have died, over 100,000 have been wounded, and hundreds of thousands of uncounted civilians have perished in Afghanistan and Iraq. Social programs have been cut to the bone, basic government services diminished; the national debt is accounted in numbers that only astrophysicists can understand; China has balked at buying more of our treasury bonds; and we are about to observe the tenth anniversary of the longest war in US history.

In the process, we have learned that great wealth, military might, and technological sophistication can be humiliated by impoverished men who live in caves, wear rags, fight with World War II assault rifles and improvised explosive devices fabricated out of stolen and surplus munitions, and who fund their operations with the national cash crop: OPIUM, which is purchased largely by impoverished, unemployed US citizens. This is not victory; this is humiliation—and thank God for that, because only out of humiliation will we learn not to do this again.

We fear that the final outcome of Osama bin Laden's demise may be the establishment of torture (which was purportedly used to extract the location of bin Laden's hiding place) and extra-judicial murder, which is the only name we can give to the execution of an unarmed man, as standard policies for our nation.

While we have no great respect for Osama bin Laden, we want to remember one of the great Christian theologians and nonviolent practitioners of our era, Dietrich Bonhoeffer, who understood that we sometimes bow to the realm of "necessity" and use violence to eliminate the practitioners of violence. When Bonhoeffer chose to participate in the plot to assassinate Adolf Hitler, he did so confessionally. When we do these things, we do not celebrate; we do not delude ourselves into thinking that we have killed the "wicked witch," the source of all evil. We do such things reluctantly and confessionally, admitting that we are violating all that the Gospels stand for and all that God asks of us. We do such things in full recognition of our own sinfulness in the participation of a sinful act, knowing full well that the death of the wicked witch is not the ending of evil, but the enabling of evil.

PART 5

RESISTANCE TO EMPIRE

Though an army encamp against me,
  my heart will not fear;
Though war be waged upon me,
  even then will I trust.

Psalm 27:1

Introduction

"Fallen, fallen is Babylon the great. She has become a haunt for demons" (Revelation 18:2). From the fall of the Tower of Babel in Genesis, the first book of scripture, to the fall of Babylon in Revelation, the last book, resistance to empire with its idols of power, military might, technological omnipotence, cultural hubris, disdain for human life, and rapacious consumption of resources, has been the singular subject of scripture. Exodus, the founding myth of the Hebrew people, is the story of a slave revolt against the most powerful empire in ancient times, and it is an account of the only successful slave revolt in history until Haitian slaves freed themselves from French domination in 1804.

After forty years of wilderness wandering, these escaped slaves entered the Promised Land and inaugurated something completely new on this earth. Rather than a nation-state like other nations, these former slaves created an anti-empire, non-hierarchical, tribal confederacy with no king but Yahweh, and made a "covenant with God" that committed themselves to a set of laws which deliberately restricted the consolidation of wealth and power to prevent the formation of oligarchies, insure justice for the least, and give Sabbath rest to humans, animals, and the land itself (Leviticus 25).

Sadly, the halcyon days of the tribal confederacy ended with the consolidation of the Davidic Empire under Solomon.

We must understand the Gospel accounts of the life of Jesus, despite domestication and spiritualization by the theologians of empire, as a re-articulation of the Exodus liberation story. The story begins with a hungry Jesus, ending a forty-day fast that recapitulates the wilderness wanderings of his escaped slave forbearers, shouting the words of the scruffy prophet Isaiah: "Liberty to the captive." It moves quickly through conflicts with local authorities to conflicts with the power elite in Jerusalem. Packed in between these conflicts, Jesus renews and rearticulates the ethical priorities of escaped slaves, who must now create their anti-empire project, no longer in a country of their own, but within the very heart of empire itself. They must be servants, they must reject the illusions of wealth and power, and end the cycle of violence through the practice of forgiveness and loving non-violence. When someone is good at this anti-empire ethic, like Martin Luther King or Mohandas Gandhi, or Monsignor Romero, they get a prophet's reward, the cross, like Jesus himself.

The primary Christian vocation is resistance to empire, but because we have listened to so many co-opted, LIMP-ASS sermons over the centuries, we think that when Jesus said something so straightforward as "render unto Caesar the things that are Caesar's and to God the things that are God's," we think that he meant we were supposed to kill whomever Caesar tells us to kill, pay taxes for nuclear weapons, and then afterwards give a donation to the Church. But in fact, any self-respecting Jew of that time would have known that "there is no king but Yahweh," and to render anything but contempt to the pagan Caesar is both blasphemous and idolatrous.

Throughout scripture, but most especially in the teachings of Jesus, the resistance story is clear. Salvation is found in resisting empire by abandoning the power, privilege, and wealth of empire, and standing in solidarity with the slaves of empire, the Anawim* of the Old Testament, the "little ones" of the Gospels, illegal immigrants, the victims of our imperial wars, and the increasingly criminalized homeless population of our own nation. I take as my mantra the lyrics of my favorite Catholic theologian, singer-songwriter Bruce Springsteen, "no retreat baby, no surrender."

---

*   Another word for the poor.

Divine Intervention

Catholic Agitator, March 2006, p. 1

In 1804, after more than a decade of fierce struggle and ruthless reprisals, the tiny Caribbean colony of Haiti finally freed itself from French rule, becoming the third democracy in modern history, preceded only by France and the United States. In addition, Haiti represents the only successful slave revolt since the Hebrew children escaped from Pharaoh and established the nation of Israel. Yet despite its great achievement, Haiti has been relegated for virtually its entire existence to pariah status by the great Western powers, most especially France, its former colonial master, and the United States, its closest continental neighbor.

It was not until 1862 into the middle of the US Civil War that the States actually recognized the second democracy in the Western Hemisphere. Prior to that time, the southern slave states had considered Haiti a terrorist state because it offered both an example of a successful slave revolt as well as succor to escaped slaves, which of course was anathema to a slave-owning nation like the United States.

In the meantime, in 1825, France demanded 150 million francs in reparations from Haiti for lost property, namely slaves, who had the audacity to free themselves. In an effort to avoid invasion and re-enslavement, Haiti agreed to pay the outrageous sum, which they continued to pay well into the twentieth century.

In 1914, at the behest of US corporations, the United States invaded and occupied Haiti until 1935, training a modern army that served largely to insure that the minority mulatto elite property owners would be protected against the black sons and daughters of former slaves.

Throughout the post-World War II/ Cold War era, the US supported and maintained the ruthless Duvalier family, Papa Doc and Baby Doc, as a bulwark against communist incursion from Castro's nearby Cuba.

But with the Fall of the Berlin Wall and the end of Communism, democracy took off, not only in Eastern Europe, but in Haiti as well. With the 1990 election of the Catholic priest Jean-Bertrand Aristide, Haitians democratically selected their first president in more than a century by an overwhelming majority.

But Aristide was opposed, not only by the United States for his communist leanings, but by the traditional mulatto elites, as well as by immigrant Middle Eastern businessmen. These two elite propertied communities, often at odds with each other, formed an alliance with the CIA and Republican neoconservatives. This alliance, with the help of paid operatives and supposed "rioters" quickly overthrew Aristide six months after his election.

Though Aristide was re-installed towards the end of his term in 1994, he was constitutionally unable to run for another term and forced to accept the election of his friend and cabinet member, René Préval. Préval was the first Haitian president to serve his full term and turned the presidency over to a democratically elected Aristide in 2000.

At that point, Aristide was quickly deposed once again by the elites. Though he was returned to power by the Clinton administration, they extracted promises from him for "structural readjustment," a euphemism that essentially meant the majority of Haitian funds would go towards the repayment of debts to US bonds, leaving nothing for health, education, and government services for the poor majority of Haitians. At that point, Aristide sealed his fate by imposing a tax upon rich property owners, as well as demanding the repayment, with interest, of the onerous French reparations, which he said amounted to $21 billion.

In 2004, the business elites, the CIA, and the French collaborated to depose the democratically-elected president Jean-Bertrand Aristide and forced him onto a plane, flying him to the French held Central African Republic. Though the business and property elite were a major factor in the disposition of power in Haiti, most observers assumed that US foreign policy was driven by the desire to eliminate any independent forces that might align themselves with Cuba's Castro and Venezuela's Hugo Chávez. Thus, Aristide had to be eliminated.

Despite enormous efforts on the part of the business elites and US functionaries to rig the recent February elections to elect a candidate favorable to the US and the world economy, the vast majority of poor people of Haiti once again elected René Préval, in the hope that he would allow their beloved Aristide to return to Haiti. Though it seems impossible for the poor of Haiti to have any hope in the face of the great powers of oppression arrayed against them, Fr. Jean-Juste points out in this issue of the *Agitator* that René Préval was only elected after thousands of stolen ballots, which someone had attempted to burn in the city dump, were doused by a fortuitous rain. These ballots were then miraculously found and turned over to the UN election authorities by "coco rats," the homeless street children of Haiti—an act of grace and God's little ones.

We pray that the poor former slaves of Haiti will continue to be blessed, as were the Israelite slaves of Pharaoh, by such divine intervention in their seemingly endless struggle for liberation.

Casting Out Demons in Iraq

Catholic Agitator, February, 2007, pp. 1 and 2

Saddam Hussein is dead and the last situation in Iraq is worse than the first. Sometimes the world seems so insane that we must turn to scripture to help explain what defies rational description, and the situation in Iraq certainly defies our rational powers.

It is the supposed wise and learned, the leaders of our nation with their penchant for power, who have created this situation in Iraq: of escalating sectarian violence that borders on civil war—3,027 American soldiers dead, over 100,000 Iraqi dead, and the promise of 21,000 more US troops as further cannon fodder. And astonishingly, they have succeeded in portraying an authentic villain, Saddam Hussein in his final days, as a sympathetic victim of kangaroo courts and petty, vengeful executioners. And it's only going to get worse.

In Chapter 12 of the Gospel of Matthew, we find the key to a better understanding of our current situation in Iraq. It is not an understanding that the "wise and learned" who make foreign policy are likely to accept, but it does, nonetheless, lend a certain clarity and illumination to the situation for the rest of us.

Chapter 12 revolves around the issue of casting out demons, and while most commentators reduce this chapter to a conflict between Jesus and the Pharisees and a struggle over religious rules, it is really a struggle about power and the demonic. Whenever issues of demons arise in the Gospels, we all tend to lose our perspective—either dismissing them as irrational superstition or diminishing them as mere personal possession. But Walter Wink says that we should rather "think of 'demons' as the actual spirituality of systems and structures that have betrayed their divine vocations" (*The Powers That Be*, p. 27). In Chapter 12, the Pharisees, already portrayed as "false shepherds," are now presented as demonic leaders, acolytes of Satan who have betrayed their divine vocation.

The central conflict of this chapter takes place in verses 12-32, in which Jesus cures a deaf, blind demoniac, and, upon receiving positive crowd affirmation, prompts the Pharisees to do what beleaguered leadership always does: demonize the opposition! Not unlike Martin Luther King and Msg. Oscar Romero, Jesus is accused of "casting out demons by the power of demons," which is the first-century equivalent to labeling someone "communist" or "terrorist." The blind, deaf demoniac in the story is, of course, emblematic of the way in which the entire population has been rendered blind and mute by a demonic system. We see that kind of blindness and silence today in our own population, unable to see the death we are causing in Iraq and unwilling to speak out against it.

The exorcism that Jesus performs is analogous to the way in which African Americans, in the presence of the "spirit-filled" Martin Luther King, were able to clearly see their bondage to Jim Crow, and were empowered to speak out against it. Such spirit-filled leaders are dangerous to the demonic status quo.

Jesus responds to the Pharisees' accusations with brilliant logic. "No town or house divided against itself will stand" (Matthew 12:25). You can't cast out Satan with the power of Satan.

Indeed Jesus has already rejected the power of Satan in the "Temptations in the Wilderness" (Matthew 4:1-11). The Temptations of Jesus are recapitulations of the three Temptations of the Hebrew people during their exodus from Egypt.

For the Hebrew people, the primordial temptation is always to "return to Egypt" by emulating the ways of empire, which is to say, the ways of Satan, who owns the kingdoms of the world (Matthew 4:8). The power of Satan, who is sometimes called the *strong man* by Jesus (Matthew 12:29), is the power of violence and death in the service of empire. But God saved the Hebrew people so that they could live a life that is an alternative to the ways of the *strong man*, an alternative to the ways of the world, to the ways of power, a life of non-violence and community. This is God's alternative vision for the Hebrew people, and for ourselves as well.

Jesus' first Temptation, to turn stones into bread, refers to the Manna story. Jesus' response to the devil's request, "One does not live by bread alone, but by every word that comes forth from the mouth of God" (Matthew 4:4), does not disparage hunger, but refers to the specific instructions the Hebrews are to follow regarding manna:

Jeff Dietrich

> So gather it that everyone has enough to eat, an omer for each person, as many of you as there are, each man providing for those of his own tent....Some gathered a large amount and some a small amount. But when they measured it out by the omer, he who had gathered a large amount did not have too much and he who had gathered a small amount did not have too little. They so gathered that everyone had enough to eat. Moses also told them, "Let no one keep any of it over until tomorrow morning."

Exodus 16:16-19

While the devil would have Jesus practice an economics of miraculously manifesting bread out of stones, Jesus would have people practice the "manna economics" of non-hoarding, sharing the gift of God's resources so that everyone would have enough to eat.

In the next Temptation, the devil challenges Jesus to prove that he is the Son of God by taking a nosedive off the Temple in Jerusalem. Just as the first Temptation relates to economic power, this Temptation relates to the power of religion to make converts and disciples through miraculous spectacles that give tangible proof of divine authority. Jesus' response to the devil's request for proof of his divinity, "You shall not put the Lord, your God, to the test," also comes from Deuteronomy (6:16); it refers to the Hebrew people putting God to the test with their demand for water at Massah (Exodus 17). It is not simply that Jesus refuses to test God's commitment to him—it is also that he refuses to give the kind of power sign that the devil and most all of us desire before we give our allegiance to God's project. By inference, this passage is a rejection of the entire temple establishment and the personnel who ultimately conspire with the Pharisees and with Rome to execute Jesus.

In the final Temptation, the devil leads Jesus to a high hill and shows Jesus all the Kingdoms of the world. "These I shall give to you, if you will prostrate yourself and worship me" (Matthew 4:9). The Temptation is a reference to the episode of the Golden Calf in Exodus 24, which is a reminder that Satan owns all of the kingdoms of the world. When Jesus says to the devil, "'Get away, Satan!' It is written: 'the Lord, your God, shall you worship and him alone shall you serve'" (Matthew 4:10) it is not merely a rejection of the "false religion" of idolatry, but it is a rejection of the awesome power of empire itself, with its military, political, and legal might all under Satan's rule. In the final analysis, Satan owns all of the "effective tools of worldly power," and to use those tools of empire to cast out demons is futile, because it only strengthens "the strongman's house."

Meanwhile, Jesus had already cast out a blind and mute demon (Matthew 12:22), but the Pharisees again ask him for a sign. What they want is something miraculous, like stones turned to bread or a freefall from a cathedral bell tower. Later they will say, "If you are the Son of God, come down from the cross" (Matthew 27:40). Jesus tells them that the only sign that will be given them is the sign of Jonah. While most commentators understand this as a reference to the Resurrection, for Jesus it is actually a reference to his own imminent Crucifixion.

We all want the signs of power. We want the effectiveness of empire, with its military, religious, or economic might. But, it is Jesus' rejection of the efficacious power of Satan that is the key that allows him to "bind the strongman and break into his house." Scripture asks us to understand that Jesus has a counter-intuitive approach—it is one of non-power. His singular power is the power of the cross. In both the Temptations and the Crucifixion, Jesus is telling us that we cannot defeat power with power. We cannot cast out Satan by the power of Satan. Ultimately, power is an addiction; it is the desire to be God.

Even though the core of Chapter 12 revolves around demons and casting out demons, Jesus understood, as did Dr. King, that these are only symptoms of the real problem. The real problem is injustice, and that is why the chapter opens with two conflicts with the Pharisees about the Sabbath.

The first conflict occurs when Jesus and the disciples walk through a grain field on the Sabbath and pick a few heads of grain to eat; the other deals with curing a man with a withered hand on the Sabbath. Typically, we understand these confrontations to be about the parsimonious and the overly scrupulous practices of the Pharisees in conflict with the mercy and humanity of Jesus, and it does mean that. But the passage goes deeper as well.

For the Pharisees, the Sabbath encompasses a set of prohibitions and strict regulations. But for Jesus, the Sabbath is the core of the tradition that distinguishes the Hebrew people from the other nations as a people of justice. It is, of course, first mentioned in Genesis, but its real roots are in the anti-slavery story of Exodus. Sabbath is a reflection of the original abundance of pre-empire creation, in which every seven days all people can rest in the abundance of creation, every seven years all debts are forgiven, and during the fiftieth "Jubilee" year, all land must be returned to the original owner (Leviticus 25:1-31). Its intent was to prevent the accumulation of wealth in the hands of a few, and to diminish the centralization of power, thus insuring justice. It is the opposite of the ways of empire, the ways of the *strong man*.

For Jesus, the Sabbath should insure the human right to eat (as with the disciples in the grain field) and the right to work (as with the man with the withered hand, handicapped and unable to provide for himself). And in claiming authority over the Sabbath, Jesus seeks to undermine the false authority of the Pharisees and establish God's kingdom of justice and compassion that is rooted in the Sabbath Jubilee Laws of Leviticus.

But ultimately, Jesus realizes that casting out demons and healing people is not the real issue. The real issue is: how did people get sick and demon possessed in the first place? This sickness, this "disease," arises when Sabbath is not observed as the practice of justice but as the practice of law. It is the primary lesson of the "Temptations in the Wilderness"; it is the primary lesson that the Hebrew people learned in their forty years of wandering in the wilderness. *Stop Hoarding. Don't take too much. Share with those who don't have enough—then people won't get so sick or demon-possessed; then people won't be so screwed up.* While it might be a bit of an over-simplification, the entire Jesus project could be summed up in the words of Catholic Worker co-founder Peter Maurin, who "stressed the need of building a new society within the shell of the old...'a society in which it is easier for people to be good'" (quoted in Day, *The Long Loneliness*, p. 170).

For Jesus, the core mission is to "enter the strong man's house and steal his property" (Matthew 12:29), liberate the captives of Satan, and steal his false authority without using the power tools of empire. He realized that we cannot cast out Satan through the miracle of globalization, or through the military and judicial apparatus of the kingdoms of the world; we cannot cast out the demons of drug addiction and homelessness on Skid Row through the punitive power of police and jails; we cannot build a better, safer world with warfare and executions.

In summation, Jesus tells us the story of casting out a demon and sweeping the house clean, but the demon goes out to the dry places and finds seven more demons and returns to occupy the house. This bizarre story is, of course, a thinly veiled reference to the violent casting out of the Roman occupiers by Israel's insurgent forces in 66 AD. In response, Rome subsequently returned to Jerusalem in 70 AD with seven times the military force to lay waste to the city. They crucified all male revolutionaries, enslaved their women and children, and banished all Jews from Palestine. This was the catalyst for the creation of Jewish diaspora, confirming that indeed "the last condition...is worse than the first" (Matthew 12:45).

34. Artist unknown, *Catholic Agitator*, 1991

Jeff Dietrich

What could better describe the situation in Iraq than this phrase from Matthew? We went into Iraq to exorcise the demons of Saddam Hussein and weapons of mass destruction. And while we never found weapons of mass destruction, we did find and execute the demonic Saddam Hussein. We have killed the demon, but we did not bind the *strong man*, because we emulate the ways of empire rather than God's alternative ways of Sabbath, Jubilee justice and compassion. And now the "last condition...is worse than the first" (Matthew 12:45).

Defeating Empire with an
Army of Dog Lappers

Catholic Agitator, February, 2009, pp. 1, 2, and 6

In the wake of the ruthless Israeli invasion of Gaza it might be helpful to review certain passages of the Hebrew Bible regarding warfare. While it is easy enough to read the scriptures as an affirmation of unrestrained warfare in the name of righteousness and entitlement, many of the stories reflect an ambiguous, if not altogether satirical, attitude toward the entire military project. David and Goliath is of course the most familiar, while the fall of Jericho may be the most edifying. Both are stories that subvert the very nature of the military project itself and lead us to a sense of ambiguity, if not outright repudiation, of military warfare. But the most subversive and outrageously humorous of all is the story of Gideon and the Midianites (Judges 6-7).

"Thus was Israel reduced to misery by Midian and so the Israelites cried out to the Lord. And the Lord sent them a prophet." The opening words of the Gideon story are meant to recall the Exodus experience of the Hebrews, in which the oppressed Israelite slaves in Egypt cried out to the Lord, and the Lord sent them a great prophet, Moses. It is a reminder to the reader that the liberation story of escaped slaves from Egypt is the very heart of the Hebrew experience, and that the God of Israel is a God of liberation, and further, that this new prophet Gideon is similar to the original prophetic prototype, Moses.

At the time of this particular story, however, the Israelites have already been residing in the "promised land" for several generations. But they have once again come under the domination of Egypt through the efforts of the Midianites, a powerful vassal client of the Egyptian empire.

When we first meet Gideon, he is "beating out wheat in the wine press." Why? As one does not beat wheat in the wine press but on the threshing room floor! This is because Gideon is hiding his crop from the Midianites, who are the tax collectors for their Egyptian overlords; in other words, Gideon is practicing an ancient form of tax resistance.

In a scene recalling the story of Abraham, an angel of the Lord appears to Gideon, telling him to tear down the altar of Baal. Of course we all know that the Old Testament God had a thing about idolatry. But that is not because God was mindlessly jealous of all those other gods or that all those other gods are phony posers without the real god-stuff. No, God hates idolatry because the real God, the God of the Hebrew people, is on the side of liberation. And idolatry represents the religion of Egypt and the surrounding nation states, who worship gods that sacralize the status quo of kings and princes and stratified hierarchy.

The altar of Baal is not just the worship site of some bogus god; it is the Internal Revenue Service for the Egyptian overlords. As theologian Anthony Ceresko writes, "The [idolatry] cult served as the occasion, religiously justified, for the transfer of large quantities of goods from the producers to the ruling elites" (*Introduction to the Old Testament*, p. 118). The sacred altar is the place where the people must bring their "tax-tribute" to the Midianites, who will then take out their portion and send the rest to the Egyptian Pharaoh. To worship at the altar of Baal is to pay taxes to the Pharaoh, and to pay tribute to the Pharaoh is to be enslaved to Egypt once again. But Yahweh supports the alternative Liberation Project of the escaped Hebrew slaves. Rabbi Michael Lerner, in an interview with Arnie Cooper, says:

> By the time the Jews came along, the world was already class stratified. A few people had great power, and most had very little. The wealthy and powerful elite traditionally maintain power through force and by convincing people that nothing can be done to change things.
>
> The Jews arrived on the scene with an ideology and a Torah that said the world can be fundamentally changed. We knew that anyone who said that hierarchical oppression is built into the structure of the universe was lying, because we'd been slaves and now we were free. It was a revolutionary message.
>
> "Resurrecting the Revolutionary Heart," *The Sun*

At the time of Gideon, this revolutionary project was in full swing, so to speak. Founded by escaped slaves, it dedicated itself to the creation of an alternative way of life that was the very antithesis of Egypt and Babylon. It received its constitution at Sinai and formalized it in the Torah. At the time of Gideon, it existed as a confederacy of tribes with no king but Yahweh, with an economic system based upon Sabbath sharing, and with no centralized cultic site. The Midianites, working for Egypt, presented a formidable threat to this fragile freedom.

So Gideon, after considerable quibbling says, "Lord, my family is the meanest in Manasseh, and I am the most insignificant in my father's house" (Judges 6:15). He then desacralizes the pagan Midianite sacred site by sacrificing a "seven-year-old spare bullock" (Judges 6:25). Not wanting to get caught, he does the dirty deed under cover of darkness.

Nonetheless he got busted anyway and the nervous townsfolk, fearing retribution, demanded his death. But, in a delightfully funny scene, Gideon's quick thinking father Joash refuses to turn him over: "If he whose altar has been destroyed is a god, let that god act for himself. So on that day Gideon was called Jerubbaal, because of the words 'Let Baal take action against him, since he destroyed his altar'" (Judges 6:31-2).

Gideon's inflammatory act of civil disobedience enraged the Midianites, who immediately mobilized against the Israelites to take revenge and collect their tribute. Jerubbaal/Gideon gathered his allies to do battle. But in an extraordinary reversal of usual military wisdom, the Lord tells Gideon, "You have too many soldiers with you for me to deliver the Midianites into their power....Now proclaim to all the soldiers 'If anyone is afraid, or fearful, let him leave'" (Judges 7:2-3).

With that outrageous announcement, 22,000 soldiers left. Can you imagine any military commander willingly relinquishing over two thirds of his fighting men? What insanity! But the insanity goes even further when the Lord tells Gideon that the fighting force is still too large, so a further test is necessary: "Lead them down to the water and I will test them for you there" (Judges 7:4). "You shall set to one side everyone who laps up the water as a dog does with its tongue" (Judges 7:5). The so-called "dog lappers" numbered only 300; Gideon is instructed to send the others home, and God says, "By means of the three hundred who lapped up the water I will save you and will deliver Midian into your power" (Judges 7:7). So Gideon had to release the other 10,000 soldiers.

Of course, the Midianites were "as numerous as locusts...their camels... were as many as the sands on the seashore" (Judges 7:12) and Gideon was afraid. So, the Lord sent Gideon under cover of darkness to spy upon the Midianites promising to give him the courage to descend upon the camp.

Upon entering the camp, he overhears a guard recounting a strange dream:

> "I had a dream," he said, "that a round loaf of barley bread was rolling into the camp of Midian. It came to our tent and struck it, and as it fell it turned the tent upside down." "This can only be the sword of the Israelite Gideon..." the other replied. "God has delivered Midian and all the camp into his power."

Judges 7:13-14

The passage comically portrays a giant wheel of a barley loaf rolling down the hill upending the tents of empire. Emboldened by this revelation, Gideon rushes back, rallies his "dog lappers," divides them into three companies, "and provide[s] them all with horns and with empty jars and torches inside the jars" (Judges 7:16). Armed with these absurd weapons, this little army descends upon the camp in darkness blowing their horns, lifting their torches, and crashing their jars, creating such noise and confusion that the Midianites begin to fight each other and flee in panic.

Like the story of David and Goliath, in which a twelve-year-old boy defeats the pride of the Philistine army with a mere sling shot, and the story of Jericho in which the mighty city walls tumble down at the sound of a trumpet call, the story of Gideon ridicules the entire military project. God does this not because of his blind affection for the Hebrew people, but because he is repulsed by the injustice of empire with its vast armies and sophisticated weaponry necessary for the maintenance of its primary activities: slavery, oppression, and surplus wealth extraction.

While the dream of the barley loaf and the defeat of the Midianites is intended to be comical and satirical, the image of the barley loaf turning the Midian world upside down actually presents an authentic image of the Hebrew Liberation Project, a world in which the most inept and incapable people, "dog lappers" armed with conviction and low-tech weapons, are actually able to defeat the world's most sophisticated army.

And the barley bread? Well, barley bread is the bread of the poor—and in this story, it represents a vision of a world liberated from the domination system of Egypt and all empires, a world in which there is a surplus of bread, enough to feed all of the poor people of the world, because the oppressive domination system of empire no longer steals the major portion off the top.

Yet even a cursory reading would seem to indicate that God takes a stand with those who wield sling shots against tanks and F-16s—that the God of Sinai confuses and overcomes those that steal the harvests of the

35. Anti-nuclear weapons protest at the Seal Beach Naval Weapons Station in Seal Beach, CA. Pictured left to right: Carol Holben, Rick Erhard, Larry Holben, Jeff Dietrich, Kent Hoffman, Debbie Garvey, Carol Kinnely, May, 1979. Photo by Don Milici

lowly, that God overturns the tents of empire with visions of justice and abundance and great wheels of barley bread. As theologian Anthony Ceresko writes:

> Israel's God was a liberating God, one who was "revealed" in the midst of a struggle for liberation and in the efforts of a people to build a more just and peaceful human community. Perhaps it is in the midst of these same kinds of struggles and efforts taking place through our contemporary world, and in solidarity with those engaged in them, that we can most adequately and authentically discover the God of Israel's scriptures today.
>
> *Introduction to the Old Testament,* pp. 118-119

How much longer can it be before the great armies of modern Israel, supported by the sophisticated weaponry of American empire, are indicted by their own stories? How much longer before it becomes clear to the world that, despite its history of suffering and victimization, the contemporary "dog lappers" are not Israeli soldiers in sophisticated American tanks and F-16s, but they are rather the hungry Palestinian "terrorists" with homemade rocket launchers protecting their last vestige of dignity, humanity, and homeland.

Torture: Exposing the Lie

Catholic Agitator, June, 2004, pp. 1 and 2

The methods and mentality of the American empire are quickly coming home to roost. In the past, it often took centuries to expose the bogus, high-minded moralisms that national leaders consistently fabricate to justify going to war. But today, one of the unintended by-products of a voracious mass media is the tendency towards instantaneous historical revisionism. In the past month, we have watched, awe-struck, as the premises for war in Iraq conveyed by President George W. Bush just one year ago have evaporated like last year's campaign promises.

We were told that Saddam Hussein had weapons of mass destruction, that he had connections with terrorists, that Iraq's people would welcome us as liberators, that a newly democratic Iraq would stabilize the Middle East and make the US safer from terrorist attacks. Now, one year later, under the scrutiny of mass media, it has become clear that there were no weapons of mass destruction or links to terrorism, and far from welcoming us as liberators, Iraqi insurgents are trying to throw us out. And most incredible of all, the man who fed us the false intelligence upon which these high moral lies were based, Ahmed Chalabi, the former darling of the Bush administration and the "voice of Iraqi freedom in exile," has been arrested and exposed as a criminal and a fraud.

The final unraveling of America's moral posturing, of course, has come in the form of hundreds of photographs of Iraqi torture victims in Abu Ghraib prison. Though the Bush administration is attempting to blame the wrongdoing on a few low-ranking military personnel, it seems clear that the responsibility goes right up the chain of command to the office of the Secretary of Defense, who authorized the use of torture in interrogating "terrorist suspects." The problem, of course, is that everyone arrested in Iraq is apparently a terrorist suspect. Nevertheless, in terms of public relations, it matters little whether it was 6 people or 600 people involved in the torture—the damage to American esteem is immeasurable and will reverberate into the next generation.

In the meantime, one can hardly imagine a more powerful set of terrorist recruiting posters than the Abu Ghraib photos. Not only do the photos confirm the worst, the very worst stereotype of conquering armies, but they affirm the absolute worst images that Arabs have of Western moral degeneracy.

What started off as a "broader strategy" for the war on terrorism has begun to ominously emerge as a broad war between the US and the entire Arab world—a religious war between Christians and Muslims. And that is definitely not a winnable situation, but it is exactly what Osama bin Laden and his fellow terrorists desired as the outcome of 9/11. Truly the American chickens have come home to roost. And we must ask ourselves in the wake of the absolute failure of this American unilateral strategy of thuggery and brutality—do we feel safer today than we did on September 11, 2001?

If anyone ever believed that the true American intention was to bring democracy to Iraq, they must surely by now see through these naïve pretensions. A Jordanian businessman quoted in *Time Magazine* perhaps sums up the general impression of American intentions in the region: "'Liberate Iraq? Rubbish,' he said. 'You occupy Iraq for the strategic and economic benefits. You are building the largest embassy in the world in Baghdad. Halliburton and Bechtel are running everything, at enormous profits'" (Klein, "The Perils of a Righteous President," p. 25). Bush claims to bring democracy and freedom to the barbarians, but who are the barbarians?

In his book, *Jihad vs. McWorld*, Benjamin Barber cites numerous scholars who suggest that Arab democracy along Western terms is wishful thinking. But he also goes on to say that the conflict is not between democracy and Islam, but between Islam and Western modernity. "Modernity," he writes, "is tantamount to secularism, and is almost by definition corrupting to all religions" (p. 210). Americans tend to think of democracy as a singular and positive good, and while it may be a profound improvement over the Taliban or Saddam Hussein, Muslim people are deeply aware that Western democracy is not a discrete entity.

Along with it comes a whole set of unwholesome Western values that many in the Arab world find repugnant. Barber quotes Hasan al-Banna, founder of the Arab Brotherhood, who said they had been, "importing 'their half-naked women into these regions, together with their liquors, their theaters, their dance halls, their amusements, their stories, their newspapers, their novels, their whims, their silly games, and their vices'" (quoted in *Jihad vs. McWorld*, p. 210). Though al-Banna's critique was written in the 1920s, it still finds strong resonance among fundamentalist Muslims who, not without some justification, perceive the West as degenerate, corrupting interlopers, and deserving objects of Holy War.

The model for this war has always been World War II, the "good war," with George W. Bush casting himself as a latter-day Winston Churchill, filled with solitary resolve in his efforts to preserve democracy and cast out the demonic enemy. While many historians might characterize this self-portrait as a bit pretentious, the deeper issue is actually whether or not there has ever been a "good war."

In spite of mainstream America's positive perception of the war, Dorothy Day believed that the fire bombings of Tokyo and Dresden and the atomic bombing of Hiroshima and Nagasaki proved that Hitler and the demonic Nazi spirit of "ends over means" were the actual victors of World War II.

Day's insight about World War II finds its foundation in Chapter 3 of the Gospel of Mark, where Jesus poses the rhetorical question: "How can Satan drive out Satan?" According to theologian Walter Wink, Satan is not simply personified in some tangible being like Hitler or Saddam Hussein who can be killed or otherwise eliminated, but rather "'Satan' is the world-encompassing spirit of the Domination System" (*The Powers That Be*, p. 27).

By Wink's account, the Domination System has been around "since the rise of the great conquest states of Mesopotamia around 3000 BCE. As warfare became the central preoccupation of states, taxation became necessary in order to support a standing army, a warrior caste, and an aristocracy" (*The Powers That Be*, p. 40). Its foundational story, says Wink, is the "Myth of Redemptive Violence" which "enshrines the belief that violence saves, that war brings peace, that might makes right. It is one of the oldest continuously repeated stories in the world" (p. 42).

The "Myth of Redemptive Violence" is the inner spirituality of militarism and the national security state:

> Not only does the myth establish a patriotic religion at the heart of the state, it gives divine sanction to the nation's imperialism. And the name of God—any god, the Christian God included—can be invoked as having specifically blessed the supremacy of the chosen nation and its ruling caste.
>
> *The Powers That Be*, pp. 56-57

36. Arlington West, Santa Monica Pier North side. Each Sunday Veterans for Peace create a symbolic military cemetery with one white cross representing each US Soldier killed in Iraq and Afghanistan. There are 6,132 crosses pictured, 2008. Photo by Mike Wisniewski

A *Los Angeles Times* article about Marine chaplain Scott Radetski, serving with troops just outside of Fallujah, illustrates Wink's point: "In their own way," Radetski writes,

> the Marines were following the same path as Jesus en route to Jerusalem. He too entered a city where some greeted him as a savior but others were plotting to kill him. He knew the risk but he went without fear because he knew his mission was just. Marines face a similar test....And God will be with them every step of the way.

quoted in Perry, "Chaplain's Iraq Flock"

While it is true that Jesus entered cities where some were plotting to kill him, he specifically did not enter with tanks and machine guns. The whole point of the Gospel lies in Jesus' effort to cast out the demonic power of Satan's myth of redemptive violence without resorting to the tools of redemptive violence. We cannot cast out Satan by the power of Satan. As Jesus said, "A house divided cannot stand," and Satan's house remains intact. When we use the tools of Satan to cast out Satan or Hitler or the Taliban, we actually empower Satan. The trick or "trap" that Jesus advocated was to "break into the strong man's [Satan's] house and "bind," or dis-empower him and "plunder his property" (Mark 3:27). The *strong man's* "property" that Jesus plunders is the divine legitimation of the myth of salvation through redemptive violence. In its place, Jesus offers us his own example of salvation through "redemptive suffering."

Just as the Crucifixion of the nonviolent Son of God exposed the authorities of Jesus' day as brutal, self-serving thugs without divine legitimacy, so do the pictures of humiliated and beaten prisoners of Abu Ghraib reveal the authorities of our own nation to be, not saviors spreading democracy and freedom in the name of God, but brutal thugs of the American empire whose high-minded moralisms for war are mere cover-ups for the baser motivations of wealth, oil, and world domination.

Critiquing the Imperial Papacy

Catholic Agitator, May, 2005, pp. 1 and 2

It's bigger than the Super Bowl, bigger than the war in Iraq, bigger than the election of a mere American president, bigger than tsunamis in Indonesia or earthquakes in Turkey. It is a spectacle of unparalleled proportions. The death of a pope is the biggest show on earth.

Ordinarily I feel quite at home in the Catholic Church. Well, at least I feel uncomfortably at home in the Catholic Church. But there are times like these—the death of a pope or the building of a new cathedral—that my discomfort level is significantly increased. It must be something akin to the level of discomfort felt by populist Britons at the coronation of a new monarch, causing a reexamination of the entire complex of antiquated, vestigial structures that remain attached to the body politic like the superfluous appendix remains attached to the human body for no apparent reason. Well, it's not quite like that, because the Papacy is hardly vestigial or superfluous to the functioning of the institutional Church.

Anyone who has taken a Western civics course is familiar with Lord Acton's aphorism: "Power corrupts and absolute power corrupts absolutely" (Dalberg-Acton, "Letter to Bishop Mandell Creighton," in *Essays on Freedom and Power*, p. 364). Some might even remember that the author was a British aristocrat. And like myself, they probably assume that Lord Acton was referring to some despotic British monarch. But they no doubt would be as surprised as I was to find out that Lord Acton was referring to the Pope—Pope Pius IX, to be exact—when he had declared himself infallible in Faith and Morals at the First Vatican Council in 1870.

In an effort to shore up waning Church authority in the face of nineteenth century attacks by science, rationalism, and democratic populism, Pius IX convened the First Vatican Council, which confirmed his infallibility and rejected almost 2,000 years of Episcopal equality and collegiality, and officially removed the supreme power of the Church from the council of Bishops and relocated it in the person of the Pope himself. Theologian Hans Küng, among others, recognizes this event as the final triumph in a lengthy historical quest for absolute Papal authority that began, at least, with the advent of the Emperor Constantine. "The Roman system...had finally and at long last found its cornerstone" says Küng in his book *The Catholic Church: A Short History* (p. 167).

I suppose that, in some ways, it is idealistic in the extreme to seek a return to a pre-Constantine church, but it is nevertheless important to reexamine the tragic turn that the Christian church took as it moved from the humble house church of the crucified Christ to the Church of empire under Constantine. As Walter Wink writes:

> Once Christianity became the religion of the empire, its success was linked to the success of the empire, and preservation of the empire became the decisive criterion for ethical behavior. Its accommodation to power politics through the infinitely malleable ideology of the just war, its abandonment of the...social theory of atonement for the blood theory, its projection of the reign of God into an afterlife or the remote future—all of this gutted the Church's message of its most radical elements. Jesus was divinized, the Mass became a perpetual sacrifice, rather than an end of all need for sacrifice, and Jews were scapegoated for the death of Jesus.

Engaging the Powers, p. 150

It is the scapegoating of the Jews, according to author and historian James Carroll in his magisterial book, *Constantine's Sword*, that forms the dark side of Christianity. While Carroll locates the roots of Christian anti-Semitism in the Early Church, and to some extent in the Gospels themselves, these were relatively benign elements until the formation of the imperial Papacy and the solidification of Church dogma, which under Constantine invested the Church with state power.

It was Constantine himself who called for and presided over the Council of Nicaea in 325 AD, the first-ever gathering of all bishops in an ecumenical council. Constantine literally imprisoned the bishops in a royal palace until they all agreed upon a unified set of principles, which later became known as the Nicene Creed. This creed laid the cornerstone of Church dogma and gave the murderous Roman Empire unwarranted spiritual authority.

It also set in place the historic mode of a legalistic, demagogic Church, which persecuted and executed pagan, Christian, and Jewish deviants from the Creed, giving rise to the horrors of the Spanish Inquisition and ultimately to the holocaust itself. In the Roman Church of empire, a heretic was quite literally a traitor.

The paradox and ambiguity of the scriptures, which in the Jewish tradition has inspired centuries of eloquent debate and dialogue, was, over time, crammed into a narrow Roman system of legality and morality that privileged orthodoxy over orthopraxy—right thinking over right action.

Jaques Ellul, the French theologian and dark visionary of our technological civilization, writes that "A moralistic attitude is essentially a masculine trait" (*The Subversion of Christianity*, p. 90). It is an attitude of judgment, of stiffness, of rigidity, of calculation of debits and assets, of classification, of designation, of the establishment of what should and should not be done.

It necessarily led to the suppression of the feminine in the entire corpus of scripture, but most especially as it is manifested in the Gospels. "Neutralizing women," Ellul writes, "was more essential precisely because the revelation of God in Jesus Christ, as it is given throughout the Bible, assigns to women...all the values of life (and not of social well-being)" (*The Subversion of Christianity*, p. 93). Thus, the Imperial Church is, and continues to be, a patriarchal, hierarchical Church. And Christian art under Constantine, according to Justo González,

> now became triumphal art, progressively centered on Christ as Lord of heaven and earth. Liturgy, which had remained relatively simple, now began to take up the uses of the Imperial court. For a parallelism was established between Christ and the Emperor. And architecture now undertook the construction of churches capable and worthy of the new liturgical developments.

A History of Christian Thought, p. 269

Like all imperial entities it was necessary for the Church to focus on the visual: art, architecture, and liturgy. While I am well aware of the momentous contributions that the Church has made to the artistic heritage of Western culture, it is important to hold that contribution in tension with the essential Biblical wisdom that forbade the Hebrew people from worshiping graven images or from making a visual representation of God or, even, of a human person. Taken in concert with the prophetic and the gospel critiques of temple liturgy, it is a formulation of the ancient Biblical recognition that the visual arts, whether manifested through the pyramids in Egypt or the Parthenon in Athens or the ziggurats in Babylon or the Colosseum in Rome, were idolatrous images that provided incarnate visual legitimation to the divine power of the oppressive and enslaving state authority.

Rich and powerful people pay for art that reinforces the status quo of the dominant power paradigm—starving artist not withstanding—and that is the essential Biblical wisdom.

"The Church," as Ellul writes in the *The Humiliation of the Word*, "allowed itself to be invaded by images. It wanted to become visible, establishing itself on the foundation of visible evidence. This developed alongside the theology of the Church's power and lust for power, which became incarnate in the institution" (p. 183).

It is this artful element of spectacle that has kept the contemporary media so focused on the Vatican—the drama and the ritual, the images of Michelangelo and the Sistine chapel, the red-robed Cardinals, the pageantry of the Mass, the processions, and the paintings of da Vinci.

And it is that same element of imperial spectacle that created the perfect stage for John Paul II, the former drama student, who with his charismatic flair and world-traveling pageantry, was able to focus world attention on the Church. John Paul II was able to use the power of his popular media-embracing personality to reinvigorate the centralized Papacy and frustrate the egalitarian reforms of the Second Vatican Council. Catholic theologian Hans Küng writes:

> He is a man with charisma…with an impressive gift for publicity…he has become a media superstar, and for many people in the Catholic Church…a kind of living cult figure. But…his course of conservatism and restoration is so clearly recognizable that in every respect he had to be be courteously but unambiguously criticized.

The Catholic Church, pp. 190-191

The unprecedented reforms of the Second Vatican Council (1958-1965) were an attempt by the Church to dismantle some of the increasing centralization of the Papacy and its administrative arm, the Curia, that had been solidified by the reactionary Pope Pius IX in 1870, and return the Church to its original populist mode of "collegiality" in which power resided not in the centralized authority of an infallible pope, but in the hands of the local bishops.

Though the Church has for centuries been one of the most centralized organizations in history, the vast distances under its watchful eye insured a

37. Guest at the Hospitality House Kitchen, 2011. Photo by Robert Radin

certain amount of autonomy to the local churches. It is only with the advent of modern technology that the Vatican has been able to utilize its centralized authority to control the actual day-to-day operations of far-flung local churches in much the same manner as a modern CEO.

Küng writes, "Meanwhile...[under John Paul] Roman legalism, clericalism, and triumphalism, which was so vigorously criticized by the bishops at the council—cosmetically rejuvenated and in modern dress—has come back with a vengeance" (*The Catholic Church*, p. 193).

John Paul, through his personal charisma and personal charm, has done more than any other pope to dash the hopes of reform that could have achieved much to move the Church from the sins of Constantinian imperial Papacy towards a more popularly-based collegial Church. My own sentiments are best summed up in the spirit of Catholic priest and theologian Richard Rohr, who writes,

> My disappointment in the present pope [John Paul II] is that he has said and written many fine and courageous things that will stand the test of time...but it is quite clear that he does not appoint cardinals or bishops or call forth a church culture that does much of the same.... We have become more and more an exclusionary institution....Our present list of necessary "purity codes" has little gospel support and does not speak to mature people.
>
> "Beyond 'Certitudes and Orders'," *Sojourners Magazine*, p. 19

You might rightly ask, why bother to remain in a Church where it doesn't look like things are going to get much better, especially with the election of our new pope? Why bother to remain in a Church that will probably continue down the road of the triumphalistic Constantinian Papacy, that continues to denigrate women, persecute free-thinking theologians, and reduce the Gospels to moralistic purity codes?

Well, I remain because it is still, paradoxically, the Church of Philip Berrigan, César Chávez, Dorothy Day, Archbishop Romero, Mother Teresa, and a whole cloud of heroes and saints who continue to inspire me. I remain because of the Mass. I remain because of the Eucharist. I remain because, despite its sinfulness and brokenness and perversions, it is where I first heard the Gospels. I remain because it is still, as Dorothy once said, the Church of the poor. I remain because we have been "commissioned" to be the tiny mustard seed of gospel "orthopraxy" stuffed down the dark, lifeless soil of an imperial Church that will, in God's good time, rend the stony monument of imperial pride. I remain because it is my home and my family.

PART SIX

TECHNOLOGY AND ALIENATION

Everything has either a price or a dignity...whatever is above all price, and therefore admits of no equivalent, has a dignity. But that which constitutes the condition under which something alone can be an end in itself does not have mere relative worth, i.e., price, but an intrinsic worth, i.e., a dignity.

Immanuel Kant,
Groundwork of the Metaphysics of Morals (1785)

It is one thing to show a man that he is in error, another to put him in possession of the truth.

John Locke,
An Essay Concerning Human Understanding (1690)

Not by the Power of Demons

Catholic Agitator, October, 1989, pp. 1 and 2

No doubt Woody Allen could make a pretty good joke about anyone living in Los Angeles with enough temerity or naïveté to speak seriously about the environmental crisis. It might go something like this: "How many environmentalists does it take to clean up Los Angeles?" The answer is "Twenty—one to talk about it, and nineteen others to take out the garbage."

Of course, it's not funny that we live in the midst of an ecological cesspool. The concrete and steel, the noxious fumes and ubiquitous garbage, the reality of our lives seems so implacable and unremitting that it is laughable to even make a serious proposal to change it. Indeed, even those who speak most eloquently on the subject of ecology rarely go beyond proposals for fine-tuning the system so that it becomes less of a burden on the environment: non-polluting automobiles, more efficient mass transit, clean energy programs and better filtration systems to purify our water.

There are very few articulate critics of our system of mass production and over-consumption who are able to criticize the basic premise of the system, partially because we are all so caught up in it that it is impossible to extricate ourselves enough to even see it clearly, much less criticize it. But it is also true that if one speaks that harsh truth too loudly, saying that the entire system is evil and unredeemable, one will be dismissed as a naysayer, thus losing effectiveness. But a prophet must speak the truth, regardless of its effectiveness.

Catholic Worker co-founder Peter Maurin, with his roots in the French peasant experience and the Catholic monastic tradition, recognized the limits of industrialism and called for a "Green Revolution," a return to the land, work with dignity, and integrated community as a response to an inhuman and unjust environment.

Jeff Dietrich

Considering the enormity of the environmental crisis, it is an easy matter to dismiss such a perspective as ineffective and idealistic. In fact, for many years I had felt exactly the same way, dismissing Peter's ideas as impractical and utopian, but over the last decade, as more and more homeless dropped through the "safety net" of the system, and decent entry-level jobs became more and more scarce for the unskilled and the unsophisticated, I began to question the prevailing mythology of progress and development and came to the reluctant realization that the system is so corrupt that it is not possible to merely reform or refine it.

For most of us in the developed world, the system works pretty well, so it is difficult to accept such a thorough condemnation. Furthermore, our faith in the power of science and technology to solve the problems of poverty and environmental decay borders on the mystical. We are enthralled and mesmerized by the work of our own hands, not unlike certain pre-Christian cults, we worship the idols of our own creation. Our machines are like gods to us. We have created our world in the lifeless image of our "machine gods."

Jacques Ellul names this world of implacable logic, rational efficiency, and infinite power "the world of techniques."

Technique gives us a way of thinking and acting and organizing based upon our pathological desire to imitate the machine. Ellul describes for us the demonic spirituality of the *principalities and powers*. Ellul writes:

> Our civilization...still attests to a secularized Christian ideology which sets the highest value on brotherly relations. But the structures of our world and its real norms represent diametrically the opposite. The fundamental rule of the world today is the rule of economic, political and class competition....The disequilibration between the traditional affirmation and the new criterion has produced the climate of anxiety and insecurity characteristic of our epoch and of our neuroses.

The Technological Society, p. 333

Though Ellul does not directly address the problem of environmental pollution, it is clear that he would remind us first, without a great deal of moralizing, that the cold reality of the situation is that such eventualities are the inevitable result of a system that is founded on the objectification and exploitation of the natural world. If we treat the planet like one enormous strip mine, then we must expect to deal with the problem of living on top of a gigantic slag heap.

He goes on to point out that technique never questions the validity of its own logic. Thus, the problem of slag heap pollution would never be solved by the abolition of planetary strip mining. Rather, it would call for the application of new ecological techniques leading perhaps to the creation of low-cost slag heap housing or recycled carbon fiber for dietary supplements.

Thus do we find the compounding of one technique upon another in order to solve the problems of each successive evolution of technology. The technique of freeway building is the inevitable result of the invention of the horseless carriage. The technique of air quality management is the necessary outcome of air pollution. So faithful are the high priests of technique that they will proceed with the development of a dangerous technology like nuclear power in complete confidence that the yet-to-be developed technology of nuclear waste disposal will ultimately be created.

Just as the nuclear arms race and economic injustice are symptoms of a deeper illness, so too is environmental pollution a symptom of a diseased culture. We suffer from a pathological pattern of behavior based on our desire to imitate the machine, which is at once infantile and megalomaniacal. It is a rejection of the restraints of traditional cultural values, as well as those of organic reality. In short, we worship our machines, which for us represent the embodiment of ultimate power and the possibility of eternal life through technical development.

We cannot cure our environmental sickness through the power of techniques. Though it seems completely ineffectual, the only cure for our illness is repentance.

The prophetic call of Peter Maurin's "Green Revolution" in 1933 or the contemporary simple life of poet and farmer Wendell Berry, seem like pathetic efforts in the face of our overwhelming crisis, and the temptation is always to be effective rather than faithful. But as Jesus said in the scriptures, we cannot cast out demons by the power of demons. Neither can we use the power of techniques to reform techniques.

Doctrine of the Common Good as Gift Relationship*

Catholic Agitator, September, 2011, pp. 1, 2 and 6

"I can't pay the rent. I'm back on the streets tomorrow cuz they cut 40 bucks off my check....Hey, they took my psych meds, they cut me off Medi-Cal, and now I heard that checks won't be sent next month." Times are tough and that is the "street talk" at the Catholic Worker soup kitchen.

The recent vitriolic debate in Congress about raising the debt ceiling, the rancor at paying taxes for other people's health care, the thought that Social Security, Medicare and Medicaid might be cut, and public education dismantled, the destruction of unions, and the denigration of voices calling for mutual responsibility all reflect the degree to which the values of the marketplace have displaced our sense of the Common Good.

When I think of the Common Good, I think of the *Commons,* the common land worked communally in pre-Renaissance Europe, and I think of Peter Maurin, co-founder of the Catholic Worker Movement, who still had a memory of the Commons—a memory of Medieval times, forged by his early village years in a part of France that was slow to develop and still lived by the old values and rhythms.

Lewis Hyde tells us in his now classic book *The Gift* that this way of life was largely destroyed throughout most of Europe, and he reminds us that it was the Reformation that changed everything. "In 1525....The Peasant's War," precipitated by the liberative aspects of the Reformation,

> broke out in Germany that year....Germany had seen over a hundred years of unrest...as feudalism faded and [Lutheran] princes began to consolidate their power by territory....The basis of land tenure had

---

* A version of this piece appeared in the *National Catholic Reporter*, September 1, 2011.

234

shifted. Now men claimed to own the [common] land and offered to rent it out at a fee.

The Gift, p. 157

The mass displacement of commoners from the common land, driven by capitalism, led to an unprecedented increase of impoverished people from rural areas migrating to the plague-infested slums of large European cities, to be exploited as cheap labor for the industrial revolution and mass consumers of its mass produced commodities.

This same process of the displacement of commoners and the commodification of the commons exported by Europeans to the New World is described by Hyde:

> The Peasants' War was the same war that the American Indians had to fight with the Europeans, war against the marketing of formerly inalienable properties. Whereas before a man could fish in any stream and hunt in any forest, now he found that there were individuals who claimed to be the owners of these commons.

The Gift, p. 157

Like the Native Americans, the ancestors of our Judeo-Christian tradition were also tribal people. The twelve tribes of ancient Israel, our forefathers, escaped slaves from the over-developed Egyptian empire, understood that development and exploitation of common creation was the primary sin of humanity. They incorporated the understanding of the gift of common creation to all from the Creator God into their very laws. "And he who had gathered a small amount did not have too little. They so gathered that everyone had enough to eat" (Exodus 16:16-30). In other words, don't take more than you need, so that everyone will have enough.

The Sabbath day prohibitions call us to stop and rest in creation, as did the Native Americans, who were regarded by European settlers as lazy. It is all gift, and the more we work the more we delude ourselves into thinking that what we have is what we *earned* and that we *deserve* what is in reality a gift. That is the meaning of Sabbath.

The Church's doctrine of the Common Good filters down to us through the scriptures. However, its moral formulation was birthed during the feudal era, a time of peasants, who like Peter Maurin, lived off the common lands and were displaced by the lords and princes of this world. The Robin Hood story of Sherwood Forest is an old memory of that struggle and our collective longings for primeval trees, large-eyed deer and doe, and the shining salmon surging up crystal streams, recall a time when the gift of creation was common to us all.

As with the story of Robin Hood in his defiance of the Sheriff of Nottingham, there are, according to Hyde, "many connections between anarchist theory and gift exchange" (*The Gift,* p. 120). As an economy—both assume that humans are generous, or at least cooperative in nature; both shun centralized power; both are best fitted to small groups and loose federations; both rely on contracts of the heart over codified contracts, and so on. But above all, it seems correct to speak of the gift as anarchist property because both anarchism and gift exchange share the assumption that it is not when a part of the self is inhibited and restrained, but when a part of the self is given away, that community is formed.

Hyde tells us "that we should understand gift exchange to be a total 'social phenomenon'—one whose transactions are at once economic, juridical, moral, aesthetic, religious, and mythological, and whose meaning cannot therefore, be adequately described from the point of view of any single discipline" (*The Gift,* xxi). The meaning of the gift, he says, is always enshrouded in mystery. However, the doctrine of the Common Good can be seen as not mysterious, but rational and reductionistic. Yet, as Catholics, we are marked in our hearts and souls by mystery, the mystery of the Eucharist.

Lewis Hyde has helped me to understand the mystery of the Eucharist, the mystery of gratitude. And it makes no difference whether we believe in the traditional Eucharistic doctrine of "transubstantiation," or we believe in the "unbloody sacrifice of Calvary," or we believe that we simply "share a meal, a common meal, so that all might be satisfied." It is still mystery.

And mystery, Hyde says, "revives" and marks us as people of the gift and the common good, causing us to remember the startling words of Isaiah: "Why spend your money for what is not bread; your wages for what fails to satisfy?" (Isaiah 55:2) I also think of Dorothy Day, who at the end of her life could say, "All is grace, all is grace, all is gift and grace." Grace and gift flow to the empty places, grace flows to the poor beggar with the empty bowl and the mystery of the Eucharist is that gift and grace flow back from the empty places, softening the hardest hearts.

As Catholics, we know intuitively and irrationally that our redemption, our very salvation, is bound up with softening hearts and the mutual reciprocity of gift that flows to the empty places. We are all people marked by mystery and the gift of the Common Good that surpasses all understanding and flies under the radar of logic and rationality, striking the core of our

39. Cover illustration by Fritz Eichenberg, woodcut. Reproduced in the *Catholic Agitator*, 1976

being. We know that in some mysterious way we are all connected, that we are all in communion, that, as Dorothy Day would say, along with the IWW (Industrial Workers of the World), "An injury to one is an injury to us all."

In addition, we know that the rancor, rhetoric, and rectitude of the current public discourse is not our language. We know that our mother tongue is the language of soft hearts, of gift, and grace, and Eucharist. We know that we cannot be whole until all empty bowls of the poor are filled and all empty spaces are filled—until "every valley shall be filled and every mountain and hill shall be made low" (Luke 3:5). We cannot be satisfied until all are satisfied.

Times are tough. The commons will continue to be rapaciously developed for the profit of the few; the poor will continue to be evicted from the commons and marginated from the common good. Wealthy capitalists will try to commodify and control every element that is common to our common humanity: food, water, earth, and even the air; and then they will try to sell it back to us for a profit.

We live in a perilous time, a time that calls for perilous action; but we cannot save the world. As Christians we are enjoined to believe that the world has already been saved, as absurd as that notion may seem. In the words of St. Teresa of Ávila, "The worst is already over."

If we believe such pie-in-the-sky nonsense, we have only one choice: we are compelled to live our lives as a testament to that very nonsense. We have to fly like a bird under the radar of marketplace rationality and marketplace logos and risk the derision, diminishment, and dismissal that comes to fools who take it all seriously. We have to risk everything on the importance of the common good and put ourselves in the flow of the gift, the gift of relationship, into the mystery of the Eucharist that is celebrated, however improbably, in such disparate places as Sunday suburban parishes, ghetto hovels, prison cells, and Papal palaces, and yes, yes the basements of tawdry Catholic Worker soup kitchens.

A Theology of Non-Power

Catholic Agitator, April, 1992, p. 1

The toilet in the first floor bathroom at the Catholic Worker farm at Tivoli, New York, was actually designed to accommodate no more than five or six good bowel movements a day. So it was completely understandable when this sterling example of the nineteenth-century plumbing technology, under the strain of a three day retreat for sixty anarchist vegetarians, experienced the plumbing equivalent of a nuclear meltdown.

After having personally cleaned the toilet and its environs several times, my wife and I finally located a five gallon plastic bucket which we conveniently placed next to the toilet with a set of helpful instructions on the process of gravity flushing: 1) fill the bucket with water 2) pour contents into toilet 3) return bucket to previous location. We, unfortunately, made the innocent mistake of signing our note "The Management."

Upon our very next visit to the bathroom, we discovered that our note had been ripped off and replaced with a barrage of angry political graffiti that made the Berlin Wall look like a kindergarten blackboard. "Eat and die, fascist scum." "Bourgeois sentimentality will never overcome the spirit of revolution." "Authoritarian dysfunctionalism begins with bad potty training: consider therapy," etc. While such sentiments were probably more prevalent at the time of this particular incident in 1975, they nonetheless illustrate the virulence as well as the absurdity, and even the impracticality, of Catholic Worker anarchism.

But as we enter yet another season of electoral circus acts with their endless rounds of vacuous candidates and authentic concerns and aspirations reduced to the packaging constraints of soap commercials, what better time to reexamine Dorothy Day's ambiguous legacy of anarchism.

For her many admirers, as well as for her numerous disciples, Dorothy's anarchism has often been a conveniently overlooked stumbling block.

But in many ways it is truly the rejected stone that eventually becomes the radical cornerstone of the foundation. Dorothy Day's great love of the Church gave her the ability to understand its call to a deeper mission and purpose as an instrument of God, one that often evades the perceptions of even its own hierarchy. Thus, she could find justification for her anarchist spirit even within an institution that has, from Constantine to Aquinas, worked toward a cozy synthesis of church and state. Dorothy Day no doubt understood that part of her own mission and gift was to live out a radical Christian witness of servanthood, sacrifice and nonviolence as a sign of contradiction to the political power, violence and self-interest of the state and as a gift of prophetic tension to the Church comfortable.

My own recent rededication to Dorothy Day's anarchist commitment was inspired in no small measure by the 1988 elections that proved that any preppy wimp with enough money, television time, and proper handling from the "spin doctors" could become president of the United States. I am more convinced than ever that her program is not just some simple-minded response, but is, in fact, a sophisticated recognition that authentic social transformation begins with personal transformation. Only by enfleshing Christ's kingdom in our own lives, only by personally feeding the hungry, clothing the naked, and sheltering the homeless, rather than calling upon the "holy mother" of the state to do it, do we create the conduit for God's transforming grace to enter the world. In this context, her admonition against voting, against taking government funds, and against filing tax-deductible status makes perfect sense.

However, I must confess that like the disciples James and John, I long for the deliverance of a political Messiah who will reorder our political structures, kick out the bad guys, and usher in a millennium of justice while appointing myself and Daniel Berrigan to the posts of Secretary of State and Attorney General respectively.

To one degree or another, this messianic hope of deliverance is the seductive element of all political involvement, from violent revolution to electoral politics. It is based upon the hope that we can be saved by some force outside of ourselves. In direct contrast to this style of political action, Jesus offers his disciples a radically different program of servanthood, sacrifice, and non-power. But very few, outside of, perhaps, Dorothy Day, really believe in the efficiency of this program. It's a nice thing for saints and holy people, but anyone who has spent upwards of $80,000 on their college education wants to do something with their lives that will "really make a difference."

The kind of difference that Jesus wishes us to make is not one of reform but of radical newness that does more than merely rearrange the pieces within the existing structures. Jesus employed a strategy of confrontational compassion that moved implacably from the peripheral provinces of Galilee to the seat of political power in Jerusalem. But Jesus did not go to Jerusalem to work out a power sharing arrangement with the Pharisees, or to lobby the high priest in the temple for a more equitable distribution of the temple taxes, or for a conference with the Roman authorities on human alternatives to the death penalty.

The core teachings of Jesus' anarchist program of personal/social transformation can be found in Chapters 9 and 10 of the Gospel of Mark. It is what Ched Myers has called the "catechism of non-violence" (*Binding the Strong Man,* p. 258), or what Jacques Ellul has called a "theology or even more so a practice of non-power" (*The Subversion of Christianity*, p. 32). It contains Jesus' patient attempt to explain his strategy of confrontational compassion to his increasingly thick-headed disciples, who can only conceive of transformation in terms of the traditional models of power politics.

The section begins and ends with Jesus exhorting his disciples to become servants: "Whoever wishes to be first among you will be the slave of all" (Mark 10:44). Presumably, this is not an euphemistic reference to contemporary politicians who are sometimes inappropriately referred to as "public servants." By turn, Jesus attacks all of the power assumptions held by his disciples as well as by ourselves. We are not to imitate the dominant subordinate relationships of the Roman military-imperialist establishment: "You know that those who are recognized as rulers over the Gentiles lord it over them, and their great ones make their authority over them felt. But it shall not be so among you" (Mark 10:42-3). Neither are they to be dependent upon economic wealth as a source of oppressive power: "It is easier for a camel to pass though the eye of a needle than for a one who is rich to enter the kingdom of God " (Mark 10:25).

Jesus said we must become as powerless as little children and, rather than overcome our political opponents with power, we must accept the cross. Sometimes we think that this radically pacifist perspective is merely a passive attitude that simply leads us away from the tainted world of politics and power, but nothing could be further from the truth. The doctrine of the cross is, in fact, a strategy of detached engagement that depends not upon direct conflict but rather upon the recognition that the real power of institutions is generated by a force greater than the people who serve them at any given time.

Jeff Dietrich

Kings, generals, legislators, judges and bureaucrats are merely replaceable functionaries. The true power of any institution is actually generated by what theologian Walter Wink calls "a king of spirituality." It is what St. Paul refers to as the *principalities and powers* or what Jesus calls a "faithless generation" (Mark 9:19). It is what the Old Testament prophets called "idolatry."

Wink speaks of the various gods of ancient times as "the actual inner spirituality of the social entity itself" (*Unmasking the Powers,* p. 88). Jesus realizes that authentic social change cannot take place by simply replacing the functionaries who serve the institutions. Rather, it is the "demonic spirituality" of the institution itself that must be "cast out."

Thus, Jesus' ministry of exorcising and healing takes him from the encounters of personal demonic possession among the poor and oppressed, at the periphery of power, directly to the source of disease and demonic possession: the Temple in Jerusalem, where he confronts the authorities and exorcises the Temple of its demonic possession.

The Christian project, according to theologian Jacques Ellul, consists in large measure, if not in total, in the process of desacrilizing the sacred. For Ellul, there are two realms: the sacred and the holy. The holy is the realm of the true God and authentic freedom, while the "sacred" is the human ordering of reality that is imbued with a false sense of transcendence. In our contemporary social order, the State represents one aspect of the sacred.

For Ellul, the sacred is nothing less than the "demonic spirituality" of institutions that has come to regard itself as ultimate power. The clearest example of this kind of idolatry happens during war time, when the choice of conscience and faith are paralyzed and we find the sacred in complete command. A recent example is the ability of the military-industrial complex to essentially maintain itself intact even though its *raison d'etre,* the Soviet threat, has completely disappeared.

Unfortunately, according to Ellul, human beings cannot live without a sense of the sacred, or they would go mad. On the other hand, the force of the sacred is such that it will become unidimensional if it remains uncriticised.

Thus, it is in this state of dialectical tension between these poles of the sacred and the holy that Christians must work to create a tiny realm of freedom where transforming grace can actually find the space to work. It is the very same project that Dorothy Day validated and witnessed to with her own life.

It may seem like a modest, even humiliating, program, but the cross of non-power and servanthood is the project that God has given us through His son Jesus Christ to desacralize the sacred. We all want to believe that

40. Volunteers preparing food at the Hospitality House Kitchen, 2011. Photo by Robert Radin

God can work through any medium, but Ellul is convinced that God has actually chosen to work through the specifically Christian medium of the cross and servanthood to desacralize the pretensions of power. Christians can, and more often than not, do choose other means of social transformation. Like the disciples, we would rather find salvation through existing systems of political power: electoral politics, legislative reforms and judicial action. But Ellul's theology of stark prophetic contrasts does tend to elevate the simple work of the Catholic Worker out of the realm of patronizing condescension and pious spirituality and into the unlikely vocation of being "a ransom for the many" (Mark 10:45).

No doubt the Catholic Worker Movement will continue to be regarded as hopelessly quixotic and idealistic as we argue endlessly, even within our own communities, about the conflicting benefits of sanitized, authoritarian bathrooms versus anarchistic, bacteria ridden toilet seats, about the benefits of incorporated, non-profit status versus personalist communitarian service, and about electoral politics versus nonviolent direct action.

My own abiding hope is that, even in the midst of the seeming absurdity and impracticality, Dorothy will continue to have the final word through her life-long anarchistic witness of service, sacrifice, and nonviolence.

PART SEVEN

THE WORLD WE HAVE LOST

Le vrais paradis, c'est le paradis qu'on a perdu.

Marcel Proust

The true paradise is the one we have lost.

The Fall into Civilization

Catholic Agitator, June, 2000, pp. 1, 2 and 6

In the beginning, there was the garden, but it wasn't good enough. Then Cain murdered Abel and Cain founded the first city. The first murderer founded the first city. The story of Cain and Abel illustrates what the writers of Genesis knew and what Jared Diamond confirms in his Pulitzer Prize winning book, *Guns, Germs and Steel*, that the powerful prey on the weak and that their pretensions to moral and intellectual superiority are baseless.

To most of us the story of Cain and Abel seems unfair. Why would God accept the gift of the shepherd and reject the gift of the farmer? In fact the authors of Genesis exhibit a profound preference for pastoralists over agriculturalists. The truth is that "farmer power," as Diamond calls it, is the very foundation of urban civilization and thus of exploitive military empire. While scripture may tell us that the meek shall inherit the earth, history reminds us that it is "the victor who gets the spoils."

In the last 500 years, since Columbus first encountered the New World and Vasco da Gama rounded the horn of Africa, the murderous march of history has indelibly inscribed the triumph of the powerful over the meek. Western technocratic society has assumed that its phenomenal ability to dominate the globe has come as a result of either God-given right or the superior intelligence and genetic qualities of the white Aryan race. Simpler tribal people were just that—simple, and thus less intelligent and less capable of managing their affairs.

Jared Diamond in his book, *Guns, Germs and Steel,* seeks to shatter this assumption of Western moral and intellectual superiority. He attempts to answer the question: how did it come to be that a small group of people, clinging precariously to the Eurasian land mass so easily dominated the world? He shows that the origins of inequality in human fortunes cannot be laid at the door of racial superiority or of the people themselves.

247

His book begins with a question posed to him twenty-five years ago by his friend Yali, an educated native of New Guinea's Trobriand Islands. "'Why is it that you white people developed so much cargo...but we black people had little cargo of our own?'" "Cargo" being a native slang word not only for modern consumer goods, but for all of the technological and cultural production of sophisticated European societies. Diamond adds, "He and I knew perfectly well that New Guineans are, on the average, at least as smart as Europeans" (*Guns, Germs and Steel*, p. 14).

Twenty-five years later, Diamond found his answer. "All human societies," he writes, "contain inventive people. It's just that some environments provide more starting materials, and more favorable conditions for utilizing inventions, than do other environments" (*Guns, Germs and Steel*, p. 408). In other words, Western nations got a head start on agriculture, writing, technology and complex societies not because they are smarter or blessed with divine direction, but rather because of the accidents of geography and climate.

Diamond examines the historic campaign of Francisco Pizarro in 1521 and explores why 168 Spanish soldiers, in unfamiliar territory 1,000 miles from any possible reinforcements, were able to capture the Incan Emperor Atahuallpa, defeat 80,000 Inca warriors, and within six months conquer the largest and most sophisticated empire in the New World. According to Diamond, Pizarro's capture of Atahuallpa, illustrates the set of proximate factors that resulted in Europeans colonizing the New World instead of Native Americans colonizing Europe. They include: military technology based on guns, steel weapons, and horses; the infectious diseases brought to the New World that were endemic in Eurasia; European maritime technology; the centralized political organization of European states, and writing (*Guns, Germs and Steel*, pp. 67-82).

He asks why is it that Europeans, and not Native Americans, were able to develop sophisticated weapons, technology and immunity to epidemic diseases like smallpox and mumps that virtually decimated aboriginal populations around the globe? He concludes that Pizarro and his men were aided in their conquest by a smallpox epidemic that virtually decimated the Inca population, killing the Emperor and throwing the country into civil war. In Mexico, the Spanish were assisted by smallpox epidemics, which, over a 100-year period, reduced the Aztec population from 20 million to less than 2 million. Much of the powerful impact that Europeans exerted on the rest of the world derived not from superior technology, but from their immunity to germs. Because of their close proximity to large domesticated animals, Europeans contracted a wide variety of animal-based epidemic diseases: measles, tuberculosis, smallpox, flu and pertussis. But over the centuries, Europeans also developed a relative immunity to these diseases, which they carried with deadly effect to vulnerable tribal populations around the globe.

Another reason for the concentration of power lies in what Diamond calls "farmer power," and especially that power as it manifested itself about 10,000 years ago on the Eurasian land mass, that largest of continental land masses, stretching from China and Japan, in the east, to all of Europe and Great Britain in the west, with Russia, India, Afghanistan, Iran and Iraq in the middle.

The largest and richest of all continents contained a veritable abundance of crops and large animals suitable for domestication. There are only fourteen domesticated animals in the modern world. Thirteen of them were to be found in the Eurasian continent. And because the Eurasian continent lies on an east-west axis with a similar climate throughout its 10,000-mile expanse, agricultural innovations and their attendant cultural innovations were able to spread quickly from place to place in a kind of synergistic fashion. Diamond writes that only a dozen species makes up 80 percent of "the modern world's annual tonnage of all crops" (*Guns, Germs and Steel,* p. 132):

> In short, plant and animals domestication meant much more food and hence much denser human populations. The resulting food surpluses, and (in some areas) the animal-based means of transporting those surpluses, were a prerequisite for the development of settled, politically centralized, socially stratified, economically complex, technologically innovative societies. Hence the availability of domestic plants and animals ultimately explains why empires, literacy, the military uses of horses and camels, and steel weapons developed earliest in Eurasia and later, or not at all, on other continents.

> *Guns, Germs and Steel,* p. 92

With the development of agriculture came greater development of surplus food resources that allowed for "leisure time" and the rise of a specialist class. Some of these specialists, like craftspeople, no doubt gave productive and creative return for the surplus they consumed. But the other specialists Diamond speaks of as "kleptocrats": kings, priests, and bureaucrats. "The difference between a kleptocrat and a wise statesman, between a robber baron and public benefactor, is merely one of degree," Diamond writes, "a matter of just how large a percentage of the tribute extracted from producers is retained by the elite, and how much the commoners like the public uses to which the redistributed tribute is put" (*Guns, Germs and Steel*, p. 276). The purpose of the "kleptocratic priest" is to provide ideological justification for the chiefs. "That is why chiefdoms devote so much collected tribute to constructing temples and other public works, which serve as centers of the official religion and visible signs of the chief's power" (*Guns, Germs and Steel*, p. 278).

Diamond points out that writing, which we think of as one of the highest achievements of civilization, was begun not for lofty literary or poetic expression, but rather to keep track of debt. "The kings and priests of ancient Sumer wanted writing to be used by professional scribes to record numbers of sheep owed in taxes, not by the masses to write poetry and hatch plots....Ancient writing's main function was [according to Claude Lévi-Strauss] 'to facilitate the enslavement of other human beings'" (*Guns, Germs and Steel*, p. 292).

The Tower of Babel story, of course, is a thinly veiled allusion to the mighty city of Babylon. It is an overt critique of the architectural hubris of the great empire. Its ability to coordinate such a vast project is premised upon the ability to speak the "same language." God's response to the project is to "scatter the people and confuse their language." This seems perverse to contemporary Americans, who believe that the solution to world belligerence is better communications. But the story is a critique of the centralizing forces of empire that destroy the multiplicity of indigenous languages and cultures, suck resources back toward the centralized capital, and consolidate their power with the construction of sacred towers or ziggurats.

This story in the "Primal Narrative" is recapitulated throughout the Bible. It is the story of the powerful empires poised against the least, the marginalized people who do not have the benefits of what Diamond calls "farmer power." This war continues today more rapaciously than ever in places like Chiapas, where indigenous people are being forced off their land; in Columbia, where the U'wa tribe is being threatened by Occidental Petroleum; in Chad, where a 650 mile pipeline built by Exxon Mobile threatens the lives of African forest dwellers.

As First World people, as Americans, as people of empire, we all believe that our dazzling cultural achievements must have come about as a result of God's blessing. We assume that it must be the Spirit of God working through the world that caused the invention of the microchip, the Internet, the world economy. But all of these achievements are, in the eyes of God, Just another Tower of Babel. None other than Jesus Christ himself has told us, that we will be judged not on our brilliance, but on how we treated the least of our brothers and sisters.

In truth, God has a preference for the simple, tribal people, the marginalized, the poor, because they do not organize themselves into empires or armies, they do not steal on a massive scale, they have no weapons of mass destruction, they do not enslave their neighbors, and whether they gather their daily bread from berries and fruit trees or along the streets and gutters of ghettos, they are still closer to the primal Garden of God's creation and thus dependent upon the beneficence of divine grace. If we seek to enter the Kingdom we must stand in solidarity with lowly and meek, whom we have been told will inherit the earth.

Anti-Christian Family Values

Catholic Agitator, February, 1997, pp. 1 and 2

If the recent elections proved anything other than the cynicism of the politicians and the naïveté of the voters, it was that whoever wraps himself the tightest in the mantle of family values will win. Followers of Jesus must, however, realize that though it sounds heretical, or outrageously biased, there is virtually no congruence between what we think of as Christian family values and the teachings of Jesus. In fact, even a cursory review of the New Testament reveals that whatever Jesus had to say about the subject of family was pretty much the opposite of what most of us think of as family values.

The very first act of Jesus' public ministry was to call the disciples into community. On the first reading this sounds like a very positive and admirable event. But we tend to forget that when the disciples ran off to join Jesus, they left their father behind in the boat with the hired hands. And though the text does not say so, we can legitimately assume that their father was pissed.

In choosing Jesus, not only have the disciples abandoned their responsibility to their parent, but they have abandoned the family business, a rare opportunity for financial security at the time. We sometimes forget that running off to join up with Jesus was not in any way equivalent to joining a religious order or entering the seminary. There were no health care plans or retirement benefits, no salary or stipend, no paid vacation or advanced study program. In other words, they were abandoning economic stability for economic precarity. Perhaps that is why Peter's mother-in-law is so sick when Jesus comes to visit. The soon-to-be head of what was to become the Holy, Roman, Catholic, and Apostolic Church could not pay the rent, support his wife, or feed her children. No wonder she took to her bed!

No doubt most of us would assume that Jesus' own family would be supportive of his ministry. Unfortunately, that doesn't seem to be the case. In Chapter 3 of Mark, it says his family came to take charge of him, for they said, "He is out of his mind" (Mark 3:21). So much for family support for the Jesus program. But what about Jesus? Did he support his family? Just about the kindest thing you could say concerning Jesus' attitude to his family is that he is blunt. If it was your mother, she would probably say that you were being cruel. In the same chapter of Mark, Jesus keeps his mother and brothers waiting at the door while he speaks to a large group of homeless people. When he is told that his family is waiting, he virtually denies them: "Who are my mother and my brothers?" he says (Mark 3:33) That is an unconscionable thing to say to people who raised you, loved you, cared for you. Most of us would at least have a guilty conscience for saying something as cold as that. But Jesus doesn't just deny his family, he looks around the room at the crowd of disciples and derelicts who are gathered there and says, "Here are my mother and my brothers. Whoever does the will of God is my brother and sister and mother" (Mark 3:34-5).

That seems harsh enough, but it gets worse in Luke, Chapter 11: "A father will be divided against his son and a son against his father, a mother against her daughter and a daughter against her mother, a mother-in-law against her daughter-in-law and a daughter-in-law against her mother-in-law" (Luke 12:49, 53).

Now one could say that I am biased, and I am just picking out quotations to fit my arguments. I know that it must seem astounding when you think of all of the radio preachers and evangelists and priests in pulpits who preach on the importance of Christian family values; you would think that there would be at least one passage in which Jesus blesses familial bliss, encourages husbands to be responsible providers, urges children to be obedient to their parents. But no, not even one. In fact, in the Gospel of John the very first and most successful evangelist is the Samaritan woman with five husbands. And Jesus doesn't even require that she repent of what appears to be a major series of sexual indiscretions.

Perhaps if we look to Jesus' early life we might find a bit more support for family values in the stories of the Holy Family. But in both Luke and Matthew we find a rejection of normal notions of family, where standard relations between husband and wife are subverted by the story of the Virgin Birth. Even if you don't accept current revisionist scholars who claim straight out that Jesus was an illegitimate child, you still must deal with the recognition that he was certainly perceived that way by his community and peers, and that such a notion demands that we at least be more tolerant of unwed welfare mothers and out-of-wedlock babies.

If you attended Catholic grade school in the 1950s like I did, you no doubt always assumed that Jesus was an obedient, compliant child just like all the students in Sister Mary Rosary's classroom. Well, guess again. The only thing that we know for sure about the adolescent Jesus comes from Luke, who tells us that the teenage Jesus was a runaway. And when he is finally found, he's smarting-off to his elders in the temple, and talking back to his mother: "Did you not know that I must be in my Father's house" (Luke 2:49), he says, which apparently is not Joseph's house. How do you think Joseph feels?

Well, one might say that I am looking for affirmation of family values in all the wrong places. Of course you're getting subversive material; you've been looking in the Gospels. You need to check out Paul, and then you'll find the conservative values of home and hearth: 'Wives be subject to your husbands, women be quiet in church,' etc. And I have to admit that I find portions of Paul that are inexplicably at variance with the radical notions of Jesus. Nevertheless, Paul, for all his apparent conservatism, thought of marriage as a last resort: "It is better to marry than to be on fire" (1 Corinthians 7:9). In other words, Paul's priority, like Jesus', was the spreading of the Gospel, which most often takes a back seat to any family obligations.

Now, clearly, I am not a scripture scholar, and my survey only includes the four Gospels, for the most part. But you don't have to be a genius to see that Jesus subverted almost every cultural structure and institution of his time. As the author Flannery O'Connor once wrote, "Jesus thrown everything off balance" ("A Good Man is Hard to Find," p. 27). Or, to quote the Catholic theologian Hans Küng,

> Jesus relativizes the law and this means the whole religio-political-economic order, the whole social system. Even the law is not the beginning and the end of all God's ways....The commandments are for man's sake and not man for the sake of the commandments. This means that service to man has priority over the observance of the law. No norms or institutions can be made absolute.

The Christian Challenge, p. 147

The current success of the Christian family values movement reflects the desire to affix blame for our contemporary social disintegration on a decline in personal moral values. Issues of crime, sexual promiscuity, pornography, and drugs will be solved by jails, censorship, and renewed moral vigor. The blame for this moral decay seems to fall unduly upon the

Advent: Birth of Hope In Central America

"As they hid from the soldiers in a ravine, a child was born to them. 'We must celebrate,' one of the women said, 'even though the Army seeks to kill us, this child's birth is a sign that God offers us life.'"

CHRISTA OCCHIOGROSSO

42. Untitled print by Christa Occhiogrosso, silkscreen. *Catholic Agitator*, 1988

immigrant, the welfare cheat, and the practitioner of gay sexuality—in other words, the political, social, and sexual outcast.

But this is a simplistic view that ignores the social, economic component of authentic Biblical ethics. The truth of the matter is that Jesus almost never addresses issues of personal morality, personal piety, personal salvation, and personal relationship. With Jesus we efface almost 95 percent of what he taught when our focus is on an exclusive, vertical relationship with God, because the whole thrust of God's incarnation in Jesus Christ is meant to deepen our awareness of God's presence in our suffering neighbor.

It is hypocritical to speak of the disintegration of civic virtue, public morals, and family values without a recognition that our current crisis has been caused in large measure by the overwhelming impact of consumer capitalism. As Robert Wright notes in a *Time Magazine* article:

> One reason the sinews of community are so hard to restore is that they are at odds with free markets. Capitalism not only spews out

cars, TVs and other antisocial technologies; it also sorts people into little vocational boxes and scatters the boxes far and wide. Economic opportunity is what drew farm boys into cities, and it has been fragmenting families ever since.. There is thus a tension within conservative ideology between laissez-faire economics and family values.

"The Evolution of Despair," *Time Magazine*

The qualities of panic and hysteria that one associates with the family values movement are a direct result of the feeling that parents have lost control over their own children. But that loss of control, as historian Christopher Lasch observes, is precipitated by the capitalism of hearth and home:

In our time it is increasingly clear that children pay the price for this invasion of the family by the market. With both parents in the workplace and grandparents conspicuous by their absence, the family is no longer capable of sheltering children from the market. The television set becomes the principal baby-sitter by default. Its invasive presence deals the final blow to any lingering hope that the family can provide a sheltered space for children to grow up in.

"Communitarianism or Populism?," *New Oxford Review*, p. 7

As sociologist Robert Wright goes on to illustrate, the marked increase in consumer propaganda leads directly to social decline: "During the 1950s, various American cities saw a rise in theft in the particular years that broadcast television was introduced" ("The Evolution of Despair," *Time Magazine*).

Much of the vitriolic bitterness of the family values debate has been fueled by the process of suburbanization, which created an ethos of estrangement. Ironically, the density and diversity of the urban experience, which so many middle-class people desired so desperately to flee, was a much more profoundly communal experience than the homogenous, isolated, "one-dimensional" environment of suburbia.

The "nostalgia for the suburban nuclear family of the 1950s," according to Robert Wright,

which often accompanies current enthusiasm for "family values,"—is ironic...to worship the suburban household of the 1950s is to miss much of the trouble with contemporary life. It was suburbanization that brought the combination of transience and residential isolation that leaves many people feeling a bit alone in their own neighborhoods. (These days, thanks to electric garage-door openers, you can drive straight into your house, never risking contact with a neighbor.)

"The Evolution of Despair," *Time Magazine*

The enhanced alienation of the suburban experience has led many middle-class people to become increasingly fearful, angry, perplexed, and vindictive towards the phenomenon of urban poverty. The process of suburbanization and its inevitable abandonment of urban areas has directly contributed to the declining quality of life for the urban poor and to a backlash against urban areas in general.

This process began in the early 1970s in California with the much touted "tax rebellion" and the passage of Proposition 13. White voters who lived in the suburbs but worked in the city rejected the notion that they had a responsibility for the urban environment in which they made their living. They didn't mind extracting wealth from the city, but they resented paying for urban services—health, welfare, police, etc.— that they did not directly benefit from, but which, nonetheless, still contributed to the overall quality of urban life.

This heartless, reactionary ethos has gathered momentum over the years and culminated in the virtual elimination of welfare payments to the urban poor with the recent passage of the Welfare Reform Act. This is essentially a cynical message from suburban taxpayers to urban residents to get your act together. But as Donella Meadows points out in an *LA Times* Op-ed piece,

> Government programs for the poor constitute one-fourth of nondefense spending but have absorbed more than half of recent budget cuts. These cuts were deemed necessary to reduce deficits caused by tax cuts for the rich. In the 1980s the real income of the top fifth of Americans rose 32 percent while their federal tax rate dropped 5.5 percent. The bottom fifth saw an income rise of 3 percent and a tax increase of 16 percent.

"The Least of These Our Brethren," *Los Angeles Times*

There is no doubt that welfare programs are inefficient and that honest labor uplifts the individual as well as the community. But it is clearly a case of blatant hypocrisy when my father, who is a wealthy, retired real estate developer, is able to have the US government pay for his quadruple by-pass surgery, and the folks in our soup line will have what little health and welfare benefits they have taken away from them. But that's the way the world works; as it says in the scriptures, "everyone who has, more will be given, but from the one who has not, even what he has will be taken away" (Luke 19:26). Jesus understood this, and that is why he said: "the poor you will always have with you" (Mark 14:7).

In the Gospel we must remember that Jesus was killed by the people who attended church regularly, refrained from immoral and criminal activity, worked diligently, and supported their families; in other words, the priests, Scribes, and Pharisees who had Jesus crucified were good, solid, upright citizens, the latter-day equivalent of the family values crowd.

When Jesus feeds 5,000 hungry, homeless, welfare cheats out in the wilderness, the immediate observation of the Pharisees is: "He did not wash his hands." Their concern was for religious ritual and a "personal" relationship with God, not with the fact that there were 5,000 people in their neighborhood who needed something to eat.

If the teachings of Jesus have anything at all to say about family values, it is that Christians must begin to treat the homeless, the outcast, the welfare cheat, and the criminal as we have been taught to treat our own families— that is what true, Christian family values means. Or as Hans Küng wrote, "Jesus expects no more and no less than a fundamental, *total orientation* of man's life toward God.... Imitating Christ in this way takes precedence even over family ties: anyone who wants to be a disciple of Christ must 'hate' father, mother, brothers and sisters, wife and children, even himself" (*On Being a Christian*, p. 249).

Burdening the Poor

Catholic Agitator, October, 1992, p. 1

The rich nations of the world, according to author Paul Vallely, are "Bad Samaritans." Though they would revel in their self-identified role as Good Samaritans who send aid and famine relief to the starving poor of third world nations, they are in reality worse than the priest and Levite who passed by the injured victim. Vallely, speaking from the "Bad Samaritans" point of view, writes:

> We cross over and announce our intention to help. We take the injured man to the inn. But we do not acknowledge that he has been injured and robbed by men who work for us. The silver we pay for his convalescence is only a small portion of what their agents have stolen from him.
>
> *Bad Samaritans,* pp. 4-5

Vallely is neither a theologian nor an economist, but he has written a superb book which illuminates the arcane system of international economics and articulates not only appropriate fiscal responses, but theological responses as well.

As a trained professional journalist, Vallely began his investigation with an assignment from the *Times of London* to report on the Ethiopian famine of the 1980s and the numerous relief efforts that were responding to that tragedy. He captured the images of refugee camps: starving children with bloated bellies, gaunt women, all eyes and cheek bones, trying in vain to nurse their crying babies with wrinkled breasts. Unlike most journalists, however, Vallely was not content with the superficial images of hunger, famine, and poverty, and set out on a quest to find the root cause of their repeated disasters that in the last decade have taken such a toll in human life.

He found that in the end everything came back to dollars and cents. It was clear that the international system of trading and finance was heavily loaded in favor of us and against them. Finally, he came to the realization that "we wealthy nations were actively contriving to make life even worse for the poorest people in the world" (*Bad Samaritans*, p. 69). The International Monetary Fund (IMF) was founded ostensibly to provide the start-up capital for poor nations, but in the last decade it has functioned as the bill collector for the First World. Even under unfair trade conditions, the Third World was able until quite recently to maintain a moderate growth rate and a reasonable balance of trade between exports and imports. But now they struggle to make loan payments that grow exponentially and that, as of 1990, have already reached $1.319 trillion. In order to repay, third world governments are being forced by the IMF to cut food subsidies to the poor and their health and education budgets. As a consequence, "more than 1,000 million people—about one in five of the entire world's population—experience hunger for at least part of every year....Some 250,000 small children die from starvation or easily preventable illness *every week*" (*Bad Samaritans*, p. 3).

And to make matters even worse, third world governments, in an effort to increase their export level, have forced peasants off of prime agricultural acreage and onto marginal land, leading to a further diminishment of food production and to deforestation and desertification of these lands, which in turn has given rise to global climate change and ecological disasters in places like the Sahel and the Brazilian rainforest.

Even though no one seems to be in control of this situation, it is the United States which must bear the greatest burden of responsibility. Because the dollar is the key currency of the international system, the US can virtually print and spend as much as it wishes, provided the rest of the world is willing to accept the dollar and attach value to it. So long as the United States government used its privilege with restraint, the system functioned.

Then came the Vietnam War, and according to Professor Robert Triffin, (economic adviser to President John Kennedy and to the European Community), rather than raise taxes, President Johnson figured, "'Why should I create problems for myself as long as the Bundesbank and the Bank of Japan are willing to finance the war?'—those two countries being the most important investors in dollars" (*Bad Samaritans*, p. 135).

The foreign debt of the United States rose from $100 billion in 1969 to over $1,000 billion in 1984 as President Reagan used Johnson's strategy of deficit financing to fund an ever-escalating arms race. The amount of dollars in foreign hands caused an inflationary growth of international monetary reserves, rising in this period to 13 percent above the world's Gross National Product.

Vallely quotes Triffin, who says, "A reform of the system would have prevented [inflation]. For, just like other countries with balance-of-payments deficits, the United States would have had to drastically cut its military expenditures or raise the money through stiff tax increases" (*Bad Samaritans*, p. 135).

The United States has used its budget deficit as a kind of back door tax upon the rest of the world, including its poorest nations, largely to finance unproductive spending on national defense.

Perhaps the most interesting chapter of the book is Vallely's Biblical examination of the Jubilee Laws in the Old Testament. The laws, as outlined in the book of Leviticus, were a means of insuring that God's gift of land to the Hebrew people remained equitably distributed. From the onset, too, the concept was established that the land belonged to God and that each individual merely held it as a trustee. "Land was capital....To deprive someone of their land was thus to deprive them of social status and rob them of their power within the community of the people of God" (*Bad Samaritans,* p. 202).

In other words, the Jubilee Laws stipulated that land could not be sold in perpetuity, and that every forty-ninth year, the land must be returned to its original owner. Their laws required that all slaves must be freed, and that every seven years all debts would be forgiven; furthermore, the Hebrew people were prohibited from loaning money at interest to fellow Hebrews. According to Vallely, "It was a mechanism which enshrined social justice above the ability to maximize profit" (*Bad Samaritans*, p. 203).

Vallely has written a superb book, thorough and readily accessible. My only criticism is that the author is just a little too balanced and rational for my tastes. In an effort to find a reasonable path out of this tragic situation, he neglects to consider the irrational nature of the consumer-driven market economy compulsively stimulated by an aggressive advertising industry and ever-evolving technologies that tend to insure permanent underclass status for the Third World.

As Wolfgang Sachs writes, the problem "is the built-in capacity of advanced societies to continuously outpace others with the latest technology—to win at the game of competitive obsolescence. The rich countries drive hard to continuously degrade and discard the achievements of

43. Catholic workers disrupt LAPD press conference to protest Safer Cities Initiative. Pictured: Katie Kelso (left); Rev. Alice Callaghan, Jeff Dietrich (center), General Dogan, Los Angeles Community Action Network (LACAN) (right), 2010. Photo by Mike Wisniewski

yesterday in order to make room for the new improved version" ("The Obsolete Race," *New Perspectives Quarterly,* pp. 53-54).

Furthermore, in his efforts to draw a reasonable and practicable ethic of wealth and debt out of scripture, Vallely diminishes somewhat its prophetic, judgmental critique. "It would be utopian," he says, "to suggest that what is required is a literal application of the Jubilee rule: that all debts should be wiped away at the stroke of the clock" (*Bad Samaritans,* p. 278). No doubt it is utopian, but it would seem that literal application of the laws by the Hebrew people expressed an explicit condemnation of the surrounding nations, whose worship of false gods led to a false understanding of human nature and created social structures of domination, oppression, and injustice. It is difficult to read this book and not see a correlation between the debt crisis and Jesus' condemnation of the Pharisees who laid "heavy burdens...on people's shoulders, but they will not lift a finger to move them" (Matthew 23:4).

Jesus' response was to forgive unconditionally and to attack unrelentingly the structures of injustice. For Jesus, the forgiveness of sin is always equated with the forgiveness of debt. The entire mission and ministry of his public life is summarized in his "inaugural address" (the beginning of his ministry in Galilee) in which he proclaimed good news for the poor, the release of captives, and a year of the Lord's favor, or "Jubilee."

While we applaud the efforts of those who seek practical solutions for the amelioration of the crisis, we must never lose sight of the fact that this system cannot be converted into a fine and beautiful thing because it is premised upon violation of divine law. The entire system of wealth and debt is one of a myriad of modern techniques. Thus, like any other "technique," its intricacies are obscure, boring, even banal; only its consequences are interesting, explosive, tragic. The system will always be idolatrous, oppressive and unjust. It is in reality a sophisticated, arcane mechanism for obscuring its true intent, which is to rob the poor and enrich the powerful. The prophetic task, which is to say the Christian task, is to unmask its true intent, withdraw from its temples of power and privilege, pray for its victims, and as grace provides, live in solidarity with the poor.

Not One Stone upon Another

Catholic Agitator, May, 1992, p. 1

From the contorted expression of subdued rage on his face, I could tell that I was about to have a less-than-pleasant experience. "You, you're not a man," he said, and hawking up a substantial wad of spit, let it fly directly into my face. I was still reflecting on my own sense of anger and humiliation when I heard the news of the Rodney King verdict and the flames of rage that began to spread throughout the city.

My initial reaction was one of quiet satisfaction in the knowledge that the entire city was now being forced to experience what we encounter every day at our soup kitchen, in front of the welfare office, among the poor huddled in their cardboard condos. It was like a collective spit in the face.

But as the chaos grew increasingly out of control, destroying all sense of order, we became frightened and uncertain, so we gathered together in our basement prayer room to do the only thing left to us, pray to our God for some insight and courage in the midst of mass hysteria and insecurity. We chose as our appropriate theme the apocalyptic vision of Mark 13.

While Mark's vision of the apocalypse was not intended to be comforting, he did give some clarity to his community about how to maintain courage, faithfulness and common sense in a time of increasing fear, chaos, and delusion.

The tribulations of Mark's community revolved around the final conflict between the flames of Jewish nationalism and the military might of Roman imperialism. Should the followers of the nonviolent Jesus take up arms to defend the corrupt structures of the very temple-state that their leader had so unequivocally repudiated?

Should they follow the false messiahs of Jewish nationalism who sought to reestablish a militant Davidic kingship? Or should they remain faithful to the nonviolent, non-aligned politics of confrontation, compassion and sharing taught by Jesus?

We already know that the disciples have hearts that are hardened resembling the magnificent stones of the Temple that they so clearly admire in the opening lines of Mark, Chapter 13. Like us, in our contemporary situation, they have internalized the structures of the prevailing social system. But Jesus predicts that the end is near and that "there will be not one stone left upon another" (13:2).

Our situation is not entirely unlike that of the disciples. "Apocalypse" means to unmask. When the stones of the social structures come tumbling down, one upon another, as they did last week, the truth becomes startlingly clear to us. If we are awake and on guard against deception, we will see the brutality and emptiness of the powers unmasked. We will see the logic of a violent, self-indulgent system played out to its brutal conclusion. It is not unlike the alcoholic who comes to a startling realization of his destructive behavior patterns after having set fire to his own home, killing his wife and children in the process.

If we are asleep, however, we will turn once again to the same destructive behavior patterns, to the false messiahs of the American Dream: the media, the politicians, the state, the market economy, and economic progress. If we listen closely to the rhetoric of the false messiahs, it begins to sound like the same salvation offered to the African American community twenty-seven years ago after the Watts Riots of 1965, hollow promises of economic reform, educational programs, and a greater share of the increasing economic pie.

The only problem is that if this strategy didn't work when the American economic empire was at its zenith, why would it work now that it approaches its nadir? If we are but awake enough to see the signs of the times, these tribulations here in Los Angeles offer a glimpse of the tumbling stones of the American Dream and clarify the potential for increased class conflict in the wake of a shrinking economic pie.

In the years immediately following World War II, it was possible to promise the poor, and especially the newly-emerging black poor, a larger share of the ever-increasing economic pie. But as Russell Mead points out, the development of the global market has changed all of that (*Mortal Splendor*, pp. 308-310). Today a shirtmaker in Taiwan can use cotton from India, dyes from Indonesia, and oil from Saudi Arabia to make shirts for Peoria. This effort can be coordinated by a head office in New York financed by a worldwide financial network. For this reason, wage rates are often the

Jeff Dietrich

most significant, if not the only, difference between a number of otherwise equally convenient manufacturing locations. Thus do we find that well-paying union jobs in manufacturing that once offered the poor some hope of economic advancement have been relocated to a third world nation.

The real wages of the American worker peaked in 1973 at $200 a week. Since that time, they have been in steady decline at approximately 2 percent a year. The realities of the global market are such that the goal of all American policy planners must be to bring American wages into line with the rest of the world. It seems most unlikely that the post-riot "healing process" will be able to fulfill the promise of the American Dream, leaving the poor doubly devastated, both by the diminishing expectations of the global job market and by the increasingly stimulated expectations of consumer capitalism.

The internal logic of the American empire, with its ideology of progress and its true religion of market economics, has come home to roost, reducing the American Dream to a nightmare of consumerism. As Christopher Lasch pointed out:

> The idea of democracy came to be associated more and more closely with the prospect of universal abundance. America came to be seen as a nation not of citizens but of consumers. [The idea of] progress [was linked] to the democratization of consumption and held out the promise of a new civilization based on leisure for all.

The True and Only Heaven, pp. 68, 70

It is this unfulfilled promise of unlimited leisure and consumption that was played out before our eyes during the riots. While looting and burning are certainly less than commendable, to simply adapt a narrow, moralistic attitude about these activities merely contributes to our increasing blindness.

Rather, we must see these activities as a mirror image of the values of the larger community. The poor, and especially our black, urban, indigenous poor, have been stripped of traditional structures of family and community, and stand naked before the propaganda and violence of the market economy. They thus reflect the authentic values of a consumerist culture. Though the immigrant poor still reflect the values of a simpler, more integrated and human culture, they too have a difficult time passing those traditional values of hard work, personal dignity, and family cohesion on to the next generation, who regard their simple, unsophisticated parents as merely out of step with the progressive American ideal of consumption and leisure.

Even the affluent, who are able to build a protective wall of money around their families, have an increasingly difficult time protecting their children from the violence and self-indulgence of the market system because, as Christopher Lasch writes:

> In our time it is increasingly clear that children [and I would add especially poor, inner city children] pay the price for this invasion of the family by the market. With both parents in the work place and grandparents conspicuous by their absence, the family is no longer capable of sheltering children from the market. The television becomes the principal babysitter by default.

"Communitarianism or Populism?" *New Oxford Review,* p. 7

Now, as we approach the demise of the American empire, the poor, increasingly stimulated by a system based on rising expectations, demand fulfillment of that promise. It should thus come as no surprise that the poor would take advantage of the recent turmoil to go shopping for those items that are tantalizingly denied to them a thousand times a day. But that promise of consumerist fulfillment has always been based not upon economic sharing, but upon increasing the size of the pie. When you allow the values of the market place to destroy the traditional human values of community, family and the common good, when you reduce the American Dream to its basest level of consumer fulfillment and leisure time activities, when you preach it to the poor ten thousand times a day, using sports figures, media icons, and sex symbols, and finally when you then refuse them access even to the minimum the system has to offer them, of course you are going to have apocalyptic disaster. The stones will come tumbling down and not one will be left upon another.

For well over a century we blindly ascribed to the illusion fostered by the American Dream, that progress would bring prosperity, that the meritocracy of the market place would foster peace and brotherhood. But now we must wake up to the apocalyptic realization that these values are not the solution. They are, rather, the problem itself that has caused and will continue to cause the disastrous consequences we have so recently experienced in the LA riots.

We must begin the difficult work, not of increasing the size of the pie, but rather slicing it up, sharing what we have now rather than what we will accumulate in the future.

44. Blood Strike. Pictured: Bill Hoard (center), Alice Callaghan (left), Ray Correio (right), 1973. Photo by Annie Leibovitz, Credit: © Annie Leibovitz/Contact Press Images courtesy of the Artist

Even now the false prophets are rushing to outdo themselves, offering multiple "signs and miracles" of a spurious salvation to our nation. Those on the right of the political spectrum proclaim the benefits of an unmediated market system, while those on the left preach the salvation of a market system mediated by the state. As Christians, we must wake up out of the American Dream and reject the very stones of the market system itself, seeking out instead the "stone rejected by the builders," basing our lives on a new foundation of radical simplicity, sharing, and community offered by the only true Savior, Jesus Christ.

Wilderness Economics

Catholic Agitator, April, 2009, pp. 1 and 2

Lent is traditionally a time of cutting back, of peeling away and doing without. Similarly, the current economic crisis actually forces us, as individuals and collectively as a nation, to live closer to the bone—a most un-American experience.

My parents, especially my father, had an unshakable faith in the American system, grounded in their experience of US victory in World War II and in the power of American technology to solve problems. They shared a vision of unending moral and social progress and an abiding conviction in the moral righteousness of an America that had defeated Nazism and restored sanity to a nightmare world. They were convinced that just as we had won the war against fascism, so we would also win the war against poverty and ignorance, and that technological progress was synonymous with moral progress.

My wife Catherine's parents, on the other hand, though just a decade older, represented quite a different vision of America. Born of immigrant parents and coming of age during the depression, they had personal memories of suffering and struggle—losing jobs, standing in food lines, burning tires to keep warm, union solidarity and labor struggle. Though later in their lives they achieved economic success and middle class status, they never abandoned their ties to the labor movement and they never voted Republican. But more importantly, they always had a healthy sense of limitations as well as a personal memory of human suffering.

On a socioeconomic level, my parents identified with the American Empire experience as the victors of history, while Catherine's parents, no less a part of the comfortable middle class, maintained a tenuous connection to the immigrant and working class, to the struggle and suffering, to the victims of history. It is that connection with the suffering victim and the repudiation of the mentality of the victor that is the essential experience of Lent.

The discipline of Lent, taught to us in our churches today, comes from the scriptural story of Jesus' wilderness experience. Essentially, the Temptations take Jesus back to the foundational Exodus journey of his people's escape from Egypt. But the term "wilderness" also implies the experience of a return to the early, precivilization beginnings of humanity.

The three Temptations, as articulated in Luke (4:1-12), focus on the basic sins of empire: turning stones into bread presents the image of exploiting nature for economic gain; the kingdoms "owned by Satan" represent military/state power; and the temple parapet represents the power of spiritual cults that validate the project of empire. Empire is a self-fulfilling and self-validating system, unlimited by the realities of nature or the demands of a just and compassionate God, and vehemently rejected by Jesus.

But with his return to the "wilderness," Jesus also returns to a more primal setting, one closer to our aboriginal hunter-gatherer ancestors. Anthropologist John Gowdy writes:

> People who lived with almost no material possessions for hundreds of thousands of years, enjoyed lives in many ways richer and more rewarding than ours....These people had structured their lives so that they needed little, wanted little, and, for the most part had all the means of fulfilling their needs at their immediate disposal. They spent their abundant leisure time eating, drinking, playing, socializing—in short, doing the very things we associate with affluence.

"Introduction," *Limited Wants, Unlimited Means,* p. xv

For Jesus, the wilderness represents a return to a time before civilization, with its economics of theft and exploitation, where the satisfaction of basic human needs took precedence over the voracious appetites of empire. Similarly, for the anthropologist, Marshall Sahlins, the wilderness offers what he calls:

> A Zen road to affluence...[tells us] that human material wants are finite and few, and technical means unchanging, but on the whole adequate. Adapting the Zen strategy, a people can enjoy unparalleled material plenty—with a low standard of living.

Stone Age Economics, p. 2

Jeff Dietrich

45. The Hospitality House Kitchen, 2011. Photo by Robert Radin

Modern western economics, on the other hand, says Sahlins, creates a situation wherein "consumption is a double tragedy….Bringing together an international division of labor, the market makes available a dazzling array of products: all of these Good Things within man's reach—but never all within his grasp. Worse, in this game of consumer free choice, every acquisition is simultaneously a deprivation" (*Stone Age Economics*, p. 4).

Sahlins (and Jesus) remind us that the basic organizing principle of our market economy (that humans are driven by greed and that more is always better than less) is not an intrinsically human characteristic, and was in fact quite contrary to the way tens of thousands of cultures were organized in the 200,000 years since the emergence of "homo sapiens." This is a timely though difficult reminder for Americans to hear, long on a binge of over-consumption and over-indulgence in the good things. The current economic crisis is a result of the recurring crisis of capitalist overproduction to meet the needs of voracious consumers. According to economic analyst Joshua Holland,

> In the booming years after World War II, the wealthy countries, led
> by the United States, did very well manufacturing goods for the entire

planet. But as Japan rose from the ashes, and, later, as production in countries like Taiwan, South Korea and Singapore increased, the industrial world simply started making more crap than there were consumers to purchase it."

"In a Perfect Storm of Economic Stagflation," AlterNet.org

This overproduction, actually surplus production, led to a decline in the profitability of investment in concrete things, which has in turn led investors scurrying for abstract financial instruments in search of a fat return. "A report in the *Economist*, cited by [social critic Walden] Bello, found that the world of Clinton's 'New Economy' was 'awash with excess capacity in computer chips, steel, cars, textiles, and chemicals' and noted that 'the gap between capacity and output was the largest since the Great Depression'" ("Meltdown and Bailout," AlterNet.org). In other words, there was an over-supply of nearly everything. According to Bello, "An inevitable result of that imbalance was a massive migration of capital from real productive industry to the 'speculative sector' run by giants like AIG and Lehman Brothers" ("Meltdown and Bailout," AlterNet.org).

In the meantime, we have created a global economy in which economic justice has been hypocritically tied to the free market's unregulated "economic growth," leading to poverty and despair for the vast majority of the world's population and the rape of global resources and the environment. According to a United Nations report, 80 percent of the world's population lives on $10 or less a day. And the global economy is in crisis, with a backlog of superfluous products aimed at a mere fraction of the world's population—who themselves can no longer afford to buy them.

The immediate solution, on one level, demands a massive regulation of the financial markets as well as the credit industry. But, on a deeper level, the crisis offers an opportunity for a complete re-evaluation of the capitalist market economy itself—one where the needs of the world's poor, as well as the needs of a planet in the midst of environmental collapse, take precedent over the needs of profit for the few.

Like my parents, who identified with the American project and its ideology of progress, and victory, most Americans, at least since the Reagan era, have tied their fate to the interests of the wealthy. But it was the era of Catherine's parents, the Great Depression, with its experience of economic failure and shared suffering, that led to the most effective and egalitarian reforms in our country's history. And while President Obama, an African American raised by a single-parent mom on welfare, is immensely closer to that experience than our former silver spoon first executive, he is hardly a radical; he will not engage in the necessary re-examination of capital demanded by this crisis unless pushed by his constituency.

During this time of Lenten stripping away, as we come closer to living lives of forced simplicity that link us more closely to our primitive ancestors as well as to poor people throughout the world, we should not think that the quaint practices of Lent are merely spiritual in nature, having no impact on the real world. The traditional Lenten practice of abstinence comes to mind—Catholics fasting from meat on Fridays during Lent results in consumption of 354 fewer million pounds of meat and the release of 2.921 billion pounds less carbon dioxide into an already overheated atmosphere for the forty days before Easter.

We can and must use this time of Lenten-like economic crisis to critically re-evaluate our most basic assumptions. We must consider practicing our Lenten disciplines on a regular basis as a means of rejecting the empire's mentality of overconsumption and overproduction. In remembering the radical call of wilderness, and identifying our lives with poor people rather than with rich people, we will find our best hope in re-aligning our economic means to meet the authentic needs of all people and to heal our planet.

PART EIGHT

IMAGE OVER SUBSTANCE

And perhaps in this is the whole difference; perhaps all wisdom, and all truth, and all sincerity are just compressed into that inappreciable moment of time in which we step over the threshold of the invisible.

Joseph Conrad,
The Heart of Darkness

Cordelia: Nothing, my lord.
Lear: Nothing?

William Shakespeare,
King Lear 1.1.87-8

Notes on Consumerism

Catholic Agitator, November, 1993, pp. 1, 5, and 7

The poor are not nice! At least twice a week the poor awaken us with the sounds of their angry gunfire in the streets below. In the last two years, our kitchen has been burglarized by the poor a total of eight times. That doesn't even count the score or so plants that the poor have stolen from our garden, the batteries lifted from our cars, and even the goldfish from our pond. The poor are not nice. Yesterday at our soup kitchen, Reuben tried to clobber a woman with a lead pipe; when my wife stepped between them Reuben assaulted her with a string of vivid metaphorical references to biological and scatological activities that would have made Henry Miller blush. The poor are not nice.

We hate the poor because they are violent, because they spend their money on entertainment rather than housing, because they prefer leisure to work. We hate the poor because they are irresponsible, depressing, and superficial. Ultimately, we hate the poor because they personify the evils of the whole society writ large.

On the other hand, we love the third world poor. The third world poor are nice. They work hard, they take care of their kids, they go to church on Sunday, they have dignity, purpose and a sense of self worth. Unlike our own poor, the third world poor are just materially impoverished, not spiritually impoverished. Third world poor are the nice poor: they fulfill our expectations that poor people should be nice folks who just need a helping hand, rather than an underclass of individuals with intractable problems that mirror our own pathological addiction to violence, consumption, and mind-numbing media propaganda.

Of course we love the third world poor: they still live in villages, they still have community, they still do meaningful work. These are precisely the values we, in the developed world, have sacrificed in the name of progress,

Jeff Dietrich

utopia, and unlimited growth. We are disappointed and frustrated when our own urban First World poor mimic the violence, rapaciousness, and acquisitiveness that form the very heart of our consumer culture. The poor are the ones who have most effectively internalized the cultural myths that character is defined by possessions, that work is onerous, and that leisure and consumption are the only important goals in life.

As a non-scholar I find myself somewhat intimidated at the prospect of writing about the impact of consumer culture. But as a Catholic Worker, I am encouraged by our co-founder Peter Maurin who, from the beginning, established a tradition in our movement of lay scholarly reflection. Without the benefit of such reflection one is left open to the constant threat of imprisonment by the banal, superficial ideologies of popular liberal culture or the encrusted moralizing of political and religious fundamentalists, neither of which is very satisfying.

While Peter Maurin's vision revolved around the critique of industrial production, contemporary Catholic Workers must reflect on the profound social change that has taken place around the patterns of capitalist consumption that have accelerated so rapidly in the post-war period. To ignore this work is to make the same mistake as the former Soviet Union. At its demise in 1990, the USSR had in place the perfect system of industrial production... for 1935. The world has changed profoundly since Josef Stalin and Peter Maurin developed their respective visions. But as Marshall McLuhan once said, "We look at the present through a rear-view mirror. [And thus do] we march backwards into the future" (*The Medium is the Massage*, p. 75).

All of us who are concerned about social justice, whether we are Catholic Workers, moral theologians, or popes who write encyclicals, have a tendency to look at the world through our rear-view mirrors. But if we spend any time among the poor or the young or the marginated, we begin to notice that there is a new social reality that reflects the profound sense of alienation, narcissistic self-indulgence, and cynical despair inherent in our system of consumer culture. Social historian Stuart Ewen notes that:

> The historic fragmentation of social life is a basic component of our understanding of the character of *mass culture*. The displacement of collective modes of living, work, ritual, and sensibility makes room for the elaboration of a media panorama, consumed and understood by people individually. Ultimately, within a rising, universal marketplace, *consumerism* is the basic social relationship replacing customary bonds.

Channels of Desire, p. 262

The only way I can make sense out of what appears to be a reality shift is to accept that theologian/sociologist Jacques Ellul is correct when he says that the "sacred" of our culture is no longer nature, but "technique."

The "sacred" is that element of culture from which all myth, ideology, and common wisdom flow. For Ellul, the "sacred" means almost exactly the opposite of the common usage of the term. The "sacred" for Ellul is that which a culture holds important (*The Subversion of Christianity*, p. 53). He reserves "holy" to designate that which is truly holy, the realm of transcendent Truth, the unnameable God.

Myths are stories about those things the society holds sacred. The primary myths of our contemporary culture, Ellul says, are the myths of history and science. From these myths flow the secondary myths of progress, youth, and utopia. Ellul's concern is not so much that there has been a transition as that the sacred technique—in the absence of any competing vision—has quickly developed into a monistic system that imprisons language, thought, and reality within the confines of its own limits. The very efficacy of technique militates against the development of transcendent thought (*The Technological Society*, pp. 92-94).

Ellul writes that the realm of technique is the realm of the primarily visual. "The image is everywhere, but now we bestow dignity, authenticity and spiritual truth on it. We enclose within the image everything that belongs to the order of truth" (*The Humiliation of the Word*, p. 95).

For all of us caught up in the contemporary reality of technique, seeing is believing; a picture is worth a thousand words. But this emphasis on the visual diminishes the power of the word in discursive or dialectical reasoning. We can see the most distressing example in our preference for television news over print news, action over reflection, reality over truth.

"Thus," writes Ellul, "in the thinking of modern individuals the image is the means *par excellence* [emphasis added] which communicates reality and truth at the same time" (*The Humiliation of the Word*, p. 31).

What appears to be the trivial, superficial activities of advertising, fashion, design, and entertainment are in fact the very heart of our culture's experience, transcending even the capitalist demands for buying and selling. They actually form the liturgies and rituals of what Neil Postman calls "Technopoly," a system in which technology of every kind is granted sovereignty over social institutions and national life. In his book of the same name, Postman decries the process of "symbol drain," in which any competing narratives, through the efforts of advertising and mass media, are drained of their motivating and energizing power. In effect, all other

Jeff Dietrich

narratives or myths are desacralized by the all-consuming myth of Technopoly ("The Great Symbol Drain," pp. 164-180).

In this system, all images are grist for the style mills, and whatever opposition that might have been contained in the historical reality from which the image emerged is eliminated. Thus, we find 60s rock and roll songs that protested conformism being used to sell Buicks. And the same has happened with the women's movement, the ecology movement, and the rap music of gang kids. What could be more trivializing than the appropriation of the ultimate black liberation figure, Malcolm X, as a fashion statement? And so, opposites become unified in the visual image.

The core of consumer culture is formed by the industries of fashion and image-making. Stuart Ewen writes, "The mechanical reproduction of styled goods, previously possessions of extreme wealth, signaled the beginnings of a mass market in style" (*All-Consuming Images,* p. 32). This process resulted in the development of what came to be known as "consumer democracy," which was founded on the idea that the symbols and prerogatives of the elite could now be made available on a mass scale. By the 1930s, with the consumer economy in serious straits, styling and "style consciousness" came to the forefront as methods designed to stimulate markets, and to keep them stimulated. Even durable goods were reconceptualized and sold as if they were non-durables.

Thus, our reference signs no longer point back to the world of nature, art, or literature, but rather to an artificial world based on old movies, television shows, commercials, video games, to the passing panoply of fashion, and the diversions of entertainment. In this hyper-reality world of simulation, it makes perfect sense to have an aging movie star as president of the United States. Ronald Reagan's ability to reconceptualize American history in terms of clips from various old movies, or refashion his own dysfunctional family as Ozzie and Harriet in the White House, and to sell public policy with the banal ease of an infomercial, made him the apotheosis of hyper-reality. And to be sure, our current president, Bill Clinton, who can work the talk show circuit, do the MTV thing, and reference himself to a black jazz saxophonist, is no slacker in the realm of hyper-reality either.

This process of substituting image for reality, surface for substance, began with the invention of photography a little more than a hundred years ago. Stuart Ewen quotes Oliver Wendell Holmes in a euphoric but prescient vision:

For Holmes, photography signaled the beginning of a time when "the image would become more important than the object itself, and would in fact make the object disposable." "*Form,*" he proclaimed, "*is henceforth divorced from matter.*" Men will hunt all curious, grand, and beautiful objects, as they hunt the cattle in South America, for their skins, and leave the carcasses as of little worth.

All-Consuming Images, p. 25

Since the time of the Enlightenment, the core of western social experience has been formed by our sacralization of the marketplace and desacralization of nature, by our faith in science, our hope in the future, and our deadly love for the individual over the communal.

We have fallen victim to the naïve assumption that unwavering adherence to these values would ultimately lead us to the Promised Land: utopian abundance in which the surplus wealth and material goods created by machine production would increase so astronomically that its abundance would be distributed lavishly throughout the planet. Such has not been the case. Rather, what we have created is a self-perpetuating, self-directing system of means without ends.

Its goal is its own growth and development without regard to its impact on humanity or the environment. Any attempt to retard this system or to redirect it will inevitably result in the unacceptable chaos of unemployment and social instability. Even something as simple as eliminating or restricting the advertising industry, which would go a long way towards humanizing our social environment, would result in an intolerable decline of the gross national product. And finally, it is sheer folly to even contemplate bringing third world countries up to First World consumption standards. "If all countries followed the industrial example," says German economist Wolfgang Sachs, "five or six planets would be needed to serve as 'sources' for the inputs and 'sink' for the waste of economic progress" (*Global Ecology*, p. 6).

The real goal of all consumption is a kind of faith commitment to the perpetuation of our system of technological and economic growth. Though this system has destroyed all traditional social structures and the values that undergirded those structures, though it has fractured the integrity of labor and degraded the environment, we nevertheless maintain our commitment to it because it has so effectively substituted the immediate gratification of products for the long-term satisfaction of psychic and emotional wholeness. But this satiation has left us empty, alienated creatures, awash in a

Jeff Dietrich

rising sea of lifeless objects that have no authentic relation to our lives. As the poet Rainer Maria Rilke writes,

> Even for our grandparents, a "house," a "well," a familiar tower, their very dress, their cloak, were infinitely more intimate: almost everything a vessel in which they found and stored humanity. Now there came crowding over from America empty, indifferent things, pseudo-things, dummy-life things....The animated, experienced things that share our lives are coming to an end and cannot be replaced. We are perhaps the last to have still known such things. On us rests the responsibility of preserving, not merely their memory (that would be little and unreliable), but their human and laral* worth.

Selected Letters of Rainer Marie Rilke, p. 129

I know that people may respond that this is a really bad situation, but it's not as though we are living in the worst social system in the world. So what if our young people are living in a state of narcissistic despair and cynical alienation? So what if the murder and suicide rates are going up astronomically? So what if we are awash in garbage? So what if the real world looks increasingly like a facsimile of Disneyland? So what if it's difficult to distinguish image from substance? These are the problems of jaded philosophers, who in another era would have wasted their time speculating on the number of angels that could dance on the head of a pin. At least here in America we aren't living in the midst of famine and rampant disease. At least we are not living in Russia, or worse, Cuba, where things are really bad. If you don't have a solution, don't bring up the problem.

Well, first of all, it's better to know the truth than not to know it. For if we know the truth, we might be inclined to accept a less arrogant self-appraisal. While we do not suffer from disease or material want, we certainly suffer from spiritual poverty and moral degradation. One wonders if places like Poland are better off today than they were before the collapse of the Soviet Union. At least then they had a clear sense of who the enemy was, of who they were and what they stood for, and why their religion was important. Today Vaclav Havel does commercials for the American Tobacco Institute, Lech Walesa enforces onerous economic sanctions, and one wonders how long religious fervor can withstand the onslaught of designer jeans, Big Macs, and TV game shows.

---

*   A reference to "Household gods."

47. Cover illustration by Gary Palmatier. *Catholic Agitator*, 1978

Jeff Dietrich

I don't know what the solution is, but to be quite honest, if we have a clearer picture of the problem we might not be so inclined to repeat the problem and call it a solution. In Los Angeles, there is much talk about healing the wounds of the riots, yet, amidst all of this talk, political and social leaders are incapable of addressing the wound of consumer culture because it cuts to the very heart of our society's disintegration. Instead, they have cut back welfare, closed county hospitals, eliminated all low-cost housing programs, increased the police force, and doubled the capacity of the county jail.

In the Bible, the prophets also talk of healing. But this healing only comes after the fall of Jerusalem and the exile of the chosen people to Babylon. Today, it is just as true that healing can only come after the hardened hearts of the rich and powerful have been circumcised by suffering and defeat. In the absence of conversion, healing is hypocrisy. It is just another name for business as usual.

True healing comes only when we realize that we cannot do the healing. At most, we can be a presence among the poor and wounded. Hence, we live in a neighborhood where gunshots are common night sounds and stripping cars is an accepted pastime; we built a soup kitchen and dining garden knowing that we will be repaid with ingratitude and burglary. Healing means going to the places of deepest woundedness, knowing that we can do nothing, but believing—against all odds—that through us, God can do everything.

Reagan's America

Catholic Agitator, April, 1987, p. 2

It is one thing to say that the emperor is wearing no clothes; it is quite another to be able to explain the process by which the emperor became naked and why the populace insist upon seeing royal finery where there is nothing but naked flesh. In the last six years there has been a chorus of insistent voices exposing the naked truth about Ronald Reagan. But Garry Wills, in his new book *Reagan's America*, is the only voice to explain in detail why Reagan's nakedness has gone so unnoticed by the general public. It becomes clear rather quickly in reading this excellent book that the fabric of the President's clothes had been cut from the material of our common mythology and that is why the vast majority of the populace refuses to see the nakedness that has been exposed before their very eyes—we ourselves are the tailors.

For Wills it is not enough to say that Ronald Reagan lies, postures, and panders to the American people. Wills forces us to take a serious look at this fabric of illusion, fantasy, and myth in which Reagan had clothed himself.

Not since Dwight Eisenhower has a president successfully completed two terms in the White House. The American empire is splitting apart, torn asunder by irresolvable inconsistencies: democratic values conflicting with imperial power, government secrecy clashing with the public's right to know, voracious consumption at odds with traditional thriftiness, and industrial capitalism conflicting with the need for full employment.

Reagan, however, has appeared to resolve our inconsistencies. According to Wills,

> He "skins and films the ulcerous place" where disparities open between what we think of ourselves and what we do. He casts a surface unity over elements that have long been drifting apart—religious beliefs away from religious posturing, conservative nostalgia from capitalist

innovation, interdependence from nonconformism. He spans the chasm by not noticing it. He elides our cultural inconcinnities.

Reagan's America, p. 459

Much like a primitive shaman, Reagan invokes the iconography of collective myth to unify and manipulate his followers. Mythology is simply the collective stories that a culture tells about itself to illustrate essential cultural values; these are always emotional and evocative to the people of the culture and have the potential to motivate individuals to action. That action can be positive, as with Christian mythology, or it can be negative, as with the Aryan mythology of Hitler's Germany.

Ronald Reagan's favorite mythic image is that of the rugged individual settling a frontier on his own, without the aid of onerous government, but as Wills points out:

> We picture the space [of the frontier] and the sparse numbers of original settlers defined against it. We think this conjunction must make for innovation, individual initiative, a break with tradition. But comparative study of frontier conditions indicates that the very reverse of these traits is more often produced. Those really without "govment" want it badly; in fact go and beg the authorities for it.

Reagan's America, p. 107

Reagan has capitalized on this myth of the independent frontiersmen by failing to acknowledge anything good about "government." Thus by evoking the inherent American distaste for bigness, he has been able to remain in public office both as governor of California and as President of the United States, despite the fact that he has created historically unprecedented budgets and deficits. He gives Americans a sense of history and identity while his policies in fact threaten to remove humanity from history itself. He is an individualist of a popular and conforming variety. Reagan's success as a communicator lies in his training as a Hollywood actor. Early in his political career, the Hollywood connection was seen as a frivolous detriment, but in actuality the entire Hollywood experience was the most crucial and seminal feature of Reagan's development as an American icon.

Hollywood is the home of modern mythmaking as well as being an epic myth itself. The role of Hollywood as dream factory and story-teller is well understood; what is more, the Hollywood star system has led to actors

48. *Catholic Agitator*, 1983. Photo by Aldon Alger

becoming heroic figures bigger than life itself. (Note all the actors endorsing political causes, both Right and Left, with their names and images).

Less understood is how Hollywood forms the conservative values of this nation as well as its President. It took no methodological break-through for anthropologist Hortense Powdermaker to conclude that Hollywood's vision was politically and culturally conservative (*Hollywood: The Dream Factory*). Many of the men responsible for the movies were anxious to achieve public respectability—Joseph Kennedy no less than Louis B. Mayer (who incidentally contributed vast sums of money to defeat progressive Upton Sinclair as governor of California in the 1930s). Financiers of the movies were and are today businessmen with large ventures to protect. Powdermaker found the film community taboo-ridden, insecure and trying to please, self-censoring, afraid, and unable to subvert society even if it wanted to, and that was the last thing it wanted: "We are allowed to dream the wildest things so long as we do not think anything new" (*Hollywood: The Dream Factory*, p. 53).

The greatest myth perpetuated by President Reagan and the one that Americans love most is the myth of innocence. Since the founding of the first American colonies, this country has been popularly conceived as the "new Eden," a place exempt from the wars, oppressions, and sins of Europe. But as Wills writes,

> There is no "clean slate" of nature unscribbled on by all one's fore-bears, no neat break from an "old world" to begin again on a "virgin continent." There is no "America" as Americans have often conceived it. The doctrine of original sin states that humankind…"has a past." And much of American theorizing has been intended to exempt this country from that stigma. Yet the only way to avoid such trammels would be to have no other person's act affect us; and the only way to do that would be to exist in a state where one's own actions were equally inconsequential in others' lives. That would be the perfect triumph of individualism, where "men should be as gods" to themselves, each ruling his own "universe."
>
> *Reagan's America*, p. 458

The appeal of this myth, wherein America is free from original sin, has grown significantly in the last two decades since the fall of Vietnam, the rise of international terrorism, and the diminishment of American prestige. President Reagan offers us a version of the past that is attractive but illusionary. The problem is that:

> If one settles…for a substitute past, an illusion of it, then that fragile construct must be protected from the challenge of complex or contradictory evidence, from any test of evidence at all. That explains Americans' extraordinary tacit bargain with each other not to challenge Reagan's version of the past. The power of his appeal is the great joint confession that we cannot live with our real past, that we not only prefer but need a substitute.
>
> *Reagan's America*, p. 458

In spite of the scandal surrounding his presidency at the moment,* the polls show that the public still likes Ronald Reagan. Perhaps it is because he

---

*   A political scandal in the US (1986) in which the Reagan administration sold arms to Iran and used the proceeds to fund the Contra insurrection in Nicaragua.

continues to tell us the tales that we want to hear and, like small children, we are eager to visit the past that our storyteller conjures up:

> Even young people who did not grow up with Reagan, or grow up hearing him on the radio or watching him at the movies, have accepted his version of the past as their own best pledge of the future. That is not as surprising as it might seem. A visit to his past is always a pleasant experience. Visiting Reaganland is very much like taking children to Disneyland, where they can deal with a New Orleans cut to their measure. It is a safe past, with no sharp edges to stumble against. The more visits one makes to such a past, the better is one immunized against any troubling incursions of a real New Orleans, a real racetrack, a real American West.

Reagan's America, p. 459

If Ronald Reagan has entranced the American public through the invocation of powerful mythic images so that they cannot see that the empire is crumbling under the weight of its own contradictions, and that the emperor himself is naked, without meaning or substance, we must remember that people are usually not fooled unless they want to be fooled. It is usually necessary to supply the wool before it can be pulled over one's eyes.

Jesus Christ, Silver Surfer*
or Suffering Servant

Catholic Agitator, August, 2007, pp. 1, 2, and 6

Jesus Christ, Silver Surfer—though it may sound a bit irreverent to speak of Jesus in terms of a comic book super hero skimming across the waves to rescue the disciples in their beleaguered fishing boat on the Sea of Galilee (Matthew 14:22-23), it is nonetheless the image of Jesus that the majority of Christians adhere to. It is an image of God that the majority of the world's population, both believers and non-believers, long for—a Savior that will allow us to practice our collective follies of greed and war-making, and rescue us at the last minute.

As a child of the Enlightenment and scientific rationalism, I am, of course, predisposed to skepticism regarding miracles. But my issue with miracles goes far deeper. It has to do more with vocation than with cultural predispositions. As a Catholic Worker, I tend to think of Jesus as sort of like us: feeding the hungry, sheltering the homeless, clothing the naked, "comforting the afflicted and afflicting the comfortable," and periodically getting in trouble for being outspoken and scandalous. I also have difficulty with creeds and dogmas that forthrightly proclaim the Virgin Birth, the divine status, and the Resurrection of Jesus as essentials of faith. On the other hand, I believe that the Gospels tell a great story and that miracles are crucial to the telling of that story.

In order to understand the walking on water scene, it is essential to realize that it comes at the beginning of an extended narrative of disciple-ship teaching that starts in Chapter 14 and culminates in Chapter 21 with the entry into Jerusalem and the ultimate Crucifixion of Jesus. This extended narrative includes two feedings, numerous healings, and a major "theophany," the Transfiguration. But it begins with the beheading of John

---

* The animated television series based on the Marvel Comics superhero.

the Baptist, a grisly foreshadowing, and includes increasingly vitriolic confrontations with the authorities, interspersed with three definitive predictions of the Crucifixion.

The high cost of discipleship is the singular lesson of this entire sixth chapter section. It is in this context of increasing political opposition and increasing discipleship demands that Matthew presents his tumultuous water crossing as metaphor for the ultimate discipleship rejection of Jesus' project.

Jesus has just fed the 5,000 in the wilderness and forced the disciples to get in the boat without him so that he can go up to the mountain to pray. The disciples row all night against the wind, still not getting to the other side. Then Jesus comes swooping in like the Silver Surfer to rescue the beleaguered boatmen, who are filled with fear because they think he is a ghost. Of course, as soon as the disciples figure out what is happening, they immediately identify him as the Son of God and fall down and worship him, which is just exactly the opposite of what Jesus wants from his disciples.

It is only natural for human beings to long for visual, manifest, incontrovertible evidence for our faith—a sign, if you will. But Jesus rejects a religion of signs and miracles, refusing to jump off the temple or change bread into stones for Satan (Matthew 4:1-11). He twice refuses the Pharisees' demand for a sign, telling them that "an evil and unfaithful generation seeks a sign" (Matthew 12:39). Obviously, for the Pharisees, exorcisms, feedings, and healings, which he has already performed, do not adequately qualify as signs. Indeed, most commentators do, in fact, make a distinction between what might be described as ministries of Jesus and such obvious transgressions of the natural order as defying gravity and death...as in the Resurrection and walking on water.

In one of his most brilliant works, *The Humiliation of the Word*, Jacques Ellul points out that there is a basic antithesis in scripture between sight and word. "The biblical revelation," writes Ellul, "is radically opposed to everything visual. The only possible relationship with God is based on the word, and nothing else" (p. 71). It is out of the question to try to grasp God through sight, to claim that what one sees can be God. Therefore, the whole visual sphere begins to be suspected Biblically.

Ellul is rigorously single-minded in his reflections on the Word. He recognizes God, the creator of the universe, to be the Word and that God's Word created all things and that that Word is all powerful. He further recognizes that human language is an intimate reflection of the Word, and it is through the Word that God speaks to every human being; so the word that humans use to communicate with each other is intimately bound up with the living Word of God. And thus it is that scripture privileges the Word over the image, the statue, the icon.

But for humans, seeing is believing; the visual is synonymous with reality, while the word is ambiguous, argumentative, dialectical. It is hard to pin down. Yet it is within that ambiguity that we find freedom. "The word is an expression of freedom," writes Ellul. "It presupposes freedom and invites the listener as well to assert his freedom by speaking. God is the liberator. We must constantly remember that the God of Israel manifests himself historically for the first time in the Exodus as the one who liberates human beings from slavery" (*The Humiliation of the Word*, p. 58).

Essentially, however, no one wants a religion of freedom, ambiguity and dialogue—we want a religion of signs, certainty, and dogma. But, "faith and sight are in contradiction," writes Ellul. "The miracle is a sign without meaning in itself. Its truth resides only in the word that accompanies it" (*The Humiliation of the Word*, p. 80). And this is precisely the case in Matthew's most visually compelling theophany: the Transfiguration (Matthew 17:1-8). Here too, it is the word that holds center stage and clarifies why the disciples got it wrong in the boat. When the disciples actually see the glory of Jesus revealed on the mountain top along with the resurrected Moses and Elijah, they betray their predisposition for a visual faith by proposing the quintessential church project: a building program. "If you wish, I will make three tents here, one for you, and one for Moses, and one for Elijah" (Matthew 17:4). Like a typical Christian, the disciples are ever ready to build a church and worship the visibly powerful transfigured Jesus. But in a very real sense, their worship of Jesus is idolatry.

We tend to think of idolatry as the false religion of images practiced by the ancient, benighted pagans, but Christian idolatry is unfortunately the religion practiced by the vast majority of Christians who separate the Word of God from the miracles of God and allow themselves to become transfixed before the power of God. Divine theophanies, tangible manifestations, miraculous events, are all manifestations of power and are problematic for human beings. In the absence of the Word, theophanies become mere images, images become idols, and idols are the image of power around which powerful institutions coalesce: Caesar, Pharaoh, and Alexander in ancient times, Hitler, Stalin, and Mao in our time. It all follows from the "building of booths"—temporary shelters become permanent edifices that over time become institutional structures for the "glory of God" and the enhancement of power for the acolytes and bureaucrats who mediate that "glory."

Ellul finds the roots of this Christian fascination with images in the post-Constantinian Church. "The Church," he says, "opted for the visible, and with it, for power, authority, efficacy, and the agglomeration of crowds around a reality that was at last seen and grasped" (*The Humiliation of the Word*, p. 191). Thus, in the Gospel of Matthew, it is the very voice of God that must speak in the Transfiguration to indisputably affirm the priority of word over image.

"Hello. This is God! Get a clue—he's my son. Listen to him!" Ironically, God confirms the disciples' original insight in the boat regarding Jesus' divine parentage, but they are deaf to the Word.

Along with the disciples, the reader also receives divine affirmation that the most important thing that we can do is not worship Jesus, but listen to him. Listening is the central motif of the Gospel, and it is first introduced at the end of the Sermon on the Mount (Matthew 7:24-28) when Jesus says, "Everyone who listens to these words of mine and acts on them will be like a wise man who built his house on a rock."

Too bad Jesus didn't copyright the image of the "rock," because in our culture it has been appropriated by the folks at Prudential Insurance Company,* who tell us that security comes from prudent financial investment. But Jesus says just the opposite because you cannot serve God and money: "Do not worry about your life, what you will eat (or drink)...what you will wear. Seek first his kingdom (of God)...and all these things will be given you besides" (Matthew 6:25,33) "Love your enemies, and pray for those who persecute you" (Matthew 5:44).

No wonder the voice of God has to confirm these words of Jesus—they are so contrary to worldly prudence and security. In truth, the bulk of Christian theology over the centuries has been dedicated to explaining why Jesus did not mean exactly what he said.

As implausible as it sounds, the "rock" of discipleship is grounded on hearing and practicing these very words. But the disciple Peter represents quite a different kind of "rock." When Jesus asks him, "Who do you say that I am?" Peter, just as he did in the boat, gets it half-right. "You are the Messiah, the Son of the living God," he says. For his insight, Jesus declares him Rock, and "upon this rock I will build my church," he says (Matthew 16:15-16,18).

But it's a pretty shaky rock. When Jesus explains what it means to be the Messiah—going down to Jerusalem to confront the authorities and getting killed—Peter protests, causing Jesus to identify him with Satan.

---

* The logo of the company is a giant, Gibraltar-like rock.

"Get behind me, Satan! You are an obstacle to me. You are thinking not as God does, but as human beings do," says Jesus (Matthew 16:23).

Ironically, Peter "the rock" has rejected the solid rock of discipleship hearing and practicing, and, like so many attracted to the power of the institution, becomes instead, a "stumbling rock." It is thus no accident that this passage comes just before the Transfiguration because only the voice of God can make these words palatable.

The critical element of the Gospels is not the miracles of Jesus, but the teachings of Jesus. The Gospels use miracles to emphasize that the very God who created the universe, the sun, the moon, the stars, the earth, and the sea, wants us to practice loving each other, turning the other cheek, giving to all who ask, giving up all our wealth—to follow him and practice not power but powerlessness. These are difficult and ineffectual actions largely ignored by most Christians. But these are the actions that keep us human and create a human world. We are not a people who are about miracles; we are a people who are about the mundane and the human, remembering that the miraculous is always on the side of those who choose to practice Jesus rather than merely worship Jesus.

For Matthew as for Ellul, the congruence of image and word is finally resolved in the implausible incarnation itself. And that incarnation is preserved for us today not in images and icons that glorify Jesus, or in shrines or cathedrals where we worship Jesus, but in the least of our brothers and sisters. As Jesus himself has told us: "What you did not do for one of these least ones, you did not do for me" (Matthew 25:45). The only living image of Christ we have in the world today resides not in images of power and glory, but in the poor, the outcast, and the victims.

We all want a Silver Surfer Super Hero Messiah to swoop in and save us at the moment of crisis. But Jesus rejects this mythic image of super hero with bands of angels who will rescue us at the last minute, and rather, insists that our sole salvation resides in the human practice of mercy, forgiveness, and confrontation with injustice. Rejecting miraculous salvation, Jesus instead embraces the cross, taking on the title not of super hero, but of "suffering servant," who accepts the cross as the fate of all who speak out against injustice and stand with the poor, the outcast, the victim.

Signs and Simulations

Catholic Agitator, May, 1995, pp. 3 and 7

Ralph sleeps in a cardboard box not far from our soup kitchen. He eats at our soup kitchen, receives a welfare check, and uses it to support his drug habit. Though he does not have so much as a dime in his pocket, he wears brand new Nikes, $100 LA Raiders jackets, and carries a boom box the size of a large suitcase. Most folks would say that Ralph and other young men like him are profligate with their money, wasting it on superfluous trivialities when they should be saving precious resources to get themselves off the streets.

If the poor seem singularly pathological to us, perhaps it is because we are blind to our own collective pathologies: the lust of fashion, the pursuit of commodities, the compulsive consumption of mindless entertainment, the substitution of the trivial and the banal for the essential and significant.

While the Papal encyclical (*Evangelium Vitae*) does an adequate job of articulating our contemporary social problems and defining a collective response to those problems based on our commitment to life, its reliance on a rational discourse causes a certain blindness to the level at which contemporary social institutions in the developed nations are demonically possessed by the *principalities and powers*.

In our efforts to name the power of death at the heart of our commodity-driven, media-hyped culture, we have turned to the work of the French philosopher Jean Baudrillard, whose "work...appeals to those who would attempt to grasp the strange mixture of fantasy and desire that is unique to late twentieth-century culture" (Poster, Introduction to *Selected Writings*, p. 2).

Most social critics believe that commodity capitalism, with its market-driven media hype, exerts a kind of mystification over human beings. In other words, they believe that people are being deluded because the commodities that they buy are superfluous and the media that they consume is trivial nonsense. As a consequence, most reform-minded individuals, whether they be Catholic bishops or Marxist revolutionaries, miss the essential point of contemporary ethos: that the trivial productions of culture—its television shows, movies, fashionable clothing, stylish automobiles, ornamental bric-a-brac, etc.—are its driving force.

Baudrillard sees these culture products as creating a kind of language of objects whose consumption is, in fact, a form of religious observance that gives expression to both a contemporary moral code and a social hierarchy. He writes, "It is certain that objects are the carriers of indexed social significations, of a social and cultural hierarchy...in short, it is certain that they constitute a code" (*For a Critique of the Political Economy of the Sign*, p. 37).

Conformity to this unwritten but powerful code is the force that drives our consumer culture. In advanced industrial societies, people no longer buy products based upon the values of need and utility but upon conformity to the code. For the wealthy and powerful, commodity consumption is a form of play, but for the poor and middle classes, it gives expression to a slave morality.

It must be asked whether certain classes (like our friend Ralph and others who eat at our soup kitchen) are not consigned to finding their salvation in objects, consecrated to a social destiny of consumption and thus assigned to a slave morality (enjoyment, immorality, irresponsibility) as opposed to a master morality (responsibility and power).

Understood in this light, consumerism does not look like an aberration, but rather like a complete system with its own internal but irrational and demonic logic. "'Consumption' has become a kind of labor," writes Baudrillard, "'an active manipulation of signs,' a sort of *bricolage* in which the individual desperately attempts to organize his privatized existence and invest it with meaning" (*For a Critique of the Political Economy of the Sign*, p. 5).

Baudrillard does not believe that there is any such thing as a false need or false satisfaction. He is convinced that within the context of the culture, consumer needs and satisfaction are not only real but are, in fact, the most essential reality. He insists that the culture cannot be understood until we recognize that it is consumer demand that drives our economic machinery and consumer satisfaction that forms the basis of our contemporary spiritual ethos.

But because Baudrillard attempts to speak from inside of this system, he can sound a little irrational himself. He actually sounds very much like any one of a number of schizophrenic friends who eat at our soup kitchen. It is almost as if he is aware of secret voices that the rest of us do not hear, of messages that constantly bombard our environment, of a transformed reality that is at once more intense and more absorbing. It is a world in which the crude, reductionistic language of "commodity signs" has meaning only as it conforms to an unwritten and unarticulated "code."

In effect, Baudrillard is reading the "subtext" of our culture. He is trying to describe the sense of psychic dislocation that exists in an advanced capitalist society where the intense, swirling energy of the media is constantly pumped into the environment to stimulate desire. Baudrillard evokes the work of 1960s media guru Marshall McLuhan by reminding us that the "media is the message." In other words, the media creates a total environment that is completely synthetic. Mundane reality pales in the face of soap operas, sit-coms, and movies. But the hyper-reality of Hollywood easily spills over into our real lives, as reported in a *Los Angeles Times* article:

> "We're not far away from whole cities being designed not only as cities but...(as) the right kind of stage that's entertaining," says Xenotec President Richard Hart. "Out cities are going to become back lots...on a grander scale. Everyone wants the Hollywood effect—it's the secret the rest of the world wants."
>
> Kotkin, "Seagram's Daring Bet"

At a very basic level, your local shopping mall is an example of hyper-reality in action. It is the marketplace re-configuring itself under the influence of the "Hollywood effect." A more spectacular example is the "City Walk" at the Universal Studios theme park here in Los Angeles. The City Walk is a megamall composed of replicas of various Los Angeles street environments, all in one, safe, condensed area. In this pre-packaged hyper-reality, it is painfully obvious what Baudrillard means by the term "simulation." All of the positive effects of the urban experience—energy, ethnicity, entertainment—are available without any of the negative ones—crime, poverty, alienation, etc. Consumers are thus immersed in a media-created, womb-like environment that maximizes their shopping activities while minimizing any sense of danger, confrontation, or tension—in short, the exigencies of life and the baggage of history.

But for Baudrillard, the paradigmatic hyper-reality is Disneyland:

> Disneyland exists in order to hide that it is the "real" country.... Disneyland is presented as imaginary in order to make us believe that the rest is real, whereas all of Los Angeles and the America

surrounding it are no longer real, but belong to the hyperreal order and to the order of simulation.

Simulacra and Simulation, p. 12

It is Disneyland that is authentic here! The cinema and TV are America's reality! The freeways, the Safeways, the skylines, speed and deserts—these are America, not the galleries, the churches, and culture.

Baudrillard, *America,* p. 104

So we live in a hyper-real environment—so what! Disneyland is fun and we prefer MTV to opera, Clint Eastwood movies to Shakespeare plays, talk shows to face-to-face discussions, the Internet to community, cyber-space to the great outdoors. But the problem is that "Hyper-reality puts an end to the system of the real, it puts an end to the real as referential by exalting it as model" (Baudrillard, *In the Shadow of the Silent Majorities,* p. 85).

Baudrillard is describing a situation in which it is possible for our hyper-real environment to absorb all potential criticism—to turn environmental catastrophe into Earth Day celebrations, to subdue and conform third world critics with syndications of *Bay Watch* and *Melrose Place,* to transform terrorist acts into breathless media stories of heroic rescues and tragic losses, to repackage our churches as simulated ski lodges with wall-to-wall carpeting, padded pews, and padded crosses.

What we seem to be dealing with is complacency beyond comprehension. We have a system that operates automatically to the benefit of increasing consumption:"Baudrillard radically confirms the theory of one-dimensionality in his vision of the potential reduction of all social, political, cultural, and economic mediations in a...correspondence with the code" (Levin, Introduction to *For a Critique of the Political Economy of the Sign,* p. 23).

It's not a happy thought. It's kind of like the movies *Invasion of the Body Snatchers* or *The Stepford Wives.* Life goes on its comfortable, secure, healthy, energetic, positive, even satisfying way, but it is somehow inauthentic, stale, and flat.

Indeed, Baudrillard is depressing because he attempts to describe our social situation as it actually exists, rather than as we hope it will one day exist. He believes that sincere social critics are often blinded by their idealism and the hopes and certainties that are grounded on that idealism.

49. Volunteers prepare food in the kitchen of the Hospitality House, 2011. Photo by Robert
Radin

But why should Christians read someone like Baudrillard? We read
him for the same reason the church has always read pagan philosophers—
so that we might better understand the world in which we live and to better
proclaim the Gospel. His work is an inoculation against the disease of
cheap grace and pie-in-the-sky spirituality. At least we know what we're up
against, and that is half of the battle. There is no liberation without a deep
understanding of our incarceration, and we cannot cast out the demons of
this world unless we can first name them. We cannot be a force for life until
we can name the forces of death. And that is what Baudrillard does in a
somewhat obscure, elegant manner.

Sacrificing the Innocent

Catholic Agitator, February, 1999, pp. 1 and 7

Until the bombs started falling, we all took a certain amusement and titillation from the entire Clinton affair. But once innocent people started to die, the entire circus began to take on a certain demonic clarity. This was imperial power in survival mode. Like King Herod,who slaughtered all of the innocent male children under the age of two when his throne was threatened by the birth of a "new king," when his own presidency was threatened by impeachment, President Clinton diverted media attention away from the scandal by bombing Iraq, thus slaughtering the innocent. Scripture is clear: power will always maintain itself by sacrificing the innocent.

President Clinton is facing impeachment for lying about his sexual indiscretions. While we would much prefer to impeach the President for the far greater crimes of bombing Iraq, sending missiles into Afghanistan, and cutting off welfare, the truth is that sex, lies, and the killing of the innocent are all constitutive to the Biblical understanding of power.

All of scripture is prejudiced against centralized political power, especially as it resides in kingship. Even David, the most beloved of kings, is castigated because he seduced Bathsheba, lied about his involvement with her, and killed her husband to cover it up. If that scenario sounds familiar, it is because scripture has always assumed, as Lord Acton once said, that "all power tends to corrupt, and absolute power corrupts absolutely" (Dalberg-Acton, *Essays on Freedom and Power*, p. 364). Nevertheless, King Herod is particularly reprehensible to the Biblical authors because he has acquired his throne through stealth, sold out his nation to the Romans, overtaxed the people, and oppressed them with military might.

Not unlike the situation with the current President, the Biblical authors mercilessly lampoon Herod as if in a segment from *Saturday Night Live.* His court is portrayed as debauched and depraved as he acquiesces to the seductive whims of a young girl who sucks up to him. He lies to the Magi, feigns piety, and slaughters the innocent to hang onto his throne. The Biblical authors blur the distinction between Herod the Great and his successor Herod Antipas. Their debauchery and ruthlessness are archetypal and are meant to recall the paradigmatic tyrant of all scripture, the Pharaoh of Egypt.

The entire ethos of the Hebrew people is directed at becoming a non-Egyptian people, who have been liberated from Egypt and have no king but Yahweh. Because we live in a democracy, we Americans do not comprehend this scriptural skepticism of state power. Most Americans naïvely believe that just because they vote every few years, their government is rational and humane. They think that government is a tool of positive and progressive values; but the truth is that we live in a plutocracy where a few powerful corporate interests control the important political decisions of the nation.

Powerful forces in the US demand the right to consume oil at cut-rate prices; many believe sanctions are in place to keep Iraqi oil off the market and allow the US to heavily influence the pricing of oil. This benefits US oil producers and oil-producing allies. Sanctions also allow the US defense industries to sell more weapons to Middle Eastern allies. Oil-producing countries that don't have to compete with Iraqi oil sales can charge more money per barrel and then have more money to buy US weapons.

In the meantime, over 200 children die in Iraq *each day* as a result of the sanctions. We do not believe that Saddam Hussein is an innocent individual. We realize that he has committed genocide. But we do believe that he has been incessantly demonized by the American propaganda machine, making us believe his slaughter of innocents (the Iranians and the Kurds) is worse than Clinton's slaughter of 700,000 Iraqi children with economic sanctions. The reason for this, of course, is that he has the temerity to be sitting on 11 percent of the world's oil reserve. It is the innocent children of Iraq who are paying the price for propping up a shaky American President and ensuring that American industry will have adequate oil to lubricate its machinery.

In Matthew's infancy narrative, the story of the slaughter of the innocents deliberately recalls the slaughtering of the Hebrew male babies by the Pharaoh in Egypt during Moses' time. This slaughter of the innocents is intimately connected with the pagan tradition of sacrificing the first-born male child to insure fertility. The repudiation of human sacrifice by the Judeo-Christian tradition signifies a commitment to living in a way that refuses to make sacrificial victims of the powerless.

Just as the pagan Egyptians were committed to sacrificing the innocent to insure abundant crop production, so too are we willing to sacrifice the innocent to insure that there is an abundant supply of oil so that, as former President Bush so aptly put it, we can "preserve our way of life."

In the pre-Vatican II Church, the Mass was often referred to as the unbloody sacrifice of Calvary. For us as Catholics, the Mass represents the highest form of this rejection of the pagan sacrificial system. Salvation can only come by embracing the "self-sacrifice" of the cross. The only way we can stop making victims of others is by our willingness to follow Christ and risk becoming sacrificial victims ourselves.

To align ourselves behind the power of empire, to allow the power of empire to kill and oppress others in our name, is to silently acquiesce to this sacrificial system. In the current world economy, we all benefit from cheap labor and cheap resources that flow so easily to the First World powers. But cheap oil and cheap clothing and cheap electronic products are all bought at the cost of sacrificial victims throughout the Third World. Laboring on plantations and in sweatshops, mines and factories, languishing in slums and shanty towns and barrios throughout the world are the powerless victims sacrificed to "preserving our way of life."

These sacrifices are what the Church calls systemic sinfulness, or original sin. But through the cross, Jesus has saved us from the effects of original sin. And thus, we are called upon to repudiate the sacrifices made in our name by following the example of the Magi, who disobeyed the king and "went home by another way." For us, the alternative way of the Magi calls us to a life of simplicity, community, and self-sacrifice that occasionally lands us in the dungeons of Pharaoh and Herod.

Propaganda:
The Death of Democracy

Catholic Agitator, March, 2003, pp. 1 and 2

I wake up each morning fearing to read the daily paper, dreading each new revelation by our government of the perversity and duplicity of Saddam Hussein. Though I disbelieve every word, I cannot help but be affected by it. I find myself bouncing between rage and demoralization, anger and impotence. Finally, I even begin to question my own sanity.

I find myself suffering from a kind of cognitive dissonance, which precisely describes the condition produced by our over-exposure to propaganda. According to Jacques Ellul, propaganda produces

> the dissociation between the verbal universe, in which propaganda makes us live, and reality. Propaganda sometimes deliberately separates from man's real world the verbal world that it creates; it then tends to destroy man's conscience.

> *Propaganda,* pp. 180-181

Continued exposure to propaganda, Ellul writes, can plunge the individual into a neurotic state:

> This is apparent from the rigid responses of the propagandee, his unimaginative and stereotyped attitude, his sterility with regard to the socio-political process, his inability to adjust to situations other than those created by propaganda, his need for strict opposites—black and white, good and bad—his involvement in unreal conflicts created and blown up by propaganda. To mistake an artificial conflict for a real one is a characteristic of neurosis.

> *Propaganda,* p. 167

Though Ellul wrote *Propaganda* in the late 50s and early 60s, well before the contemporary sophistication of the "Wag the Dog" critique, his perspective remains not only relevant, but singularly profound. While most of us assume that propaganda is primarily endemic to totalitarian regimes and used in democracies only on a periodic basis, Ellul believes that all contemporary mass societies, whether totalitarian or democratic in structure, are incapable of functioning without propaganda. Propaganda is to contemporary society what religion was to ancient society; it is the glue that binds the whole thing together (p. 121).

"The democratic State, precisely because it believes in the expression of public opinion and does not gag it, must channel and shape that opinion if it wants to be realistic and not follow an ideological dream" (*Propaganda*, p. 126). The problem is that in a modern technological media-driven society, public opinion is stimulated and activated by such a massive flow of information that no single individual can possibly process it. Ellul writes:

> A surfeit of data, far from permitting people to make judgments and form opinions, prevents them from doing so and actually paralyzes them....The mechanisms of modern information induce a sort of hypnosis in the individual.

Propaganda, p. 87

Thus, our attitudes and dispositions must be shaped for us by advertisements, public relations, political parties, and the government. Without such structuring, mass society would quickly disintegrate. Some of us think that might not be a bad idea, but it is certainly antithetical to generally accepted ideological predispositions.

Most of the time the impact of propaganda functions at a level that operates below the level of the conscious mind. Currently we are in the throes of a particularly powerful form of propaganda, which is why many of us wake up each morning with our stomachs churning.

The two primary forms of propaganda, writes Ellul, are "propaganda of integration" and "propaganda of agitation" The former is a mild, pervasive form of propaganda deployed on advanced literate societies. "Integration propaganda aims at stabilizing the social body, at unifying and reinforcing it....The more comfortable, cultivated, and informed is the milieu to which it is addressed, the better it works" (*Propaganda,* pp. 74-75). Integration propaganda seeks to align and solidify the populace around

50. Image compiled by Jeff Dietrich from *The Image Book*, *Catholic Agitator*, 2002

dominant myths and ideologies such as "technology," "progress," "democracy," "freedom," "the nation."

"Agitation propaganda" on the other hand, as the name implies, is a much more vigorous form of propaganda that seeks to compel a particular form of action:

> It is led by a party seeking to destroy the government or the established order. It seeks rebellion or war. Governments also employ this propaganda of agitation when, after having been installed in power, they want to pursue a revolutionary course of action. In all cases, propaganda of agitation tries to stretch energies to the utmost, obtain substantial sacrifices, and induce the individual to bear heavy ordeals. It operates inside a crisis or actually provokes the crisis itself.
>
> *Propaganda,* pp. 71-72

It is Mao's "Great Leap Forward;" it is Churchill's "Blood, Sweat, and Tears;" it is Hitler's "Deutschland über alles;" it is George W. Bush's "Liberation of Iraq." All of these propaganda efforts represent national historic turning points that require participation and sacrifice.

For us it will mean more than just higher gas prices. It will entail the diminishments of civil rights, the acceptance of a permanent war status, high civilian and military casualties in Iraq, as well as an increasing number of terrorist casualties here in the US, and finally, the possibility of nuclear conflict with the risk of in-kind terrorist reprisals: all of this done in the name of democracy and freedom.

For Ellul, propaganda has destroyed the very things that our nation is being called to sacrifice for in Iraq:

> The means employed to spread democratic ideas make the citizen, psychologically, a totalitarian man. The only difference between him and a Nazi is that he is a "totalitarian man with democratic convictions"....And the citizen can repeat indefinitely "the sacred formulas of democracy" while acting like a storm trooper.
>
> *Propaganda,* p. 265

Rejecting the Temptation to Tall Towers

Catholic Agitator, September, 2002, p. 1

We find ourselves protesting both the opening of the new Cathedral here in Los Angeles as well as America's ongoing "War on Terror." The common theme that we see tying the two events together is tall buildings and victimized humanity. Victims of war, victims of sexual abuse, victims of poverty.

Historically speaking, tall buildings are, with no exceptions that come readily to mind, built by men: military men, business men, and church men. As a class, these men are not overly concerned about the victims of war, poverty, or sexual abuse; victims are just the collateral damage endemic to their lofty project.

Biblically speaking, lofty, man-made edifices—pyramids, ziggurats, and towers, which are the material manifestation of "manly" aspirations— are doomed to deconstruction. As Jesus said of the Jerusalem Temple, built by Herod, "There will not be one stone left upon another" (Mark 13:2). This theme of fallen towers bookends the entire Bible, from the fallen Tower of Babel in Genesis to the fall of Babylon in the book of Revelation.

The common cliché that "pride goeth before the fall" is a powerful reflection, which has been trivialized by being applied solely to the personal, when in fact it applies primarily to the political and the powerful. The "fall" is not about personal pride. It is about empires and kingdoms, *principalities and powers,* justice and judgment. And it is Biblically articulated, epito- mized, and symbolized by the toppling of tall towers.

The World Trade Center were the tall towers that dominated world trade. A cathedral is a tall tower that, like the temple in Jesus' time, is a symbol of religious and political domination. The vision of Jesus was a vision that recognized the best in the Jewish tradition. Jesus recognized that the Hebrew people were called to be a people unlike other nations. God called his people to build an alternative society—the very opposite of the warring empires that surrounded them: a decentralized tribal society with no central government and thus, no king but Yahweh, and an economic system based upon mutual aid and Jubilee redistribution of the wealth. This God had no permanent cultic shrine or temple, but rather accompanied his people in the Ark of the Covenant, a kind of "mobile suitcase," and slept in a tent (the tabernacle) at night.

The God of suitcases, tents, and tribal confederacies abhors tall towers, temples, and sky scrapers because these edifices are emblematic not merely of human pride and self-sufficiency, but of imperial domination, military supremacy, international theft, and the cultic sanctification of all of the above.

In Biblical times, the erection of temples and towers required the assembling of vast cadres of slave labor. In modern times, they simply require the assembling of vast amounts of capital. In either case, from the scriptural perspective they are always built by the wealthy and powerful upon the backs of the poor.

Though it is vastly unpopular, even heretical to say so, the targeting of the World Trade Center, while it may have been inhuman and unfair, was not an irrational act or even an act of jealousy at our "freedom and lifestyle." It was rather an expression of rage and frustration unleashed upon the quintessential target of American territorial and financial domination. American banks and oil companies own the world, and their lofty skyscrapers are emblematic of the distance between rich and poor.

Scripture is pretty clear: if we have more than "enough" (Exodus 16), it must be shared with those who have less. If we have way too much it has not been earned, it has been stolen. Historically speaking, the super rich don't want to give their wealth back to the poor in the form of food and shelter. What they give away at the end of their lives, they give away in the form of endowments to grandiose projects of art and architecture, museums and cathedrals. Like Marie Antoinette, they cry out, "Let them eat art!"

From a Biblical perspective you get the sense that God has some doubts about the human project. Oh I know that part about "God so loved the world that he sent his son, etc." But then look what the world did to him. We must not forget that it was the men who build tall buildings: priests, scribes, and Roman governors, presidents, generals and businessmen, who killed the Son of God.

Blind to Our Sin of Usury

Catholic Agitator, August, 1997, pp. 1 and 2

Usury. The very word conjures up notions of archaic Medieval practices like alchemy and numerology, the Inquisition, and Papal indults. Yet, unlike these other mysterious practices, usury lies at the very heart of contemporary life. It is the driving force of our credit economy, the very center of the capitalist ethos.

So entrenched is the concept of usury—the practice of lending money at interest—that even most Catholic Workers have a difficult time understanding why our founders, Dorothy Day and Peter Maurin, were so opposed to this ubiquitous and seemingly beneficial practice.

After all, most of us come from middle-class, suburban homes that could never have been purchased without a bank loan. Most of us were taken to the local bank at an early age and, with as much ceremony as attended our First Communion, opened our first interest-bearing savings account.

Our parents put us through college with the interest from their investments and eventually retired on the interest from those very same investments. Most people we know have house payments, car payments, credit cards, and student loan debts.

Debt, credit, and interest are an essential part of people's lives. With it, people purchase the "good life." But there is a high price to be paid for this.

While a small minority are able to reap the gains and benefits of the "good life," the vast majority of the world's population find themselves drained of resources by this process.

As Kevin Phillips points out, there is a debtor class in America and there is a creditor class:

> The conservative columnist George Will came to more or less the
> same conclusion: to pay the interest component of the 1988 budget
> will require a sum ($210 billion) equal to approximately half of all

the personal income-tax receipts. This represents...a transfer of wealth from labor to capital unprecedented in American history. Tax revenues are being collected from average Americans...and given to the buyers of US government bonds—buyers in Beverly Hills, Lake Forest, Shaker Heights, Grosse Point, and Tokyo, and Riyadh.

The Politics of Rich and Poor, pp. 90-91

In America, we are so imbued with the ideology of democracy that we are blind to the ways in which large concentrations of wealth undermine the practice of authentic "government by the people."

But Phillips reminds us that the historic struggle between Alexander Hamilton and Thomas Jefferson over national monetary policies is emblematic of the American political experience as a whole. Our struggle has always been over the issue of whether or not democratic freedom, in the absence of some semblance of economic equality, has any substantive meaning at all.

The servicing of the national debt and the payment of interest to the wealthy holder of US Treasury Bonds is just one of the many hidden ways in which the employment of usury inevitably drains resources from the poor to the wealthy, from the "debtor class" to the "creditor class." This is the reason that both scripture and Church teaching condemned the practice of usury.

Of course the debilitating dynamic of usury is most apparent in third world countries where the payment of massive interest rates to First World banks has caused the restructuring of entire national economies, eliminating government services and food subsidies for the poor, and emphasizing the priority of cash crop production for export over the basic nutritional needs of citizens. In Mexico, the cost of beans, rice, and tortillas is increasingly beyond the means of the poor for whom it is the very staff of life.

It is not really big news that the rich get richer and the poor get poorer. But it is worth reflecting on the realization that the writers of the Jewish Torah understood this dynamic all too well and sought to create a society in which this process of wealth concentration, if not eliminated, was diminished.

The Jubilee Laws of the book of Leviticus called for the forgiveness of debt and the freeing of debt slaves at seven year intervals, while every fifty years the law further required that all land be returned to its original owners. In other words, land, as the primary wealth in the ancient world, was a gift from God and could not be sold outright. The whole intent of these laws was to "re-shuffle the deck" every fifty years and start over again,

51. Cover illustration by Gary Palmatier, pen and ink. *Catholic Agitator*, 1975

thus insuring that resources would never accrue in perpetuity to the benefit of a small wealthy elite.

It was very much this Jubilee tradition, "a year acceptable to the Lord," that Jesus proclaimed at the beginning of his public ministry in the Gospel of Luke. Jesus' ministry was based on the forgiveness of debt, liberation to the captives of debt slavery, and the recognition that Creation is a gift given by God to all and should be shared by all. But this "economy of grace" is elusive and seems utopian to us.

We cannot imagine a world without capitalism, and thus do we remain captive to a "debt economy" in which the poor are over-burdened with heavy interest payments, marginalized by unemployment, and imprisoned by a justice system that is utterly blind to the true causes of crime. But our faith in Jesus Christ requires that we begin to re-imagine a transformed social environment, to look upon the world with eyes that see and ears that hear so that we might not be deaf to the cries of the poor, nor blind to the effects of our sin of usury.

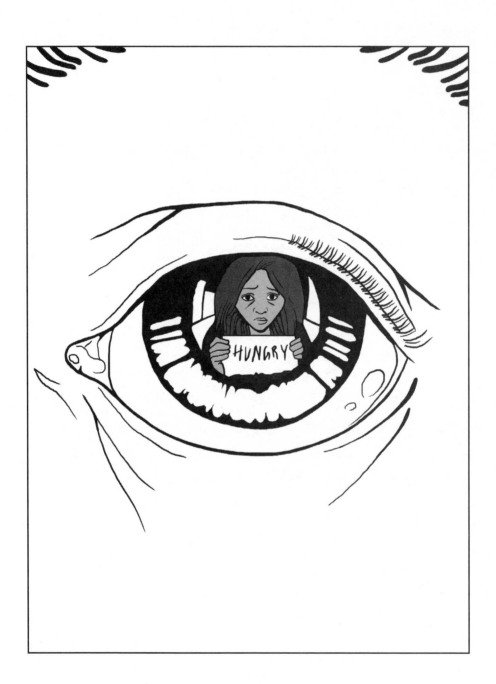

PART NINE

COMPASSION AS AN ACT OF SEEING

compassion

(first usage in English, 1340);
suffering together with another;
participation in suffering;
fellow-feeling, sympathy. 1 *OED*

seeing

(first usage in English, 1300);
having the ability of sight;
discerning, possessing insight;
gifted as a seer. 1 *OED*

Introduction

The essential gospel value is the cultivation of the ability to see. The core gospel passages that come to mind are "Lord, when did we *see* [emphasis added] you hungry, or thirsty or...in prison" (Matthew 25:41) and the parable of the Good Samaritan. In the first passage, it is the disciples who are blind to Christ's presence in the hungry, thirsty, and the incarcerated "little ones," the victims of an unjust system. In the second passage it is the righteous religious authorities who are blind, and it is only the despised Samaritan who can see the victim by the side of the road.

Like these same religious authorities and the disciples themselves, we are blind to the suffering victim right in front of us. Though traditionally understood as acts of pious charity, the practice of the Works of Mercy, "feeding the hungry, sheltering the homeless, visiting the imprisoned," are better understood as radical acts of personal transformation. Only by abandoning the comfortable confines of our suburban ideologies, where everything is in good running order, rules are rational, authorities are just, and everyone enjoys abundance, can we begin to lose our blindness and recover our sight. Christ sent us out to look for him among the poor and suffering so that we might be disabused of our ideological blinders, recover our sight, and be restored to our humanity.

The daily practice of the Works of Mercy brings us into human contact with the victims of our social and ideological structures. I think of Martin Russell, a young African American man with a drug problem, caught up in the criminal justice system. After spending a year in prison as a very minor drug dealer, he admirably performed all of the many probation

53. *Skid Row* by Ted Miller, serigraph, 1965. Reproduced in the *Catholic Agitator*, 1976

requirements demanded of him: living in a group home, attending regular Narcotics Anonymous meetings, remaining drug-free for over sixteen months, finding a job in the midst of the recession after hundreds of rejections, going to school, and receiving high marks from his professors. At a recent court appearance, the judge, though congratulating him for his exemplary behavior, refused to forgive Martin's $4,000 fine. Martin was emotionally crushed and relapsed. He is back in jail now again on minor drug charges, and the prosecutor has offered him a deal: five years in state prison.

Over the period of his first incarceration and recovery, a member of our Catholic Worker community visited Martin in jail regularly, went to all of his court appearances, ran errands for him, helped him with his defense, supported him, both spiritually and even to some extent financially, during his period of release and recovery. She was gratified at the great success that he achieved and devastated at his current situation. One could easily say, "Why bother? The guy is obviously a loser."

On the contrary, what we learn in the practice of the Works of Mercy, in the practice of our presence to the victim, as we navigate the frustrating procedures of jail visitation, the callousness of the court system, and the gratuitous demands of the probation system, is that our own judgmental attitudes, our own sense of superiority, our own punitive predispositions, our own sense of middle-class entitlement, is founded on an exclusionary and unjust system. We are challenged to see with "new eyes" that the poor are not losers but rather they are often heroic individuals who struggle mightily in their efforts to overcome the burdens of injustice heaped upon them by an ideological system that is blind to their humanity.

May the Angels Guide You to Heaven

Catholic Agitator, January, 1995, pp. 1 and 7

Kieran died on Christmas morning, and with his death we have entered fully into a territory previously explored only at its periphery. For all intents and purposes, death in all its forms describes and proscribes the human condition. Kieran's death on Christmas morning was a gift that allowed us to explore that foreign territory of death and grief.

Over the last few years, our work with AIDS patients has led to the development of a hospice ministry to not only those with AIDS, but also to any transient individual with a terminal illness. In the last year we have lost six of our friends, three of these deaths coming within ten days of Christmas. It is our increasing intimacy with death and dying that has led us to reflect upon all of the ramifications of this universal human experience.

Contrary to the lyrics of an old popular song, it is not love that makes the world go around, it is death—death as social purpose. As William Stringfellow writes,

> The truth is that human beings are concerned with nothing else but death, though that be seldom realized....The moral reality of death involves death comprehended sociologically and anthropologically, psychologically and psychically, economically and politically, societally and institutionally. Death as a moral power means death as social purpose.

An Ethic for Christians and Other Aliens, p. 69-70

We fear and deny death. It is this fear and denial of physical extermination that infuses death with its social power and demonic purpose. As Christians, our essential call is to be people of life, but a society committed to life is an anomaly. This is why Christians must live in tension, "in the world, but not of it." Social conformity is extracted through the coercive

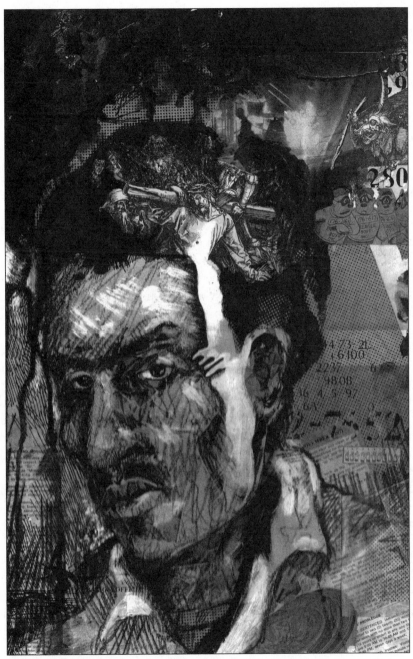

54. Untitled collage by Gary Palmatier, circa 1970s

sanctions of death in all its forms: genocide, war, jail, taxes, capital punishment, social, and economic discrimination. However, we as Christians must come to know the meaning of eternal life, which is nothing other than the refusal to use the means of death, the tools of death, the forces of death for mere survival.

Only those who grieve will come to the meaning of eternal life. Through Kieran's death we have been able to bring to culmination our efforts to re-create an authentic ritual of mourning.

After Kieran died, Lisa cleaned him up, put him in his favorite Lady of Guadalupe T-shirt, and laid him out on his bed. The entire community gathered to recite the "liturgy of the dead" that Donald and Sandi put together for all of the deaths that we experience here at our house.

We then canceled our usual Christmas celebration and invited friends and extended community members to come over to the house. For the next fourteen hours we sang and prayed, drank whiskey, cried, ate, and exchanged stories around Kieran's bed in the tradition of a good old-fashioned Irish wake, as people paid their respects and said good-bye to Kieran. The wake was followed by a memorial service the following Wednesday, and a two hour funeral service on Saturday. We closed our soup kitchen and spent the entire week grieving for Kieran.

Just days before he died, Kieran told us that his death was not a tragic thing. He had indeed come to the Catholic Worker to die. More precisely, he had come to the Catholic Worker to teach us how to die. Through Kieran we have learned more deeply how to be present to the dying, how to grieve the dead, and how to face our own deaths with courage, dignity, and grace.

To give expression to our grief is to give expression to our essential humanity and its limitations. As local columnist Michael Ventura writes, "My grief allows me to cleanse and purify some bit of [the madness that swirls around and through me]. Cleansed, I can act. My anger can be turned against me...but not my grief. Grief hurts no one, yet it softens the air about one and increases possibility. In that softening, love moves—a little" (*Letters at 3AM*, p. 146).

In our tenderheartedness, we recognize that our lives and all of creation are a gift from God, and that try as we might, we cannot control that gift. Our hearts of stone have been transformed into hearts of flesh. In grieving Kieran's death we grieve our own deaths. In facing death we turn control of our lives and creation over to our Creator God.

On Wednesday, January 11, we buried the ashes of Kieran Prather under a Celtic cross, hand-carved by our friend Karen Roarke. The cross stands in our garden dining area, right near the entrance to our soup kitchen, where Kieran often stood to smoke a cigarette.

Joe Prather, Kieran's father, spoke of Kieran having been born at home, and of holding him at birth and how grateful he was to have been able to hold Kieran at the moment of his death as well.

We said our final good-byes to Kieran and recited together the *In Paradisium*: "May the angels guide you into heaven."

My Continuing Education*

Catholic Agitator, September, 1995, p. 3

Monday, August 21, 1995

Dear Catherine,

It's only been twelve days since I saw you last, but it seems like twelve months. I miss you terribly, but as always, your singular faith and strength give me courage. To me you are gift and grace.

But for the loss of your company, my incarceration is hardly penitential. My greatest difficulty is trying to stay focused in the midst of twenty-four hour television bombardment. Enduring the torture of Regis and Kathy Lee, Montel Williams, and Bob Baker are more than I can bear. You would think that after having done civil disobedience so many times I would be a pro at this kind of thing. You would think that I would be strong and confident. You would think that I would be convinced of my own righteousness. Rather, this time of enforced solitude convinces me more deeply of my brokenness, my own sinfulness, my own flawed integrity.

I am more convinced of the wrongfulness of what our government does at the Test Site than I am of the rightness or efficaciousness of my own action. In this, I take strength from William Stringfellow, who said that when we act on the Word of God, we do so in fear and trembling, because we can never know for certain whether we act upon the Word of God or the word of our own arrogant ego. In this I am also reminded of the Thomas Merton prayer that we recite so often: "Lord God, I do not know if I am following your will, but I hope my desire to do your will does in fact please you."

---

*   Jeff Dietrich appeared before Justice of the Peace Bill Sullivan of Nye County, Nevada and was sentenced to thirty days in the Nye Court Detention Center for cutting the fence at the Nevada Test Site. He refused to pay a $1,157.00 fine for the cost of repairs.

August 22

The mornings are, thank God, quiet. Everyone goes back to sleep after breakfast. So I can spend the time exercising and praying. I turn the TV down to just below audible rather than completely off. That way if someone wakes up they won't be alarmed at the change in their environment and go turn the damn thing back on!

This is the most unusual jail environment that I have ever been in. Its small Western town location reflects the demographics: this is the last bastion of a dying breed—the white American male. As you might expect, the values in here are decidedly racist and passionately sexist. "Thick-lipped monkeys" and "ball-busting bitches" are symptomatic of our national decline. I am grateful that these attitudes only tend to manifest themselves in response to television news shows or talk shows. O.J. Simpson is a "guilty mother-f-----, but his ball-bustin' wife deserved to die."

Despite a feeling of initial repulsion, I must admit a certain feeling of compassion for these men. Unlike inner-city, black inmates, they cannot blame their misfortune on systematic oppression. There is, however, a deep sense of alienation from mainstream liberal culture, a disdain for big money and especially big government. There is a feeling that they have been robbed, cheated out of their birthright, and in its emptiness, there is only anger.

Jerry is a warrior. Though he is over sixty, his lean, muscular body, covered with tattoos and thick bristly hairs, is still lethal. Tall and foreboding, with long grey hair and beard, he looks something like a cross between the pre-Civil War Abolitionist John Brown and an aging Hell's Angel biker. Since 1967, Jerry has been out of custody for a total of four months. His original charge of killing a policeman, for which he received fourteen years, was later extended for killing a fellow prison inmate. He is a former Green Beret and expert in small arms and explosives and a self-proclaimed white supremacist. He claims to be connected with that White Supremacist guy in Idaho who shot it out with the FBI, and whenever news information comes on about the Oklahoma bombing, he just perks right up. He hates cops and he hates the prison system. He hates the government and he hates "n------." And he doesn't trust women either—"they'll screw you every time." Yet despite the anger and cynicism and the violence, there is a kind of nobility and compassion about him. He'll stand up for anybody he thinks the system is trying to screw, whether that means connecting you with legal help or physically duking it out with the authorities. But his sense of compassion goes even further. This rough, violent man is also a healer. "People laugh," he says, "but I have the healin' power in my hands. Everyone in my family does." And indeed, Jerry is a natural chiropractor. He has cracked every vertebra in my spine. He claims that he can feel in his hands an emanation of heat wherever the vertebrae are "hung up." In an atmosphere rife with prohibition against male touching, Jerry has touched me with his strong, gentle hands of healing. The power of the human touch calls me to reconsider my own tendency to stereotype people like Jerry and thus diminish their humanity.

August 23

It is morning everyone is sleeping. I have turned the TV down so it is blessedly quiet. I have been praying for the last two hours, trying to be present to the Spirit, or as Stringfellow would say, to the "Word of God" in creation and history. I put myself with the Catholic Workers as you vigil, as you pray, but most of all, as you turn to the Word of God in scripture. I count myself blessed to be here in this jail. My ability to be here is a gift from the community. My presence here is a gift that I give back to the community.

55. Los Angeles Catholic Worker house on Brittania Avenue, circa 1930s. Photo from the Los Angeles County Archives

Without community we are lost, abandoned to the allure of the world. But through the gift of community, we are connected to that great cloud of witnesses, that Communion of Saints and martyrs who renew the face of the earth, bringing the spirit of life into the structures of death, light into the darkness of the world.

My deepest love and gratitude,
Jeff

I Saw Satan Fall Like Lightning

Catholic Agitator, June, 2003, p. 2

"I saw Satan fall like lightning from heaven" (Luke 10:18)*. It seems like a bizarre, mystical, metaphorical passage. But for Jesus, it is the key to the entire gospel message. While many contemporary people are dismissive or even scornful of the entire concept of Satan, linking it with images of a little red man with horns and pitchfork, the Gospels were pretty clear that Satan was not just a comic book character, but is in truth the ruler of the world, whose primary tools include violence, robbery, and the making of victims.

The fall of Satan is situated, oddly enough, directly in the middle of a whole set of passages that deal with hospitality food, and prayer (Luke 10:11-13). It begins with Jesus sending out seventy-two disciples (Luke 10:1-12) who are to be dependent upon hospitality, and "stay in the same house and eat and drink what is offered to you (Luke 10:7), and ends with a section on the Lord's Prayer and a story about getting bread at midnight from a locked house by persistent knocking (Luke 11:1-13).

As we reflected on these passages in our community Bible study sessions, we couldn't figure out what all this stuff about food and praying had to do with the fall of Satan. But as we began to study more deeply on the Good Samaritan passage (Luke 10:29), which comes pretty quickly after the fall of Satan, things began to be clarified.

Clearly, the Good Samaritan passage is definitively related to this section on hospitality. It is about the moral blindness of the religious leaders to the plight of the victim, who has been beaten, robbed, and left for dead along the side of the road. The compassion and hospitality of the "unlearned", "unclean" Samaritan exposes the ideological blindness of the "wise" religious leaders. The real issue is blindness to the victim. And we thought that the deeper meaning of the passage might be that the religious

---

*   The title of René Girarad's book.

leaders are, in fact, blind to the ways in which they are beneficiaries of a social and economic system that is based upon theft and victim-making.

It suddenly became clear that in this entire section, hospitality and prayer is much, much more than some quaint Christian practice. Luke considers the practice of hospitality and solidarity with the victims as the very heart of the alternative Christian economy, and the complete antithesis of "Satan's" worldly economy, which is based on robbery and victim-making. While our Biblical interpretation may seem a bit fanciful to hard-core scripture scholars, it is nonetheless impossible to deny that our contemporary post-Iraq war economy is designed to rob and victimize the poor. While the wealthy of our nation receive tax breaks, it is the poor who pay for the multi-billion dollar war in Iraq, through cuts in public health care, transportation, and education. It is the poor in Iraq, and the poor in our own nation, who pay for the war and continue to be victimized by an economy centered on wealth accumulation. We believe that is the very issue Jesus was attempting to address in his own time, through the creation of what might be called "kingdom economics."

When Jesus sends out the seventy-two disciples, he insists that they take nothing with them: "Carry no money bag, no sack, no sandals." (Luke 10:4). They are to be powerless victims, "like lambs among wolves" (Luke 10:3). Totally separated from the money economy, they rely completely upon the grace and kindness of hospitality for their very sustenance. And when they are welcomed, Jesus tells us that "The kingdom of God is at hand for you" (Luke 10:9).

When food and hospitality are shared outside of the money economy, the kingdom of God has come near, and that is about as close as humans get to the divine. It is the essence of the Lord's Prayer (Luke 11:1-13), which is in fact a prayer about the divine economy of hospitality and bread sharing, and forms the closing passages of this section.

It is easy enough to read the Lord's Prayer as a strictly spiritual exercise, but in truth it is all about the kingdom and bread. "May your Kingdom come," says Jesus. "Give us day by day the bread we need." This sense of material urgency is further underscored by the pithy manner in which Jesus explains his prayer, through the example of a man who goes to a friend's house at midnight, a very inconvenient hour, seeking bread for "a friend of mine [who] has arrived at my house" (Luke 11:6). Clearly the man is not begging for himself; one is tempted to imagine that he is seeking food for one of the seventy-two disciples sent out by Jesus. But the important point is that the man gains the necessary food, not through the compassion and mercy of his friend, who has already locked his door and gone to bed, but through persistent, shameless knocking and begging at midnight.

Jesus is aware that the world is full of tough, mean-spirited, and hard-hearted people like ourselves, and that the new economy requires more than mere compassion. It will require the particular discipleship virtue of shameless, persistent, faithful begging that is undeterred by locked doors, inconvenient hours, and hardened hearts. In the Gospel of Luke, this discipleship virtue is best exemplified by women: "the anointing woman," "the bleeding woman," and most especially, the impoverished widow, who obtains justice from the unjust judge, who "neither fears God nor respects people" (Luke 18:2). The widow won her rights not because of compassion or even because of justice, but "because this widow keeps bothering me." She was persistent and shameless and finally the judge said, "While it is true that I neither fear God nor respect any human being, because this widow keeps bothering me I shall deliver a just decision for her lest she finally come and strike me." (Luke 18:5). And that is, I suspect, the singular discipleship virtue, to keep coming and knocking and persisting until we finally wear down the system of injustice and Satan finally "falls...like lightning."

The Homeless and Hopeless[*]

Catholic Agitator, October, 1988, p. 1

It is like a dance—they circle around and around, eyes fixed on each other. Suddenly, a clenched fist finds a landing place, with the slap of flesh on flesh, just below the eye.

Words are flung like weapons. Bodies crouch into defensive positions, as hands quickly reach into pockets. "Show me your stuff, mother-fucker." Is that just a butane lighter, buried inside of deep pockets, or is it a buck knife—tempered steel that can cut an iron bolt, folded into brass and old-fashioned wood—ready to leap out of dark pockets into deadly flashing action?

"Where's my fifty bucks? You asked me for fifty bucks, and like a man I reached into my pocket and gave it to you. Now I want it back."

"What fifty bucks? You never gave me fifty bucks."

"I'll kill you. I just done thirteen years in the pen, and I don't care if I go back or not. I'll kill you. I am a Crip."

He is short, thick-necked and muscular, and his name is Cartoon. That's his *placa*, his street name, his gang name. He has only been coming to our soup kitchen since last June when he got out of Folsom State Prison. Fortunately, he recognizes me, and because he has "respect," decides not to kill anyone while he is here at the soup kitchen.

At approximately thirty years of age, Cartoon has exceeded by eight to ten years the life expectancy of the average gang member. I don't know why he is called Cartoon, but to me it is a deadly accurate name, suggesting one who is not real, a mere sketching of reality, lacking in substance, merely a facsimile of a person.

Increasingly, the homeless population on Skid Row is coming to resemble Cartoon: young, black and angry. The depths of their despair and alienation finds its roots in a negative self-image, developed from a lifetime of being a non-person, a mere cartoon. Without family, community

[*] A version of this piece appeared in the *Los Angeles Times*, November 26, 1988.

or cultural roots, they are the victims of institutional racism, poverty, and social and political disenfranchisement. They know intuitively as well as from pragmatic experience that the doors to full participation in American community life are firmly locked to them.

They are poor in the economic sense, but more importantly, they are poor in the spiritual sense as well. They come from broken families, perhaps generations of broken families. If they are not dropouts, then the diplomas they have received from substandard ghetto schools are worthless. Having been robbed of any authentic cultural experience, their values are derived from the subtext of Western culture, steeped in violence, materialism, and instant gratification. They are faithful adherents to the religion of consumerism, and fervently believe the constantly repeated media message that salvation comes through consumption.

If you do not have the money to be a consumer, then you are a non-person, you do not exist. Therefore, you steal, deal, get high or do all three. The values of the streets are the values of mass culture. Reality for these people consists of a constantly stimulated set of expectations, mixed with diminishing possibilities for fulfillment.

We believe that the problem of homelessness goes to the heart of our problems as a culture, and with our founder, Dorothy Day, we would say, "The problem is this filthy rotten system" (*On Pilgrimage*, p. 45). Culture is such an ephemeral entity, not unlike the bacteria in yoghurt or the yeast in bread, that we are not aware of it until it has gone bad, leaving our yoghurt tasteless, our bread flat, and our lives without substance.

Thus, we are appalled at the facile pronouncements on the homeless, purveyed by a growing cadre of self-proclaimed experts and homeless administrators who seem to imply that the problem might be solved by funding a new program, passing a new piece of legislation, or even changing the presidential administration.

No, the problem is deeper, darker, and more profoundly disturbing than any mere public policy change could address. It is not that we would ever want to deny the poor funding for any program designed to ease their situation, but the problem goes much farther. As the homeless population grows in size and degree of alienation, neither the economy nor the once traditional enclave of the marginated, the Skid Row neighborhood, can accommodate them.

The driving force of the culture seems to be the elimination of all those who do not have a degree in computer science, sell Tupperware, or offer courses in aerobics or Tai Chi. The once vigorous US economy that offered unskilled people the opportunity to at least hit the beachhead of the mainstream no longer exists. At the same time, it is these same values that, since the mid-1950s, have systematically eliminated the neighborhoods of the marginally poor. Under the banner of redevelopment, so called blighted inner city neighborhoods were upgraded to office buildings, singles bars, and gourmet restaurants. In the last two decades, New York City has lost over 20,000 units of single room occupancy hotels. A portion of this substandard housing was replaced with low-cost housing, but even low-cost housing is too expensive for marginal people. In the final analysis, the only thing standing between a marginalized person and homelessness is substandard housing.

Less than ten years ago, it was possible to rent a Skid Row hotel room for as little as $50 per month. Today, because of the attrition rate of this kind of housing and the increased demand by the newly marginated poor, these rooms rent for as much as $400 per month, complete with rodents, roaches, and dysfunctional bathrooms at the end of the hall.

The homeless situation is alarming in the extreme. It offers a perverse paradigm of our cultural and economic dysfunction. As the homeless population increases, the new poor, in their alienation, grow less tolerable, and the culture, caught up in its narcissism, grows less tolerant.

We believe the situation is hopeless, given the set of public policy alternatives and the predisposition of the American public. This isn't to say that we indulge in despair, because our hope doesn't lie in changing public policy or public opinion. Neither do we find hope in the stopgap measures of politicians, nor in the bureaucratized compassion of administrators of homeless assistance programs. The system cannot be fine tuned; it is rotten to the core. Rather, we find hope in the God of life and the power of personal witness through the Works of Mercy: feeding the hungry, clothing the naked, and sheltering the homeless.

It is a scandal that in a nation as rich as ours, the Works of Mercy remain a necessity. Our acts give daily testimony to the emptiness at the center of our culture. We are not naïve; we realize that we will not change the world through these simple personal acts of compassion. We do these things not to change the world, but rather that the world might not change us.* The poor will always be with us. Our calling, as followers of Christ, is to be always with the poor.

Jesus did not transform public policy; he transformed human hearts. The daily practices of the Works of Mercy are merely exercises in compas-

---

* A pharaphrase of Rabbi Abraham Heschel.

Jeff Dietrich

sion. Jesus said that he would take away our hearts of stone and give us hearts of flesh, that we might love. The regular exposure of our stony hearts to the experience of the poor insures that we remain tender to their suffering and travail.

To sit down each day and break bread with the poor, to offer some sense of community and connectedness is to say that even the least tolerable of our brothers and sisters has dignity and worth. All humans are animated with the fullness of life. No one is merely a cartoon.

Prophetic Hospitality

Catholic Agitator, January, 1992, p. 1

Jesus said to His disciples: "Be watchful! Be alert! You do not know when the time will come. It is like a man traveling abroad. He leaves home and places his servants in charge...watch, therefore; you do not know when the lord of the house is coming....May he not come suddenly and find you sleeping. What I say to you, I say to all: 'Watch!'" (Mark 13:33-37).

Hector is a periodic visitor at our hospitality house, usually coming to stay after a stretch in jail or in the hospital. While our guest, he works regularly, takes his medicine at scheduled times, and, in general, gets healthy. But one morning, just as he seems to be adjusting comfortably, he disappeared. In the ensuing weeks, we will see him on Skid Row, underweight, haggard, and drawn in the face, nervous and tense from lack of medication. Then we won't see Hector for a while—perhaps a long while—until he again contacts the house from a hospital or from jail.

Cheryl, the mother of three children, is addicted to crack and alcohol. Because she is HIV positive, she can only last three or four weeks on the streets before she arrives, abruptly, at the threshold of death. Last night she left us to return to the streets. When she comes back in three or four weeks, the question will be whether we take her in again. If we don't, she will surely die in a matter of days; if we do, we are, God forbid, her co-dependents.

Leroy is perhaps our greatest success: he doesn't do drugs or alcohol; he doesn't have AIDS; he's never even been in jail; and he is hard-working. In the four months that he was here, he gained the distinction of being the first person in over a decade to actually save more than $200 while living with us. Working at a job that he detested, telephone sales, he was able to save almost $1,500. We urged him to keep saving until he had enough for first and last month's rent on an apartment. But, alas, the only thing that he wanted was a car. The last we heard from Leroy was a call from the discount jewelry store, which wanted to know if he was a good credit risk. Now Leroy has his own transportation, nice clothes, and jewelry—and sleeps in his car.

What are we really doing here anyway?

When we are really honest with ourselves, when we wake up in the darkness of the early morning, plagued with doubt and even despair, we must admit that we have not accomplished all that much. We have not changed the world; the poor and the hungry are still with us in even greater numbers than when we started. Though we write and speak unceasingly, though we appear with some frequency in the media, though our founder, Dorothy Day, is considered by many to be the single most important Catholic in the history of the American Church, we remain virtually a secret movement. What are we doing here, making beds, preparing soup, and cleaning toilets? What are we doing here, breaking up fights, arguing with community members, and battling unceasingly with petty bureaucrats? What are we doing here, going to endless meetings, talking to high school students who would rather be watching MTV, explaining to our parents for the millionth time why we don't get a salary or have health insurance or pay into Social Security, apologizing to them again for that time their new Buick got graffitied while visiting us?

What are we doing here, wasting our time on folks who are probably going to die on the streets anyway? What are we doing here, wasting our time on losers and drug addicts, people who are never going to make it?

We feed the hungry, clothe the naked, shelter the homeless; we offer hospitality, community, and friendship to the poor; but in twenty years of doing this work, what have we really accomplished?

When we first started, it was easier for me to dismiss our failures because we were just a bunch of hippies running a free soup kitchen. No wonder we failed; we simply didn't know what we were doing. We used to envy all of the professional agencies filled with certified experts, who ran effective programs that claimed to reconnect the poor or mainstream the poor or empower the poor.

I have come to realize that we are not failures because of our lack of knowledge, education, sophistication, or professional staff. We are not even failures because the poor whom we serve fail so consistently. We are failures because we are in intimate contact with the failure and brokenness of our culture. When Jesus told us to feed the hungry, shelter the homeless, and visit the imprisoned, he knew that such activities would take us directly to the heart of all the injustice, oppression, and brokenness in our society.

He assumed that such simple activities would cause us to ask questions about both ourselves and our society. He assumed that such activity would involve us in a continuing process of becoming increasingly human. He assumed that it would cause us to deny both power and status. He assumed that this ministry of prophetic compassion would be the ongoing work of his church.

As Walter Brueggemann writes,

> Compassion constitutes a radical form of criticism, for it announces that the hurt is to be taken seriously, that the hurt is not to be accepted as normal and natural but it is an abnormal and unacceptable condition for humanness. Thus compassion that might be seen simply as generous goodwill is in fact criticism of the system, forces, and ideologies that produce the hurt. Jesus enters into the hurt and finally comes to embody it.

Prophetic Imagination, p. 88

Our task is to do the same. To enter into the hurt is to realize that the system is rigged. It is to realize that the poor can never be conformed to the rigorous, self-serving standards of progress, education and consumption—patterns demanded by our culture for even minimal social acceptance. To enter into the hurt is to realize that these standards are the exact parallel to the Pharisaical codes of first-century Palestine that kept the poor of Jesus' time landless, marginated, and debt-ridden.

The great temptation for people in our line of work is to abandon the basic human effort of responding compassionately in favor of a so-called "effective strategy." But whether those strategies of salvation are job training programs, political action, substance abuse therapies, or just simple-minded religion, their predisposition toward operational effectiveness and quantifiable results tends to cover over the depth of the woundedness.

We are not here to cure the poor or to fix the poor or to mainstream the poor; we are not here to create programs, make converts, raise money, or build great buildings. We are here to enter into the pain of the poor, to expose the wounds that make the suffering of the poor inevitable. We are here to offer healing and compassion. We are here in response to Jesus' challenge to be human. We are here to submit to that radical surgery which will take away our hearts of stone and exchange them for hearts of flesh. We are here to mourn with the poor and to tell their stories. Anything less than this witness of prophetic compassion covers over the wound without healing it. Anything less than this is pious self-aggrandizement or pompous professionalism.

It is not enough for us to be merely people who have faith and hope in Jesus Christ. We must also be people who have a corresponding lack of faith and hope in the institutions and structures of worldly power. We must not be seduced by professional technique or therapeutic jargon or political power or mindless religion.

To be an instrument of God's grace is to reject the idols of power; it is to reject the instruments of professional religion and professional bureaucracies. To be an instrument of God's grace is to be human and to respond to hurt in a human manner, which is to say personally and communally, rather than collectively and bureaucratically. The personal, communal witness is the only means that opens a path for our God to act in the world. Only by personally emulating, however imperfectly, the values of God's kingdom, do we open an avenue for grace, healing, and transformation. Only by being human can we make the world more human. Only by being Christian can we make the world more Christian. Only by exposing the wound as terminal can we then make room for our God to work.

While it does not seem very effective, this work of cleaning toilets, making soup, healing wounds, and offering prophetic hospitality is what our God asks of us in order that we might be human. To be human is to recognize that we are not God, that we are not all-powerful. The greatest evils in all of history have been perpetrated by good people who thought that they could fix all human problems in one great "final solution." Whether through war, revolution, or technological progress, these strategies of effectiveness share a common disregard for the relationship between means and ends.

Our collective experience of the last century demonstrates so clearly that the "little way" of Dorothy Day and Peter Maurin is not some outdated, pious, pie-in-the-sky theology, but it is rather the only appropriate means of achieving our noble end—a more humane world. The instruments of power, whether political, military, or bureaucratic, can achieve only disaster, even though the world would wish us to believe otherwise.

As Dorothy wrote so many years ago,

> One of the greatest evils of the day…is a sense of futility. Young people say, "what good can one person do? What is the sense of our small effort?" They cannot see that we must lay one brick at a time, take one step at a time; we can be responsible for only the one action of the present moment. But we can beg for an increase of love in our

hearts that will vitalize and transform individual actions, and know that God will take them and multiply them, as Jesus multiplied the loaves and fishes.

Loaves and Fishes, p. 176

Finally, we must ask ourselves what it is that the Master should expect to find us doing when he returns. Running successful programs? Acquiring advanced degrees? Transforming political systems? Should He find us filling stadiums with converts, administering massive building programs, developing sophisticated fundraising strategies? No, the Master has a right to expect that the servants to whom he entrusted His house will be serving still, cleaning toilets, making soup, binding wounds. This is what it means to be human and not to be God. This is what it means to be faithful and not to be effective. This is what it means to be an instrument of grace and not an instrument of power, to be servants of the poor and not administrators of poverty programs.

We may not be able to cure Cheryl, Hector, or Leroy, but we can serve them and welcome them as best we can. We can embody their hurt and tell their stories. And we can let our God do the rest.

Appropriate Medicine

Catholic Agitator, July, 1986, p. 1

There's a stack of onions where "examining room number one" used to be and the tiny pharmacy is now a paint closet. The linoleum is peeling from the floor, and I can hear in the background the clank of metal trays as they are being washed and sent back out to the soup line.

It is hard to believe that this humble, lackluster storeroom once served as a medical facility. Not that the present location of the Hospitality Clinic across the parking lot, in a squat, two-story cinderblock building, represents the height of medical technology, but it is a tremendous improvement on this original *ad hoc* space behind our soup kitchen.

In the early days, when our scruffy little MASH unit* was forced to share its back room location with our clothing distribution program, I had considerable doubts about the ability of a Catholic Worker community to provide medical services. It is such a sophisticated undertaking and we had no special skills or training. Surely there were other more appropriate organizations with better funding that could provide this service. Fortunately, we overcame those early misgivings and took the advice of Dorothy Day, founder of the Catholic Worker, who said sometimes it is better just to begin. So each Monday and Friday we trundled the used clothing out of our makeshift clinic and scrubbed every square inch with disinfectant until it was suffused with the aroma of a Johns Hopkins Hospital. Then several Catholic Workers covered their soup-splattered Levis and faded T-shirts with gleaming white lab coats, rolled out the medical files and opened the front door of the kitchen for intake. What it lacked in amenities it more than made up for in accessibility and warmth. It was unpretentious, but not unprofessional. Our early staff included Dr. Brian Henderson, Director of Family Practice at USC, as well as Sister Antoinette, a Franciscan regis-

---

*   A reference to *Mobile Army Surgical Hospital*, first deployed in the Korean War, and the subject of 1970s and 80s TV sitcom and movie.

tered nurse and missionary. Despite occasional setbacks, like the time a slightly inebriated patient wandered into our makeshift lab and mistook a urine sample for a glass of juice, we persisted in our audacious assumption that a soup kitchen could be a medical clinic.

What this soup kitchen clinic provided, as it continues to provide today with considerably more sophistication, was a warm and supportive setting in which medical professionals could treat the poor. In fact, the greatest strength of the Hospitality Clinic has always been its power to attract a core of dedicated professionals who are motivated by their desire to practice medicine within the context of a community that invites the poor in, rather than a bureaucracy that shuts the poor out. The Catholic Worker community is rooted in the compassionate healing ministry of Christ and the early monastic orders that offered simple hospitality to the sick and the dying, the same ministry practiced today by Mother Teresa and her sisters on the streets of Calcutta.

The needs of the poor are often elementary: food, clothing, a sense of community, meaningful work. But less and less are the complicated economic and social structures of our culture able to meet those needs. Nowhere is this complexity of organization and allocation of resources more apparent than in the practice of medicine. Both in philosophy and actual practice, the medical profession had isolated itself from the needs of the poor with a complex, arcane bureaucracy and expensive, inappropriate technology.

There is money for sophisticated research into heart disease and for lengthy hospital stays, but there is little money for clinics, health education or preventative medicine. Thus, when a poor street person just simply needs antibiotics for the treatment of an infected toe, the length of the wait, the lack of accessible facilities, and the endless red tape of bureaucratic forms effectively prevents them from receiving timely, appropriate, medical care. However, once the infected toe reaches the stage of gangrene, the medical system functions beautifully. Transportation is made available at great expense in a fire department ambulance, and immediate entrance to the hospital is facilitated through the emergency room. Several specialists, including an orthopedic surgeon, a resident physician, two interns, and an anesthesiologist, are attached to the case. After the infection has been stabilized with massive doses of antibiotics, the amputation can usually proceed within a few days.

Several units of fresh, whole blood are kept on hand in case of emergency, but normally only one unit is utilized for the amputation of a leg below the knee. Complete recovery from the procedure occurs within a

Jeff Dietrich

week to ten days, but sixty to ninety days are required for physical therapy and the arduous process of learning how to walk with a prosthesis.

The entire service from ambulance ride to brand new plastic leg is offered free of charge to the medically indigent while costing the taxpayer in excess of $100,000. Clearly, both the taxpayer and the poor could be better served.

That is why over ten years ago we had the hubris to move the used clothing out of our storeroom, put in some basic plumbing, shelving and partitions, and open our soup kitchen for medical service.

For a clinic that started out competing for space with a bunch of used clothing, it is presently doing quite well with a core of fifty volunteers, including ten doctors, twenty nurses and nurse practitioners, a pharmacy, and a bi-weekly dental clinic. While the Hospitality Clinic continues to grow in its professional quality, sophistication and variety of services, it is still as basic, accessible, and unpretentious as the soup kitchen that spawned it.

The Skid Row Death Row Connection

Catholic Agitator, July, 1992, p. 3

Big Louie is a singular anomaly, the only black former biker in Skid Row, or anywhere, for that matter. Actually, I don't think that he was ever really a biker, but he likes to wear Harley-Davidson T-shirts and black leather bracelets with silver studs on them, and he has a really bad temper.

"How can you be so stupid?" he shouts at me, his breath redolent with the aroma of his favorite wine cooler—unmistakably peach. As he presses his face insistently closer to my own, I find myself unconsciously counting his rotting teeth: there are five of them. "A man kills another man, he deserves to die. You hippie types care more about baby whales and murderers than you do about real people."

Well, maybe we aren't stupid. Perhaps we are just a little naïve in thinking that frequenters of our soup kitchen here on Skid Row might share a mutual concern for Robert Harris.* Since most of the people on death row are, like themselves, poor and black, it seemed reasonable to think that we could obtain a large number of sympathetic signatures on our clemency petition in Harris' behalf.

And, indeed, as they filed into the kitchen, a number of individuals did sign, but most shared Big Louie's sentiments. "Fry him man." "Yeah, it's an eye for an eye, that's what it says in the Bible."

While I'm constantly amazed at how often the poor reflect attitudes that appear to be contrary to their own best interests, I suppose that it shouldn't come as a real surprise that they would want the same security, police protection, and freedom from fear desired by any Republican matron.

But when your home is the streets of Skid Row and not Beverly Hills, and police protection is often indistinguishable from police abuse, it is pretty irrational to identify with attitudes of the affluent. On the other hand

---

* Robert Harris was executed in 1992 in San Quentin's gas chamber by the state of California.

though, it is self preservation that usually determines our basic attitudes and interests in life.

It is out of a sense of fear and self-preservation that the affluent have deserted our urban streets and the people who live in them for the placid comfort and security of gated communities and vacuum-sealed shopping malls. Along with their abandonment of the common space has come the concurrent abandonment of the common good, the rejection of a common connectedness and common fate of rich and poor.

No one knows better than the poor themselves how dangerous these streets are and how casually human life is regarded here. They teach the lesson of brutality to each other every day with sticks and knives, crack pipes and syringes. But they learn it also in welfare lines and food lines and in increasingly futile job searches. They are without intrinsic value as human beings, brutalized by their environment. Thus do they support the death penalty in the hope that it will afford them some measure of security in an otherwise desperate environment.

But even as the county criminal justice system proceeds to double its present capacity with the completion of its new high-tech, high security jail, Universal Studios has begun construction on its "City Walk" project, a simulated urban theme park for "those who find real cities too much of a hassle." There can be little doubt who will occupy which environment.

Unlike other soup kitchens in the area, it has been our tradition here at the Catholic Worker to avoid giving sermons to our diners. But under the circumstances, I could not hold back. "You are the ones who are stupid," I shouted. "Don't you realize that 40 percent of the people on death row are black, that a black man convicted of killing a white man stands a far higher chance of being executed than a white man convicted of killing a black man, that the number of executions always goes up when the economy goes down because it's easier for politicians to give the voters a sense of security by executing a few people than it is for them to fix the economy? And while I may like baby whales and have sympathy for murderers, I am not so stupid that I don't know that there is a direct connection between Skid Row and Death Row."

Though they still wouldn't sign my petition, they did pay me something of a compliment: "Hey, you should be—"

"A preacher?" I said.

"No, a politician," they laughed.

Compassionate Response to Suffering[*]

Catholic Agitator, January, 1995, pp. 6 and 7

The pungent odor of feces wafts its way to the third floor as a fragrant reminder that Norma is slowly dying down below. Her diapers are full and I desperately hope that someone other than myself will take notice and change her.

She will no doubt die before Christmas. Ravaged by stomach cancer that went undiagnosed for years as she self-medicated with street doses of heroin, Norma lived on the sidewalk in a "cardboard condo" not far from our soup kitchen where she took her meals, her welfare check going to pay for her "medicine." Even on her deathbed she is hounded by the loan shark to whom she no doubt owes more than she will ever be able to pay before her imminent death.

Our old, Victorian home is, in fact, filled with dying people. Our home has become a hospice—our response to the growing number of AIDS victims on the streets of Skid Row. Our care has since expanded to include any homeless victim of a terminal illness. Increasingly, I have come to recognize that our ministry to the dying indigents is the single appropriate response to the current plight of the poor in our society.

This work with the dying poor rankles the American character. We like to think of ourselves as a people of hope. We have hope in the future, hope in ever-changing technologies that will improve the lot of the marginalized as all boats rise on the tides of progress. The thought that something like Mother Teresa's work with the dying street people of Calcutta might apply to our own American experience is repugnant to the vestigial liberal sensibilities of most of Americans.

The Enlightenment gave birth to the liberal notion of an ever-growing economic pie whose benefits will increasingly diffuse throughout the

---

[*]   A version of this piece appeared in the *Los Angeles Times*, December 23, 1994.

culture, but the Enlightenment has died a painful death. And the current conservative resurgence bears little resemblance to any authentic conservatism, which was based on the preservation of traditional values grounded in a common commitment to ideology and place and a reciprocal relationship of mutual responsibility.

We live in a "meritocracy," according to Christopher Lasch. A meritocracy is a society in which the wealthy and powerful feel they have earned their privileges and recognize no sense of obligation to the disadvantaged:

> Meritocracy, however, turns out to be a contradiction in terms: the talented retain many of the vices of aristocracy without its virtues. Their snobbery lacks any acknowledgement of reciprocal obligation between the favored few and the multitude.

"The Revolt of the Elites," *Harper's Magazine,* p. 44

Furthermore, meritocracy simply drains off the best brains of the lower classes while depriving the majority of the poor of any reasonable excuse for their own poverty—they just didn't try hard enough.

Our current social policies reject the possibility of reforming criminals or mainstreaming the poor. Rather, we prefer to segregate them into prisons, orphanages, and skid rows. A local disc jockey even goes so far as to voice the general but unspoken feelings: "Do them a favor," he said, "and put them to sleep."

We are surrounded by death at our house, but there is a refreshing honesty about facing death directly. We particularly appreciate the attitude of the medical professionals who care for AIDS patients. In the face of this plague, they lack the hubris so endemic to their peers. Because there is no cure, all the physician can offer her patients is compassion and anesthetics. They cannot cure, but they can heal. For there is a difference.

In his ministry, Jesus healed a great number of sick people. But these miraculous healings were not cures in the medical sense of the word so much as they were healings of a breach in the social environment. A handicapped person who lives in a loving, supportive environment does not necessarily need to feel actual physical regeneration in order to feel a sense of wholeness. Jesus' healings were a sign of reconciliation and acceptance to those who had been shunned by the dominant culture. It was the moral disgust of the religious and political elites that resulted in sickness and death for the rejected—the bleeding woman, the lepers, the crippled poor.

The pungent odor of feces intensifies now, taking on the acrid smell of burnt cabbage, indicating that someone other than myself has, thank God, changed Norma's diapers.

I guess all of us have a desire to avoid the messier problem of our social environment. But in abandoning these problems, both liberals and conservatives have abandoned their commitment to the "common good." Here in California our current governor has insisted in his inaugural address that "all citizens meet the demands of common decency, respecting of the rights of others." Yet common decency presupposes a universal commitment to the common good. Without such a commitment, we "may yet unleash a war of all against all" (Lasch, "The Revolt of the Elites," *Harper's Magazine,* p. 49).

Every Simple Thing

Catholic Agitator, August, 1986, p. 1

The majority of his life he lived alone without family or friends, sleeping in parks, under bridges, and in all-night movie theatres. Indeed, with his rotting teeth, thinning hair, and ill-fitting clothes draped over a slope-shoul-dered, one-armed body, he was at sixty-four the archetypal Skid Row man.

But the humbleness of his worldly position was belied at his funeral by the presence of over 200 people from around the city who came to pay their last respects to this gentle, simple, meek man of the streets whom they counted as a friend.

Eugene Fejnas came to live with us here at the Catholic Worker almost ten years ago. At that time he was sleeping in Elysian Park in the shadow of Dodger Stadium, or when it rained he would sleep hidden inside the hard steel abutment of the Sixth Street Bridge, listening to the splash of automobiles as they passed in the cold, wet night.

The uniqueness of Eugene is not so much that he survived the travails and hardships of his difficult life: the automobile accident that killed both his immigrant parents and left him without the use of one arm, the years in prison, the disdain of a cold, harsh society. No, it's not that he survived these things, it is that he survived them with grace, gentleness, and, yes, even with dignity.

Through the experiences that would justifiably transform most of us into cynical misanthropes, Eugene miraculously maintained a childlike joy and enthusiasm. It was easy to give to Eugene. To the casual observer it would seem that the relationship was one-sided. But what we got back was that great feeling of joy you always get when you take an eager child to the beach or the ballgame.

The reality of our work with the poor is sometimes pretty grim: generations of brokenness, poverty, and unemployment, drugs, alcohol, and family violence. What we can give to those who come to us is so meager compared to their needs, and it is often ineffective and unappreciated.

So the gift that Eugene gave to us was appreciation and unabashed enthusiasm for every simple thing we did for him. Nothing went unnoticed or unthanked.

His needs were simple and his tastes were without pretension—an ice cream cone, a soda, a ride in the car, a day at the beach. The secret was he never asked for more than we could give. Thus, we gave freely and often. He hated rock music, long hair, and granola. He loved Dolly Parton, the Dodgers, and hot dogs without mustard or catsup. Before he died, a good friend arranged for him to meet Dodger general manager Tommy Lasorda. Eugene was thrilled. He never tired of showing everyone the baseball Lasorda signed for him. And the Dodgers won that night, breaking a thirteen-game losing streak. In the end, perhaps the greatest gift Eugene gave to us was his death. For weeks afterwards I would continue to feel absurd because in response to queries about his passing I would say, "It was wonderful," or "It was beautiful."

In his simplicity, Eugene had made a simple choice for quality over quantity when it came to deciding about chemotherapy and other life-extending measures. "I don't want to be sick or in the hospital," he said. "I just want to be with my friends and go for rides as long as I can." And so he stayed with us until the end.

When he died, the room was packed with his friends. Bob held Eugene's hand and Nancy sat at the foot of the bed, while the rest of us gathered around in a circle. He had vomited several times that morning and each time Catherine had cleaned him up and put on fresh sheets and pajamas. Now there were brand new sheets on the bed with a sky blue pattern and the whir of the electric fan managed to keep the heavy, slightly fetid, summer air moving about the room.

As we pressed around him, we could see the great tumor bloating his stomach like a woman heavy with child and we knew that his time had come, that his mission here had been fulfilled. Rather than the fear and dread one normally associates with death, we felt the sense of hope that usually comes only with a birth, for we believed that Eugene was about to be born into a new life, a life everlasting in a Kingdom where he would be accorded high station.

56. Guest outside the Hospitality Kitchen dinning garden, 2011. Photo by Robert Radin

At about 2:00 p.m., the loud rattle of his breathing diminished progressively and for a few moments we were not sure if he was truly dead. But when it became clear that he was, Catherine handed me the breviary and I began to read from the Prayers of the Dead.

"Withhold not, O Lord, your compassion from me; may your kindness and truth ever preserve me."

"Though I am afflicted and poor, yet the Lord thinks of me."

"You are my help and my deliverer; O my God, hold not back!"

Afterwards, I sat alone in the room with his lifeless body, knowing that Eugene's spirit was still present. I wanted to speak to him, but I was afraid that others would hear and think me crazy for communing with the dead.

What I wanted to say was: "Eugene, thanks for being here. Thanks for letting us give our meager gifts to you. And thank you for appreciating them so much."

Part of the sorrow is that we never took the opportunity to thank Eugene for so joyfully allowing us to be a part of his life, thus insuring that we too might be among those who inherit the earth.

PART TEN

ABANDONING THE POOR

To none shall we sell, to none deny or delay, right or justice.

Magna Carta, 1215

Poor naked wretches whereso'er you are,
That bide the pelting of this pitiless storm,
How shall your houseless heads, your unfed sides,
Your looped and winow'ed raggedness defend you
From seasons such as these? O I have ta'en
Too little care of this! Take physic pomp;
Expose thyself to feel what wretches feel,
That thou myst shake the superflux to them
And show the heavens more just.

William Shakespeare,
King Lear, 3. 4. 28-36

Hurricane Katrina Reveals a Nation in Which the Poor Are Abandoned

Catholic Agitator, November 2005, pp. 1 and 2

It has been two months since the devastating Hurricane Katrina hit the gulf shores of the United States, and, in the interim, the disasters in Guatemala and Pakistan have far surpassed the devastation and death toll of our domestic tragedy. Katrina nonetheless remains, along with the Iraq War, as a persistent thorn in the side of the Bush Administration, making a mockery of its self-proclaimed efficacy, and revealing the depths of its ineptitude and contempt for the poor.

The apocalyptic image of the disastrous flood in the Gospel of Matthew has profound implications for an administration that claims to rely so heavily upon scripture. Coming as it does at the conclusion of the "Sermon on the Mount," the storm and flood are, in effect, salutary images that separate the "wise man" who builds the foundation of his house on the rock of "hearing and practicing" the Word of God from the "foolish man" who builds the foundation of his house on the sandy ground of hearing the Word but not putting it into practice.

The vivid media images of floating bodies and desperate African Americans stranded in flood-drenched New Orleans continues to indict the Bush Administration, as well as haunt our collective national conscience, revealing, despite disclaimers to the contrary, that our nation has built its house on foundations of shifting sand. The ensuing floodwaters have exposed us as a nation that has no real connection to the Gospel, because we have abandoned the poor, who are at the very heart of that document. The Sermon on the Mount does briefly address the narrow fundamentalist agenda of personal sexual morality espoused by the President and the religious right, calling for the hyperbolic excising of the eye and hand of any man who merely looks lustfully at a woman. The vast majority of the three-chapter-long sermon, however, focuses almost exclusively on the demands of justice and concern "for the least." It starts off by blessing the poor, the sorrowing and the lowly, and promising that they will receive the kingdom, be consoled and inherit the land. And that's just the introduction!

The Sermon further exhorts us to "give to all who beg from you...love your enemy, pray for your persecutors," and refuse to "lay up for yourselves earthly treasures," because "you cannot give yourself to God and money." Finally, in the ultimate summation of justice and reciprocity, it insists that we are supposed to "treat others the way you would have them treat you." And that, Jesus says, "sums up the law and the prophets."

The United States has never had a domestic policy even remotely based on the compassion and justice of the Sermon on the Mount, and social critic Noam Chomsky reminds us that our current public policy amounts to an all-out war on the poor. The fate of poor African Americans, abandoned in the floodwaters of New Orleans, has been compounded by the regressive social policies of the last five years—policies designed to benefit the rich at the expense of the poor.

Money and resources that should be dedicated to social services, education and infrastructure, including the maintenance of dikes and levees, have been drained by the war in Iraq. "Empires are costly" Chomsky says,

> running Iraq is not cheap. Somebody's paying. Somebody's paying the corporations that destroyed Iraq and the corporations that are rebuilding it. In both cases, they're getting paid by the U.S. taxpayer. Those gifts from U.S. taxpayers to the U.S. corporations. Who pays Halliburton and Bechtel? The U.S. taxpayer. The same taxpayers fund the military-corporate system of weapons manufacturers and technology companies. So first you destroy Iraq, then you rebuild it. It's a transfer of wealth from the general population to the narrow sectors of the population.

Imperial Ambitions, pp. 56-57

This overt transfer of wealth from the poor sectors of the economy to the wealthier sectors is reflected most clearly in the so-called Social Security reforms of the Bush Administration. The drive to destroy Social Security is quite transparent, according to Chomsky:

> Instead of a highly efficient government system, with very low administrative costs, we're moving toward a system with very substantial

administrative costs, but costs that will be transferred to the right pockets, namely, Wall Street firms and big money managers.

Imperial Ambitions, p. 145

But even more than the vast transference of wealth, the Bush Administration is bent upon destroying the last vestiges of community and solidarity:

But that idea has to be driven out of people's heads. There is huge pressure to turn people into pathological monsters who care only about themselves, who don't have anything to do with anyone else, and who therefore can be very easily ruled and controlled. That's what lies behind the attack on Social Security.

Imperial Ambitions, p. 146

In addition to Social Security,

they want to destroy the whole array of progressive achievements of the past century. They've already more or less gotten rid of the progressive income tax. They're trying to destroy the limited medical care system. They'll probably go after schools. They don't want a small government anymore than Reagan did. They want huge, massively intrusive government, but one that works for them.

Imperial Ambitions, p. 113

But the massive robbery of the poor and working class taxpayers of this country is more than mere theft of the commonwealth; it is also a conscious effort to institutionalize conservative heartlessness by insuring government parsimony through long-term national indebtedness. Chomsky writes:

They will have left the economy in a very serious state, with huge deficits....And then it will be somebody else's problem. Meanwhile, they will have undermined social programs and diminished democracy, which of course they hate, by transferring decisions out of the public arena into private hands....The legacy they leave will be painful and hard, but only for the majority of the population. The people they are concerned about are going to make out like bandits.

Imperial Ambitions, pp. 15-16

It is not that the poor and working class of New Orleans are particularly different from similar populations in any other large city. It is simply that the hurricane and flood have compounded and revealed the extent to which

Jeff Dietrich

58. Jeff Dietrich observes the picket line during the Blood Strike of 1973. Photo by Hank Lebo

360

the poor everywhere in this country, but particularly in New Orleans, have been increasingly victimized and abandoned by a heartless and punitive national policy.

Theologians, both Catholic and Protestant, have argued for centuries that the Sermon on the Mount was merely a personal ethic, and that Jesus never intended it to be the basis of a rational governmental policy, indeed, such policies such as loving our enemies, turning the other cheek, and giving to all who beg would be absurd governmental policy.

On the other hand though, the corollary to the Sermon on the Mount is Matthew 25:44: "Lord, when did we see you hungry or thirsty,...or in prison?" It seems pretty clear that the entire Gospel of Matthew is bracketed by the Sermon on the Mount at the beginning and Matthew 25 at the end, with Matthew 25 essentially repeating and re-emphasizing the compassion of the Sermon on the Mount. What is typically overlooked by theologians is that Matthew 25 is not a personal ethic, but is actually the basis of the Last Judgment. And the Last Judgment is not a judgment of individuals; it is, rather, a judgment of "the nations of the world."

"When the Son of Man comes in his glory...all of the nations will be assembled before him, and he will separate them one from another as a shepherd separates sheep from goats" (Matthew 25:31-2). Incredible as it may seem, America, along with "all of the nations of the world," will be assembled before the royal throne of the "Son of Man," and judged on the basis of how we as a nation treated the least of our brothers and sisters. If New Orleans is an example of our public policy towards "the least of our brothers and sisters," then we might want to start looking for a good defense attorney.

Renaissance or Resurrection

Catholic Agitator, May 2006, pp. 1 and 6

With bodies lying huddled in blankets, tents, and cardboard condos and reeking of urine and human excrement, it is difficult to believe that Gladys Street is located in Los Angeles, one of the richest cities in the world, and not in some impoverished slum of Calcutta or Jakarta. But it is true that the street directly in front of the Catholic Worker soup kitchen, at the corner of Sixth and Gladys, looks more like a third world refugee camp than a First World thoroughfare.

Though a perennial source of concern and distress to the powers that be, the homeless poor and their deviant activities have, in the wake of what the developers and realtors call the "Downtown Renaissance," come under unprecedented scrutiny by police, politicians, and reporters who are suddenly, and rather uncharacteristically, focused on "solving the problem of homelessness."

Rallied by Police Chief Bratton and a brigade of *LA Times* reporters and editorial writers, city, county, and state politicians have responded to a media campaign of historic proportions with a dazzling array of bills, plans, and proposals. All of them share two common features: one, they all were developed in a knee-jerk response to media pressure without much thought, planning, or consultation; two, they all seem to dovetail rather neatly with the agenda of the business and real estate interests, who would, in reality, prefer to remove the homeless rather than assist them.

The issue of homelessness has been on LA's front burner ever since 2003, when former New York City Police Commissioner William Bratton became LA's new chief of police and began to implement his signature Broken Windows strategy of policing, which entails the stringent enforcement of so called "quality of life crimes:" begging, loitering, jaywalking, sleeping on the streets, etc. But in the last few months, it has become clear that the driving force of homeless concern has been the super-heated downtown real estate market. After decades of stalled attempts to attract the middle class back to the central city, the market seems to have taken off with a vengeance.

Spurred by recent architectural projects like the new Cathedral, the Disney Concert Hall, the Staples Center sports arena, and the proposed $1.2 billion Grand Avenue project, Los Angeles has become a destination for professionals, artists, and others who are moving into long-vacant former office buildings, lofts, and new condos.

Buyers are standing in line and falling all over themselves to pay $500 thousand to $1 million for one and two-bedroom condos. With suburban housing starting at well over $1 million, that sounds like a reasonable entry price into the exorbitant LA real estate market. And it is a small price to pay to be part of the "Downtown Renaissance, and own a piece of history," as one condo sales advertisement promises.

As a result, downtown has begun to fill with a critical mass of condo and loft owners who perceive the homeless poor as intrusive interlopers with a deleterious impact on both property values and "renaissance panache." But it is in fact the wealthy condo owners who are the interlopers while the poor have actually been the historic residents of this Skid Row area for over a hundred years.

It is hard to believe that the Catholic Worker soup kitchen and the fifty surrounding blocks that comprise the urban tawdriness of Skid Row is identified in county land records as part of the Wolfskill Orchard Tract. But it is true that a little over a hundred years ago, this urban nightmare was a bucolic orchard and vineyard watered by the Los Angeles River. It was only with the coming of the railroad in 1887 that the sleepy pueblo of Los Angeles began to spread south and east of its central plaza area to include the rural acreage that now comprises Skid Row.

The Skid Row area east of downtown began to evolve from its original agricultural nature into an industrial district. "Even in the early days, a lot of the industrial activity in Los Angeles was seasonal, so there was historically a very transient population that came to Los Angeles for work" (Spivack, "History of Skid Row," *Skid Row Journal*). This temporal population gave rise to the need for, and thus the development of, hotels that provided living space for a primarily single, male population coming into Los Angeles. Because the area had a predominantly single adult male population, it attracted services that catered to that population, including small shops, bars, saloons and restaurants, brothels, and other social and recreational meeting places. "So there was a demand for additional social services. These were initially delivered by organizations such as the religious-based missions" (Spivack, "History of Skid Row," *Skid Row Journal*). Many of those that now deliver social services have roots that go back over a hundred years.

In short, the entire Skid Row area developed expressly to serve a marginal, transient population; it has been around for a very long time, and it is not going anywhere any time soon. In the 1970s and 80s, under the Bradley Administration, the city developed what, in retrospect, was a humane and realistic plan for the Skid Row area. Sometimes called the "containment plan," it was a plan that recognized the fact that Skid Row was a permanent institution for the homeless. The plan called for the preservation of the transient SRO (single room occupancy) hotels while providing funding for the consolidation of Skid Row by moving the two largest missions, the Union Rescue and the Midnight, off of Main Street and further east to San Pedro Street. It worked to save and upgrade housing, while improving and augmenting social services in the area. It was a recognition that this area was a permanent setting, a last enclave for poor and marginally-employed males. It also recognized that other areas of the city and county were permanently hostile to this population, and thus resistant to the placement of service facilities for the homeless in their communities.

What's happening in LA is no different from any other city—white flight and suburban malls deplete the urban core, then developers come in with cultural, entertainment, and tourist attractions, luring the middle class back to refurbished "Old Towns" and "Main Streets." What these new urbanites want is an "urban" experience with the comfort, convenience, and blandness of the suburbs and none of the crime, poverty, and grittiness of a real downtown. According to Mark Lacter the editor of the *Los Angeles Business Journal*, there are "more than 12,000 condominium units under construction between now and 2013," putting enormous pressure on the homeless and marginal population of Skid Row ("Downtown's Renewal Testing 'Containment' of Homeless Problem").

Led by local councilwoman Jan Perry, new residents have created a "Take Back Our Streets" campaign, pressuring police and city government to arrest the homeless and remove city-funded porta-potties and demanding a safer, cleaner neighborhood.

In the meantime, a Ninth Circuit Court decision has raised the hope of slowing down the gentrification process somewhat. Initiated by the Catholic Worker and Las Familias del Pueblo, the ACLU secured the right

59. Catholic Workers disrupt Mayor's press conference. Pictured: Mayor Antonio Villaraigoso, Councilwoman Jan Perry (foreground), Jeff Dietrich, Clare Bellefeuille-Rice (background), 2009. Photo by Mike Wisniewski

of the homeless poor to sleep through the night without being harassed by the police. The court ruled that in the absence of shelter alternatives, jailing the homeless poor was a violation of their Eighth Amendment protection against "cruel and unusual punishment." While the police will no doubt find other ways to harass the homeless, this nevertheless is a significant victory for the poor. Just solutions to this dilemma must be struggled for by people throughout the continent, indeed, the world, since the powers that be would be happy to leave us divided and conquered.

But lawsuits notwithstanding, the most important advantage that the poor and homeless of Skid Row have in their favor is inertia. While current plans call for the dispersal of homeless services and populations to regional areas, the reality is that, even as downtown property owners fight to push the poor out, suburban property owners will fight just as tenaciously to protect their own property values that are endangered by this dispersal process.

In the final analysis, it seems pretty clear that this enormous population of over 10,000 marginal people is not going anywhere. Skid Row is, in effect, an institutionalized entity that has existed for over a hundred years, almost as long as the "modern" city of Los Angeles itself has existed. The century-old missions, as well as the city-funded SRO hotels and homeless services, have anchored this population as an unmovable mass. As *Los Angeles Business Journal* editor Lacter writes, "Trouble is Skid Row... [is] too big to fail. Its residents cannot be put in buses and shipped to some other neighborhood, because there is no better place to take them. This is, after all, the largest service-dependent ghetto in the nation" ("Downtown's Renewal Testing 'Containment' of Homeless Problem"). While Lacter goes on to point out that the poor will ultimately win and the developers and new downtown residents surrounding Skid Row will ultimately lose by experiencing falling property values, the homeless will nonetheless continue to experience intense harassment as the "Renaissance War on the Poor" plays out on LA's Skid Row.

The poor continue to suffer, and the Catholic Worker, as their advocates, will continue to be increasingly vilified as people who support deviance, criminal activity, and sleeping on the streets.

Our desire, of course, is not that the poor should sleep on the streets, but it is rather that, in the absence of housing or suitable shelter, their suffering should not be hidden from view by incarceration or dispersal to obscure locations. Their presence is like an open wound.

It is just this kind of woundedness that theologian Roberto Goizueta speaks of in his article on the Resurrection in the Easter issue of *America Magazine*. "The refusal to acknowledge Christ's wounds," says Goizueta, "...is a mortal sin (in the most literal sense of the term) for it leads inevitably to the death of others....By denying death we inflict it" ("From Calvary to Galilee," p. 2). Goizueta equates the experience of touching Christ's wounds with the post-Resurrection command to return to Galilee, the wounded borderland of Israel filled with "unclean contaminated lawbreakers," not unlike the people of Skid Row, according to Goizueta. "If we are to recognize the crucified and risen Lord, we must risk defilement. We must touch the untouchable" ("From Calvary to Galilee," p. 3). So, perhaps what we struggle for is not a downtown renaissance, but a downtown resurrection, in which we acknowledge our common woundedness, our common humanity, and our solidarity with the suffering.

The Story of Jacob and the Homeless with a Stone for a Pillow

Catholic Agitator, November 2006, pp. 1 and 2

It must have been that bit about a stone for a pillow, "taking one of the stones at the shrine, he put it under his head and lay down to sleep at that spot" (Genesis 28:11) that made me think of Jacob, the Biblical patriarch, as a homeless person. As I listened to this typically boring church sermon on the story of Jacob's Ladder (Genesis 28:10-20), I had a hard time focusing on the prosaic theme.

Like most commentators on this odd text, the priest who gave the sermon offered little illumination, focusing instead on the image of angels running up and down a ladder, and on God's promise of abundance and on the wonderful gifts that God has given us. But, perhaps because I was so focused on the harassment of the homeless in downtown Los Angeles, I tended to see everything in terms of the problems of the homeless. As the story of Jacob was being read, I could not help but hear it, not from the perspective of abundance and gifts, but from the perspective of the homeless poor.

Just a few days prior to this sermon, Mayor Villaraigosa and Police Chief Bratton held a press conference to announce something they call the "Safer Streets Initiative." As part of this project, the city has assigned fifty extra police officers to the streets of downtown. At the behest of civic leaders and Chief Bratton, the new officers will patrol the streets of downtown, implementing Bratton's notorious Broken Windows theory of policing, which maintains that overall crime rates in a particular area will diminish if the "criminal environment" is diminished.

The primary tactic of this theory rests on the strict enforcement of so-called quality of life crimes, essentially misdemeanor offenses like littering, loitering, or urinating in public, jay walking, sleeping, sitting, or standing in public, as well as vigorous enforcement of parole violations and petty drug offenses. We have known people who have been ticketed for dropping a cigarette butt on the street, or simply putting one foot in the street after the *Don't Walk* sign lit up.

As the police patrol the streets in groups of two to six officers at a time, downtown Los Angeles has begun to look as if we were under a state of siege. In the first week of the program, the police claimed to have made over 600 arrests of what they call drug dealers. Though I have doubts that they have made that many arrests, I have no doubt the amount of drugs they have confiscated can be counted in ounces rather than pounds.

In Los Angeles, the poor have been effectively demonized and marginalized by a public relations campaign that covers over a basic hostility to the homeless with euphemistic rhetoric about tough love, safe streets, and a desire to get everyone into a program. There is almost unanimous cooperation between police, politicians, business interests, social services, and the press, who attempts to discredit supporters of the homeless who speak out for basic justice and civil rights of the poor.

But the truth is that all of this focus on homelessness, though cloaked in high moral jargon, is really about profits and property. Downtown Los Angeles is quickly becoming a desirable housing location for young, wealthy elites, and developers are falling all over themselves to cater to that market at the expense of the Skid Row poor, who, like Jacob the ancient patriarch, are homeless.

The primary element of the Jacob story that jumped out at me was that before he went to sleep and had his dream of angels, Jacob chose to lay his head on a stone for a pillow. Now, while most commentators identify the stone to be a sacred element of the holy site at Bethel, I could not help but remember that many of the folks that we know in downtown Los Angeles go to sleep each night with a concrete sidewalk for a pillow and a piece of cardboard for a mattress, and wake up each morning saying, "I am blessed, because I woke up today." And it struck me with the force of lightning that the reason Jacob used a stone for a pillow was because, he too, was actually at that point in his life, an authentically homeless person.

Like many of the folks on the streets of Skid Row, Jacob was not only homeless, but he was also a fugitive and a refugee fleeing for his very life. Perhaps one of the most morally ambiguous figures in the scriptural pantheon of ambiguous heroes, Jacob had lied to his father, deceived his brother, and stolen his patrimony. Now he had to flee from the wrath of his sibling, who had vowed to kill him.

But his status as a refugee, "a criminal," and homeless person puts him squarely within the very core of the scriptural tradition. In truth, the entire scriptural opus not only privileges the estate of homelessness, but it casts a critical eye upon the project of urban civilization itself. From the toppled Tower of Babel in Genesis, the first book of the Bible, to the fall of Babylon in Revelation, the last book of the Bible, the urban project is consistently condemned.

The Scriptural critique of cities begins by identifying the founder of the first city as the perpetrator of the first murder. Cain, who killed his own brother Abel, responded to God's query about his brother with the paradigmatic urban response: "Am I my brother's keeper?" Of course not; in alienated cities, there are only strangers to be found. It is only after the fall of the Tower of Babel, that ultimate symbol of urban hubris, that God begins the project of salvation. And the first step in that salvation program is "urban flight." "Get out of town," God tells Abraham. And Abraham leaves his comfortable existence in Ur to become a homeless wanderer in the hostile land of Canaan.

This urban critique finds deep resonance in the anti-hospitality story of Sodom and Gomorrah, in which these cities are destroyed because their hostile citizens attempted to rape Lot's two angelic visitors. But the paradigmatic anti-urban narrative of scripture is the Exodus story. With its epic depiction of slave revolt, urban flight, and wilderness wanderings, it offers the essence of scriptural preference for the homeless fugitive and rejection of the urban project.

Jacob is indeed promised abundance and progeny and wealth and angels, but these things come only after he has experienced servitude and slavery at the hands of his treacherous uncle Laban and takes fugitive flight once again, this time fleeing the hot pursuit of his enraged uncle.

The subsequent wound that Jacob receives when he wrestles the angel at the Jabbok River is a symbolic reminder of his homeless fugitive origins, a permanent physical handicap that forces him to remain always compassionate to the "handicapped" homeless, because his wound will never completely heal.

For Jacob, like the Hebrew people themselves, abundance and the promised land only come after a time of servitude and slavery and homelessness. The Hebrew people are commanded, as a requirement for entering the promised land, to keep their status as homeless fugitives at the forefront of their memories. In fact, the law of Deuteronomy is replete with divine commands to remember "that you were too once slaves in the land of Egypt" (Deuteronomy 15:15).

Jeff Dietrich

That memory of homelessness is at the forefront of Jesus' mind as well when he boldly states that "Foxes have dens, birds of the sky have nests, but the Son of Man has nowhere to rest his head" (Matthew 8:20). Jesus is, in fact, a homeless person! Thus, when he sends his disciples on their first mission, they are told to take "no sack for the journey, or a second tunic, or sandals, or walking stick. Whatever town or village you enter, look for a worthy person in it, and stay there until you leave. As you enter a house, wish it peace" (Matthew 10:10-12). In other words, the disciples are supposed to be homeless, defenseless, and dependent on the "kindness of strangers."

In keeping with the entire opus of scripture, Jesus has insisted that his disciples and his church must have an actual experience of homelessness, because it is that experience, and the memory of that experience of suffering, which keeps us tender-hearted and human, ever mindful that all gifts come from God.

Conversely, from the perspective of scripture, people who are housed and live in cities have a tendency to lose their humanity, thinking that they are independent and self-sufficient, believing that their wealth and security are the result of their own efforts. And thus they repeat, if only unconsciously, the original mantra of urban alienation: "Am I my brother's keeper?"

The answer, of course, is that we are. But we forget it, and it is that condition of amnesia that allows us to tolerate and perpetrate urban war on the homeless poor in the phony moral jargon of Safe Streets and tough love.

Like homeless Jacob who slept with a stone for a pillow and woke in the morning saying, "Truly the Lord is in this spot" (Genesis 28:16), the homeless poor of our city rise from their concrete and cardboard mattresses each morning saying, "I am blessed," because they too have dreamt of angels watching over them, and where they have slept is holy ground indeed.

The Shopping Cart Campaign[*]

Catholic Agitator, August, 1998, p. 3

The caller was outraged. "It is criminally irresponsible and a pernicious waste of money to give shopping carts to the homeless," he said, "and I intend to hold you personally responsible if one of your carts is used in a theft from my business."

It's OK for the Catholic Worker to run a free soup kitchen, but giving out one hundred free shopping carts to the poor has inspired unprecedented anger and even violent reactions from the community. The police have intimated that we are abetting criminal activity; numerous irate and sometimes anonymous callers have castigated us for trashing the city, degrading the homeless, and wasting resources, while some members of the business community have actually screamed angry epitaphs at us, saying that we are providing the homeless with a license for vagrancy.

On the one hand, our action is a simple, human response to the anger we felt at watching homeless people harassed and jailed for up to thirty days for the mere crime of possessing a shopping cart. We wanted to prevent homeless people from going to jail and give them what they needed to survive on the streets by providing them with shopping carts complete with a written statement giving our permission to use the cart, thereby eliminating all legal impediments to such use.

This is a provocative action that flies in the face of cherished beliefs held by most Americans. Nothing symbolizes more graphically the desperation and degradation of homeless poverty than a shopping cart. To give a shopping cart to a homeless person is an act of complicity and co-dependency, if not outright criminal conspiracy. Rather than reforming the poor or mainstreaming the poor, we are affirming the reality of their dead-end poverty.

---

[*] A version of this piece appeared in the *Los Angeles Times,* August 4, 1998.

Jeff Dietrich

60. Cover illustration by Gary Palmatier, pen and ink. *Catholic Agitator*, 1976

However, social service agencies continue to foster the illusion that it is the fault of the poor that they have not reaped the bounty of the American Dream. Over the past several decades our nation has consistently eliminated the lifelines, step ladders, and safety nets that historically have made it possible for the poor in a complex industrial society to transition out of poverty. Our collective parsimony has precipitated the elimination of every social program from free higher education to job training to low cost housing. And now this month, with the elimination of 80,000 people from the welfare rolls, we have virtually slammed the door on the poor, creating a permanent homeless underclass.

The result of these cuts has led to an increase in the homeless population which is aesthetically unpleasant, bad for business, and has a chilling effect on tourism. It thus becomes the responsibility of the police to insure that the public need never encounter the odious consequences of its own hard-heartedness.

In San Francisco it is illegal to serve food to homeless people in the downtown area. In Seattle it is illegal to sit in certain areas of the city. And in Orlando, Florida street beggars will be arrested unless they possess a city-issued license to beg.

Here in Los Angeles the police zealously enforce anti-camping, anti-begging, anti-loitering as well as anti-shopping cart laws, thus sanitizing public contact with the poor.

The real purpose of our free shopping carts is not simply to help the poor or to keep them out of jail, though it is definitely that. The real purpose is actually to insure that the poor, with the emblem of their poverty and suffering, will not be entirely invisible to the community.

We expect more angry phone calls in the coming weeks when we announce our next distribution of one hundred free, street-legal shopping carts. Anger and violence are part of the process of breaking through the veil of public denial to expose and heal the wounds of homelessness and poverty.

The Universe Bends Towards Justice*

Catholic Agitator, August 2011, p. 4

Our street looked like the Nazi *blitzkrieg*. Instead of the Nazi's attacking England or France, the Fascists were targeting four red shopping carts piled high with the belonging of homeless people who'd joined us at the Catholic Worker Soup Kitchen for lunch. The men had parked their carts in front and had been gone no longer than ten minutes when five police cars, a city dump truck, a skip loader and ten police officers swooped in, and dumped the men's meager belongings into the street. The dismal pile was quickly picked up by the skip loader.

Hearing the commotion, the homeless owners of the shopping carts came rushing out into the arms of the police, who pushed them back and told them that their belongings were gone and could not be retrieved. "No, this is abandoned property. Get back or you will be arrested."

Had I been there in time I would have attempted to jump into one of the shopping carts, because I actually possessed a bill of sale, and I could prove that the Catholic Worker owned the carts. Over the last ten years the Catholic Worker, in an effort to assist homeless people, thwart police malfeasance, and piss off the business community, has purchased over 50,000 shopping carts for homeless people. We don't often tell our donors about this secret project, because we fear that our most faithful supporters might consider it a bit too profligate, even for the Catholic Worker.

Even though we actually own the shopping carts, when police and city agencies confiscate them they often don't return them. Despite numerous court rulings in our favor, police and city officials continue to act with impunity. Along with destroying personal property they seize such things as pillows, milk crates, and excess blankets as contraband, because they are items that give comfort. Like battle-weary soldiers, our hearts get hardened.

---

* A version of this piece appeared in the *Los Angeles Times*, August 8, 2011.

But on this particular occasion, one of our soup kitchen volunteers from the suburbs observed the police onslaught.

Richard was shocked: "Can't we do something about this? They just took everybody's stuff. They were just eating lunch, and when they rushed out to grab their shopping carts, and the police just said, 'This is abandoned property!'"

It's embarrassing when volunteers come from the suburbs. They think that the same rules that apply there apply everywhere. But that's not how it works on Skid Row. If you are gone for five minutes to wash, eat, or relieve yourself, you lose all of your possessions. If you leave a friend in charge of your shopping cart and the police suspect that your friend is not the actual owner—boom—gone to the city dump. I felt like the cop in that old Jack Nicholson movie. I imagined myself saying to our suburban volunteer, "Forget it, Jake. It's Chinatown."

So inured had I become to the way things are on Skid Row that I did not even bother to contact our civil rights attorney, Carol Sobel, who years ago in Federal Court affirmed the right of homeless people to security in their person and property. Fortunately, mutual friends did contact her. She came, took depositions, collected photos, and took the case back to Federal Court.

I was heartened, but still did not expect any results. The way city officials and police articulate their story of Skid Row, everyone on the streets is either a drug addict or a drug dealer, and those people do not actually have a constitutional right to security in their person or property. In August, when a rag-tag group of soup kitchen workers gathered in a Federal courtroom, the room began to fill up with off-duty police officers dressed in suits and ties, the very officers who had participated in the attack and actually planned and ordered the property theft in front of our soup kitchen. I recognized the captain of the Central Division as well as the Senior Lead Officer, Dion Joseph, who is also the head of the Safer Cities Initiative. Given the turnout of such impressive police brass, I was expecting an affirmation of police impunity. In other words, I thought they'd get away with it.

So, I was as unprepared as the City Attorney when Judge Philip S. Gutierrez made his announcement: "Before we begin today," he said, "I need to inform the court that in 1980 I was a summer intern at the Catholic Worker Soup Kitchen. I chopped onions. I served food. I cleaned toilets. And Catherine Morris was my supervisor. But I have had no contact with them since, except that I do see Ms. Morris periodically protesting the war in Iraq. But, I do not speak to her. Therefore, I see no reason to recuse myself from this case."

Whoa! You could have heard the City Attorney's jaw drop to the table from here to Santa Monica. And quite frankly, mine as well. We were all shocked; none of the old-timers at the Catholic Worker recognized Judge Gutierrez's face or his name.

Miraculously, two days later we got a permanent Federal injunction, affirming the right of homeless people to security in their person and property. Richard was elated. For him, it was an affirmation that the system works; I was in a state of shock. Where did this come from?

We are all formed by our own individual life experiences. We were raised Republican or Democrat, Protestant, Jewish, or Catholic, pro-life or pro-choice. But Judge Gutierrez was formed in some measure by his experience chopping onions, cleaning toilets, and serving food to the homeless at the Catholic Worker Soup Kitchen. All formations being equal in the eyes of the law, it was appropriate that he did not recuse himself from this case.

From our perspective, and the perspective of the folks who push shopping carts containing the last of their earthly treasures, it is like one of those unlikely biblical stories. Just when you had given up all hope, just when you thought the authorities had the final words, just when you thought that the rules of the suburbs did not apply on Skid Row, there is a parting of the waters, and the universe, in the words of Dr. King, "bends towards justice."

Declaring a Cease-Fire in the Drug War

Catholic Agitator, August, 2009, pp. 1 and 2

It's a no-brainer. It's time to legalize drugs and empty our bloated, over-crowded prison system of all nonviolent drug offenders. It's time to put an end to this insane, money-sucking, ineffective, hypocritical, War on Drugs that is really a war on the poor, the unemployed, the unemployable, and, to a large extent, on black males.

It's a no-brainer. Decriminalize drugs: free the captives; close 75 percent of the prisons; put the savings into job creation, health care, substance abuse counseling, education, and recapitalizing bankrupt state govern-ments. Retrain prison guards to work in organic gardens; lay off all of the extra police and help find them jobs as chauffeurs and body guards in the film industry.

For forty years we have been fighting a war on drugs and now it's time to admit defeat. It's time to stop demonizing the poor. It's time to stop eroding civil rights with no-knock laws, warrantless searches, and asset forfeiture laws that give the police the right and the incentive to seize bank accounts and property of suspects before they are proven guilty in a court of law.

According to Bureau of Justice statistics from 2006, we have over 7.3 million people in criminal custody in the United States—there are over 2.3 million in jails and prisons, and another 5 million on parole or proba-tion. Approximately 3.2 percent of the US adult population, or 1 in every 32 adults, was incarcerated or on probation or parole as of year end 2006. That number will no doubt be higher for 2009. There is no other nation in the world that has more of its citizens in criminal detention than the United States of America. According to FBI crime reports, over 1 million people were arrested for drug law offenses in the year 2008.

When we first began to research this issue, we thought that a call for legalized drugs was the most radical, idealistic statement one could make, short of, say, peace on earth. However, even a cursory examination of our almost half-century war on drugs reveals that it is nothing more than a war on the poor, the unemployed, and more specifically, a war on poor, unemployed black men. It is a racist, hypocritical, recapitulation of the southern chain gang system that sucks vast chunks of the commonwealth out of the social safety net of health care, welfare, housing, and education, and places it directly into the hands of the social repression network of the USA's vast gulag known as the prison industrial complex.

"No one will convince me that racism and discrimination does not take place in this issue," says Norm Stamper, former Seattle police chief, who currently works for drug law reform. He goes on to write:

> Wildly disproportionate numbers of people of color, young people, poor people have gone to jail and ultimately to prison behind this drug war for decades now....These people have been uprooted from their communities, detached from their families. They've lost employment. They've lost student loans. They've lost public housing. And they've lost their freedom.

> "Citing Failed War on Drugs," *Democracy Now*

When you think of the huge number of people who have been imprisoned for non-violent drug offenses—and most of those for simple possession of marijuana—it's just heartbreaking.

The effects of this racism are enhanced by the power of mandatory minimum sentences, which mandate a five-year sentence for the mere possession of crack cocaine, the inexpensive drug-of-choice among poor black men, while possession of a hundred times that amount of the similar, but more expensive cocaine, the white man's drug, is required before a felony charge is pressed. Of the 2.3 million people incarcerated in the US, 1 in 9 are black males ages 20 to 34. For black women ages 35 to 39, the figure is 1 in 100, compared with 1 in 355 for white women in the same age group.

In his seminal book, *Smoke and Mirrors: The War on Drugs and the Politics of Failure*, former *Wall Street Journal* reporter Dan Baum documents the racist origins of the drug war and the prison industrial complex, tracing it back to Richard Nixon's successful 1968 presidential campaign, in which he focused on "Law and Order":

> For the GOP to bury the Great Society, it would have to convince Americans that people are poor and violent not because of social pressures the mainstream can correct, but because they are bad indi-

viduals deserving of discipline and punishment. In this context, drug use was the perfect crime on which to focus. While stealing to feed one's family could conceivably be excused, drug taking can be framed as purely escapist and pleasure driven. In the War on Drugs, users would come to provide a bottomless well of villains and scapegoats for administrations looking to unburden the electorate of taxes, shed federal responsibilities, and divert attention from their own failures.

p. 6

Though conceived by Richard Nixon and the Republicans, politicians of both parties over the decades realized that fear and scapegoating and veiled racism, in short, demonizing drug addicts and poor people, was a very effective election strategy. In the process, we have created powerful vested interests among law enforcement and prison bureaucracies, while enhancing the wealth and power of third world drug cartels and destabilizing nation states throughout Latin America, Afghanistan, and Pakistan.

The US drug war is big business—a multi-billion dollar venture that radically inflates the value of illegal drugs and is used to criminalize the poorest people of color, trapping them in a vicious cycle of addiction, unemployment, and incarceration. Last year alone, the US spent $27 billion for interdiction and law enforcement. In the year 2000, we spent almost $10 billion to incarcerate 500,000 non-violent drug offenders, 75 percent of whom were black.

According to the United Nations' international drug control program, the international illicit drug business generates as much as $400 billion in trade annually. Profits of this magnitude invariably lead to corruption and complicity at the highest levels. We clearly see, in places like Mexico, Colombia, Pakistan, or Afghanistan, that the heroin trade has essentially paid for the cheap victory by our Northern Alliance allies, who are nothing more than drug lords, now operating with the tacit consent and support of the United States government.

But this drug war does not target failing nation states and our allies, rather it targets the poorest of the poor, the economically disadvantaged, ethnic minorities, and indigenous people in the US, Mexico, Colombia, Peru, Bolivia, Afghanistan, Pakistan, Laos, Thailand, and Vietnam. Discussing the legal apartheid that keeps the developing world poor, economist Matthew Miller observes that "The poor live outside the law...because living within the law is impossible: corrupt legal systems and warped rules force those at the bottom of the world economy to spend years leaping absurd hurdles to do things by the book" ("The Poor Man's Capitalist," *New York Times*). In a criminalized economy, the risk of imprisonment is almost a form of business license tax.

Arianna Huffington reports,

> a major shift in the global drug policy debate, a Latin American commission, headed by former presidents Fernando Cardoso of Brázil, Ernesto Zedillo of Mexico, and Cesar Gavaria of Colombia issued a devastating report condemning the US 40-year war on drugs.

> "Prohibitionist policies based on eradication, interdiction, and criminalization of consumption simply haven't worked," the former presidents wrote in a joint op-ed. "The revision of US inspired drug policies is urgent in light of rising levels of violence and corruption associated with narcotics. The alarming power of the drug cartels is leading to a criminalization of politics and a politicization of crime."

> "Ending the War on Drugs," *Huffpost Politics*

In other words, Latin American leaders want the US to rethink the drug problem from the consumer end rather than the production end. And that's a lot harder for us. It is simply easier to declare war on poor people than it is to figure out why so many people in the richest society in the world, both wealthy and poor, have such a huge consumer demand for drugs. Collective soul-searching is painful; it's easier to just demonize and punish the visible substance abuser on the streets and forget the hard questions of why drugs seem so essential to our nation's social fabric.

Domestically, the most visible result of the drug war has been the development of the prison industrial complex. Short of war, mass incarceration has been one of the most thoroughly implemented social programs of our time. The dramatic increase in funding for prison expansion and criminal justice has come at the expense of education. From 1987 to 1995, General Fund expenditures for prisons throughout the country increased by 30 percent, while General Fund expenditures for universities decreased by 18 percent. In 1995, the National Crime Bill was passed, resulting in the construction of 150 new prisons and the expansion of 171 existing prisons. States around the country spent more on building prisons than colleges, and there was nearly a dollar for dollar trade-off between corrections and higher education—with university construction funds decreasing to $2.5 billion while corrections funding increased to $2.6 billion.

Social critic Michael Parenti reveals that the premise of the drug war is to incarcerate the nation's superfluous population of poor people, mostly black males, eviscerate the social safety net, and transfer funds into the hands of the social control network—prisons and law enforcement. But with an overall budget approaching almost half that of the Pentagon, Parenti theorizes that the prison industrial complex begins to take on a role similar to the military industrial complex in its ability to infuse massive amounts of Keynesian capital back into the system:

> While the estimated spending on prisons overall is $30 billion dollars annually, the overall tab on police, courts, prosecutors, probation, parole, bail bond, bounty hunting, drug treatment, and prison is estimated to be as high as $150 billion annually.

"Beyond the Prison Industrial Complex," *Covert Action Quarterly*

But, like the military industrial complex, the prison industrial complex is not a wealth creating system; it is a wealth destroying system.

Economic consultant Lisa Hammond points out that "the economics of the private prison industry are in many respects similar to those of the lodging industry" ("Drug War Policy and the Prison Industrial Complex," *The Addiction Web Site of Terence T. Gorski*). An inmate at a private prison is like a guest at a hotel, and the economic incentive is to book every available room and encourage every guest to stay as long as possible.

In California, the prison guards' union is the most powerful of all unions, and they join with private prison operators and prosecutors and police departments to lobby legislators who are already predisposed to punitive drug laws and the massive incarceration of poor people. So if you are worried about the radical screams of crazed Catholic Workers crying for legalization of drugs and massive prison depopulation, fear not. There are plenty of beneficiaries of this corrupt, racist, unjust system who will make sure it is not dismantled. But, we remember that the very first public cry of our crazed founder Jesus Christ was *liberation to captives*!

The Soloist:
Fiddling while Los Angeles Burns

Catholic Agitator, June, 2009, pp. 1 and 2

The streets of Skid Row are clean now. Where once there were hundreds of homeless people living in tents and cardboard condos with a welter of trash and discarded clothing strewn about, there are now vacant and sanitized sidewalks. Where once shopping carts and cook stoves packed the sidewalks and drug dealers swarmed every car and people sat about openly smoking crack, now no one is in sight. Gladys Street, in front of our soup kitchen, is a ghost town. But back in 2006, when the *LA Times* reporter Steve Lopez came to Skid Row to write the series of articles that eventually became the book and then the feature film called *The Soloist*, it resembled a slice of Calcutta in the USA.

It was frightening and shameful that such a situation could possibly exist in the richest nation in the world. Shock and outrage are the only proper human responses to that sight, and Lopez mobilized that shock and outrage, causing the powers that be to, as he said, "respond correctly." And to do something about Skid Row.

I had not originally intended to see *The Soloist*, because I date the beginnings of our most difficult times on Skid Row to the advent of Steve Lopez in our neighborhood. But because so many of our supporters have seen the film and it has become the virtual public image of Skid Row, I finally decided it was important for me to view it after all. I was hoping the movie would be a bomb. Unfortunately, it was pretty good. How could it not be with Robert Downey Jr. starring in a DreamWorks production?

The movie tells the heartfelt story of a crusading reporter befriending Nathaniel, a homeless, mentally ill man who turns out to be a Juilliard dropout and a musical savant. It is a wonderful American success story in which the reporter cleans up Skid Row, gets a Press Club award, a book deal and a movie contract, while restoring a homeless, schizophrenic musical genius to, if not complete recovery, at least a more stable, secure life. I was impressed by the manner in which so many of our Skid Row friends, as well as the exemplary services of the Lamp mental health community, were portrayed with such accuracy, dignity, and compassion.

So, what's not to like? Maybe the movie grates on me because I was responsible for creating the very mess that Lopez takes credit for cleaning up!

The fifty square blocks that comprise LA's Skid Row are unusual. Most American cities simply bulldozed their blighted Skid Row areas during the 50s and 60s in a paroxysm of urban renewal. But what was not well understood at the time was that, while these areas indeed might be blighted, they also comprised a vast reservoir of extremely low-cost housing, and even when these units were replaced with low-cost market rate housing, many people were left out of the market. This was a significant contributing factor to the great surge of homelessness beginning in the 1970s.

But due to the efforts of many homeless activists, the Catholic Worker among them, an unusual convergence of atypical allies joined forces to commit the city to preserving the so-called blighted housing of Skid Row and to put much of it into the hands of nonprofit corporations, who were required by law to make this housing available to the poorest of the poor. In the meantime, as part of its redevelopment plan, the city spent millions, not only in housing preservation, but also in relocating Skid Row missions and services from the periphery into the very heart of Skid Row. The final stages of that plan were completed a mere five years ago. This strategy of preserving housing and centralizing services was only possible because central city property values were so diminished at that time that no one really cared what happened in Skid Row. Today however, the area around the periphery of Skid Row is prime development territory for lofts and condominiums.

In the meantime, during the 80s, as the first wave of globalization and deindustrialization combined, Skid Row was hit with a surge of unemployed, mostly young black males, who pressed into the area seeking assistance available nowhere else in the county. Housing and services were quickly over-taxed, and after a three-week camp-out protest in 1985 organized by members of the LACW and Inner City Law Center, the homeless began to create shelter for themselves on the streets of Skid Row.

Throughout the decades, activists worked diligently to preserve peoples' civil rights and protect them from police abuse, from unlawful seizure of property, as well as assaults from city cleaning crews and private security guards. One of our many successes was the securing of the right of home-less people to sleep on the streets at night, undisturbed by the police. We also provided free shopping carts to the homeless in the wake of a police campaign to arrest people for possessing carts "stolen" from local markets. But our lengthiest and most hard-fought ten-year campaign was the success of winning from the city thirty-two porta-potties for the homeless. For the ten years that these ad hoc amenities were on the streets, we fought the police and business community to maintain them as an act of both human dignity and public health.

Yes, we were responsible for the porta-potties; we were responsible for the shopping carts homeless people push down Skid Row sidewalks; we were responsible for court orders that prohibit police from summarily stopping and questioning individuals without probable cause; we were responsible for court rulings that gave the homeless the right to sleep on the streets. And we were guilty of having maintained the scandalous mess of Skid Row homeless encampments. Why did we do all this? Because we hoped that the sight of these suffering masses of forgotten marginal people might inspire the powers that be to do something for them. Well, thanks to Steve Lopez and the *LA Times*, they did.

Lopez's serialized articles on Skid Row appeared on the front pages of the *Times* over a period of days, one after another, and mobilized public opinion and outrage.

Over a period of two weeks, there were more column inches devoted to Skid Row than in all the previous ten years combined. The whole thing had the feel of a well-orchestrated public relations campaign, creating a demand for the city to act. And indeed the city already had a well prepared plan of action just waiting for the right moment. And whether by coinci-dence or by design, Lopez's articles provided just the right moment for the city to act.

The first thing the city did was to remove the porta-potties so despised by the police and the business community, and decried in Lopez's first *Skid Row* article. Yes, some of them were used for prostitution and drug sales, as Lopez said, but they were also emptied twice daily because they were filled to the brim with human excrement and urine.

Then both the mayor and Police Chief Bratton, under "great pres-sure" from Steve Lopez and the community, announced their master plan for Skid Row. Was it more housing, better toilets, employment programs, social service, or mental health services?

61. Jeff Dietrich marching with Skid Row residents during the Blood Strike, 1973. Photo by Hank Lebo

No, it was the Safer Cities Initiative. The 50 square blocks of Skid Row would get 50 extra police officers who systematically enforced every petty ordinance on the books. In the first year, 12,000 citations were issued to the citizens of Skid Row, 85 percent for pedestrian violations. There were 9,000 arrests made in 1 year (2007) but only 22 were for "violent crimes": 1 homicide, 8 robberies, no rapes, 13 aggravated assaults. The same 24 people were arrested a total of 210 times! In that same one-year period the city spent a total of $10 million on 50 extra police, while spending only $100,000 on housing the homeless. For further statistics and analysis, see Blasi, "Policing Our Way Out of Homelessness?"

They put the poor in jail, and they put the fear of God and the LAPD in them, so that now the streets of Skid Row are clean and clear of homeless. If they're not in jail or an institutional program of some kind, they are hiding out under freeway off-ramps, shrubs, and bridges, but they must come back to Skid Row for the vital services that the city has centralized here. And we have encountered numerous incidents where individuals are stopped, searched, and ticketed multiple times by a zealous police force before they can reach the safety of our soup kitchen.

Thanks to Steve Lopez, the *LA Times,* Mayor Antonio Villaraigosa and Chief Bratton, the scandalous mess of Skid Row has been cleaned up, and the poor and homeless are where they are supposed to be—locked up, scattered, hidden, and blessedly invisible.

Out of sight, out of mind—problem solved. Now the streets of Los Angeles are safe for real estate developers and loft dwellers to walk about downtown without encountering the human cost of an economy that creates homeless people forced to live on sidewalks.

My frustration with Steve Lopez's superficial reporting style was peaked by a television interview between David Simon, the creator of the HBO TV series *The Wire,* and Bill Moyers. Like Steve Lopez, Simon once was a reporter. And, like Lopez, he also wrote a popular book about his experience as a reporter with the *Baltimore Sun,* which later became the basis for a hit TV show. He said:

> Even the highest ambition of the people at my newspaper, was to bite off a small morsel of the actual problem. Surround one little thing. And maybe we'll get a law passed. And we'll write the react to our stories. And then we'll submit it for a prize. And that was the highest ambition of people who were regarded as very good journalists.
>
> "Transcript," *PBS's Bill Moyers Journal*

Simon found that within the fictional format of television he was better able to tell the story of the larger social problem, rather than the "small morsel." The larger story is that inner city Baltimore, as well as inner city Skid Row and for that matter all inner cities, are composed of what Simon calls "the superfluous people." Simon states, "It's the abandoned inner cores of our urban areas. And...economically, we don't need these people. The American economy doesn't need them" ("Transcript," *PBS's Bill Moyers Journal*). So why seriously assess what you are doing to your poorest and most vulnerable citizens? There is no profit to be had in doing anything other than marginalizing them and discarding them.

But it is impossible to tell that story because, while it may be true, it doesn't sell newspapers.

Conversely, the story of Nathaniel sold newspapers, books, and motion picture tickets; it won awards, furthered the career of Steve Lopez, and enhanced the *LA Times'* reputation. And, as I said, *The Soloist* is a very fine, uplifting film. But if you left the theater with the impression that the lives of anyone on Skid Row, other than Nathaniel's, were improved by the efforts of the intrepid *Times* reporter played by Robert Downey Jr., you are quite wrong. In fact, life has become substantially more difficult for the poorest of the poor on LA's Skid Row.

Epilogue

Often when I hear criticism of our Los Angeles soup kitchen, I realize that similar criticisms were leveled at Dorothy Day in the past. "You are just putting a band aid on the cancer," they would say. We know that we are not going to fix this American system of inequality and injustice. As a people we are inexorably mired in the sludge of consumptive over indulgence. The only thing that we can really do is to live our lives in such a way that we might serve as an example of a different way to live.

For me, the huge wooden chopping table in the middle of our soup kitchen is emblematic of that different way to live. It symbolizes what we do every day: feed the hungry, clothe the naked, and shelter the homeless, the most singular, important, and efficacious things that we could be doing. We chop lettuce for the salad and onions for the soup, we butter bread and put it in the baskets. In the morning we gather around the table for prayer: "You are the servant of the poor, the uglier and dirtier they are, the more unjust and insulting, the more love you give them. It is only for your love alone that the poor will forgive you the bread that you give to them," *Prayer of St. Vincent de Paul.*

Our chopping table is sacred space, a place for food preparation, conversation, prayer and yes, Eucharist. Not that everyone who comes to us is actually familiar with the Catholic tradition of the Eucharist, because they are not all Catholics. We are a diverse group: Catholics, Protestants, Jews, atheists, communists and anarchists. But we all gather together for this experience of transubstantiation, for this experience of communion, for this experience of community, for this opportunity to teach the real presence of Jesus Christ in the bread and soup, salad and ice cold water, that we share with the poor, the homeless, the beggar, the drug addicted, the drug dealer, the physically maimed, the spiritually abused, the criminalized, and the marginalized. When it works the way it's supposed to with minimal rules and conflicts, which is most of the time, we serve over a thousand meals, and it is like a great party with little distinction between server and served.

We need at least twenty-five people to "transubstantiate" the lettuce, onions and carrots into food that nourishes both body and spirit. But there are only ten full-time Catholic Worker community members, so we are gratefully dependent upon the scores of volunteers who show up both regularly and periodically to give us essential assistance in this work. In addition to the high school students who come from St. Paul, Damian and Sacred Heart Academy, we are blessed on given days with the likes of Ted, the actual heir to significant shopping market wealth, who comes every Tuesday and Thursday and does "food flow," making sure that the food line runs smoothly, getting the soup and salad on the line without interruption. If there are too many people working at the Kitchen he takes a step back and washes the walls and floorboards on his hands and knees. Sometimes, he brings retired Maryknoll sisters to work with us.

John Owen is a retired employee of the city of Los Angeles. For the last ten years in his chosen job as "waterboy," John has made a science of producing, especially in the hot summer months, the kind of cold water that freezes your eyeballs and gives you a headache if you drink it too fast. The word on the streets is that our water is actually piped into the kitchen from a mountain spring that funnels it into our fountain that gushes directly into the fishpond in the middle of the "soup garden."

Polish Paul is a stubborn, atheist, anarchist, vegan, and self-styled Pollack. Though he does not believe in Jesus, he nevertheless thinks that Christians who eat meat are hypocrites. He does not hold hands around the chopping table, and he does not pray. He refuses to touch the hands of those who have touched dead meat. We're not sure that he actually likes us, but he likes what we do, and he keeps coming back every Saturday to run the kitchen in his white clothes and chef's hat.

Carol Taunton is one of twelve children born to Honey and Bob. Fifteen years ago her father was a regular volunteer. He was old and a bit infirm, so we gave him lots of "sit down" jobs, but still he would all asleep on the stool, which was OK with us, but when he started to fall asleep at the wheel of his forty-year-old Volkswagen his family became concerned. Rather than make him stop what he loved to do, Carol appointed herself his designated driver and brought him to the soup kitchen every Thursday. After he died, Carol took her father's place at the Kitchen. She doesn't fall asleep on the job, and she has been with us for fifteen years, brightening our kitchen with her smile and enthusiastic energy.

Richard is a seventy-year-old former Chicano gang member. He lives in a Skid Row hotel not far from our soup kitchen and regularly attends a tattoo removal clinic. Every Thursday he comes early, around 6:30 a.m., to set up the onion-chopping table. He drives my wife Catherine crazy, because he starts the day by grinding his knife on the electric knife sharpener for what is actually only two or three minutes, but seems like two or three hours, at least to her. He spends his day at that table chopping fifty to one hundred pounds of onions, half to go into the soup of the day and half to be dispersed as minced condiments on our beans and salad.

Ben Sullivan came to us in 1983 as a seventeen-year-old volunteer from Loyola High School. He is the one who told me to watch *Saturday Night Live*. I did, and I have never been the same since. Ben left us to go to college, tour Europe, and ultimately start the first English speaking newspaper in the newly found Czech Republic, where he lived and worked for ten years. When he returned to the States, he resumed volunteering with the Catholic Worker. For the last decade he has chopped onions, served soup and, more importantly, picked up Bill Board* every Saturday. Bill is a long time friend from the streets whose ill health now confines him to a convalescent hospital. Ben picks him up and brings him to the Kitchen, but even more important, he sometimes takes him to the beach, the park, and to nice restaurants.

I don't know exactly how this happened, but in the last few years my sister Nancy has sent her daughters Colleen and Paige to work at the Kitchen. They were the tender ages of sixteen and twelve when they first came. We packed them into the van and took off to a protest at Vandenberg Air Force Base. Security forces were immediately on us, arresting several people. My nieces were excited and took pictures with their cell phones, sending them home to Mom. They have come back for the last three years. I feel validated that my sister would trust me with her children, even more so do I have a sense that she wants her children to have an experience beyond the comfort zone of most Americans.

Sister Gloria is a retired Maryknoll nun who is also a doctor. At the end of next September she will travel to Hong Kong for the hundredth anniversary of the founding of her order.

Doran is a clinical psychologist, who once worked for a Skid Row service agency. When she began volunteering at the soup kitchen she ran into a former client who requested weekly therapy sessions with her. Now she works at the Kitchen buttering bread and chopping lettuce from 8 a.m. to 10 a.m. and meets with her client in our new dental clinic from 10 a.m.

---

*   Pictured in his younger days in Illustration 44.

to 11 a.m., returning to finish out her day at the Kitchen serving soup and salad on the line. Her client insists on paying her a nominal fee of $30 which she donates each week to the Catholic Worker.

Kate Haight is a thirty-five-year-old film editor with a major Hollywood studio. She was born in France and raised in Canada. Her mother continues to live in France in a Zen Buddhist monastery where she is one of the few women Zen masters in the country. Kate is a regular volunteer.

At the beginning of this book I wrote that, "I believe that the Gospels are the best story that we have. They are the singular counter narrative to our consumerist, war mongering, media saturated, technologized, dehumanized, and death-oriented culture. The story of the Gospels, the triumph of goodness and mercy over the powers of death and domination, cannot be proven. The only way to make that story true is to live our lives as if it were true."

Chopping lettuce, buttering bread, serving soup, making the ice water cold enough to freeze your eye balls, these simple acts of compassion and mercy and shared humanness practiced day after day, week in and week out, season after season, year after year, are compounded, and thus do they give witness to our deepest desires for humanity, which is our desire to make the Gospel story a living reality.

Jeff Dietrich
Los Angeles
September 22, 2011

CATHOLIC WORKER

The Los Angeles Catholic Worker (LACW), founded in 1970, is part of the larger Catholic Worker Movement founded by Dorothy Day and Peter Maurin in 1933 in the midst of the Great Depression, "to comfort the afflicted and afflict the comfortable," and to put into practice the social justice agenda of the Catholic Church.

There are over 250 such communities of lay Catholics throughout the world—the majority within the United States, with a few located in Europe, England, Ireland, Australia, New Zealand, and Mexico. Most communities have between two and five members; the Los Angeles Worker, with fourteen full-time members, is probably one of the largest.

The original house founded by Day in New York City continues to exist as a thriving community twenty years after her death, and the original Catholic Worker newspaper is still published by the New York community. While both that community and newspaper are generally recognized as the titular mother house and voice of the movement, the Catholic Worker remains a decentralized organization, with each community assuming full responsibility for choosing its various ministries and providing staffing and financing for those efforts.

The Los Angeles Catholic Worker has two locations—one is its community house in Boyle Heights just east of downtown and the other is its soup kitchen and service center in LA's Skid Row district. In contrast to the many conservative evangelical missions and tax-exempt non-profit organizations located within the fifty block Skid Row area, the Los Angeles Worker identifies as a personalist, deliberately non-institutional community that operates a free soup kitchen which serves over 4,000 meals a week. The kitchen also serves as a more generalized service center, which includes a medical and dental clinic. The fourteen members of the LACW live together at their Boyle Heights location in community with fourteen formerly homeless people from Skid Row. There is no board of directors, CEO, or professional staff. All members receive room and board and $15 a week; there is no health care plan or retirement program.

Because of its location in the nation's second largest city, a city with the greatest concentration of homeless people in the country, the LACW has

62. Prayer circle, Hospitality House Kitchen, 2011. Photo by Robert Radin

been able to generally attract a larger number of community members than most other houses, to assist in serving the patently obvious needs of the thousands of poor and needy who have been herded into the Skid Row area by the city's policy of "centralization of services."

The population of the fifty square blocks of LA's Skid Row is generally agreed to be around 1,000 people. The majority of that population is precariously housed in single room occupancy hotels, while 2 percent to 3 percent sleep outside on any given night.

The Los Angeles Catholic Worker serves over 4,000 meals a week, which means that in the forty years of its existence, the LACW has served over 8 million meals to the homeless of LA's Skid Row.

CHRONOLOGY

While the majority of LACW community activities are really about changing beds linens, cleaning toilets, and preparing and serving over a thousand meals a day, certain events stand out over the course of the last forty years.

1970 Easter Sunday

Dan and Chris Delany initiated the Los Angeles Catholic Worker by serving their first meal to the homeless poor in front of St. Vibiana Cathedral, out of the trunk of their old '57 Pontiac, as a gentle reminder to the Church of Christ's call to put service to the poor and homeless first.

1970 September

Jeff Dietrich arrives at the LACW after refusing induction into the military and spending six months traveling in Europe and North Africa.

1972 August-September

The Delanys leave after a significant struggle with the "young Turks," led by Jeff Dietrich, who had, at this time, only a minimal conception of what the Catholic Worker was and what it meant to live in community.

1973 January-March: The Blood Strike

In the early 1970s, when the LACW first came to Skid Row, a significant portion of income for poor and homeless people was obtained by selling their whole blood and plasma to one of the many commercial blood banks that were, at that time, located on Skid Row. Following the model of the United Farm Workers Union, Catholic Workers organized numerous homeless blood donors in a strike and boycott to obtain higher remuneration and better health care from the blood banks. The actions received much press coverage, and thus the Workers were unwittingly instrumental in ultimately closing down the blood banks altogether. But the original objectives of the Blood Strike were not met.

1974 Jeff Dietrich Marries Catherine Morris

Jeff Dietrich marries soup kitchen volunteer Catherine Morris, who had been a Catholic nun and held the position of Head Mistress of Mayfield School, an elite Catholic preparatory school for young women in Pasadena, California.

At the time, he had only a minimal sense of his future wife's organizational acumen that would obviate his most glaring deficiencies in logistics and management, and in the future, make him look like he knew what he was doing.

1978 November: The Arms Bazaar

Beginning in November 1978, the LACW joined with the Alliance for Survival, a grassroots anti-nuclear group, to protest what came to be called the "Arms Bazaar," a gathering of arms merchants at the Anaheim Convention Center convened to sell military armaments to third world countries. In November 1978 the Alliance for Survival led a candlelight vigil of 2,000 people to protest the convention, and the next morning four Catholic Workers were arrested for blockading the conference.

1979 June-November: Arms Bazaar Continues

In the summer of 1979, the Catholic Worker organized a campaign in Anaheim and circulated a petition opposing the Arms Bazaar, signed by 10,000 citizens of Anaheim, which at that time represented 10 percent of the city's population. The city council rejected the petition, and over 2,000 people showed up to protest on the opening night of the conference. A civil disobedience action, organized by the LACW, took place the next day, and resulted in the arrest of 30 people. Two of those people, Kent Hoffman and Jeff Dietrich, received six-month sentences because they had violated their probation from the previous year's arrest. Because of extensive media coverage, as well as a massive LACW letter-writing campaign, the two were released after having served only two months.

The next year, the Arms Bazaar was dis-invited by the city of Anaheim and subsequently relocated to Wiesbaden, Germany, home of two former Catholic Workers, who organized a die-in protest that caused the Arms Bazaar to ultimately be relocated to the US Canal Zone in Panama.

Jeff Dietrich

1980-1986 WINCON Protests

The Winter Conference of Electrical Engineers (WINCON), a symposium of military and Pentagon officials along with scientists and engineers, who gathered to reflect on more efficient and creative ways of spending the huge US military budget and killing more third world people. This was a six-year campaign that ultimately resulted in the permanent relocation of WINCON, fostered a vibrant anti-war community, and led to the birth of a new Catholic Worker community in Orange County that will celebrate its 25th anniversary this year.

1980-1983 Rockwell/El Segundo Campaign: "Santa Claus Action"

A three-year campaign in the very heart of the aerospace industry in El Segundo, CA that included numerous civil disobedience actions, daily vigils, and a "Santa Claus" action that culminated with a rally of 5,000 and the mass arrest of 100 people at various military production plants.

1984-1986 LACW the "Big Break-Up"

In a major community conflagration, the LACW, over a period of two and a half years, collapsed, going from thirty live-in members, to just six. The core community of six began rethinking and re-articulating their mission, their goals, their beliefs and values.

1985-1986 Central America Intervention Protests

The LACW joined the "Wednesday Morning Coalition" in a weekly civil disobedience protest for the murder of the seven Jesuits and their housekeeper in El Salvador; protests also were organized against the US-funded Contra War in Nicaragua.

1986 Inauguration of "Sister House Project"

After the big break-up, the remaining LACW members rejected the model of a large community with numerous projects and chose instead to embrace the traditional CW model of a "Catholic Worker School" designed to recruit, train, and send forth "disciples" to found "Sister Houses." To date, there are a total of twelve "Sister Houses" founded by the LACW.

1986 First Sister House

The first Sister House was founded in Las Vegas, Nevada at the behest of Franciscan Father Louis Vitale, who had organized protests at the Nevada Nuclear Test Site for decades.

1986 First Summer Program

In an effort to rebuild community after the "great break-up," the LACW began a summer program as part of their recruitment efforts.

1986 First Nevada Test Site Action

With the inauguration of the Las Vegas Catholic Worker, a civil disobedience action began at the Nevada Test Site. The Las Vegas Catholic Worker celebrated its 25th anniversary with a national call to civil disobedience at Creech Air Force Base, the Nevada site responsible for unmanned drone aircraft attacks in Afghanistan and Pakistan.

1987-1990 Earthquake Destroys LACW Kitchen

After the 1987 Whittier Narrows earthquake rendered the LACW soup kitchen and hospitality house uninhabitable, our resident homeless guests were moved to the main house in nearby Boyle Heights. Subsequently, Catholic Workers chose to rebuild, on the site, a smaller "prep-kitchen" with a spacious outdoor dining area with flowers, trees, fountains, fish, and birds.

1993-1997 Porta-Potty Campaign

The LACW and Rev. Alice Callaghan engage in a series of civil disobedience actions which ultimately result in the commitment by the city of Los Angeles to provide thirty-two outdoor porta-potties for the use of the hundreds of homeless people living on the streets of Skid Row.

1995 "Defencing" Action

In commemoration of the fiftieth anniversary of the dropping of the first nuclear bomb on Hiroshima, members of the Los Angeles Catholic Worker cut the perimeter fence around the Nuclear Test Site. Jeff Dietrich received a sentence of thirty days.

Jeff Dietrich

1996-2001 Anti-Cathedral Actions

The Los Angeles Catholic Workers engage in a series of protests and civil disobedience actions throughout the five-year construction of the new Cathedral to give public expression to the primacy of buildings over people.

1996-2010 Shopping Cart Campaign

The LACW focus attention on the plight of homeless peoples, whose shopping carts, filled with their meager belongings, are consistently confiscated by the police, who then routinely crush them and issue their owners a citation for possessing a stolen cart. At a press conference held in front of LAPD's Central Division, Catholic Workers distributes a hundred free street legal shopping carts to the homeless of Skid Row. Since then, the LACW has distributed over 20,000 free shopping carts to the homeless poor.

2001-Present Anti-"Star Wars" Campaign

In conjunction with the Guadalupe Catholic Worker and other local activists, the LACW join in a campaign against the so-called Missile Defense Shield or "Star Wars." The US spent close to a trillion dollars on a project designed to shoot down incoming ballistic missiles. In its twenty-year existence the project has not had one successful test and most leading scientists agree that it will never work. Catholic Workers begin their campaign with a "backcountry" action for which Jeff Dietrich receives a six-month sentence. The campaign has continued with regular vigils in front of Vandenberg Air Force Base, as well as numerous civil disobedience actions.

September 11, 2001 Opposition to War in Afghanistan

Many community members, including Jeff Dietrich, are in jail at the time of 9/11 for the backcountry action at Vandenberg. Members not in jail gather with West Coast Sister House communities to issue a collective statement reaffirming a firm commitment to Catholic Worker pacifism, even in the wake of the 9/11 tragedy.

2003 Iraq War Protests

From January through March of 2003, the LACW protest the imminent Iraq invasion with six civil disobedience actions, including a blockade of the Rose Parade in Pasadena as well as a "die-in" at the Federal Building, downtown Los Angeles, and a blockade of the streets around the building. Dietrich was arrested and sentenced to forty-five days in jail for a prayer action on the steps of the Federal Building. When he is released, his wife Catherine has just entered county jail to serve her forty-five-day sentence for blocking the city streets to protest the Iraq invasion.

2006-2008 Anti-Recruitment Actions

Over a period of two years, the LACW joins with the American Friends Service Committee, to protest the US war in the Middle East with a series of civil disobedience actions blockading various US Army recruiting centers.

2006-Present Anti-Safer Cities Campaign

The Safer Cities Initiative is announced by Mayor Villaraigosa and Police Chief William Bratton, based on the so-called Broken Windows theory of policing, which focuses on the "visual blight" of poverty in neighborhoods. Rather than addressing the social causes of crime: lack of jobs and housing, poor education, racial injustice, the Broken Windows perspective addresses only the visual aspects of poverty and homelessness, suggesting that if we repair the broken windows and eliminate the unsightly, broken people, we will eliminate the problem.

In the first year under the Safer Cities Initiative, within the 50 square blocks of Skid Row, the police issue over 12,000 citations, 85 percent of which are for pedestrian violations. The LACW opposes the Safer Cities Initiative since its inception through acts of protests and civil resistance, as it is clear that Safer Cities and Broken Windows policing are code words for incarcerating the poor, most specifically the homeless African American poor.

2007 Loretta Sanchez Action

Jeff Dietrich joins with Military Families of the Iraq War in a sit-in at the offices of Congresswoman Loretta Sanchez to protest the war in Iraq.

2010 No Peace, No Prize Action

In January, members of the LACW are arrested on the steps of the Federal Building, downtown Los Angeles, while protesting the award of the Noble Peace Prize to a president whose country was at war.

2010 Hiroshima Day

Seven Catholic Workers, including Jeff Dietrich, are arrested at Vandenberg Air Force Base protesting the dropping of the atomic bomb on Hiroshima and Nagasaki.

Bibliography

Albertson, Clint. "A Notre Dame for Los Angeles," *Los Angeles Times,* September 17, 1997. http://articles.latimes.com/1997/sep/17/local/me-33058.

Barber, Benjamin. *Jihad vs. McWorld* (New York: Times Books, 1995).

Baudrillard, Jean. *Simulacra and Simulation,* trans. Sheila Faria Glaser (Ann Arbor, MI: The University of Michigan Press, 1994).

———. *America,* trans. Chris Turner (New York: Verso, 1988).

———. *Selected Writings,* ed. Mark Poster (Stanford, CA: Stanford University Press, 1988).

———. *In the Shadow of the Silent Majorities,* trans. Paul Foss, John Johnston, Paul Patton and Andrew Beradini (New York: Semiotextle, 1983).

———. *For a Critique of the Political Economy of the Sign*, trans. Charles Levin (St. Louis: Telos Press Ltd., 1981).

Baum, Dan. *Smoke and Mirrors: The War on Drugs and the Politics of Failure* (Back Bay Books, 1997).

Berry, Wendell. *Continuous Harmony: Essays Cultural and Agricultural* (New York: Harcourt Brace Jovanovich, 1972).

Blasi, Gary. "Policing Our Way Out of Homelessness? The First Year of the Safer Cities Initiative on Skid Row." *Los Angeles Catholic Worker.* Last modified September 24, 2007. http://lacatholicworker.org/agitator/blasi_study.pdf.

Brueggemann, Walter. *The Prophetic Imagination,* 2nd ed, (Minneapolis, MN: Fortress, 2001).

Camara, Dom Helder. *Dom Helder Camara: Essential Writings*, ed. Francis McDonagh (New York: Orbis Books, 2009).

Carroll, James. *Constantine's Sword: The Church and the Jews: A History* (New York: First Mariner Books, 2002).

Ceresko, Anthony R. *Introduction to the Old Testament: A Liberation Perspective* (New York: Orbis Books, 2001).

Chomsky, Noam. *Imperial Ambitions: Conversations on the Post-9/11 World, Interviews with David Barsamian* (New York: Metropolitan Books, 2005).

Colbert, Stephen. *Jesus is a Liberal Democrat, Friends. Episode no. 153, first broadcast 16 November 2000 by NBC. Directed by David Schwimmer and written by Scott Silveri.*

Cooper, Arnie. "Resurrecting the Revolutionary Heart of Judaism: An Interview with Michael Lerner." *The Sun,* Issue 340. Last modified April 2004. http://www.thesunmagazine.org/_media/article/pdf/340_Lerner.pdf.

Crossan, John Dominic. *Jesus: A Revolutionary Biography* (New York: Harper Collins Publishers, 1994).

Dalberg-Acton, John Emerich Edward, Baron. *Essays on Freedom and Power* (Boston: The Beacon Press, 1948).

Day, Dorothy. *Selected Writings: By Little and By Little*, ed. Robert Ellsberg (New York: Orbis Press, 2005).

———. *On Pilgrimage* (Grand Rapids, MI: Wm. B Eerdmans Publishing, 1999).

———. *Loaves and Fishes* (New York: Orbis Books, 1963).

———. *The Long Loneliness: The Autobiography of the Legendary Catholic Social Activist, Dorothy Day* (New York: Harper Collins Publishing Inc., 1952).

Diamond, Jared. *Guns, Germs and Steel: The Fates of Human Societies* (London: Vintage, 1998).

Dietrich, Jeff. *Reluctant Resistor* (Greensboro, NC: Unicorn Press, Inc., 1983).

Eisenberg, Evan. *Ecology of Eden* (New York: Alfred A Knopf, Inc., 1999).

Ellul, Jacques. *The Technological Bluff,* trans. Geoffrey W. Bromiley (Grand Rapids, MI: William B. Eerdmans Publishing Co., 1990).

————. *The Subversion of Christianity,* trans. Geoffrey W. Bromiley (Grand Rapids, MI: William B. Eerdmans Publishing Co., 1986).

————. *The Humiliation of the Word,* trans. Joyce Main Hanks (Grand Rapids, MI: William B. Eerdmans Publishing Co., 1985).

————. *Propaganda: The Formation of Men's Attitudes,* trans. Jean Lerner and Konrad Kellen (Vancouver, WA: Vintage Books, 1973).

————. *The Meaning of the City,* trans. Dennis Pardee (Grand Rapids, MI: William B. Eerdmans Publishing Co., 1970).

————. *The Presence of the Kingdom* (New York: Seabury, 1967).

————. *The Technological Society* (New York: Vintage Books, 1964).

Ewen, Stuart. *All-Consuming Images: The Politics of Style in Contemporary Culture* (New York: Basic Books, 1988).

———— and Elizabeth Ewen. *Channels of Desire: Mass Images and the Shaping of American Consciousness* (New York: McGraw-Hill Book Co., 1982).

Girard, René. *Things Hidden Since the Foundation of the World* (New York: Continuum, 2003).

Goizueta, Roberto S. "From Calvary to Galilee." *America Magazine,* April, 17, 2006, Vol. 194, No. 14.

González, Justo L. *A History of Christian Thought: From the Beginnings to the Council of Chalcedon,* Vol. 1 (Nashville: Abingdon Press, 1970).

Gottwald, Norman K. *The Tribes of Yahweh: A Sociology of the Religion of Liberated Israel, 1250-1050 BCE* (New York: Orbis Books, 1979).

Gowdy, John. *Limited Wants, Unlimited Means: A Reader on Hunter-Gatherer Economics and the Environment* (Washington, D.C.: Island Press, 1998).

Halberstam, David. "We Were Led by the Children." *Parade.* Last modified March 22, 1998. http://www.parade.com/features/halberstam-children.html.

Hammond, Lisa. "Drug War Policy and the Prison Industrial Complex." *The Addiction Web Site of Terence T. Gorsk.* Last modified May 9, 2002. http://www.tgorski.com/articles/Drug%20War%20&%20The%20Prison%20Industrial%20Complex.htm.

Hedges, Chris. "Gravel's Lament: Fighting Another Dumb War." *Truth Dig: Drilling Beneath the Headlines.* Last modified December 14, 2009. http://www.truthdig.com/report/item/gravels_lament_fighting_another_dumb_war_20091213/.

Herzog, William R. *Parables as Subversive Speech: Jesus as Pedagogue of the Oppressed* (Louisville, KY: Westminster/John Knox Press, 1994).

Holland, Joshua. "In a Perfect Storm of Economic Stagflation, the Yachting Set Says: 'Let Them Eat Pizza'." *AlterNet.* Last modified July 31, 2008. http://www.alternet.org/economy/92910/in_a_perfect_storm_of_economic_stagflation,_the_yachting_set_says:_%22let_them_eat_pizza%22/?page=entire.

———. "Meltdown and Bailout: Why Our Economic System Is on the Verge of Collapse." *AlterNet.* Last modified September 22, 2008. http://www.alternet.org/economy/99703/meltdown_and_bailout:_why_our_economic_system_is_on_the_verge_of_collapse/.

Howard-Brook, Wes and Anthony Gwyther. *Unveiling Empire: Reading Revelation Then and Now* (Maryknoll, NY: Orbis Books, 1999).

Huffington, Arianna. "Ending the War on Drugs: The Moment is Now." *Huffpost Politics.* Last modified May 14, 2009. http://www.huffingtonpost.com/arianna-huffington/ending-the-war-on-drugs-t_b_203768.html?show_comment_id=24362440.

Hunter, Robert. *Ripple* (London: Warner Brothers, 1970).

Hyde, Lewis. *The Gift: Creativity and the Artist in the Modern World* (New York: Random House Inc., 2007).

Johnson, Chalmers. "Ending the Empire." *TomDispatch: A Regular Antidote to the Mainstream Media.* Last modified May 15, 2007. http://www.tomdispatch.com/post/174784/chalmers_johnson_ending_the_empire.

Johnson, Elizabeth. *Truly Our Sister: A Theology of Mary in the Communion of Saints* (New York: Continuum International Publishing Group, 2003).

Kahl, Brigitte. "Reading Luke Against Luke," in *A Feminist Companion to Luke,* ed. Amy-Jill Levine (Cleveland: The Pilgrim Press, 2001).

King, Martin Luther Jr. *A Testament of Hope: The Essential Writings and Speeches of Martin Luther King, Jr.,* ed. James M. Washington (New York: Harper Collins, 1986).

Kingsolver, Barbara. *Small Wonder: Essays* (New York: Harper Collins Publishers, 2002).

Klein, Joe. "The Perils of a Righteous President." *Time Magazine,* Vol. 163, Issue 20, May 09, 2004.

Kotkin, Joel. "Seagram's Daring Bet: The Future is Fantasy," *Los Angeles Times.* Last modified April 16, 1995. http://articles.latimes.com/1995-04-16/opinion/op-55251_1_entertainment-centers.

Kraay, Robert and Jan Kiefer, Patricia Lynn, Suzanne Frei, Claudia Schmitz eds. *The Image Book* (Hickory, NC: C. I. Publishing, 1993).

Küng, Hans. *The Catholic Church: A Short History,* trans. John Bowden (New York: Modern Library, 2003).

———. *On Being a Christian,* trans. Edward Quinn (Garden City, NY: Image Books, 1984).

———. *The Christian Challenge: A Shortened Version of on Being a Christian,* trans. Edward Quinn (New York: Doubleday, 1979).

Lacter, Mark. "Downtown's Renewal Testing 'Containment' of Homeless Problem." *Los Angeles Business Journal.* Last modified September 5, 2005. http://www.allbusiness.com/government/561919-1.html.

Lasch, Christopher. *The Revolt of the Elites and the Betrayal of Democracy* (New York: W. W. Norton & Company, 1996).

———. "The Revolt of the Elites: Have They Canceled Their Allegiance to America?" *Harper's Magazine,* Vol. 289, Issue 1734, November 1, 1994.

———. "Communitarianism or Populism?" *New Oxford Review.* May 1992.

———. *The True and Only Heaven: Progress and Its Critics* (New York: W. W. Norton & Company, 1991).

———. *The Culture of Narcissism: American Life in an Age of Diminishing Expectations* (New York: Norton & Company, 1978).

Levin, Charles. "Introduction," *For a Critique of the Political Economy of the Sign* by Jean Baudrillard (St. Louis: Telos Press Ltd, 1981).

Manning, Richard. "The Oil We Eat: Following the Food Chain Back to Iraq." *Harper Magazine.* February 2004, Vol. 308, Issue 1845.

McLuhan, Marshall. Quentin Fiore, illustrator. *The Medium is the Massage: An Inventory of Effects* (New York: Random House, 1967).

Mead, Walter Russell. *Mortal Splendor: The American Empire in Transition* (Boston: Houghton Mufflin Company, 1987).

Meadows, Donella. "The Least of These Our Brethren." *Los Angeles Times.* Last modified December 22, 1996. http://articles.latimes.com/1996-12-22/opinion/op-11602_1_moral-majority.

Miller, Matthew. "The Poor Man's Capitalist: Hernando de Soto." *The New York Times.* Last modified July 1, 2001. http://www.nytimes.com/2001/07/01/magazine/01DESOTO.html.

Morris, Errol, director. *The Fog of War: Eleven Lessons from the Life of Robert S. McNamara* (Los Angeles: Sony Pictures Classic Industry. 2003).

Myers, Ched. *Binding the Strong Man: A Political Reading of Mark's Story of Jesus* (New York: Orbis Books, 1988).

Nouwen, Henri J.M. *The Wounded Healer: Ministry in Contemporary Society* (New York: Doubleday & Company, Inc., 1972).

O'Connor, Flannery. *Flannery O'Connor: Collected Works*, ed. Sally Fitzgerald (New York: Library Classics of United States, 1988).

———. *The Complete Stories* (New York: Farrar, Straus and Giroux, 1971).

———. *A Good Man is Hard to Find and Other Stories* (New York: Harcourt Inc., 1955).

Parenti, Michael. "Beyond the Prison Industrial Complex," *Covert Action Quarterly,* Spring/Summer 2000, Issue 69. Last modified August 29, 2001. http://www.globalresearch.ca/articles/PAR108B.html.

Perry, Tony. "Chaplain's Iraq Flock is Battle-Scarred Marine Unit." *Los Angeles Times*. Last modified May 22, 2004. http://articles.latimes.com/2004/may/22/local/me-beliefs22.

Pfeiffer, Dale Allen. *Eating Fossil Fuels: Oil, Food and the Coming Crisis in Agriculture* (Gabriola Island, BC, Canada: New Society Publishers, 2006).

Phillips, Kevin P. *The Politics of Rich and Poor: Wealth and the American Electorate in the Reagan Aftermath* (New York: Random House, 1990).

Pollan, Michael. *In Defense of Food: The Myth of Nutrition and the Pleasures of Eating* (New York: Allen Lane, 2008).

Postman, Neil. "The Great Symbol Drain" in *Technopoly: The Surrender of Culture to Technology* (New York: Alfred A. Knopf, Inc., 1992).

Powdermaker, Hortense. *Hollywood: The Dream Factory* (Boston: Little, Brown and Company: 1950).

Reich, Robert. "Why the Rich are Getting Richer and the Poor, Poorer." *UTNE Reader* (January 1990).

Rilke, Rainer Maria. *Selected Letters of Rainer Marie Rilke, 1902-1926*, trans. R.F.C. Hull (London: MacMillan & Co. Ltd., 1947).

Rohr, Richard O. F. M. "Beyond 'Certitudes and Orders'." *Sojourners Magazine*, March 2005, Vol. 34, No 3.

Ruether, Rosemary Radford. *Sexism and God-Talk: Toward a Feminist Theology* (Boston, MA: Beacon Press, 1993).

Sachs, Wolfgang, ed. *Global Ecology: A New Arena of Political Conflict*, (Canada: Fernwood Publishing, 1993).

—— and Ali A. Mazrui. "The Obsolete Race: Development After East-West Rivalry." *New Perspectives Quarterly*, Vol. 7, No. 2. (Spring 1990).

Sahlins, Marshall. *Stone Age Economics* (Chicago: Aldine-Atherton Inc., 1972).

Saint Joseph Edition of The New American Bible. (New York: Catholic Book Publishing Co., 1970).

Simon, David. "Transcript," *PBS's Bill Moyers Journal.* Radio Interview by Bill Moyer. Last modified 2009. http://www.pbs.org/cove-media/http/PBS_CP_Bill_Moyers/58/1000/transcript1.html.

Sobrino, Jon. *Archbishop Romero: Memories and Reflections* (New York: Orbis Books, 1990).

Spivack, Donald R. "History of Skid Row," *Skid Row Journal* (1998): 1, http://www.skidrowjournal.org/history-of-skid-row.html.

Stamper, Norm. "Citing Failed War on Drugs, Former Seattle Police Chief Calls for Legalization of Marijuana and All Drugs." *Democracy Now.* Interview by Juan González, March 30, 2009. http://www.democracynow.org/2009/3/30/citing_failed_war_on_drugs_former.

Stringfellow, William. *An Ethic for Christians and Other Aliens in a Strange Land* (Waco, TX: Word Books, 1973).

Vallely, Paul. *Bad Samaritans: First World Ethics and Third World Debt* (New York: Orbis Books, 1990).

Ventura, Michael. *Letters at 3AM: Reports on Endarkenment* (Dallas: Springs Publications, 1993), 146.

Wills, Garry. *Reagan's America* (New York: Penguin Books, 1988).

Wink, Walter. *The Powers That Be: Theology for a New Millennium* (New York: Doubleday, 1999).

———. *Engaging the Powers: Discernment and Resistance in a World of Domination* (Minneapolis: Fortress Press, 1992).

———. *Unmasking the Powers: The Invisible Forces That Determine Human Existence* (Philadelphia: Fortress Press, 1986).

———. *Naming the Powers: The Language of Power in the New Testament* (Philadelphia: Fortress Press, 1984).

Wright, Robert. "The Evolution of Despair." *Time Magazine.* Last modified August 28, 1995. http://www.time.com/time/magazine/article/0,9171,983355,00.html.

Index

A

Abel 46-48, 97, 125, 247, 369
abortion 114, 123, 147
Abraham 45-46, 57, 125-26, 212, 369
Abu Ghraib 217-18, 221
Acts of the Apostles 30
adultery 65
advent 83, 88, 223, 226, 382
Afghanistan 174, 188, 191, 193, 220, 249, 302, 379, 397-98
African Americans 42, 44, 101, 205, 357-58
agriculture 90-93, 248-49
AIDS 322, 337, 347-48
Albertson SJ, Clint 141
Allen, Woody 231
al-Qaeda 181, 191
America Magazine 366
American Civil Liberties Union (ACLU) 364
American Dream 159, 161, 265-67, 269, 373
Amos 114, 141
anawim 200
Annunciation 124
Anti-Ballistic Missile Treaty 186
anti-Semitism 223
Antoinette, Marie 310
Aquinas, Thomas, Saint 191, 240
Arab Brotherhood 218
Arabs 49, 176, 218
Aryan 247, 288
Aristide, Jean Bertrand 69, 73, 202
Armageddon 180, 185
Arms Bazaar 395
arms race 30, 114, 233, 260
Assyria 191
Aztec 248

B

B-52 103, 166
Baal 212-13
Babylonia 176, 187
Baltimore Sun 386
Bank of Japan 260
Banna, Hasan al- 218-19
Barber, Benjamin 218
Baudrillard, Jean 297-301
Bechtel Corporation 218, 358
Berlin Wall 161, 175, 202, 239
Berrigan SJ, Daniel xix, 11, 21, 110, 112, 186, 240
Berrigan, Philip 227
Berry, Wendell 84-85, 233
blitzkrieg 33, 374
blood: 75-77, 98, 161, 163-64, 168, 176, 183, 308, 343, 394; bloodshed, 163, 176, 183; and Christian theology of sacrifice, 43, 97, 223; and the Eucharist, 23, 236; and the prophets' deaths, 70, 97, 125; used in protest demonstrations, 5, 163-65, 178
blood bank strikes 75-77, 268, 360, 385394
Bloomingdale, Betsy 40, 142
Bolivia 379
Bonhoeffer, Dietrich 165, 186, 194
Book of Revelation 185-86, 190, 309
Borlaug, Norman 91
Boyle Heights 392, 397
Bradley Administration 364
Bratton, William 362, 367, 384, 386, 399
Brazil 380, 260
Britain 191, 249
Broken Windows Initiative 362, 367, 399
Brown, John 327